ROYAL HISTORICAL SOCIETY

GUIDES AND HANDBOOKS

No. 16

A HANDLIST
OF BRITISH DIPLOMATIC REPRESENTATIVES

1509 – 1688

ROYAL HISTORICAL SOCIETY
GUIDES AND HANDBOOKS
ISSN 0080 – 4398

MAIN SERIES

1. *Guide to English commercial statistics 1696 – 1782.* By G. N. Clark and Barbara M. Franks. 1938.
2. *Handbook of British chronology.* Edited by F. M. Powicke, Charles Johnson and W. J. Harte. 1939. 2nd edition, edited by F. M. Powicke and E. B. Fryde, 1961. 3rd edition, edited by E. B. Fryde, D. E. Greenway, S. Porter and I. Roy, 1986.
3. *Medieval libraries of Great Britain. A list of surviving books.* Edited by N. R. Ker. 1941. 2nd edition, 1964.
4. *Handbook of dates for students of English history.* Edited by C. R. Cheney. 1945. Reprinted, 1982.
5. *Guide to the national and provincial directories of England and Wales, excluding London, published before 1856.* By Jane E. Norton. 1950.
6. *Handbook of oriental history.* Edited by C. H. Philips. 1951.
7. *Texts and Calendars. An analytical guide to serial publications.* By E. L. C. Mullins. 1958. Reprinted (with corrections), 1978.
8. *Anglo-Saxon Charters. An annotated list and bibliography.* By P. H. Sawyer. 1968.
9. *A Centenary Guide to the publications of the Royal Historical Society 1868 – 1968 and of the former Camden Society 1838 – 1897.* By Alexander Taylor Milne. 1968.
10. *Guide to the local administrative units of England.* Volume I. *Southern England.* By Frederic A. Youngs, Jr. 1979. 2nd edition, 1981.
11. *Guide to bishops' registers of England and Wales. A survey from the middle ages to the abolition of episcopacy in 1646.* By David M. Smith. 1981.
12. *Texts and Calendars II. An analytical guide to serial publications 1957 – 1982.* By E. L. C. Mullins. 1983.
13. *Handbook of Medieval Exchange.* By Peter Spufford, with the assistance of Wendy Wilkinson and Sarah Tolley. 1986.
14. *Scottish Texts and Calendars. An analytical guide to serial publications.* By David and Wendy Stevenson. 1987.
15. *Medieval libraries of Great Britain.* Edited by N. R. Ker. *Supplement to the second edition.* Edited by Andrew G. Watson. 1987.

SUPPLEMENTARY SERIES

1. *A Guide to the papers of British Cabinet Ministers, 1900 – 1951.* Compiled by Cameron Hazlehurst and Christine Woodland. 1974.
2. *A Guide to the reports of the U.S. Strategic Bombing Survey.* I *Europe.* II *The Pacific.* Edited by Gordon Daniels. 1981.

A HANDLIST OF BRITISH DIPLOMATIC REPRESENTATIVES

1509 – 1688

BY

GARY M. BELL

LONDON
OFFICES OF THE ROYAL HISTORICAL SOCIETY
UNIVERSITY COLLEGE LONDON, GOWER STREET
LONDON WC1E 6BT
1990

© Royal Historical Society 1990

First published 1990

Distributed for the Royal Historical Society
by Boydell & Brewer Ltd
PO Box 9 Woodbridge Suffolk IP12 3DF
and Boydell & Brewer Inc.
PO Box 41026 Rochester NY 14604 USA

ISBN 0 86193 123 8

British Library Cataloguing in Publication Data
Bell, Gary M.
A handlist of British diplomatic representatives, 1509 –
1688. — (Royal Historical Society guides and handbooks;
no. 16)
1. Great Britain. Foreign relations. Diplomacy, history
I. Title II. Royal Historical Society III. Series
327.20941
ISBN 0-86193-123-8

This publication is printed on acid-free paper

Printed in Great Britain by
Woolnough Bookbinding, Irthlingborough, Northants

CONTENTS

PREFACE

In a work that has been as long in development as this one has, one accumulates a large number of debts that a brief mention in this section will not even start to repay. There are however several whose help has been crucial and to whom I would like to express appreciation. I am especially grateful to Dr. De Lamar Jensen of Brigham Young University, whose inspiration instigated and whose encouragement was pivotal in this particular project. Dr. Arthur J. Slavin of the University of Louisville was similarly supportive in both graduate studies and subsequently. His advice, direction and insights are fundamental to my own work. Professor Sir Geoffrey Elton and Professor R. B. Wernham have been most helpful in providing suggestions as the project unfolded, and then graciously evaluating the final results. To Professor Ron Fritze and Professor Richard Poll, I am indebted for their reading and commenting on the final manuscript. To the late Professor Donald Sutherland I owe appreciation for his support and comments during a beneficial summer spent in part on the project under NEH auspices at the University of Iowa. Mr. Norman Evans at the Public Record Office was generous with information and suggestions in the section dealing with ambassadors to Russia. To Dr. Donald Coers of Sam Houston State University I express special thanks for both his help in research, and also for undertaking what could only have been an unusually tedious task in carefully proofreading the final manuscript. Finally, I acknowledge with gratitude Dr. Ian Roy and Dr. Colin Matthew for their continuing helpfulness in their roles as Literary Directors of the Royal Historical Society.

Despite received wisdom about the impersonality of institutions, I found during this project several institutions in which the staffs made it a pleasure to work. To the professionals of the Public Record Office, the British Library, and the Institute of Historical Research, I must express great appreciation for their willingness to accommodate the often special circumstances that the need to see large amounts of documentary material entailed. The staff at the Newton Gresham Library (Sam Houston State University) — with a special expression of thanks to Dr. Marie Hayden — and the staff at the Perry-Casteñada Library and the Humanities Research Center (the latter two at the University of Texas) also did a great deal to facilitate the research demands that I often placed upon them. In all cases, I have marvelled at the cooperation and friendliness at these institutions.

The American Philosophical Society supported the outset of the work with a most timely grant; and Sam Houston State University at Huntsville, Texas, was unusually generous in its willingness to underwrite financially the work that had to be done.

Finally, to my sons Ryan, Darin and Loren, and most significantly to my wife Marilyn, to whom this effort is dedicated, I am sensitive to the sacrifices you have made, the notes you have taken and the typing you have done. Thank you for your enduring patience and unstinting assistance.

INTRODUCTION

I

The following list is designed to continue the publications of D. B. Horn and S. T. Bindoff, who have, in separate volumes, catalogued diplomatic representatives for the period 1689 to 1852. That there has been no comparable effort for the years before 1689 seems surprising. Statesmen, historians and antiquarians have provided numerous partial listings over the last four centuries—some only cursory and some quite sophisticated—that collectively indicate a continuing fascination with the question of diplomatic representation in the early modern era. Clearly this current handlist both owes a substantial debt to all of them and is an attempt as well to unify and expand what collected information exists.[1]

The principal objective in providing a handlist of Tudor and Stuart ambassadors is to push our knowledge about the men and missions of English

---

[1] A Listing of Previous Handlists and Compilations of British Diplomatic Representatives:

    a. Anonymous, 'A List of Persons as have been employed by the Kings and Queens of England to negotiate (either as ambassadors, envoys, residents, com[missione]rs, or agents) in foreign kingdoms and states,' from BL, Stowe 548, ff. 85-9.

    b. Anonymous, [List of Ambassadors], from BL, Birch 4164, f. 76.

    c. Beck, Brandon, *From the Rising of the Sun. English Images of the Ottoman Empire to 1715* (New York, 1986), p. 145.

    d. Bent, J. Theodore, 'List of English Ambassadors to the Porte in the 16th and 17th Centuries,' *Early Voyages and Travels in the Levant...*(1893), p. xlii.

    e. Bittner, Ludwig and Gross, Luther, *Reportorium der Diplomatischen Vertreter aller Länder seit dem Westfälischen Frieden* (1648) (Berlin, n.d.), 2 v.

    f. Bliss, W. H., 'Reports on Materials Relating to England in Swedish Archives and Libraries,' *Report of the Deputy Keeper of the Public Record Office*, xliii, app. II, (1882), pp. 26-8.

    g. [Cecil, William, Lord Burghley?], 'Noblemen and gentlemen that have served and are fitt to be employed in forrein messages,' from BL, Lansdowne 683, ff. 49-50.

    h. Firth, C. H. and Lomas, S. C. (eds.), 'English Ambassadors and Diplomatic Agents in France (1603-1688),' *Notes on the Diplomatic Relations of England and France,1603-1688* (1906), pp. 5-27.

    i. Great Britain, Public Record Office, 'Diplomatic Agents accredited by the Crowns of England and Scotland and by Great Britain to the Republic of Venice,' *Calendar of State Papers, Venetian, 1202-1509*, table 7.

    j. Lachs, Phyllis S., 'Personnel,' *The Diplomatic Corps under Charles II and James II* (New Brunswick, N.J., 1965), Appendix II, pp. 190-201.

    k. Spuler, B., 'Europäische Diplomaten in Konstantinople...(to 1739),' *Jahrbuch Geschichte Osteuropas*, i (1936), pp. 247-55.

    l. Thomas, F. S., *Historical Notes. 1509-1714.* (1856), i.

    m. [Thomas, F. S.], 'Catalogue of Ambassadors in Foreign Countries,' from BL, Add. 20765.

    n. Weaver, F. J., 'Anglo-French Diplomatic Relations, 1558-1603,' *Bulletin of the Institute of Historical Research*, iv-vii, (1926-9).

diplomacy well back into the Renaissance, beginning with the reign of Henry VIII; and then concluding the effort where Professor Horn began his, in 1689. The 179 years under scrutiny are especially significant. It was in this period that the foundations of modern English diplomatic practices and institutions were established. Knowing the diplomats and their assignments is crucial to understanding how the evolution of diplomacy occurred. Furthermore, such detailed knowledge seems essential in more fully analyzing and then presenting the narrative of England's relations with foreign powers. Finally, it might also be noted that this collection can serve as a useful reference for dating and understanding other, non-diplomatic events.

With respect to the information in this compilation, the principal purpose has been to identify names—the names of diplomats, some of whom are well known, but others of whom are obscure and in several instances forgotten altogether in the historical record. The next important objective has been to provide as accurate a beginning and termination date as possible for the multifarious assignments that the ambassadors undertook abroad. It is often the case that understanding the course of foreign relations hinges on precisely who was where and exactly when their assignment occurred.

In an attempt to discover and then isolate the large number of ambassadors (602) and their missions (1320), I have systematically surveyed several sources. Most are obvious for a study of this nature. Among the essential collections subjected to a page-by-page search were the various *Calendar of State Papers* (foreign, Roman, Spanish, Milanese, Venetian, Scottish, etc.) as well as the *Letters and Papers of Henry VIII* and the 'Descriptive Lists of the State Papers' (which consist of manuscript volumes located in the reference rooms of the PRO and the Institute of Historical Research). This same page-by-page treatment was accorded to the *Calendar of Treasury Books* and several classes of unpublished Exchequer documents (dormant privy seal books, payment books and registers of orders for payments). In fact, these financial records proved to be the key to accurate mission identification and dating.

In addition, as need dictated, I utilized the *Calendar of State Papers, Domestic*, the calendars and lists of the Historical Manuscript Commission, and various collections of correspondence—especially the State Papers located at the Public Record Office, although I did not subject these items to a page-by-page scrutiny.[2] Finally, I identified and consulted the vast majority of all secondary sources relevant to British diplomatic history for the period.

II

Information contained in this handlist met strict guidelines for inclusion. To be incorporated in the listing, a man, in the final analysis, needed to have been warranted by his sovereign to represent, officially, the English

[2] In citing sources for information, I have generally used the printed Calendars where they exist rather than the original State Papers, assuming that this is an adequate beginning point for consulting the original documents. Where the Calendars leave off, I have whenever possible consulted the original State Papers, and these are then cited.

government to a foreign power or interest, located outside of English territorial boundaries. Generally, this involved a negotiating role. In this period of unsettled diplomatic procedures and indistinct diplomatic status, this criterion led to fairly arbitrary decisions about who was, and who was not a representative. Some types of representatives are easy to delete; others call for a rather closer judgment. Generally, the following guidelines have been observed in deciding those who would be *excluded*. Those who *do not* find a place include:

1. Anyone sent by, or representing a person other than the prince, or established English government. For instance, Cecil's or Buckingham's representatives, if not officially sanctioned by the monarch or government, are not included. The one exception to this rule is some of the men who went abroad at the behest of Thomas Wolsey. The great Cardinal was for a time so much the *alter ego* of Henry VIII that he was virtually as much the ultimate authority in government as the King.

The situation is similarly ambiguous between 1642 and 1649. Typically, representatives of both the King and Parliament are noted (when they are discoverable in this confused period).

2. Men sent simply to convey messages or presents (usually falcons, horses, foodstuffs, or the like). I assume they were not really diplomats. They did not negotiate, they usually were not invested with royal authority, and they were typically paid far less than their ambassadorial brethren. The one exception to this category would be those men, usually peers, who convey honorary titles or membership in orders (the Garter, the Bath, etc.) to a foreign dignitary. Their pay was usually inflated, they frequently became involved in diplomatic exchanges, and the honor they conveyed typically had diplomatic significance.

3. Military men, who assumed a negotiating assignment while engaged principally in military operations. A good example would be the Earl of Essex in France in the late 1590s. He certainly dealt diplomatically with Henry IV, but his principal assignment was in another sphere. Other examples would include the many sea-captains who went to Morocco or the Barbary Coast in the mid-seventeenth century, who had some negotiating role, but who were principally operating as mariners and military commanders, not diplomats.

The same reasoning applies to a miscellaneous group of people such as Sir Thomas Gresham in the 1550s and 1560s, or in many instances to Stephen Vaughan in the 1530s and 1540s, who operated overseas, but who, in most cases, were principally involved in something other than diplomacy (i.e. borrowing or repaying money).

Finally, representatives to continental religious assemblies, such as Biondi who went to the Calvinist assembly at Grenoble in 1615, do not find inclusion, primarily because their objectives were typically something other than diplomatic.

4. Merchants. Although they may have had some modest negotiating assignment in the course of their trading activities, or they may have conveyed messages, unless they were formally accredited for a specific purpose, they are not included. The distinctions here might best be understood in terms of William

Harborne. While a merchant at Constantinople, he was not considered an ambassador, even though he actually negotiated trading privileges for the English. Once he carried the Queen's credentials, as he did for the first time in 1584, he then begins to appear on the list. In the same sense, the governor of the Merchant Adventurers in the Low Countries seldom would be included.

5. Consuls, men assigned to work in major overseas trading centers for the purposes of facilitating commerce. This category would include both the formally designated consuls of the seventeenth century and the men who acted in an untitled consular role in the sixteenth century, such as Thomas Ferrers at Stade in the 1590s. Although usually paid by the English government, their responsibilities lie much more in the economic than the political/diplomatic sphere.

6. Heralds. They are of course included when they were involved in a mission of substantial negotiation, but typically this was not the case, and thus they are usually excluded.

Geographically, I have again imposed fine distinctions when compiling this list. Given England's location, an ambassador had to cross the sea on an assignment, Scotland before 1603 being the only exception. But at the same time, he also had to leave English territory. Thus before 1558, men might negotiate with their French counterparts at Calais, but this is treated as being no different from their fellows treating with French counterparts in London. Similarly, I have not tried to sort out the various commissions at Berwick or along the Scottish border, but have only included those Englishmen who actually negotiated on Scottish territory. It would be simple to specify that a diplomat had need go to a foreign court, but the complications here become insurmountable. Included are the men who treated with the Huguenots in France, for instance, or with rebels in the Low Countries, and they of course never set foot into a formal court setting.

There is no listing of any diplomat to Ireland during the period, nor to Scotland after 1603, although in both of these instances a debate could be generated.

So far as the vast diplomatic netherworld of spies, unofficial contacts, travellers, informers, intriguers, and men-on-the-make abroad is concerned, they find no place in this list. These people were surely an important diplomatic conduit in an era before the systematic use of residents in neighboring countries was practiced, and their presence permits us to understand some of the gaps that exist in relations between England and her neighbors that we find in the following list. But their contribution to diplomacy must await another study.

It also bears mentioning that I have deleted representatives or their missions for whom there is no persuasive evidence that in fact an embassy was undertaken. If a diplomat and his mission appear, this means that there is *substantial* documentation for the mission. As a general rule, the tendency was to *exclude* rather than include. Despite this conservatism, and despite efforts to identify all official representatives, there will surely be omissions of legitimate diplomats, either through simple oversight, or through a mistaken assessment of an assignment.

III

With regard to the format of the list, the entries are arranged principally by geographical area, and chronologically within those categories. The ambassadors are understood to have been sent to the sovereign political unit in the region, such as the court of Sweden (usually at Stockholm), or, the court of France (typically at Paris). Where numerous political sub-units occur, such as in Germany (labelled 'Germany and Central Europe') or Italy, careful distinctions are made about the prince, state or city to which a diplomat was assigned. Equally careful designations are made when the diplomat contacted a rebellious faction or force in an area. When an ambassador was dispatched to a prince who was not currently in his normal residence, such as Gustavus Adolphus, the Swedish King who was often campaigning in Germany, this also is noted. Finally, because the Holy Roman Emperor was important indeed throughout our period, the imperial court, wherever it may have been located, is given a separate category.

In a specific entry, the object of the mission determines the geographical arrangement. If an ambassador went to Venice, then it is under Venice that his embassy will be found. However, if he stopped in other courts, such as at the Hague, in Savoy, or in France, either en route to or returning from Venice, these will be noted in the main entry, and brief entries will also be included under the secondary areas where he had some diplomatic role.

Entries will normally take the form of the following sample (drawn from the general designation of 'France'):

F275.
MONTAGU, Ralph (later 1st Duke of Montagu; 1638-1709)*

1 Sept. 1676[a] - 12 July 1678[e]	Ambassador Extraordinary
Audience: *c.*20 Dec. 1676	£100/wk.
Secretary: John Brisbane	

He left his post without permission—12 July represents the date upon which his successor was appointed to assume the Paris residency. He had returned briefly to England, autumn 1677.

Instructions: PRO, SP/104/239, ff. 9-13; Bodl., Rawlinson Mss. A.255, ff. 265-6; BL, Add. 25119, f. 13; HMC *4th Report*, p. 232.

Correspondence: PRO, SP/78/142, SP/104/18 & 185-6; BL, Add. 25119, 28054, 32680, 38849B, Harl. 1516, 1523, Eg. 2540, 3326, Stowe 191; HMC *Buccleuch*, i; Oxford, Mss. in All Souls Lib., clxix, ccliii; HMC *4th Report*, p. 245; Browning, A., *Thomas Osborne, Earl of Danby*...(Glasgow, 1944-51), ii.

Identification number: One such number is assigned to each mission to facilitate identifying individual men and missions.

Names: The first part of the entry includes not only the name and appropriate titles of the diplomat or diplomats (listed in order of status when there is more than one) sent on the assignment, but as much biographical detail as necessary to allow precise identification of the individual(s). The list makes an effort to standardize names, titles and dates with those found, most importantly, in the

History of Parliament Trust publications, and secondarily, with those found in the *Dictionary of National Biography* and the *Complete Peerage*. Names to be found in one of these sources are so indicated by an asterisk next to the biographical entry.

Dates: The dates of the mission form the next body of information. The system of dating missions warrants a detailed explanation. All missions are considered to have begun from the first day the diplomat was paid for his assignment; and to have terminated with the 'return to presence,' the date he made his official report to his sovereign. This latter date usually coincided with the last day of pay. Unfortunately, such precision is in many cases not possible, and a variety of beginning dates that only approach the ideal had to be used for many missions. The various dates used have been listed, in order of descending desirability (the most accurate or most credible dates are those that come first), in the table immediately below. For greater precision, the source for a date has been indicated through a code system—an italicized lower case letter, which follows the beginning date in all entries. In the case of truly vague origination dates, that is, as indicated by the last three italicized letters ('f' through 'h'), a '*c.*' (*circa*) often appears *before* the date indicating that the beginning date is only approximate.

Greater imprecision frequently attends the return date. Existing financial records are substantially less informative about the conclusion of missions than they are about the outset. Since we are typically dependent on domestic correspondence for that day, and such letters have long since disappeared, or would be impossibly time consuming to discover, or never existed in the first place, these dates are often provided based upon corroborating evidence (estimates of travel time from the host court, the date of the last known overseas correspondence, etc.). They too are listed in the table immediately below in a descending order of 'goodness,' with the italicized letter code again providing insight into how that date was determined. In some instances, the beginning or the end dates cannot with any assurance be established; the notation 'n.d.' (no date available) is then inserted. The following tables provide the codes for origination and termination dates:

Dating for the Beginning of an Embassy

a — first day of pay (this corresponds in the late seventeenth century with the day the ambassador 'left the royal presence')

b — date of the privy seal or some other warrant (i.e. royal sign manual or royal commission issued under the Great Seal) issued to authorize the mission

c — date upon which instructions, or letters of appointment were issued

d — date of the credentials or of the letters to a foreign potentate that the ambassador carried; or the date of the English pass he carried authorizing him to go abroad.

e — date of leave-taking from the English monarch (always the date upon which pay began in the last two thirds of the seventeenth century, but not the case before then) f — date of departure from London (usually from a letter or other documentary reference)

g — date of departure from English territory (i.e. from Dover or from another station such as Berwick or Calais)

h — date of first employment given by other sources (usually from comments in peripheral documentation or epistolary allusions). This date would include the point upon which the secretary of a legation assumed responsibilities as the chargé d'affaires. In other words, this is as close a date as possible upon which it can be established that diplomatic responsibilities of some type began

Dating for the Termination of an Embassy

a — date of 'return to presence'

b — date of cessation of pay (these first two are usually, but not always, identical)

c — date of arrival (at court or in London) or when it can be established that diplomatic duties ceased, typically based on relevant epistolary allusions. This usually represents a more credible date than the one followed by an 'h,' defined below

d — date of re-credentialling (issuing of leave-taking papers) by the host court combined with an average travelling-home time

e — date of formal leave-taking or identifiable departure from the host court, combined with an average travelling-home time

f — date of leave-taking from the host court, when travelling to another diplomatic or non-diplomatic assignment; or date of simply ceasing diplomatic responsibilities at that geographical location

g — date of last letter or documentary allusion (including the date of a recall letter from home) plus a plausible elapsed time until the 'return to presence'

h — an educated guess based on circumstantial evidence

It must be stressed that all dates given are 'Old Style,' conforming to English and not continental usage after 1582. The year is also reckoned to begin on January 1.

Diplomatic Rank: Following the dates of the mission is an indication of the rank, status or function of the diplomat. This is a notoriously imprecise business. During most of the sixteenth century there was no clear designation for different representatives, and in the seventeenth century, terms kept altering in meaning. The guidelines in this handlist are expressed by the use of brackets. If a diplomatic designation is bracketed, that is an indication that no precise title for the man on that mission has been discovered, and thus his function, or presumed title is given. For instance, in all probability no one in sixteenth century England called the lesser man or secretary who assumed the legation once a resident left and ran it until his successor arrived, a chargé d'affaires, but that name is so aptly descriptive that in the absence of a sixteenth century term (other than the indistinct title 'agent') this title has been used. In the seventeenth century, as French diplomacy began to make its mark, contemporaries would have recognized a 'chargé.' The English themselves began to use the title after the Civil War. Thus the brackets begin to disappear from the term 'chargé.'

The same imprecision leads to the widespread use of the bracketed term 'special ambassador.' The term would have evoked some recognition at the time, but more generally the man who went overseas for a short period for a specific negotiating or message conveying purpose was called variously an orator, a procurator, a nuncio, a legationibus, an envoy or simply an ambassador, based on unclear and only dimly perceived Roman precedents. So far as can be determined, there was no pattern of rank or specificity, as indicated by some credentials that use all of these titles and more. Thus for purposes of simplicity, [Special Ambassador] is used as more descriptive than specific. It is unbracketed if the man was actually labelled a 'special ambassador.' Resident or resident ambassador is usually found unbracketed, because that term, in the sixteenth century, was widely utilized. By the seventeenth century, a more precise terminology was emerging. Resident ambassadors were typically known as 'ambassadors ordinary,' or, if their social status was exalted, 'ambassadors extraordinary.' Special ambassadors were usually called 'ambassadors extraordinary' in the case of the greater men, 'envoys extraordinary' in the case of the lesser (a titling subtlety that was hardly yet systematically applied or even very precise in the seventeenth century). Men who represented their sovereign at special congresses or negotiating sessions were more often than not designated 'plenipotentiary.' And finally, agents, chargé d'affaires, and commissioners continued in much the same way that they had always both functioned and had been titled. My practice is, once again, to give, if it can be discovered, the title that the ambassador's contemporaries employed; otherwise to continue the use of the sixteenth century terms, placing them in brackets (resident, special, etc.) if no specific designation has been identified.

Remuneration: Pay scales are noted under the title, both as another indication of status, and to provide additional information that can be a key element in understanding the mission. An underpaid ambassador, for instance, could be a less effective one.

Pay rates could change in mid-embassy, especially during prolonged missions. I try, through the figures given, to trace these changes, but the general rule is that the pay rate indicated, if it stands alone, indicates rate of remuneration at the outset of the assignment.

Audiences: On the same line with pay scales, but on the left-hand side of the entry, one finds the audience, or, less desirably, the arrival date of the diplomat. It often happened that extended preparation periods in England followed the start of pay, and in isolated instances, men were paid who never went abroad. Thus the date of the first audience with the foreign power is also given, to allow the distinction to be made between when the mission was initiated and when the ambassador officially first began to conduct business. The dates for audiences are frequently much more difficult to determine than are origination and termination dates. They are based, in many cases, upon incidental information from correspondence that permits only an estimate of when the reception of the diplomat occurred. It should also be noted that when a choice is available, I use the date of the first public audience, as contrasted to the first private audience. The former was considered the point at which formal duties begin; the latter was relevant in those cases when an English ambassador arrived in a foreign country, but for some reason could not immediately assume his official duties. If there is a great disparity in the two, I cite both. An arrival date is utilized when a diplomat's audience date is undiscoverable, or when his responsibilities include contact with several people or groups, so that no one audience marks the inauguration of the embassy.

Secretaries: The list notes the name of the secretary of the legation under the audience date. The office of diplomatic secretary grew in importance as the period progressed. Few are noted in contemporary documents of the sixteenth century, although these assistants to ambassadors certainly existed. By the seventeenth century, the secretary was the second ranking official in the embassy, was usually appointed independently by the crown, and was the designated successor of the ambassador when the latter left, died, or otherwise ceased to function in his office. When more than one secretary was found, their names are listed and no attempt has been made to determine ranking.

Explanatory Notes: Beneath the data about legation secretaries often comes a section, in paragraph form, that provides other essential information about the mission. Notations relate to the dates during which the ambassador was absent from his post, about where the person to whom he was accredited was found, about unusual circumstances in the embassy, etc.

It should be noted that all geographical designations, spellings and usages have been modernized.[3]

Instructions and Correspondence: Finally, all the references to instructions and correspondence that could be discovered are provided. In each case, the instructions cited are those carried at the outset of the mission, and the vast body of subsequent instructions that most ambassadors received is merely considered part of the correspondence of the embassy. Often instructions are either summarized or inferred in peripheral sources. When authentic instructions are missing, I resort to this type of source (frequently the reports of Venetian ambassadors in London, for instance) and the reader is warned with such phrases as 'implied by,' 'inferred from,' or 'suggested by.'

The correspondence citations contain a representative sampling, but not necessarily an exhaustive list, of where correspondence, both sent to and written by the diplomat (or his secretary) while on assignment, may be found. In some cases, where an embassy or an ambassador is particularly obscure and little or no correspondence has been found, I have listed contemporary correspondence *about* the mission. Most references are to collections of letters, but a

---

[3] Based on the usages in William L. Langer (ed.), *An Encyclopedia of World History*, 4th ed. (Boston, 1968); and *Rand McNally New Cosmopolitan World Atlas* (Chicago, 1965).

number of citations do note single items. Finally, important diaries, journals, revealing financial memoranda, third person commentaries about or summaries of reports dealing with an embassy are typically incorporated under the correspondence section. It should be noted that the vast majority of references are to sources printed in English or to collections in English archives.

I would introduce a cautionary codicil to all of the above. The information regarding sixteenth and seventeenth century diplomacy is extensive—and maddeningly incomplete in many instances. The more one works in the sources, the clearer it becomes that to pretend to have produced an exhaustive list would be, without a lifetime's commitment, presumptuous. What I present here is as complete as ten years of work, and several trips to English collections can make it. But it also should be understood simply as the most thorough list produced to date from a long history of such efforts.

IV

Finally, an introduction of this nature is not the place to give a detailed analysis or summation of the Handlist material. It is instead to be hoped that this now more organized data, with its accurate dating, names of personnel, and sources of additional information, will lay the foundations for further systematic investigation of Tudor-Stuart diplomatic history. There are, however, some initial patterns and several new avenues of inquiry that have suggested themselves while I was compiling the list.

English Foreign Policy

Much has been made by historians of England's moats, the great protective seas that surround her. In fact, such an emphasis in the literature on her insular status has been at the expense of what most contemporary English governments perceived as the country's true first line of defense—an effective diplomatic network. This network would, it was hoped, forestall the moats ever being put to the test. It was the ambassadors who collected vital information, manipulated foreign powers in the interests of English policy, first countered threats, and then, if necessary, sounded the initial tocsins of danger. It was the diplomatic corps who served as the vital early warning and defense system of the realm.

One can trace the significance of this diplomatic defense structure by noting simply the numbers and locations of ambassadors abroad at any one time. During placid periods in British history, there were the usual residents in the usual courts—especially in France and the Low Countries. When crises loomed, however, such as with the Armada in 1588 or the Dutch threats of the early 1660s; or when the English government felt unusually beleaguered, as during the early years of Elizabeth's reign or during Edward's minority; or when major policy initiatives required attention, as with the divorce in the 1530s or relations with France in the 1670s, the *tempo* of diplomatic activity escalated sharply.

The deployment of ambassadors in the Elizabethan period is a prime example of the correlation between diplomatic activity and national perceptions. Queen Elizabeth is arguably one of the English monarchs who felt most threatened in the post-Anglo-Saxon period by overseas forces. Certainly, as a declaredly bastard, female ruler, hewing moreover to a Protestant line (however middle of the road it might be) and governing a relatively weak, poor and sparsely-populated country on the fringes of the continent, she was anything but comfortably secure during the greater part of her reign. It is an indication of the importance she placed upon her diplomatic corps that hers was the largest commitment to diplomacy in the 179 years under review. This commitment is measured by, among other things, the number of people involved overseas, the number of man-days officially employed in diplomatic activity, and seemingly by the resulting expenditures made on ambassadors.

In the same sense, it is abundantly clear where the *foci* of English interest lay during the entirety of the period under review. France and the Low Countries were dominant military and economic concerns. Here, in these areas that were also most proximate to England, the need for observation was unceasing. Here, England's leaders maintained the diplomatic web most consistently. In point of fact, more missions, of longer duration, were served in these two regions than in all other areas of diplomatic activity combined. Other areas were contacted only periodically as need dictated: Central Europe, Spain, the Italian states, and Scandinavia.

The shifting emphasis of policy is equally fascinating. Anyone doubting the extent of Elizabethan overseas expansion need only note the sudden appearance in this reign of English representatives in Turkey, Russia, North Africa, southern Italy, and the Baltic area. Similarly, as Eastern trade and interests in the Mediterranean developed in the Stuart era, an ambassador at Venice became a necessity. In all, much has already been written about the nature and course of early modern English foreign affairs. Many of the old interpretations are reenforced; others may need reinterpretation as we analyze the precise patterns of where, how long and with what rank English diplomats served.

Diplomatic Personnel

One established notion already deserves to have short shrift made of it due to the information in this *Handlist*. Received wisdom suggests that the men who served as ambassadors overseas were haphazardly chosen and at best a randomly-prepared lot.[4] This hardly seems credible if monarchs placed the value upon their ambassadors (in the defense of royal and national interests) that they seemingly did.

Preliminary analysis of the personnel suggests, on the contrary, that in the main they were an unusually well-trained and reasonably carefully selected

[4] A frequent assertion, but most recently articulated in Susan Doran, *England and Europe, 1485-1603* (London, Longman, 1986), p. 13.

11

group of royal servants. Striking commonalities emerge. The ambassadors all seem to have been well-educated, which is not surprising given the responsibilities in which they were engaged. They required an unusual breadth of knowledge about historical precedents, the mores of the countries with which they were dealing, and legal theory. The majority (65 percent) had some formal education, and not a few held doctorates in their professions.

At first, many were the learned doctors of the church. But this soon changed. Churchmen, used extensively by Henry VIII, who had feet planted firmly in both the medieval as well as the modern world, gave way to lay ambassadors by the middle of the sixteenth century. It was a rare churchman who went abroad after 1600. Long-standing conclusions about the secularization of the state after the Reformation now receive support in the diplomatic sphere.

Lack of formal education did not of course preclude other types of preparation. Most of the diplomats, if not the products of universities or inns of court, could at least claim the benefits of the informal educational process of the age. Private tutors or the grand tour abroad were both acceptable substitutes and generally a part of many diplomat's repertoire of experience. There were also those few whose education came practically, through the process of long service overseas in foreign armies; as merchants abroad; or in the service of a prince or government beyond the Channel. The conclusion is that the vast majority of ambassadors were something other than whimsical selections out of an available pool of courtiers ready-to-hand; or that they were simply patronage appointments. Those selected were usually well prepared by education or practical experience for their responsibilities.

A significant number of the diplomats were also men 'brought up through the ranks.' The progression is traceable. A man, usually in his youth, first appears in the documents as part of a serving ambassador's entourage, then is found as a secretary of the legation. Subsequently, he undertook assignment to one of the less important posts overseas, first as a temporary, and then possibly as a resident envoy. This process of diplomatic career development was especially pronounced in Elizabeth's reign, but clearly experience had a bearing on ambassadorial selection in all reigns. In one instance, the embassy of Sir Nicholas Throckmorton to France in the early 1560s, so many later diplomats are to be found involved that it is tempting to refer to that embassy as a 'school for ambassadors.' Not a few of the men were thus trained in diplomacy, and seemingly much more systematically prepared than previously suspected.

It was also the case that every successive government relied upon its skilled men—and thus it is an unusual ambassador, even among the nobility, who served but once on a mission. Of all the men, a total of 602, who went abroad between 1509 and 1688, each served an average of 2.5 missions. If one eliminates those who served only once, the average jumps to 3.8 missions for the rest—a majority (53 percent) of the 602. Repetitive service also belies the notion of random or whimsical selection.

At the apex of those conducting foreign affairs are the principal secretaries, men drawn heavily from diplomatic backgrounds. Fifty-seven per cent of all principal secretaries had been in charge of a diplomatic legation before their appointment. Perhaps more tellingly, there was never a period, but for the

Interregnum, when at least one of the principal secretaries had not had previous and extensive ambassadorial responsibilities overseas.[5] Tudor-Stuart monarchs relied upon experience, at the highest levels, to guide their kingdom's foreign affairs. This also suggests, of course, a division within the secretariat that foreshadows the home/foreign office split of a later era.

With notable exceptions, men seemed to desire, even to solicit diplomatic service. They did so with good reason. Diplomacy may not have been an assured path to greater preferment and influence in the government, but it clearly constituted one important component in the successful building of careers by Tudor-Stuart courtiers and officials. We can dispel at the outset the notion that diplomatic service, with its long tenures abroad, its isolation from the English court, and its association with often highly suspect strangers was the wrong avenue for advancement.[6] Nor was it just the principal secretaries who began or enhanced their careers as ambassadors abroad. The overwhelming majority of men who participated in a diplomatic assignment were to be found at some point in their lives in a variety of other significant domestic offices of state. Sixty-three percent of the men who served at the rank of ambassador or above had careers distinguished enough to be found in the *Dictionary of National Biography*. In excess of eighty percent are found either in the *DNB* or were members of Parliament, as listed by the History of Parliament Trust. Indeed, the administrative experience acquired through diplomatic service combined with the other roles undertaken abroad gave a man an enormously valuable background. He became, after an ambassadorship, a prime candidate to serve his government in responsible and often remunerative domestic positions.

It was moreover the case that diplomacy itself was remunerative. Besides very large salaries, detailed herein, ambassadors could claim, as well, compensation through their bills of extraordinaries—their expense account statements (for the heavier of their overseas expenditures).[7] Salaries also rose with the passage of time. In fact, average increases in diplomatic pay slightly outran inflation. While inflation increased prices by a factor of 4.1, reimbursement for diplomatic 'diets' rose by 4.7 between the decade of the 1520s and that of the 1670s.[8] A note of warning imposes itself here however. There is enough preliminary evidence to indicate that irrespective of official rates of pay, some ambassadors were compensated only slowly, if at all. This is to be expected during the reign of Charles I, and that pattern is in fact observable in existing correspondence from the period. His father's reign also established a bad, although not quite as egregious a record as that of Charles for letting diplomatic pay lag behind promised pay dates. Other reigns exhibit an admittedly mixed record. The major

[5] E. B. Fryde, et al., *Handbook of British Chronology*, 3rd ed. (London, Royal Historical Society, 1986), pp. 116-18.

[6] Garrett Mattingly, *Renaissance Diplomacy* (London, Jonathan Cape, 1963), p. 236.

[7] A thesis more amply developed in: Gary M. Bell, 'Elizabethan Diplomatic Compensation: Its Nature and Variety,' *Journal of British Studies* (Spring, 1981), pp. 1-25.

[8] Developed from information provided in: Peter Ramsey, *The Price Revolution in Sixteenth Century England* (London, Methuen and Co., 1971), combined with information derived from pay averages of all ambassadors of the 1520s and 1670s.

exception to such generalizations was that of Queen Elizabeth. Her pay, although perhaps less generous, was promptly remitted, possibly reflecting again the central role of the diplomatic cadre in this Queen's reign.

There are numerous other patterns that knowledge of the men who served can now provide. With sure identification of who they were, we can begin to accumulate their life stories, and their general qualifications, strengths, liabilities, and contributions.

Structure

The *Handlist* also suggests the evolution of the diplomatic structure. For instance, an ambassadorship, at the outset of our period, had often been a solitary responsibility, but one involving an increasingly large entourage of attendants by the Stuart era. Above all, the embassy secretary emerged as a distinct officer. The secretary developed from what was a purely personal servant who accompanied the Henrician ambassadors to a formal diplomatic official, usually paid independently by the government, often nominated separately, and functioning as the second ranking individual in the legation by the Stuart era. He handled not only 'secretarial chores'—producing correspondence, securing information, conveying messages, and attending to the desiderata of ambassadorial responsibilities—but frequently he negotiated autonomously. In a number of instances, he assumed the legation outright, such as when the ambassador died in office. This was no trivial role when one understands that approximately 10 percent of all embassies ended fatally for the principal diplomat. It was the secretary, as chargé d'affaires, who provided continuity.

It is hard to say whether or not the ambassador could draw, as our period progresses, upon other skilled subordinates for support in his assignment. This would require the detailed analysis that only long familiarity with ambassadorial correspondence could provide. There is, however, some evidence that this was the case. Sir Thomas Chudleigh, recommended in 1680 as a possible substitute for Sir Philip Warwick in the assignment to Sweden, was cited as having a vast background of a varied nature in previous legations.[9] One is struck with the fact that he, and certainly others like him, would have been distinct assets in the embassies that encompassed their services.

The professionalization of the diplomatic corps is unmistakable during our two-century period. With the often systematic preparation of diplomats, with the frequently clear criteria employed in selection, and with repeated usage of the same men besides, it is no longer possible to assert glibly that there were no professional diplomats. In reality, certain men, such as Sir Dudley Carleton, Sir Henry Killigrew, Thomas Randolph, and Sir William Temple, in various reigns, give very clear evidence of being preoccupied with diplomacy at home and abroad; they were used extensively in overseas assignments, and could, with further study, prove to be the prototypes of an emerging, professional diplomatic bureaucracy.

[9] Great Britain, Public Record Office, *Calendar of State Papers, Domestic, 1680-1* (1860-1939), p. 53.

To take this generalization one step further, it is also clear that even at home men continued to serve the demands of diplomacy. By the Elizabethan period there had emerged a clear conception of area specializations. Daniel Rogers dealt continuously with the business of the Baltic, while Thomas Randolph had clearly become the Scottish expert (as Sir Ralph Sadler had been before him), and Wilkes, Wilson, and Davison were the men called upon to deal with the Low Countries. There was emerging an unmistakable professionalization by function.

As the ambassador's function and the structure of his legation become more specific and more formalized, so too did ambassadorial titles become specialized. For the first time we have a rather complete idea of what each legate was called by his contemporaries. When we move from the sixteenth to the seventeenth centuries, titular distinctions become far less quixotic, as section II, above, indicates.

The legation became more formalized, the responsibilities more extensive, and indeed, even the personnel seem to have grown increasingly professional. The *Handlist* gives evidence, in the most cursory of ways, that between 1509 and 1688 there is to be found the modernization of the English diplomatic service.[10] There are of course numerous other possibilities for inquiry that the *Handlist* suggests. It is to be hoped that the information herein will suggest the need for future work on the nature of diplomatic administration and practices and also help revitalize a venerable and honourable historical genre — the history of foreign affairs.

---

[10] Based on criteria presented in Henry Parris, *Constitutional Bureaucracy: The Development of British Central Administration Since the Eighteenth Century* (London, 1969); H. E. Dale, *The Higher Civil Service of Great Britain* (Oxford, 1941).

ABBREVIATIONS AND SYMBOLS USED

Add	British Library, Additional Collection
APC	*Acts of the Privy Council*
BIHR	*Bulletin of Institute of Historical Research*
Bodl.	Bodleian Library, Oxford
BL	British Library
c.	circa
Calig.	British Library, Cotton Collection, Caligula
CO	Colonial Office
CSPCol/EI	*Calendar of State Papers, Colonial, East Indies* (as differentiated from Colonial, West Indies)
CSPD	*Calendar of State Papers, Domestic*
CSPF	*Calendar of State Papers, Foreign*
CSPM	*Calendar of State Papers, Milan*
CSPR	*Calendar of State Papers, Roman*
CSPS	*Calendar of State Papers, Spanish* (including the 13 vols., 1485-1558, and the 4 vols., 1558-1603, which constitute two different series)
CSPScot	*Calendar of State Papers, Scottish* (1898-1952 edition)
CSPScot (1858 ed.)	*Calendar of State Papers, Scottish* (1858 ed.)
CSPV	*Calendar of State Papers, Venetian*
CTB	*Calendar of Treasury Books*
d.	died
E	Exchequer
Eg.	British Library, Egerton Collection
EHR	*English Historical Review*
Faust.	British Library, Cotton Collection, Faustina
fl.	flourished (dates when diplomat was active)
Harl.	British Library, Harleian Collection
HMC	Historical Manuscripts Commission
KL	Kervyn de Lettenhove, *Relations politiques de Pays-Bas...*
L&A	*Lists and Analyses of State Papers, Foreign*
L&P	*Letters and Papers of Henry VIII*
PRO	Public Record Office
RHS	Royal Historical Society
Salisb.	Manuscripts preserved at Hatfield House, reported by the HMC
SP	State Papers
ThSP	Thurlow, John, *A Collection of State Papers of John Thurloe...*(1742)

TRHS	Transactions of the Royal Historical Society
Vesp	British Library, Cotton Collection, Vespasian
Vitel.	British Library, Cotton Collection, Vitellius
*	an asterisk next to a name indicates that it is to be found in one, two or all of the major biographical collections of the Tudor/Stuart era — the *DNB*, the publications of the History of Parliament Trust or the *Complete Peerage*.

BRITISH DIPLOMATIC REPRESENTATIVES
1509-1688

CONFERENCES, CONGRESSES

These entries include peace conferences, commercial negotiations, and similar conventions where specific geographical designations do not seem especially informative or accurate. These conferences usually involved multiple participants (bilateral negotiations are for the most part included under the foreign country or prince involved).

C1.
TUNSTALL, Cuthbert, Bishop of London (later Bishop of Durham; 1474-1559)*
KNIGHT, Dr. William (later Bishop of Bath and Wells; 1476-1547)*
MORE, Thomas (later Sir Thomas; 1477/8-1535)*
HACKETT, John (later Sir John; *d*.1534)

29 June 1529*a* - *c*.22 Aug. 1529*b*	Peace Commissioners
First meeting: *c*.6 July 1529	53*s* 4*d*/d (Tunstall),
	26*s* 8*d*/d (More)

They met at Cambrai in Flanders to conclude the Treaty of Cambrai. The resident in the Low Countries (q.v.) John Hackett was included in the commission.

Instructions: *L&P*, iv, 3, no. 5818; Rogers, E. (ed.), *The Letters of Sir John Hackett, 1526-1534* (Morgantown, W. Va., 1971), p. 277.
Correspondence: *L&P*, iv, 3; Rogers, *Letters of Hackett*.

C2.
WOTTON, Dr. Nicholas (later Sir Nicholas; 1497?-1567)*

c.15 Sept. 1558*h* - 21 Nov. 1558*c*	[Peace Commissioner]
First meeting: 22 Sept. 1558	

He met with the French representatives at Lille.

Correspondence: BL, Cotton, Galba C.i; *CSPF, 1553-8*; *APC, 1556-8*; KL, i.

C3.
FITZALAN, Henry, 12th Earl of Arundel (1511?-1580)*
THIRLBY, Dr. Thomas, Bishop of Ely (1506?-1570)*

28 Sept. 1558[h] - 21 Nov. 1558[c]   [Peace Commissioners]
First meeting: 23 Oct. 1558   £5/d (Thirlby)

They were sent to join with Wotton for formal peace negotiations at Cercamp. Guido Cavalcanti was seemingly an adjunct to this diplomatic group. Their commissions expired with the issuance of updated commissions by the new Queen, Elizabeth I.

Correspondence: *CSPF, 1553-8, 1558-9*; KL, i.

C4.
HOWARD, William, 1st Baron Howard of Effingham (1510?-1573)*
THIRLBY, Dr. Thomas, Bishop of Ely (1506?-1570)*
WOTTON, Dr. Nicholas (later Sir Nicholas; 1497?-1567)*

7 Nov. 1558[a] - 7 Apr. 1559[c]   [Peace Commissioners]
(Thirlby)   £6/d (Howard), £5/d
21 Nov. 1558[b]   (Thirlby), £4/d (Wotton)
(Howard and Wotton)

They were joined for a time in late 1558-early 1559 by William Lord Cobham (Low Countries, q.v.). The commissioners were involved first at Brussels, and then Câteau-Cambrésis, where they negotiated variously with representatives of the Scottish monarchs, the Spanish King, and the French King. Once again, Cavalcanti seemingly served as a diplomatic adjunct. Wotton was engaged, late Dec. 1558, to late Jan. 1559, in a special mission to Philip II at Brussels (Low Countries, q.v.).

Instructions: BL, Cotton, Calig. E.v, f. 42, Galba C.i, ff. 22-5; *CSPF, 1558-9*, nos. 23, 174-6.
Correspondence: *CSPF, 1558-9*; BL, Cotton, Galba C.i, Calig. E.xii; KL, i; plus others as listed in Weaver, F., 'Anglo-French Diplomatic Relations, 1558-1603,' *BIHR* (1926-9), iv, p. 76.

C5.
MASON, Sir John (1503-1566)*

7 Mar. 1559[c] - 7 Apr. 1559[a]   [Peace Commissioner]
Arrived: 16 Mar. 1559

He joined with the other commissioners at Câteau-Cambrésis (see above).

Instructions: *CSPF, 1558-9*, no. 374; KL, i, pp. 458-9.
Correspondence: *CSPF, 1558-9*; KL, i.

C6.
BROWNE, Anthony, Viscount Montagu (1528-1592)*
WOTTON, Sir Nicholas (1497?-1567)*
HADDON, Dr. Walter (1516-1571)*

5 Mar. 1565[b] - *c.*1 July 1566[e]	Commissioners
Beginning of negotiations:	£5/d (Montagu), £4/d
*c.*30 Mar. 1565	(Wotton), £2/d (Haddon)
Secretary: John Shers?	

They met at Bruges with the Spanish commissioners to resolve commercial differences. The conference was prorogued from 29 Sept. 1565 until 15 Apr. 1566 (during which time the commissioners returned to England). After negotiations terminated, Wotton apparently remained in the Low Countries until *c.*Oct. 1566, perhaps for health reasons.

Instructions: BL, Add. 19400, 32091, Cotton, Galba C.ii, ff. 18-34, 268-79; Eg. 2790, ff. 165-72, Lansd. 155, ff. 113b-24, Sloane 2442, ff. 28-33; *CSPF, 1564-5*, no. 1036; HMC *Salisb.* i, p. 318; HMC *2nd Report*, p. 97; HMC *Pepys*, p. 43.
Correspondence: BL, Cotton, Galba C.ii; *CSPF, 1564-5*; KL, iv; HMC *Salisb.*, i; HMC *Pepys*.

C7.
ROGERS, Dr. John (*c.*1540-1603)*
JENKINSON, Anthony (1530?-1611)*

1 July 1577[a] - 28 Oct. 1577[a]	[Special Ambassadors]
First meeeting: 10 Aug. 1577	40s/d (Rogers)

This meeting with Danish commissioners was to have taken place in Emden, but actually took place in Hamburg. Jenkinson returned but Rogers went to the Hanse towns and possibly Germany (qq.v.), from which he did not return until 7 Dec. 1577.

Instructions: BL, Lansd. 155, ff. 201-02, Sloane 2442, p. 97; *CSPF, 1577-8*, no. 28-30; HMC *2nd Report*, p. 97; PRO, 'Report on the Royal Archives of Denmark,' *Deputy Keeper Reports*, xlv (1884) app. ii, p. 48.
Correspondence: *CSPF, 1577-8*.

C8.
STANLEY, Henry, 4th Earl of Derby (1531-1593)*
BROOKE, William, 7th Baron Cobham (1527-1597)*
CROFTS, Sir James (*c.*1518-1590)*
DALE, Dr. Valentine (by 1527-1589)*
ROGERS, Dr. John (*c.*1540-1603)*

20 Jan. 1588*a* - 10 Aug. 1588*c*	[Peace Commissioners]
(Rogers)	£6/d (Derby), £5/d (Cobham),
30 Nov. 1587*a*	£4/d (Croft), 53*s* 4*d*/d
(all others)	(Dale), 40*s*/d (Rogers)
Arrived (Ostend): 26 Feb. 1588	
First meeting (Bourbourg): 27 May	
1588	

Secretary: Richard Spencer?

This mission involved the peace negotiations with Spain that occurred just prior to the Spanish Armada. Despite the names listed in the original commission, Rogers was substituted at the last minute for Sir Amias Paulet. The others joined with Dale, who had apparently left early and was already in the Low Countries (q.v.). This mission included meetings by Croft, Dale and Rogers, at separate times, with the Duke of Parma at Bruges. Croft also returned to England briefly in late Mar. through early April.

Instructions: PRO, SP/77/2, no. 7; BL, Cotton, Galba D.ii, f. 3; Vesp. C.viii, ff. 18-21, Lansd. 103, no. 53, Sloane 2442, f. 89; Oxford, Mss. at All Souls Lib., ccxix, ff. 37-9; *CSPF, 1588* (xxi-4), pp. 32-3, 43-6, 84.

Correspondence: BL, Cotton, Add. 4105, 14027, 35841, 38823, Galba D.iii, Vesp. C.vii-viii, Harl. 286, 287, 6994, Lansd. 57; *CSPF, 1588* (xxi-4), *1588* (xxii); HMC *Ancaster.*

C9.
HERBERT, Dr. John (later Sir John; *c.*1540-1617)*
BEALE, Robert (1541-1601)*
NEVILLE, Sir Henry (1562-1615)*
EDMONDES, Thomas (later Sir Thomas; *c.*1563-1639)*

20 Apr. 1600*a* - 8 Aug. 1600*a*	[Peace Commissioners]
Arrived: 16 May 1600	60*s*/d (Herbert and Beale each),
	66*s* 8*d*/d (Neville),
	40*s*/d (Edmondes)

The commissioners met at Boulogne with Spanish representatives, including the Regent of the Spanish Netherlands, the Archduke, to discuss Anglo/Spanish peace. Neville briefly returned to England in late June 1600.

Instructions: PRO, SP/78/44, ff. 129-36; BL, Lansd. 161, ff. 338-46, Stowe 179, f. 163; HMC *Salisb.*, x, pp. 145-6. PRO, SP/78/44, ff. 112 and Harl. 4715, ff. 183-240 (for Neville only).

Correspondence: PRO, SP/78/44; BL, Add. 22591, 48035, Cotton, Vesp. C.viii (including a journal of negotiations), Hargrave 226, Sloane 1786,

Stowe 145, 167, 179; Oxford, Mss. at Exeter College Lib., cxli; *APC, 1599-1600*; HMC *Salisb.*, x.

C10.
EURE, Ralph, 3rd Baron Eure (1558-1617)*
DUNN, Dr. Daniel (*c*.1550-1617)*
HERBERT, Sir John (*c*.1540-1617)*

16 July 1602*ᵃ* - 27 May 1603*ᵇ*　　Commissioners
Audience: *c*.2 Oct. 1602　　　　　100*s*/d (Eure),
Secretary: Stephen Lesieur　　　　60*s*/d (Herbert)

They were sent to Bremen to negotiate with the Danes and the Hanse.

Instructions and Commissions: BL, Cotton, Nero B.iv, ff. 43, 46-60, B.vi, ff. 252-7; Rymer, *Foedera* ..., xvi, p. 429.
Correspondence: PRO, SP/75/3; BL, Cotton, Nero B.iv; HMC *Salisb.*, xii, xv; Rymer, *Foedera*, xvi.

C11.
ROE, Sir Thomas (1581?-1644)*

8 Apr. 1638*ᵃ* - 2 June 1640*ᵃ*　　Ambassador Extraordinary
Arrived: *c*.8 June 1638　　　　　£6/d
Secretary: Mr. Westphalus

He participated in the peace negotiations at Hamburg. During this engagement, he seemingly functioned as well as an ambassador throughout the Hanse towns (q.v.). He went to Denmark (q.v.) after the negotiations concluded.

Instructions: PRO, SP/81/44, f. 72.
Correspondence: PRO, SP/81/44-6; BL, Add. 4168-72, Harl. 1901, Eg. 2533; *CSPD, 1637-8, 1639-40, 1640*; Baker, L., *The Letters of Elizabeth of Bohemia* (1953).

C12.
MONTAGU, Edward (later 1st Earl of Sandwich; 1625-1672)*
SIDNEY, Algernon (1622-1683)*
HONYWOOD, Sir Robert (1601-1686)*
BOONE, Thomas (*fl*.1650s)

11 Mar. 1659*ᶜ* - 13 Sept. 1659*ᵍ*　　Plenipotentiaries
(Montagu)　　(Montagu)
30 June 1659*ᵇ*　　*c*.1 July 1660*ᵉ*
(the other plenipotentiaries)
Began work (Montagu): 6 Apr. 1659
Audience (all commissioners together):
　3 Aug. 1659

They met with representatives of the Swedes, the Danes and the Dutch at Elsinore, Denmark, in a conference about trade into the Baltic. The Lord Admiral Montagu's fleet was already in the Sound, and thus he began his involvement before the other commissioners. Sidney, Honywood and Boone were appointed to the commission 30 Jun. 1659, opened negotiations with the Danes on 3 Aug. 1659, and did not conclude their responsibilities until 21 June 1660. As the events of the Restoration became more compelling, Boone may have returned to England in Dec. 1659, much as Montagu had already returned earlier (13 Sept. 1659) with the fleet for the same reasons. The various commissioners also made contact with the Swedish court (q.v.) at different times.

Instructions: PRO, SP/75/16, ff. 262-70; BL, Add. 40796, ff. 17, 32; *ThSP*, vii, pp. 680, 727-8.

Correspondence: PRO, SP/75/17; BL, Add. 4158; Bodl., Tanner Mss. 51, Rawlinson Mss. A.65; *ThSP*, vii; Ewald, A., *The Life and Times of the Hon. Algernon Sidney*...(1873); Montagu, E., *The Journal of Edward Montague, the Earl of Sandwich*...ed. R. Anderson (1929); Carte, T. (ed.), ...*Ormonde Papers*...(1739), ii.

C13.
TEMPLE, Sir William, 1st Bart. (1628-1699)*

2 Apr. 1668[b] - 2 July 1668[a] Ambassador Extraordinary
Arrived: 19 Apr. 1668

He was the English representative at the conference at Aix-la-Chapelle.

Correspondence: PRO, SP/81/58; Temple, W., *The Works of Sir William Temple, Bart.*,...ed. J. Swift (1720), iii; Haley, K. H. D., *An English Diplomat in the Low Countries*...(1986).

C14.
HOLLES, Denzil, Baron Holles of Ifield (1599-1680)*
COVENTRY, Henry (*c*.1618-1686)*

22 Mar. 1667[b] - 13 Sept. 1667[a] Plenipotentiaries
First general meeting: 25 May 1667 £100/wk. (each)
Secretary: Nicholas Morice

They were the English delegates to the peace conference at Breda. Holles came directly from his residency in France (q.v.). Coventry returned briefly to England for further instructions, mid-June - July 1667.

Instructions: PRO, SP/84/182, f. 95 *et seq.*
Correspondence: BL, Add. 32074.

C15.
VILLIERS, George, 2nd Duke of Buckingham (1628-1687)*
SAVILE, George, Viscount Halifax (later Earl of Halifax; 1633-1695)*
BENNET, Henry, Earl of Arlington (1618-1685)*

21 June 1672[d] - 21 July 1672[a] [Plenipotentiaries]
First session: 26 June 1672 £4754 (shared between
Secretary: Sir Joseph Williamson Villiers and Bennet)

They participated in the Franco-Dutch peace negotiations in the Low Countries; and were also accredited to the French and Dutch sovereigns in the same area (Low Countries, France, qq.v.).

Instructions: PRO, SP/104/64, ff. 25-6, SP/105/101, ff. 6-7; Foxcroft, H., *The Life and Letters of Sir George Savile...* (1898), i, pp. 72-5.
Correspondence: PRO, SP/84/189-90, SP/105/101; BL, Add. 22878, 28953; Foxcroft, *Life and Letters of Savile*, i.

C16.
JENKINS, Sir Leoline (*c.*1625-1685)*
WILLIAMSON, Sir Joseph (1633-1701)*

6 May 1673[a] - 5 May 1674[b]   Plenipotentiaries
Secretaries: Thomas Chudleigh and   £100/wk. (each)
    Réné Petit

They attended the Congress at Cologne. Robert Spencer, 2nd Earl of Sunderland was scheduled to attend, although owing to sickness, he never went.

Instructions: PRO, SP/81/60, ff. 110-51, SP/104/64, ff. 50-6, 61-5.
Correspondence: PRO, SP/81/60-74, SP/105/229; BL, Add. 28937, 34346, Stowe 203-05; Oxford, Mss. at All Souls Lib., ccxli; Christie, W. (ed.), *Letters Addressed from London to Sir Joseph Williamson while Plenipotentiary at the Congress of Cologne...*, Camden n.s., viii-ix (1874).

C17.
BERKELEY, John, 1st Baron Berkeley of Stratton (1606?-1678)*
JENKINS, Sir Leoline (*c.*1625-1685)*
HYDE, Laurence (later Viscount Hyde of Kenilworth, Earl of Rochester; 1642-1711)*
TEMPLE, Sir William, 1st Bart. (1628-1699)*

13 Dec. 1675[a] - 26 Aug. 1679[a]   Plenipotentiaries
Arrived: 24 Dec. 1675   £1300/qtr. (Jenkins)
Secretary: Thomas Chudleigh

These delegates attended the Congress at Nimwegen. The permanent plenipotentiary was Sir Leoline Jenkins. Berkeley, the resident in France (q.v.), joined him 7 Oct. 1676. Berkeley returned to England 16 June 1677. Hyde was a participant in the Congress from 30 Aug. 1677[a] through 14 Feb. 1679[a], with a return to England from June to Aug. 1678. Temple, the resident in the Low Countries (q.v.), joined the Congress from 28 June through early March 1679, when he returned to the Low Countries.

Instructions: PRO, SP/81/76, ff. 263-7, SP/84/199, ff. 268-71, SP/104/66, ff. 85-7; Courtenay, T., *Memoirs of the Life, Works and Correspondence of Sir William Temple, Bart.* (1836), ii, pp. 412-24.
Correspondence: PRO, SP/84/207, 209-14, SP/104/184; BL, Eg. 3682, Add. 5819, 9801, 17016-7, 25119, 28054, 28103, 28896, 28953, 32095, 34274, Eg. 3325, 3354, Harl. 1514-23, Stowe 210-11; Oxford, Mss. at All Souls Lib., ccxii, ccxl, cclii; *CSPD, 1678*; HMC *Hodgkin*; Browning, A., *Thomas Osborne, Earl of Danby and Duke of Leeds, 1632-1712* (Glasgow, 1944-51).

DENMARK

DK1.
BAKER, John (later Sir John; *c*.1489-1558)*

17 Mar. 1514^d - *c*.15 Sept. 1514^d [Special Ambassador]

Instructions: *L&P*, i, 2, nos. 2721, 2731.
Correspondence: *L&P*, i, 2; PRO, 'Report on the Royal Archives of Denmark...,' *Reports of the Deputy Keeper of the Public Record Office*, xlv (1884), app. ii.

DK2.
LEE, Dr. Thomas (later Sir Thomas; by 1511-1545)*

21 Dec. 1532^a - 28 Mar. 1533^a [Special Ambassador]
20*s*/d

He also went to Hamburg (Hanse, q.v.).

Instructions: Inferred from *L&P*, v, no. 1633; *CSPS, 1531-3*, pt. 2, p. 818.

DK3.
31 Jan. 1534^b - early July 1534^g Special Ambassador

He also went to Lübeck and Hamburg (Hanse, q.v.).

Instructions: Suggested in part in *L&P*, vii, no. 167.
Correspondence: BL, Cotton, Galba, B.x; *L&P*, vii.

DK4.
BONNER, Dr. Edmund (later Bishop of Hereford, London; 1500?-1569)*
CAVENDISH, Richard (*fl*.1530s)

20 July 1535^b - 27 Apr. 1536^a [Special Ambassadors]
Audience: mid-Sept. 1535 13*s* 4*d*/d (Cavendish)

Besides Denmark, they visited the Duke of Holstein, the court of Sweden, and some of the Hanse towns (qq.v.).

Instructions: Inferred from *L&P*, x, nos. 24, 303.
Correspondence: *L&P*, viii-x; BL, Cotton, Vitel. B.xxi, Nero B.iii, Add. 48036; Merriman, R., *The Life and Letters of Thomas Cromwell* (1902).

DK5.
BARNES, Dr. Robert (1495-1540)*
ST. LEGER, George (*fl*.1530s)

10 Mar. 1539^a - *c*.15 June 1539^c Special Ambassadors
Audience: *c*.12 May 1539 20*s*/d (Barnes), 10*s*/d (St. Leger)

Instructions: Inferred from *L&P*, xiv, 1, no. 955.
Correspondence: *L&P*, xiv.

DK6.
MORISON, Richard (later Sir Richard; by 1514-1556)*

23 Dec. 1546[b] - early Mar.? 1547[h]   [Special Ambassador]
Secretary: Jacques Granada?   26s 8d/d

He also visited some of the Hanse towns (q.v.). He served as well as Henry
    VIII's delegate to a peace conference between the Duke of Holstein and King
    Christian of Denmark, held in Holstein.

Instructions: *L&P*, xxi, 2, no. 647 (50); suggested in *CSPS, 1545-6*, p. 543.
Correspondence: *L&P*, xxi, 2; *CSPF, 1547-53*.

DK7.
BORTHWICK, Sir John (*fl.*1540s-1550s)

12 Nov. 1548[c] - n.d.   Agent

While an agent in the Baltic area, presumably stationed at Danzig, (German
    States; Hanse qq.v.), he undertook this and the following missions to
    Denmark.

Instructions: PRO, 'Report on the Royal Archives of Denmark...,' *Reports of
    the Deputy Keeper...* xlv, app. ii, p. 21.
Correspondence: *CSPF, 1547-53*.

DK8.

10 Dec. 1550[c] - n.d.   Agent

He was dispatched from England, to where he had apparently returned
    temporarily.

Instructions: BL, Add. 5935, ff. 86-8, Sloane 2442, f. 27, Lansd. 353, ff. 38-
    40(?).

DK9.

19 June 1552[d] - *c.*15 Nov. 1552[g]   Agent

Correspondence about: HMC *Salisb.*, i; PRO, 'Report on the Royal Archives of
    Denmark...,' *Reports of the Deputy Keeper...* xlv.

DK10.
SPITHOVIUS, John (*fl.*1560s)

Jan.? 1560[h] - July? 1560[h]   [Special Ambassador]
Audience: 22 Feb. 1560

Instructions: Inferred from *CSPF, 1559-60*, no. 806, *1560-1*, no. 181.
Correspondence: *CSPF, 1559-60, 1560-1*.

DK11.

ALLEN, Richard (*d.*1602)

*c.*11 Sept. 1577[h] - *c.*7 Nov. 1577[e]   Special Ambassador
Audience (with Danish Council):
  *c.*15 Oct. 1577

Instructions: Inferred from CSPF, 1577-8, no. 364.
Correspondence about: *CSPF, 1577-8*; PRO, 'Second Report on the Royal Archives of Denmark...,' *Reports of the Deputy Keeper of the Public Record Office*, xlvi (1886), app. ii.

DK12.

ROGERS, Dr. John (*c.*1540-1603)*

*c.*6 Aug. 1580[d] - autumn 1581[h]   [Special Ambassador]
Audience: *c.*1 Sept. 1580

He also went to Poland, Sweden, and the Hanse (qq.v.). William Salkins, a merchant, accompanied him.

Instructions: BL, Sloane 2442, ff. 41-3, Harl. 36, f. 319.
Correspondence: PRO, SP/88/1; Talbot, C., *Res Polonicae Elisabetha...* (Rome, 1961).

DK13.

BERTIE, Peregrine, Baron Willoughby d'Eresby (1555-1601)*

28 June 1582[b] - by 1 Nov. 1582[h]   [Special Ambassador]
Investiture: 14 Aug. 1582

He conveyed the Garter to Frederick II.

Credentials: Inferred from *CSPF, 1582*, no. 130.
Correspondence: HMC *Ancaster*.
Correspondence about: *CSPF, 1582*.

DK14.

HERBERT, John (later Sir John; *c.*1540-1617)*

16 May 1583[b] - *c.*1 Sept. 1585[e]   [Special Ambassador]
Audience: mid-June 1583

He went from Denmark in autumn 1583 to Prussia (German States), Poland, and the Hanse towns (qq.v.).

Instructions: PRO, SP/88/1, no. 26.
Correspondence: BL, Cotton, Nero B.iii, Galba D.xiii; *CSPF, 1583*; Talbot, *Res Polonicae*; PRO, 'Report on the Royal Archives of Denmark...,' *Report of the Deputy Keeper...*, xlv.

DK15.
BODLEY, Thomas (later Sir Thomas; 1545-1613)*

27 Apr. 1585[b] - *c*.15 Aug. 1585[g]   [Special Ambassador]
Audience: 12 Jun. 1585

He also visited the Duke of Brunswick (German States, q.v.).

Instructions: BL, Cotton, Julius F.vi, f. 63, Nero B.iii, ff. 271-4; *CSPF, 1584-5*, pp. 415-6; HMC *Ancaster*, p. 16; PRO, 'Report on the Royal Archives of Denmark...,' *Reports of the Deputy Keeper...* xlv, p. 26.
Correspondence: PRO, SP/82/3; BL, Cotton, Galba C.viii, D.ix, D.xiii; *CSPF, 1584-5*.

DK16.
BERTIE, Peregrine, Baron Willoughby d'Eresby (1555-1601)*

28 Jun. 1585[b] - *c*.1 Mar. 1586[h]   [Special Ambassador]
Audience: *c*.18 Oct. 1585   £4/d

He also visited the Duke of Brunswick (German States, q.v.).

Instructions: BL, Cotton, Julius F.vi, f. 184b, Nero B.iii, ff. 244- 6; inferred from *CSPF, 1585-6*, pp. 255-7; HMC *Ancaster*, p. 17.
Correspondence: BL, Cotton, Nero B.iii, Titus C.vii, ff. 226-35 (a summary of the mission by Willoughby); *CSPF, 1585-6*; HMC *Ancaster*.

DK17.
ROGERS, Daniel (*c*.1538-1591)*

18 Sept. 1587[a] - *c*.25 Jan. 1588[c]   [Special Ambassador]
                                 40s/d

He apparently stopped in the Low Countries (q.v.) both going to and returning from Denmark.

Instructions: *CSPF, 1586-8*, pt. 1, pp. 369-71; PRO, 'Report on the Royal Archives of Denmark...,' *Reports of the Deputy Keeper...* xlv, pp. 30, 49.
Correspondence: BL, Cotton, Nero B.iii; *CSPF, 1586-8*.

DK18.

12 June 1588[b] - *c*.1 Sept. 1588[e]   [Special Ambassador]
Audience: 7 July 1588

This was a mission to negotiate trading rights in the Baltic and fishing rights off Iceland, but it also became a mission of condolence upon the death of the Danish King. Anthony Jenkinson was apparently associated with Rogers in the negotiations.

Instructions: BL, Cotton, Nero B.iii, ff. 330-2, 335b, Eg. 2790, f. 230; HMC *Salisb.*, iii, p. 329.
Correspondence: BL, Cotton, Nero B.iii, Harl. 57, 168, Lansd. 57, Sloane 2442; *CSPF, 1588* (xxii).

DK19.
BODLEY, Thomas (later Sir Thomas; 1545-1613)*

11 Aug. 1588[c] - *c.*1 Oct. 1588[h]　　　　[Special Ambassador]

He also apparently went to the Hanse towns (q.v.) although the documentation that he actually went on this mission cannot be located.

Instructions: BL, Cotton, Nero B.iii, ff. 333-4.

DK20.
DYER, Edward (later Sir Edward; 1543-1607)*

1 Oct. 1589[f] - mid-Mar. 1590[c]　　　　[Special Ambassador]

He travelled home through Bohemia on private business.

Instructions: Inferred from *APC, 1588*, pp. 228-9.
Correspondence about: PRO, SP/82/3, SP/84/35; *L&A, 1589-90*.

DK21.
PARKINS, Dr. Christopher (later Sir Christopher; *c.*1543-1622)*

9 May 1590[b] - *c.*26 July 1591[c]　　　　[Special Ambassador]
Audience: 21 June 1590　　　　　　　　£300 (total)

He also went to Poland, Prussia and the Hanse towns (qq.v.), with a great deal of travelling between these areas.

Instructions: Inferred from PRO, SP/75/2, ff. 128-33; *L&A, 1591-2*, nos. 885, 890; PRO, 'Report on the Royal Archives of Denmark...,' *Reports of the Deputy Keeper*... xlv, p. 31.
Correspondence: PRO, SP/75/2; *L&A, 1589-90, 1590-1*; PRO, 'Report on the Royal Archives of Denmark...,' *Reports of the Deputy Keeper*... xlv; Talbot, C., *Res Polonicae Elisabetha*... (Rome, 1961).

DK22.
CAREW, George (later Sir George; *d.*1612)*

20 May 1598[a] - 21 Dec. 1598[b]　　　　[Special Ambassador]
　　　　　　　　　　　　　　　　　　40s/d

He also went to Poland, Germany and some of the Hanse towns (qq.v.).

Instructions: PRO, SP/88/2, ff. 48-58; Talbot, *Res Polonicae Elisabetha*, pp. 212-16.
Correspondence: PRO, SP/88/2; Carew, G., 'A Relation of the State of Polonia and the United Provinces of the Crown anno 1598,' in Mews, G., *Deutschland und der Osten* (Leipzig, 1936)—a report on the mission; Talbot, *Res Polonicae Elisabetha*.
Correspondence about: HMC *Salisb.*, viii.

DK23.
ZOUCHE, Edward la, 11th Baron Zouche of Harringworth (1556?-1625)*
PARKINS, Dr. Christopher (later Sir Christopher; *c.*1543-1622)*

26 May 1598*a* - 31 July 1598*b*	Ambassadors Extraordinary
Audience: 25 June 1598	£5/d (Zouche),
	40s/d (Parkins)

Instructions: PRO, SP/75/3, ff. 17-24, 42-3; BL, Cotton, Nero, B.iv; PRO, 'Report on the Royal Archives of Denmark...,' *Report of the Deputy Keeper...,* xlv, p. 32.
Correspondence: PRO, SP/75/3; *CSPD, 1598-160*1; HMC *Salisb.,* viii; PRO, 'Report on the Royal Archives of Denmark...,' *Reports of the Deputy Keeper...* xlv.

DK24.
PARKINS, Dr. Christopher (later Sir Christopher; *c.*1543-1622)*

1 Sept. 1598*a* - 10 Dec. 1598*b*	[Special Ambassador]
Audience: 6 Nov. 1598	40*s*/d

Instructions: PRO, SP/75/3, ff. 51-60.
Correspondence: PRO, SP/75/3; PRO, 'Report on the Royal Archives of Denmark...,' *Reports of the Deputy Keeper...* xlv.

DK25.
FERRERS, Thomas (*fl.*1590s)

10 Apr. 1599*a* - 30 Aug. 1599*a*	[Special Ambassador]
Audience: 1 May 1599	30*s*/d

Instructions: PRO, SP/75/3, ff. 91-3.
Correspondence: PRO, SP/75/3; BL, Stowe 150; HMC *Salisb.,* ix.

DK26.
LESIEUR, Stephen (later Sir Stephen; *d.*1627)*

21 Sept. 1599*a* - 1 Dec. 1599*a*	[Special Ambassador]
Arrived: 26 Oct. 1599	30*s*/d

Instructions: PRO, SP/75/3, ff. 154-8.
Correspondence: PRO, SP/75/3.

DK27.
BANCROFT, Dr. Richard, Bishop of London (later Archbishop of Canterbury; 1544-1610)*
PARKINS, Dr. Christopher (later Sir Christopher; *c.*1543-1622)
SWALE, Richard (later Sir Richard; 1545?-1608)*

25 Mar. 1600*a* - 11 July 1600*b*	[Commissioners]
	50*s*/d (Swale and Parkins each)

They were sent to Emden to treat with Danish commissioners on commercial matters.
Instructions: PRO, SP/75/3, ff. 204-10
Correspondence: PRO, SP/75/3; HMC *Salisb.,* x.

DK28.
LESIEUR, Stephen (later Sir Stephen; *d*.1627)*

14 Mar. 1602*b* - 3 July 1602*b*   [Special Ambassador]
                                          30*s*/d

This mission included stops in some Hanse towns (q.v.).

Instructions: PRO, SP/75/3, ff. 251-60; Rymer, T., *Foedera*...xvi, p. 440;
    PRO, 'Report on the Royal Archives of Denmark...,' *Report of the Deputy
    Keeper*..., xlv, p. 33.
Correspondence: PRO, SP/75/3; BL, Cotton, Nero B.iv; HMC *Salisb.*, xii.

DK29.
MANNERS, Roger, 5th Earl of Rutland (1576-1612)*
NAUNTON, Robert (1563-1635)*

1 June 1603*a* - 8 Aug. 1603*b*   [Special Ambassadors]
Audience: 10 July 1603   £6 13*s* 4*d*/d (Rutland)
                                          20*s*/d (Naunton)

Correspondence: PRO, SP/75/4; BL, Stowe 150; HMC *Salisb.*, xv.

DK30.
PACKER, John (1570?-1649)*

4 Sept. 1610*b* - 1611*g*   [Special Ambassador]

Instructions: PRO, SP/75/4, ff. 191-201.
Correspondence: PRO, SP/75/4; Birch, T. (comp.), *The Court and Times of
    James I*...(1849), i.

DK31.
ANSTRUTHER, Sir Robert (*fl*.1600s-1640s)

30 Apr. 1612*b* - 12 Apr. 1613*c*   [Agent]
Audience: *c*.3 June 1612

Instructions: Inferred from PRO, SP/75/5, f. 55.
Correspondence: PRO, SP/75/4-5; *CSPV, 1610-13*.

DK32.

4 Feb. 1615*d* - *c*.27 May 1615*c*   Special Ambassador

Instructions: PRO, 'Second Report on the Royal Archives of Denmark...'
    Reports of the Deputy Keeper..., xlvi, p. 11.
Correspondence: PRO, SP/75/5.

DK33.

8 Mar. 1620*b* - 15 Sept. 1620*c*   [Special] Ambassador

Instructions: Inferred from PRO, SP/75/5, f. 261.
Correspondence: BL, Add. 38597.

DK34.

8 Jan. 1621[b] - *c*.20 July 1621[c]　　　　[Agent]

He also stopped in the Low Countries (q.v.) and visited the Duke of Brunswick and the Count of Oldenburg in Germany (q.v.).

Instructions: Inferred from PRO, SP/75/5, f. 261; *CSPD, 1619-22*, p. 213; PRO, 'Second Report on the Royal Archives of Denmark...,' *Reports of the Deputy Keeper...*, xlvi, p. 15.
Correspondence: PRO, SP/75/5.

DK35.

1 Dec. 1623[a] - *c*.10 Apr. 1625[c]　　[Resident Ambassador]
Audience: *c*.mid-Aug. 1624　　　　　£4/d

Between Oct. and Nov. 1624, he went to Saxony, German States (q.v.) during his sojurn in Denmark. He also visited the Hague, Low Countries (q.v.) both going to and returning from Denmark.

Instructions: Inferred from PRO, 'Second Report on the Royal Archives of Denmark...,' *Reports of the Deputy Keeper...*, xlvi, p. 17.
Correspondence: PRO, SP/75/5; BL, Add. 35832, Stowe 176, 258, 272, 274.

DK36.

1 Mar. 1625[a] - 26 Apr. 1635[a]　　　Ambassador Ordinary
Audience: *c*.mid-June 1625　　　　　£4/d
Secretaries: Joseph Avery and
　　Mr. Hurst (after 1628)

His responsibilities in Denmark were repeatedly interrupted by assignments into Germany—being sent both to individual princes and to the Imperial Court (qq.v.). This was especially the case when he was directed to attend the Prince of Brandenburg, mid-1627; the Diet at Ratisbone, 29 June 1630 to *c*.Jan. 1631; the Emperor (after a brief return to England) 3 Dec. 1632 until 28 July 1633; and the Diet at Frankfurt, Apr. 1634 to Sept. 1634. He may well have relocated to Hamburg for the latter part of his embassy, Nov. 1627 through 1635 (also Hanse, q.v.). He returned to England briefly at least in Dec. 1628, besides Dec. 1632.

Instructions: PRO, SP/75/6, f. 72; BL, Add. 35832, f. 179.
Correspondence: PRO, SP/75/6-13, SP/104/167, 169; BL, Add. 4474, 35832, 38669, Eg. 1820, 2553, Harl. 1583; *CSPD, 1625-6, 1628-9, 1629-31, Add. 1625-49*; PRO, 'Third Report on the Royal Archives of Denmark...,' *Reports of the Deputy Keeper...*, xlvii (1886), app. i.

DK37.
GORDON, Francis (*fl.*1620s-1640s)

c.30 Jan. 1627 - n.d.　　　　　[Special Ambassador]

While ambassador to Poland (q.v.), he visited Denmark.

DK38.
CLERKE, Edward (*fl.*1620s)

26 July 1627^d - *c.*20 Oct. 1627^d [Special Ambassador]
Audience: 20 Aug. 1627

Instructions: PRO, SP/75/8, ff. 232-4.
Correspondence: PRO, SP/75/8; PRO, 'Third Report on the Royal Archives of Denmark...,' *Reports of the Deputy Keeper...*, xlvii.

DK39.
ROE, Sir Thomas (1581?-1644)*

2 Apr. 1629^a - 4 July 1630^a Ambassador Extraordinary
Audience: 4 Aug. 1629   £4/d

Roe also went to Sweden, Poland, Germany and the Hanse towns (qq.v.).

Instructions: PRO, SP/104/170, pp. 31-40; HMC *3rd Report*, p. 190; Gardiner, S. R., 'Letters...of Sir Thomas Roe...1629-30,' *Camden Misc.*, vii (1875), pp. 10-21.
Correspondence: PRO, SP/75/10-11, SP/88/5, SP/104/170; *CSPD, 1629-31*.

DK40.
VANE, Sir Henry (1589-1655)*

1 May 1631^a - late Nov. 1632^c Ambassador Extraordinary
    £6/d

He was not granted an audience in Denmark. He also went to Sweden and Germany (qq.v.).

Instructions: PRO, SP/75/12, ff. 204-09.
Correspondence: PRO, SP/75/12; *CSPD, 1631-3, Add. 1625-49*; PRO, 'Third Report of the Royal Archives of Denmark...,' *Reports of the Deputy Keeper...*, xlvii.

DK41.
SIDNEY, Robert, 2nd Earl of Leicester (1595-1677)*

6 Apr. 1632^a - 3 Dec. 1632^c Ambassador Extraordinary
Audience: 1 Oct. 1632   £8/d
Secretary: James Howell

Instructions: PRO, SP/75/12, ff. 396-9, 406-10; Bodl., Rawlinson Mss., C.354, ff. 34-8; Cant, R., 'The Embassy of the Earl of Leicester to Denmark in 1632,' *EHR*, ccxiv (1939), pp. 253-6.
Correspondence: PRO, SP/75/12; Bodl., Rawlinson C.354; HMC *3rd Report*; HMC *De Lisle and Dudley*, vi (journal of the mission); PRO, 'Third Report on the Royal Archives of Denmark...,' *Reports of the Deputy Keeper...*, xlvii.

DK42.
AVERY, Joseph (*fl.*1630s-1660s)

While serving as an agent in the Hanse towns (q.v.), he saw intermittent service in Denmark, especially in 1631, Oct. 1632 (with Sidney), June 1636, July 1637 and 1641.

Instructions: PRO, SP/75/12, ff. 232-5.
Correspondence: PRO, SP/75/12.

DK43.
DE VIC, Sir Henry (later Bart.; *d.*1671)

1 Jan. 1637[a] - 29 Jun. 1638[a]   [Agent]
                                          40s/d

Although accredited to Denmark, he apparently spent the latter part of this mission at Hamburg (Hanse, q.v.) with Avery.

Instructions: PRO, SP/75/14, ff. 5-7; inferred from PRO, 'Second Report on the Royal Archives of Denmark...,' *Reports of the Deputy Keeper...*, xlvi, pp. 51-2.
Correspondence: PRO, SP/75/14-15.

DK44.
ROE, Sir Thomas (1581?-1644)*

After participating in the peace negotiations at Hamburg (Conferences, q.v.), he paid a brief visit to Denmark in the summer of 1640.

DK45.
JENKS, Richard (*fl.*1640s)
BARKER, William (*fl.*1640s)

24 Nov. 1643[c] - Apr. 1644[d]   [Special Ambassadors]

They were seemingly sent by Parliament to Sweden and the Hanse towns (qq.v.), as well as Denmark.

Instructions: Bodl., Tanner Mss. 62, f. 379.

DK46.
JENKS, Richard (*fl.*1640s)
SKINNER, Thomas (*fl.*1640s)

6 Sept. 1644[c] - 27 May 1645[a]   [Special Ambassadors]

They were sent by Parliament.

Instructions: Bodl., Tanner Mss. 61, ff. 132-3.

DK47.
JENKS, Richard (*fl.*1640s)

9 Mar. 1646[d] - summer 1646[h]   [Special Ambassador]
Audience: *c.*3 June 1646

Correspondence: PRO, 'Third Report on the Royal Archives of Denmark...,' *Reports of the Deputy Keeper...*, xlvii.

DK48.
BRADSHAW, Richard (*fl.*1650s)*

9 Nov. 1652[d] - 10 Feb. 1653[h]   Agent

He undertook this mission while stationed as resident at Hamburg (Hanse, q.v.).
  He may have been denied audience in Denmark.

Instructions: Inferred from *CSPV, 1647-52*, p. 311.
Correspondence about: *HMC Portland*, i; *CSPV, 1647-52, 1653-4*.

DK49.
MEADOW, Philip (later Sir Philip; 1626-1718)*

3 Sept. 1657[c] - *c.*1 Oct. 1659[e]   Ambassador Extraordinary
Audience: 20 Sept. 1657   £1000/an.
Secretary: Isaac Ewers

He went to Sweden (q.v.) July through Aug. 1658, and Aug. through Sept.
  1659. He also had responsibilities in Poland and the Hanse (qq.v.).

Instructions: PRO, SP/75/16, ff. 241-4; Abbott, W. (ed.), *The Writings...of
  Oliver Cromwell* (Cambridge, Mass., 1937-47), iv, pp. 605-07; *ThSP*, vi,
  p. 478; Weiss, J., 'Propositio Legati Protectoris Angliae ad Regem Daniae,'
  Historisches Jahrbuch, xiv, p. 608.
Correspondence: *ThSP*, vi-vii; Jenks, E., 'Some Correspondence of Thurlowe
  and Meadowe,' *EHR*, vii (1892), pp. 720-42; Montagu, E., *The Journal of
  Edward Montague, the Earl of Sandwich...*ed. R. Anderson (1929); PRO,
  'Third Report on the Royal Archives of Denmark...,' *Reports of the Deputy
  Keeper...*, xlvii.

DK50.
EWERS, Isaak (*fl.*1650s)

26 Mar. 1658[d] - 1659[h]   [Agent]

He served in Meadow's absences.

Correspondence about: *ThSP*, vii.

DK51.
MONTAGU, Edward (later 1st Earl of Sandwich; 1625-1672)*
SIDNEY, Algernon (1622-1683)*
HONYWOOD, Sir Robert (1601-1686)*
BOONE, Thomas (*fl.*1650s)

11 Mar. 1659[c] - 13 Sept. 1659[g]   Plenipotentiaries
(Montagu)   (Montagu)
30 June 1659[b]   *c.*1 July 1660[e]
(the other plenipotentiaries)
Began work (Montagu): 6 Apr. 1659
Audience (all commissioners together):
     3 Aug. 1659

See 'Conferences and Congresses' for full citation.

DK52.
HOWARD, Charles, 1st Earl of Carlisle (1629-1685)*

20 June 1663[b] - 31 Jan. 1665[c]   Ambassador Extraordinary
Audience: 30 Oct. 1664   (reimbursed for expenses)
Secretaries: Andrew Marvel and Guy
  de Miege

He also went to Russia and Sweden (qq.v.).

Correspondence: PRO, SP/91/3, SP/95/5A-B, 7; Bodl., Clarendon Mss., 80-1;
  CSPD, 1664-5; Konovalov, S., 'England and Russia: Three Embassies,'
  Oxford Slavonic Papers, x (1962), pp. 59-101; and a contemporary narrative
  in: [Miege, Guy], *A Relation of Three Embassies...*(1669).

DK53.
TALBOT, Sir Gilbert (*c.*1606-1695)*

30 July 1664[b] - *c.*10 Apr. 1666[g]   Envoy Extraordinary
Audience: 21 Sept. 1664   £5/d
Secretary: Peter du Moulin

Correspondence: PRO, SP/75/17-18; Bodl., Clarendon Mss. 82-3.

DK54.
CLIFFORD, Sir Thomas (later 1st Baron Clifford of Chudleigh; 1630- 1673)*

29 Aug. 1665[b] - *c.*1 Feb. 1666[c]   Ambassador Extraordinary
Audience: 6 Sept. 1665
Secretary: Peter du Moulin

He also went to Sweden (q.v.).

Instructions: Clifford Mss. as cited in Hartmann, C., *Clifford of the
  Cabal...*(1937).
Correspondence: PRO, SP/75/17; Coventry Mss. as cited in Hartmann.

DK55.
HOWARD, Charles, 1st Earl of Carlisle (1629-1685)*

He stopped in Denmark on his way to Sweden (q.v.) and had audience of the
  Danish King, 26 Mar. 1669.

DK56.
CAPEL, Arthur, Earl of Essex (1631-1683)*

29 Sept. 1669[a] - 1 Sept. 1670[a]   Ambassador Extraordinary
Audience: 16 May 1670   £10/d
Secretary: William Loving

Instructions: Suggested in *CSPV, 1669-7*, p. 181.
Correspondence: PRO, SP/75/18; BL, Add. 40629, Sloane 1003; Bodl.,
  Rawlinson Mss. A.477.

DK57.
LOVING, William (*d*.1670)

7 Nov. 1670^a - *d*.mid-Nov. 1670   [Special Ambassador]

He drowned on his way to his assignment.

Instructions: Inferred from *CSPD, 1660-70, Add.*, p. 498.

DK58.
BERTIE, Charles (*c*.1641-1711)*

4 Mar. 1671*ᵃ* - 28 Feb. 1672*ᵃ*   Envoy Extraordinary
Audience: 27 May 1671   £4/d

He visited Hamburg (Hanse, q.v.) on his journey to Denmark.

Instructions: PRO, SP/75/19, f. 3; Oxford, Mss. at All Souls Lib., ccliv, f. 1;
    Bertie, C., 'Copies of Several Letters...by... Charles Bertie...,'
    Retrospective Review, 2nd ser., i, pt. 2, (1827), pp. 181-2.
Correspondence: PRO, SP/75/19, SP/82/11; Oxford, Mss. at All Souls Lib.,
    ccliv; Bertie, 'Copies of Several Letters...,' pp. 177-205.

DK59.
PAULL, Sir John (*fl*.1660s-1680s)

9 Dec. 1671*ᵃ* - 31 May 1679*ᵇ*   Resident Ambassador

He had previously been a consul in Denmark, and his consular responsibilities
    continued during his residency.

Correspondence: PRO, SP/104/1-2, 56; BL, Add. 25117, Harl. 1515; *CSPD,
    1672-3.*

DK60.
**STUART, Charles, 10th Signeur d'Aubigny, 6th Duke of Lennox and 3rd
    Duke of Richmond** (1639-1672)*

28 Feb. 1672*ᵃ* - *d*.12 Dec. 1672   Ambassador Extraordinary
Audience: 14 June 1672   £100/wk.
Secretary: Dr. Thomas Henshaw and
    William Blathwayt

Additional instructions: PRO, SP/104/64, ff. 9-10.
Correspondence: PRO, SP/75/19; BL, Add. 36988; *CSPD, 1671-2.*

DK61.
HENSHAW, Dr. Thomas (1618-1700)*

12 Dec. 1672*ᵃ* - 16 Jan. 1673*ᶠ*   [Chargé d'Affaires]
                                        40*s*/d

He assumed his duties upon Richmond's death, and remained ultimately as
    envoy extraordinary (see next entry).

DK62.

17 Jan. 1673*ᵃ* - 15 July 1674*ᵃ*   Envoy Extraordinary
                              £5/d

Correspondence: BL, Add. 25117.

DK63.
WYCHE, Sir Peter (1628-1699?)*

While ambassador at Hamburg (q.v.), he conducted a special embassy to
Denmark in Oct. and Nov. 1679.

DK64.
ROBARTES, Robert, Viscount Bodmin (1633-1682)*

6 Mar. 1680*ᵃ* - *c*.1 July 1681*ᵈ*   Envoy Extraordinary
Private audience: 10 Apr. 1680   £5/d

Instructions: PRO, SP/75/21, ff. 344-9, SP/104/2, pp. 15-20, 23-6, 28-30, 31-
8, SP/104/153, p. 14.
Correspondence: PRO, SP/75/21, SP/104/3; BL, Add. 35104.

DK65.
CHURCHILL, John, Baron Churchill (later 1st Duke of Marlborough; 1650-
1722)*

In a quasi-diplomatic status in June 1683, he accompanied Prince George from
Denmark, who came to England to marry Princess Anne. He found the Prince
at Glückstadt.

DK66.
SKELTON, Bevil (*died c.*1692)*

He was accredited as ambassador to various German courts and the Hanse towns
(qq.v.), 1681-1685, and undertook a visit to Denmark in the spring of 1684,
receiving an audience *c.*28 May 1684.

DK67.
SILVIUS, Sir Gabriel (*fl.*1660s-1680s)

29 May 1685*ᵃ* - 12 Aug. 1689*ᵃ*   Envoy Extraordinary
Secretary: Thomas Fotherby   £5/d

Instructions: PRO, SP/104/2, pp. 164-9.
Correspondence: PRO, SP/104/187; BL, Add. 41828, Bodl., Rawlinson Mss.
A.480, C.417.

These entries include any envoy sent to the Imperial Court, wherever that constantly moving body might have been at any given date.

E1.
WINGFIELD, Sir Robert (*c*.1470-1539)*

30 May 1510*ᵃ* - by 21 Aug. 1517*ᵍ*   Resident Ambassador
Audience: mid-July 1510   20*s*/d

Originally finding the Emperor at Innsbruck, he resided with that monarch in his various peregrinations around central Europe. Wingfield returned to England Jan. - Feb. 1511, and Oct. 1512 - Mar. 1513. He visited the Regent in the Low Countries (q.v.) on his journey to the Emperor. He may have visited the Pope (Italian States, q.v.) in spring 1512.

Instructions: Suggested in *L&P*, i, 1, nos. 450, 455, 476.
Correspondence: BL, Cotton, Vitel. B.xviii-xx; *L&P*, i, 1-2, ii, 1-2.

E2.
YOUNG, Dr. John (1467-1516)*
BOLEYN, Sir Thomas (later Viscount Rochford, Earl of Wiltshire; 1477-1539)*

16 May 1512*ᵈ* - *c*.25 May 1513*ᶜ*   [Special Ambassadors]
Audience: *c*.22 May 1512   20*s*/d (each)

The Emperor was at Brussels. They later joined with Wingfield and Poynings (see both below and Low Countries). Young and Boleyn seemingly returned briefly to England *c*.Feb. 1513.

Correspondence: BL, Cotton, Galba B.iii, viii; *L&P*, i, 1-2.

E3.
WINGFIELD, Sir Richard (1469?-1525)*
POYNINGS, Sir Edward (1459-1521)*

8 Jan. 1513*ᵃ* - *c*.25 May 1513*ᶜ*   [Special Ambassadors]
            (Poynings)
            24 June 1513*ᵇ*
            (Wingfield)

They joined with the above ambassadors and negotiated at Brussels and Mechlin for the formation of a Holy League (also Low Countries, q.v.). Poynings also was sent to secure men and supplies for the upcoming war with France.

Instructions: Inferred from *L&P*, i, 1, nos. 1524.39, 1680, 1745.
Correspondence: BL, Cotton, Galba B.iii, viii; *L&P*, i, 1-2.

E4.
POYNINGS, Sir Edward (1459-1521)*
KNIGHT, Dr. William (later Bishop of Bath and Wells; 1476-1547)*

7 May 1515*c* - *c*.21 Sept. 1515*e*   [Special Ambassadors]
Arrived (Bruges): 23 May 1515

The Emperor was at Brussels and Bruges.

Instructions: *L&P*, ii, no. 423.
Correspondence: *L&P*, ii.

E5.
PACE, Richard (later Sir Richard; 1482?-1536)*

24 Oct. 1515*g* - *c*.20 Dec. 1517*c*   [Special Ambassador]
Audience: *c*.24 Feb. 1516

He originally found the Emperor in southern Germany around 8 Nov. 1515. No
    audience is recorded during this original contact. He visited almost
    immediately the Swiss cantons (q.v.), and returned there at least once more
    during this sojurn. He also visited the Regent Margaret in the Low Countries
    (q.v.), both going to and returning from his assignment.

Instructions: BL, Cotton, Nero. B.vi, f. 36; *L&P*, ii, 1, nos. 1065, 1095.
Correspondence: BL, Cotton, Vitel. B.xviii-xx; *L&P*, ii, 1-2.

E6.
SOMERSET, Charles, 1st Earl of Worcester (1460?-1526)*
KNIGHT, Dr. William (later Bishop of Bath and Wells; 1476-1547)*

28 Dec. 1516*b* - *c*.10 Mar. 1517*e*   [Special Ambassadors]
                (Knight)
                c.25 May 1517*e*
                (Worcester)
Audience: 31 Jan. 1517

They found the Emperor at Brussels. Sir Robert Wingfield, resident with the
    Emperor, and Cuthbert Tunstall, an ambassador already in the Low
    Countries (but at that moment in Tournai) joined with them in negotiations.
    Knight had specific responsibilities with the Regent, Lady Margaret (Low
    Countries, q.v.) but apparently did not replace Tunstall as resident, which
    was originally envisioned.

Instructions: *L&P*, ii, 1, no. 2713.
Correspondence: BL, Cotton, Galba B.v; *L&P*, ii, 2.

E7.

SPINELLY, Sir Thomas (*d.*1522)

mid-July 1517[d] - *d.*26 Aug. 1522   Resident Ambassador
Audience: 3 Aug. 1517   20*s*/d

He was resident with Charles, Prince of Castile, beginning in 1517. He attended
  Charles in Brussels, and then moved with him to Spain (q.v.). He
  accompanied Charles to Aachen when the Prince was crowned Emperor, 28
  July 1519. Spinelly died at Valladolid not long after the Imperial Court
  returned to Spain.

Correspondence: BL, Cotton, Galba B.vii, Vitel. B.xx; *L&P*, ii, 2 - iii, 1-2.

E8.

PACE, Richard (later Sir Richard; 1482?-1536)*

11 May 1519[a] - 10 Aug. 1519[a]   [Special Ambassador]
Arrived (Frankfurt): *c.*10 June 1519

Instructed to attend the imperial elections at Frankfurt, he also spent extensive
  time with Margaret of Savoy, Regent (Low Countries, q.v.). He visited as
  well various German rulers (German States, q.v.).

Instructions: In part in *L&P*, iii, 1, nos. 239-41.
Correspondence: *L&P*, iii, 1.

E9.

TUNSTALL, Dr. Cuthbert (later Bishop of London, Durham; 1474-1559)*

1 Sept. 1519[b] - 25 Apr. 1521[c]   [Special Ambassador]
Audience: 25 Sept. 1519   40*s*/d

The Emperor Charles V was in the Low Countries and Germany. Tunstall also
  visited the Regent (Low Countries, q.v.).

Instructions: Inferred from BL, Cotton, Galba B.i, f. 200; *L&P*, iii, 1, nos. 892,
  969.
Correspondence: BL, Cotton, Galba B.iii, Vitel. B.xx; *L&P*, iii, 1.

E10.

WINGFIELD, Sir Richard (1469?-1525)*

*c.*1 May 1521[c] - by 24 Jan. 1522[c]   [Special Ambassador]
Audience: *c.*28 May 1521

He resided with the Emperor in the Low Countries and other parts of Germany.
  He returned briefly to England 22 June to 13 July 1521. He also visited
  Margaret of Savoy in Low Countries (q.v.).

Instructions: BL, Cotton, Vitel. B.xx, ff. 236-42; *L&P*, iii, 1, no. 1270, iii, 2,
  no. 1394.
Correspondence: BL, Cotton, Calig. D.viii, Galba B.vii; *L&P*, iii, 1- 2.

E11.
WOLSEY, Cardinal Thomas (1475?-1530)*
SOMERSET, Charles, 1st Earl of Worcester (1460?-1526)*
RUTHAL, Dr. Thomas, Bishop of Durham (*d.*1523)*
WEST, Dr. Nicholas, Bishop of Ely (1461-1533)*
DOCWRA, Sir Thomas (*d.*1527)*
TUNSTALL, Dr. Cuthbert (later Bishop of London, Durham; 1474-1559)*

29 July 1521*b* - 30 Nov. 1521*c*   [Commissioners]
Arrived at Calais: 2 Aug. 1521;
  audience with Emperor at Bruges:
  18 Aug. 1521

Much of the conference was held at Calais, but it did involve negotiations with
  the Emperor Charles V at Bruges. Docwra joined with Boleyn (immediately
  below) partway through the mission.

Instructions: Inferred from *L&P*, iii, 2, nos. 1443, 1448.
Correspondence: BL, Cotton, Galba B.vii; *L&P*, iii, 2.

E12.
DOCWRA, Sir Thomas (*d.*1527)*
BOLEYN, Sir Thomas (later Viscount Rochford, Earl of Wiltshire; 1477-
  1539)*

20 Oct. 1521*c* - *c.*24 Nov. 1521*e*   [Special Ambassadors]
Audience (at Courtraye and
  Oudenarde): 25 Oct. 1521

Instructions: *L&P*, iii, 2, no. 1694.
Correspondence: BL, Cotton, Galba B.vii; *L&P*, iii, 2.

E13.
WINGFIELD, Sir Robert (*c.*1470-1539)*
KNIGHT, Dr. William (later Bishop of Bath and Wells; 1476-1547)*

*c.*29 Jan. 1522*g* - 26 May 1522*c*   [Special Ambassador]
Audience: 10 Feb. 1522 (Knight);
  11 Feb. 1522 (Wingfield)

The Emperor was in the Low Countries, where the ambassadors joined with
  Spinelly. Knight continued immediately to Switzerland (q.v.) on diplomatic
  assignment, while Wingfield apparently returned to England on the date cited
  with the Emperor when that sovereign paid a visit to Henry VIII.

Instructions: Summarized in Wingfield, J., *Some Records of the Wingfield
  Family* (1925), pp. 81-2.
Correspondence: BL, Cotton, Galba B.vii; *L&P*, iii, 2.

E14.
WINGFIELD, Sir Richard (1469?-1525)*

Late Apr. 1522*g* - 26 May 1522*c*   [Special Ambassador]
Audience: 6 May 1522

He joined with Sir Robert Wingfield and Thomas Spinelly who were with the Emperor at Brussels. He also apparently accompanied the Emperor to England.

Instructions: Inferred from *L&P*, iii, 2, no. 2246.
Correspondence: BL, Cotton, Galba B.vii; *L&P*, iii, 2.

E15.
BOLEYN, Sir Thomas (later Viscount Rochford, Earl of Wiltshire; 1477-1539)*
SAMPSON, Dr. Richard (later Bishop of Coventry and Lichfield; *d*.1554)*

25 Sept. 1522*c* - *c*.30 May 1523*d*   [Special Ambassadors]
Audience: 1 Nov. 1522

The Emperor was at Valladolid in Spain. Sampson remained as resident ambassador (see below).

Instructions: BL, Cotton, Vesp. C.ii, ff. 14-24, Harl. 297, ff. 51- 9, Sloane 3839, ff. 116-18; *L&P*, iii, 2, nos. 2481, 2567.
Correspondence: BL, Cotton, Vesp. C.ii, Add. 5860, 48045, Harl. 295, 6260, Sloane 3839, Stowe 147; *L&P*, iii, 2.

E16.
SAMPSON, Dr. Richard (later Bishop of Coventry and Lichfield; *d*.1554)*

25 Sept. 1522*c* - *c*.20 Feb. 1526*e*   Resident Ambassador
Audience: 1 Nov. 1522

Inasmuch as Spinelly had recently died, Sampson remained in Spain with the Emperor after Boleyn's return (above).

Instructions: *L&P*, iii, 2, nos. 2481, 2567.
Correspondence: BL, Cotton, Vesp. C.ii, Add. 5860, 48045, Harl. 297, 6260; *L&P*, iii, 2, iv, 1.

E17.
JERNINGHAM, Sir Richard (*d*.1525)

19 May 1523*b* - mid-Apr. 1524*g*   [Special] Ambassador
Audience: 22 June 1523

He visited the Emperor in Spain, joining with Sampson there.

Instructions: *L&P*, iii, 2, no. 3059.
Correspondence: BL, Add. 5860, 48045, Harl. 297, 6260, Stowe 147; *L&P*, iii, 2 and iv, 1; *CSPS, 1509-25*.

E18.
TUNSTALL, Dr. Cuthbert, Bishop of London (later Bishop of Durham; 1474-1559)*
WINGFIELD, Sir Richard (1469?-1525)*

26 Mar. 1525[b] - *d.*22 July 1525   [Special Ambassadors]
       (Wingfield)
       early April 1526[g]
       (Tunstall)
Audience: 24 May 1525

The Emperor was in Spain at this time. They joined with Sampson. Tunstall and Sampson also visited the captured French King at Madrid (France, q.v.).

Instructions: BL, Add. 48045, ff. 135-95, Lansd. 6260, ff. 70b-96, Stowe 147, f. 67b; *L&P*, iv, 1, no. 1212.
Correspondence: BL, Cotton, Vesp. C.iii, Lansd. 6260; *L&P*, iv, 1.

E19.
LEE, Dr. Edward (later Archbishop of York; 1482?-1544)*

2 Nov. 1525[g] - 21 Oct. 1529[a]   Resident Ambassador
Audience: 10 Jan. 1526   26*s* 8*d*/d
The Emperor was in Spain.

Instructions: *L&P*, iv, 1, no. 1798.
Correspondence: BL, Cotton, Vesp. C.iv, Harl. 295; *L&P*, iv, 1-3; *CSPS*, 1527-9.

E20.
GHINUCCI, Jerome de, Bishop of Worcester (*fl.*1520s-1530s)

*c.*23 Nov. 1526[h] - *c.*10 Sept. 1529[f]   [Special Ambassador]
Audience: 26 Jan. 1527

He joined with Lee in Valladolid to meet with the Emperor. During this rather vaguely defined assignment, he also apparently made numerous trips to France (q.v.), including Dec. 1526 and upon the conclusion of his stay with the Emperor, 1529.

Instructions: Inferred in *L&P*, iv, 2, nos. 2705, 2638, 2828.
Correspondence: BL, Cotton, Galba B.ix, Calig. D.ix, Vesp. C.iv; *L&P*, iv, 2-3.

E21.
POYNTZ, Sir Francis (*d.*1528)*

*c.*15 May 1527[h] - *c.*10 Dec. 1527[c]   [Special Ambassador]
Audience: 2 July 1527

He joined with Lee and Ghinucci to meet with the Emperor in Spain.

Instructions: *L&P*, iv, 2, nos. 3143-5, 3179.
Correspondence: BL, Cotton, Vesp. C.ix; *L&P*, iv, 2.

E22.
DARIUS, Sylvester (*fl.*1520s)

$c.1$ May 1528[h] - 9 Feb. 1529[b]   [Special] Ambassador
Audience: $c.15$ Aug. 1528

He was a papal nuncio and proctor to the Bishop of Worcester. Henry VIII used Darius as an ambassador to the Emperor in Spain. He found the Emperor at Madrid.

Instructions: Suggested in *L&P*, iv, 2, nos. 4637, 4909.
Correspondence: *L&P*, iv, 2.

E23.
CAREW, Sir Nicholas (*c.*1496-1539)*
SAMPSON, Dr. Richard (later Bishop of Coventry and Lichfield; *d.*1554)*

4 Oct. 1529[a] - $c.1$ May 1530[e]   [Special Ambassadors]
Audience: 3 Dec. 1529   26*s* 8*d*/d (each)

They visited the Emperor at Bologna, as well as the Pope (Italy, q.v.). They joined with Dr. William Benet, ambassador with the Pope.

Instructions: *L&P*, iv, 3, no. 6069.
Correspondence: BL, Add. 29597, 35838, Eg. 3315 (diary of mission); *L&P*, iv, 3.

E24.
BOLEYN, Thomas, Earl of Wiltshire (1477-1539)*
STOKESLEY, Dr. John (later Bishop of London; 1475?-1539)*
LEE, Dr. Edward (later Archbishop of York; 1482?-1544)*

20 Jan. 1530[a] - 3 Aug. 1530[a]   [Special Ambassadors]
Audience: $c.15$ Mar. 1530   £5/d (Wiltshire),
                                    26*s* 8*d*/d (Lee)

They visited the Emperor and the Pope (Italy, q.v.) at Bologna, where they joined with Dr. Benet. On their return journey, they visited the French King (France, q.v.).

Instructions: *L&P*, iv, 3, no. 6111.
Correspondence: *L&P*, iv, 3.

E25.
HARVEY, Nicholas (later Sir Nicholas; by 1491-1532)*

$c.1$ June 1530[h] - $c.20$ Feb. 1531[d]   [Resident Ambassador]
Audience: 10 July 1530   26*s* 8*d*/d

The Emperor was in the Low Countries and Augsburg during these years.

Instructions: Partially suggested in *L&P*, iv, 3, no. 6511.
Correspondence of and about: *L&P*, iv, 3.

E26.
HACKETT, Sir John (*d.*1534)

27 Jan. 1531[d] - *d.*27 Oct. 1534	Resident Ambassador
Audience: 12 Feb. 1531	20*s*/d

At the outset he was resident with the Emperor's court at Brussels and Malines, but from Apr. 1532, he shifted assignments to become the resident with the Regent Mary of Hungary (Low Countries, q.v.)

Correspondence: *L&P*, vi; Rogers, E. (ed.), *The Letters of Sir John Hackett, 1526-1534* (Morgantown, W. Va., 1971).

E27.
ELYOT, Sir Thomas (*c.*1490-1546)*

7 Oct. 1531[c] - 2 June 1532[c]	[Resident Ambassador]
Audience: late Oct.? 1532	20*s*/d

The Emperor was to be found both at Brussels and in Germany during this period of service.

Instructions: BL, Cotton, Vitel. B.xxi, f. 60; *L&P*, v, app., no. 15.
Correspondence: BL, Cotton, Vitel B.xxi; *L&P*, v.

E28.
CRANMER, Dr. Thomas (later Archbishop of Canterbury; 1489-1556)*

25 Jan. 1532[h] - *c.*1 Jan. 1533[e]	[Resident Ambassador]
Arrived: 14 Mar. 1532	20*s*/d?

He arrived at Ratisbone, but was granted no immediate audience due to the Emperor's illness. He served in Germany and Italy. He also visited Saxony (Germany, q.v.).

Correspondence: BL, Cotton, Vitel. B.xxi; *L&P*, v; Cranmer, Thomas, *Works*, ed. J. Cox, (Parker Society, 1844-6).

E29.
HAWKINS, Dr. Nicholas (*d.*1534)*

2 Oct. 1532[b] - *d.*Jan. 1534	[Resident Ambassador]
Audience: 16 Nov. 1532	30*s*/d

The Emperor was originally at Mantua. Hawkins followed him into Spain, where the ambassador died.

Instructions: Suggested in BL, Cotton, Vitel. B.xxi, ff. 74-8.
Correspondence: BL, Lansd. 1045; *L&P*, v - vi.

E30.
PATE, Richard (later Bishop of Worcester; *d.*1565)*

15 Nov. 1533[a] - 30 Sept. 1537[b]	Resident Ambassador
	30*s*/d

The Emperor was in Spain during most of these years.

Correspondence of and about: BL, Harl. 282-3; *L&P*, vii - xii.

E31.
WYATT, Sir Thomas (1503-1542)*

10 Mar. 1537[a] - 17 June 1539[b]   [Resident Ambassador]
Audience: 22 June 1537   41s/d, 53s 4d/d (after
Secretary: Peter Rede   8 Apr. 1538)

The Emperor resided mostly in Spain. Wyatt returned briefly to England June - July 1538.

Instructions: *L&P*, xii, 1, no. 637; Nott, G. (ed.), *The Works of...Sir Thomas Wyatt* (1815-16), p. 312.
Correspondence: BL, Harl. 282; *L&P*, xii, 2 - xiv, 1; Muir, K., *Life and Letters of Sir Thomas Wyatt* (Liverpool, 1963); Merriman, R. B., *The Life and Letters of Thomas Cromwell* (Oxford, 1902); Nott, *Works*.

E32.
BONNER, Dr. Edmund (later Bishop of Hereford, London; 1500?-1569)*
HEYNES, Dr. Simon (*d*.1552)*

6 Apr. 1538[a] - 24 July 1538[f]   [Special Ambassadors]
   (Bonner)   40s/d (each)
   31 Aug. 1538[a]
   (Heynes)
Audience: early May 1538

The Emperor was in Spain. Bonner went directly from this assignment to assume the residency in France (q.v.); while Heynes returned directly to London.

Instructions: *L&P*, xiii, 1, no. 695.
Correspondence: *L&P*, xiii, 1-2.

E33.
HOBY, Sir Philip (1505-1558)*

10 Oct. 1538[c] - 17 Dec. 1538[c]   [Special Ambassador]
Audience: 1 Nov. 1538

He joined with Wyatt (see above) in attendance upon the Emperor in Spain.

Instructions: BL, Cotton, Vitel. B.xxi, ff. 170-6; Add. 5498, ff. 2- 6; *L&P*, xiii, 2, no. 622; Nott, G., *The Works of...Sir Thomas Wyatt* (1815-16), p. 494.
Correspondence: BL, Add. 5498.
Correspondence about: *L&P*, xiii, 2.

E34.
TATE, Richard (*fl.*1530s)

26 Mar. 1539[a] - 6 Feb. 1540[b]   Resident Ambassador
Audience: *c*.3 June 1539   40s/d

He found the Emperor in Spain, where Tate replaced Wyatt.

Correspondence: *L&P*, xiv, 1-2.

E35.
WYATT, Sir Thomas (1503-1542)*

15 Nov. 1539[b] - c.28 Apr. 1540[c]   [Special Ambassador]
Audience: 3 Jan. 1540   53s 4d/d

Wyatt, who joined with Tate, had audience with the Emperor at Paris. The
ambassador then accompanied the Emperor to Flanders. Wyatt also had
contact with the court of France (q.v.).

Instructions: BL, Harl. 282, f. 78; *L&P*, xiv, 2, no. 524.
Correspondence: BL, Harl. 282; *L&P*, xiv - xv; Nott, *Works*.

E36.
PATE, Richard (later Bishop of Worcester; *d*.1565)*

9 Apr. 1540[d] - c.15 Dec. 1540[f]   [Resident Ambassador]
Arrived: 14 Apr. 1540   30s/d

The Emperor was in the Low Countries. Pate, a Roman Catholic, fled to Rome
for sanctuary in 1540, carrying with him the Emperor's commendations.
Correspondence: *L&P*, xv - xvi.

E37.
GARDINER, Dr. Stephen, Bishop of Winchester (1483?-1555)*
KNYVETT, Sir Henry (*d*.1546)

1 Nov. 1540[a] - 8 Oct. 1541[b]   [Special Ambassadors]
Audience: 25 Dec. 1540   66s 8d/d (Winchester);
                                         53s 4d/d (Knyvett)

The Emperor was in the Low Countries and Knyvett subsequently remained as
resident ambassador (see below).

Instructions: Inferred from *L&P*, xvi, no. 269.
Correspondence: *L&P*, xvi.

E38.
KNYVETT, Sir Henry (*d*.1546)

1 Nov. 1540[a] - 30 Apr. 1542[b]   [Resident Ambassador]
Audience: 25 Dec. 1540   53s 4d/d

He went with Gardiner initially, and then remained with the Emperor in Spain
and Germany as the resident ambassador.

Instructions: Inferred from *L&P*, xvi, no. 269.
Correspondence: *L&P*, xvi - xvii.

E39.
BONNER, Dr. Edmund, Bishop of London (1500?-1569)*

5 Feb. 1542[d] - *c*.15 Dec. 1543[e]   Resident Ambassador
Audience: 5 Apr. 1542

The Emperor was first in Spain, and then Bonner followed him to the Low
   Countries.

Instructions: Inferred from *L&P*, xvii, no. 292.
Correspondence: *L&P*, xvii - xviii, 1-2.

E40.
BRYAN, Sir Francis (*c*.1492-1550)*

6 Oct. 1543[a] - 28 Dec. 1544[b]   [Special Ambassador]
Audience: 24 Oct. 1543

He was joined with Bonner, and had audience at the town of Avesnes, France,
   during the Emperor's military campaign.

Instructions: Inferred from *L&P*, xviii, 2, no. 305.
Correspondence: BL, Add. 32649; *L&P*, xviii, 2.

E41.
THIRLBY, Dr. Thomas, Bishop of Westminster (later Bishop of Norwich,
   Ely; 1506?-1570)*

30 June 1542[a] - 10 Oct. 1542[c]   [Special Ambassador]
                                           53s 4d/d

The Emperor was in Spain.

Instructions: *L&P*, xvii, no. 447.
Correspondence: *L&P*, xvii.

E42.
WOTTON, Dr. Nicholas (later Sir Nicholas; 1497?-1567)*

24 Nov. 1543[c] - *c*.15 Sept. 1545[c]   Resident Ambassador
Audience: 5 Dec. 1543   26s 8d/d, 40s/d (after June 1544)

He was with the Emperor in the Low Countries and Germany.

Instructions: BL, Cotton, Galba B.xi, f. 1, Sloane 2442, f. 34, Add. 2442, f. 34,
   Harl. 289, f. 158, 297, ff. 60-2; *L&P*, xviii, 2, no. 420.
Correspondence: BL, Harl. 283; *L&P*, xviii, 2 - xx, 2.

E43.
PAGET, Sir William (later 1st Baron Paget of Beaudesert; 1505-1563)*

c.19 May 1544[h] - 14 June 1544[a]   [Special Ambassador]
Audience: 28 May 1544

He found the Emperor at Speyer. He also visited the Regent in the Low
   Countries (q.v.).

Instructions: Inferred from *L&P*, xix, 1, nos. 530, 578, 619.
Correspondence: *L&P*, xix, 1.

E44.
GARDINER, Dr. Stephen, Bishop of Winchester (1483?-1555)*
SEYMOUR, Edward, 1st Earl of Hertford (later Duke of Somerset; 1506?-1552)*

23 Oct. 1544^g - c.25 Nov. 1544^g Special Ambassadors
Audience: 27 Oct. 1544

They left from Calais, and met the Emperor in Brussels. Dr. Nicholas Wotton, the resident, was included in this commission.

Instructions: HMC *Salisb.*, i, p. 44; inferred from *L&P*, xix, 2, nos. 492, 661.
Correspondence: *L&P*, xix, 2; Gardiner, S., *The Letters of Stephen Gardiner*, ed. J. Muller (New York, 1933).

E45.
PAGET, Sir William (later 1st Baron Paget of Beaudesert; 1505-1563)*

15 Feb. 1545^b - 10 Apr. 1545^a [Special Ambassador]
Audience: 28 Feb. 1545

He also visited the Regent in the Low Countries (q.v.), where the Emperor was residing.

Instructions: *L&P*, xx, 1, no. 227.
Correspondence: BL, Add. 5753; *L&P*, xx, 1.

E46.
THIRLBY, Dr. Thomas, Bishop of Westminster (later Bishop of Norwich, Ely; 1506?-1570)*
PETRE, Sir William (1505/06-1572)*
CARNE, Sir Edward (1495/6-1561)*
CHAMBERLAIN, Thomas (later Sir Thomas; c.1504-1580)*
VAUGHAN, Stephen (by 1502-1549)*

27 Apr. 1545^e - c.25 July 1545^h Commissioners
Arrived: 8 June 1545

These men served as commissioners to the Imperial Diet at Bourbourg to discuss commercial differences and claims. Dr. Edward Carne was already resident ambassador with the Regent in the Low Countries (q.v.). Thomas Chamberlain was also resident in the Low Countries as governor of the Merchant Adventurers, and participated only minimally in the proceedings. Although part of the original commission, Stephen Vaughan seems to have participated not at all. Thirlby remained as a resident with the Emperor (see below).

Instructions: Suggested in *L&P*, xx, 1, no. 590.
Correspondence: BL, Cotton, Galba B.x; *L&P*, xx, 1.

E47.
THIRLBY, Dr. Thomas, Bishop of Westminster (later Bishop of Norwich, Ely; 1506?-1570)*

27 Apr. 1545*e* - *c*.18 July 1548*c*   [Resident Ambassador]
Audience: 30 Aug. 1545
Secretary: John Bernardino (towards
  conclusion of mission)

The Emperor was at Brussels. Thirlby, initially part of the above commission, assumed the duties of a resident from Wotton upon having his first audience with the Emperor.

Correspondence: BL, Add. 25114, Cotton, Galba B.x, B.xii, Harl. 523; *L&P*, xx - xxi; *CSPF, 1547-53*; Tytler, P. (ed.), *England under the Reigns of Edward VI...*(1839), i.

E48.
GARDINER, Dr. Stephen, Bishop of Winchester (1483?-1555)*

16 Oct. 1545*c* - 21 Mar. 1546*a*   [Special Ambassador]
Audience: 4 Nov. 1545

He found the Emperor at Bruges. He also visited the Regent, Mary of Hungary (Low Countries, q.v.).

Instructions: *L&P*, xx, 2, no. 604.
Correspondence: BL, Add. 25114; *L&P*, xx - xxi; Gardiner, *The Letters*.

E49.
BELLINGHAM, Edward (later Sir; by 1507-1550)*

1 Feb. 1547*c* - *c*.5 Mar. 1547*c*   [Special Ambassador]
Audience: *c*.15 Feb. 1547

He went first to the Regent in the Low Countries (q.v.) to announce the death of Henry VIII, and then to the Emperor, who was at Ulm.

Instructions: *CSPF, 1547-53*, no. 5.
Correspondence: *CSPF, 1547-53*.

E50.
HOBY, Sir Philip (1505-1558)*

15 Apr. 1548*c* - *c*.20 Oct. 1550*d*   Resident Ambassador
Audience: 6 June 1548
Secretary: John Bernardino

After the initial audience at Augsburg, the Emperor's residence varied between the Low Countries and Germany. Hoby returned briefly to England in Oct. 1549.

Instructions: *CSPF, 1547-53*, no. 82.
Correspondence: BL, Add. 5828, 5935, 46367, Cotton, Titus B.ii, v, Calig. B.xii, Galba B.xii, Harl. 284, 353, 523; *CSPF, 1547-53*; *APC, 1550-2*; HMC *Salisb.*, i; Tytler, *England...*, i.

E51.
PAGET, Sir William (later Baron Paget of Beaudesert; 1505-1563)*

2 June 1549*c* - *c*.30 July 1549*e*   [Special Ambassador]
Audience: 22 June 1549

The Emperor was at Brussels, where Paget joined with Hoby.

Instructions: PRO, SP/68/3, ff. 110-16; BL, Add. 5935, ff. 82-4, Burney 390,
    f. 1, Cotton, Galba B.xii, ff. 90-1, Sloane 2442, ff. 35-6, Harl. 297, ff. 63-5;
    CSPF, 1547-53, no. 160.
Correspondence: PRO, SP/68/3; BL, Cotton, Galba B.xii, Titus B.v, Harl. 523,
    Add. 5935, 46367; *CSPF, 1547-53*; *CSPS, 1547-8* (report on mission);
    Paget, William Lord, *The Letters of William Lord Paget...* ed. Beer, B. and
    Jack, S., Camden Misc., xxv (1974); Tytler, *England...*, i.

E52.
CHEYNE, Sir Thomas (1482/7-1558)*

22 Oct. 1549*c* - *c*.30 Nov. 1549*e*   [Special Ambassador]
Audience: early Nov. 1549

He went with Sir Philip Hoby, resident at the Imperial Court. Hoby had briefly
    returned to England. They found the Emperor at Brussels.

Instructions: *CSPF, 1547-53*, no. 207.
Correspondence: BL, Cotton, Galba B.xii.

E53.
MORISON, Sir Richard (*c*.1514-1556)*

1 July 1550*a* - *c*.1 Sept. 1553*d*   Resident Ambassador
Audience: *c*.9 Nov. 1559   £1000/an.
Secretary: Roger Ascham

The Emperor was resident primarily in Germany.

Instructions: BL, Sloane 2442, f. 37, Cotton, Galba B.xii, ff. 221- 6, Add.
    5935, ff. 84-5, Harl. 353, ff. 103-04; *CSPF, 1547-53*, no. 229.
Correspondence: BL, Cotton, Galba B.xi-xii, Harl. 353, 523; *CSPF, 1547-53*;
    APC, 1552-3; HMC *Salisb.*, i; Lodge, E. (ed.), *Illustrations of British
    History...*(1838); Tytler, *England...*, i, ii.

E54.
WOTTON, Dr. Nicholas (later Sir Nicholas; 1497?-1567)*

10 Apr. 1551*c* - mid-Oct. 1551*e*   [Special Ambassador]
Audience: 23 June 1551

The Emperor was at Augsburg.

Instructions: BL, Cotton, Galba B.xii, ff. 3-9, Add. 5935, ff. 80-2; *CSPF, 1547-
    53*, no. 318.
Correspondence: BL, Cotton, Galba B.xi-xii; *CSPF, 1547-53*; HMC *Salisb.*, i;
    Haynes and Murdin, *Collection of State Papers*.

E55.
DUDLEY, Sir Andrew (*c.*1507-1559)*

27 Dec. 1552*[c]* - *c.*19 Feb. 1553*[a]*   [Special Ambassador]
Audience: 25 Jan. 1553

He found the Emperor at Luxemburg. He also visited the Regent in the Low
    Countries (q.v.).

Instructions: *CSPF, 1547-53*, no. 599.
Correspondence: *CSPF, 1547-53*; *APC, 1552-4*.

E56.
THIRLBY, Dr. Thomas, Bishop of Norwich (later Bishop of Ely; 1506?-
1570)*
HOBY, Sir Philip (1505-1558)*

2 Apr. 1553*[d]* - *c.*1 Sept. 1553*[d]*   Resident Ambassador
    (Hoby)   66*s* 8*d*/d
    *c.*19 May 1554*[e]*   (Norwich)
    (Norwich)
Audience (Regent): 7 May 1553
Audience (Emperor): *c.*mid-Aug. 1553

They joined with Morison, already with the Emperor at Brussels. They found
    that monarch so indisposed due to illness that, after a long delay, they had
    only the briefest of audiences with him. Hoby remained in Brussels as
    resident with the Regent (Low Countries, q.v.) whom they all had visited
    extensively; while Thirlby (whose entry this primarily represents) remained
    as the resident with the Emperor. He was accredited 8 Aug. 1553 and
    replaced Morison. Thirlby returned briefly to England *c.*15 Oct. to *c.*15 Dec.
    1553.

Instructions: BL, Add. 5498, f. 61; *CSPF, 1547-53*, no. 646.
Correspondence: BL, Harl. 523; *CSPF, 1547-53, 1553-8*; *APC, 1552-4*; Tytler,
    England..., ii.

E57.
SHELLEY, Sir Richard (1513/14-1587)*

11 July 1553*[c]* - Aug.? 1553*[h]*   [Special Ambassador]

He was sent by Lady Jane Grey's Council to announce to the Emperor her
    accession to the crown. It is unlikely that he ever had audience with the
    Emperor, if in fact he even left England.

Instructions: BL, Harl. 523, no. 33.
Correspondence about: *CSPS, 1553*.

E58.
CHEYNE, Sir Thomas (1482/7-1558)*

8 Aug. 1553*[d]* - *c.*1 Sept. 1553*[d]*   [Special Ambassador]
Audience: 21 Aug. 1553

He was equally an ambassador to the Regent (Low Countries, q.v.) and to the Emperor, both residing at Brussels.

Instructions: Inferred from *CSPF, 1553-8*, nos. 18, 22; *CSPS, 1553*, pp. 181-2.
Correspondence: *CSPF, 1553-8*.

E59.
MASON, Sir John (1503-1566)*

19 Sept. 1553[b] - *c*.10 Feb. 1554[c]   [Special Ambassador]
Audience: *c*.12 Oct. 1553   66*s* 8*d*/d

Besides diplomatic responsibilities that he had in Brussels with the Emperor, he also participated in money securing and conveying activities in the Low Countries. These he undertook in conjuction with Sir Thomas Gresham, the Queen's financial agent there.

Correspondence: *CSPF, 1553-8*; Tytler, *England...*, ii.

E60.
5 Apr. 1554[d] - 26 Oct. 1555[f]   [Resident Ambassador]
Secretary: John Shers?   66*s* 8*d*/d

The Emperor was at Brussels during this period. Mason was revoked as ambassador by a letter of 26 Oct., but remained at Brussels, by the Queen's command, to attend upon King Philip II. He seemingly returned to England in May 1556.

Correspondence: *CSPF, 1553-8*; *CSPS, 1554*; *APC, 1552-4, 1554-6*; KL, i; Tytler, *England...*, ii.

E61.
CLINTON, Edward Fiennes de, 9th Baron Clinton and Saye (later 1st Earl of Lincoln; 1512-1585)*

On a mission to convey the Garter to the Duke of Savoy, he also visited the Emperor at Brussels, *c*.15 Nov. 1554.

E62.
PAGET, William, Baron Paget of Beaudesert (1506-1563)*
HASTINGS, Sir Edward (later Baron Hastings of Loughborough; by 1519-1572)*

5 Nov. 1554[c] - 24 Nov. 1554[a]   [Special Ambassadors]
Audience: 11 Nov. 1554

They consulted with the Emperor in Brussels, and then conveyed Cardinal Pole to England as part of their assignment.

Instructions: BL, Add. 5935, ff. 82-4; *CSPF, 1553-8*, no. 285.
Correspondence: Paget, W. Lord, *The Letters of William Lord Paget...*, ed. Beer and Jack, Camden Misc., xxv (1974); *CSPF, 1553-8*.

E63.
HOWARD, Sir George (by 1519-1580)*

Late May 1555[h] - c.16 June 1555[e]   [Special Ambassador]
Audience: c.1 June 1555

The Emperor was at Brussels.

Instructions: Inferred from *CSPF, 1553-8*, nos. 384-7.
Correspondence about: *CSPF, 1553-8.*

E64.
RADCLIFFE, Thomas, Viscount Fitzwalter (later 3rd Earl of Sussex; 1526?-
    1583)*

c.24 Mar. 1556[h] - c.7 Apr. 1556[e]   [Special Ambassador]

The Emperor was at Brussels.

Correspondence about: *CSPF, 1553-8.*

E65.
PAGET, William, Baron Paget of Beaudesert (1505-1563)*

6 Apr. 1556[a] - 17 May 1556[b]   [Special Ambassador]
Audience: 13 Apr. 1556   £4/d

He met with the Emperor at Brussels.

Instructions: Inferred from *CSPV, 1555-6*, pt. 1, nos. 448, 460; *CSPF, 1553-8*,
    no. 503.
Correspondence: BL, Cotton, Galba B.xi, Stowe 147; Paget, W. Lord,
    Letters...

E66.
MOUNT, Dr. Christopher (1497-1572)*

14 Dec. 1558[b] - d.Oct.? 1572   Agent

He remained in Germany as Queen Elizabeth's representative to various German
    princes (q.v.) and to the Emperor and the Imperial Diets as well. He
    specifically attended Diets at Augsburg in the spring of 1559 and again in
    1566.

Correspondence: *CSPF* (all vols. from 1558 to 1572).

E67.
CHALONER, Sir Thomas (1521-1565)*

26 Nov. 1558[d] - c.20 Jan. 1559[e]   [Resident Ambassador]
Audience: 2 Jan. 1559

The Emperor Ferdinand II was at Augsburg. Chaloner was also accredited to
    Maximilian, King of Bohemia, but this Prince was not at Augsburg, and there
    is no evidence that Chaloner saw him.

Instructions: BL, Cotton, Galba C.i, f. 27, Nero B.ix, f. 90; *CSPF, 1558-9*,
    nos. 38-9.
Correspondence: BL, Royal, 13.B.1; *CSPF, 1558-9.*

E68.

ALLEN, Edmund (1519?-1559)*

c.5 June 1559[f] - *c*.1 Aug. 1559[h]   [Agent]
Arrived: 20 June 1559

He was sent to attend the Imperial Diet at Augusta and joined with Mount.

Correspondence: *CSPF, 1558-9.*

E69.

KNOLLYS, Henry (*c*.1515-1582)*

25 Sept. 1562[d] - 4 Feb. 1563[c]   [Special Ambassador]
Audience: 18 Nov. 1562
Secretary: Thomas Windebank?

Besides visiting various Protestant princes throughout Germany (q.v.), he
attended upon the Emperor and the Imperial Diet at Frankfurt. Mount joined
with him. In Dec. 1562 he accompanied the Emperor to Strasbourg.

Instructions: Inferred from *CSPF, 1562,* no. 434; Wright, T. (ed.), *Queen
Elizabeth and Her Times...*(1838), i, p. 95.
Correspondence: *CSPF, 1562, 1562-3.*

E70.

DANNET, Thomas (*c*.1525-1569)*

30 Apr. 1566[c] - *c*.15 June 1567[h]   [Special Ambassador]
Audience: 25 May 1566

He and Christopher Mount met with the Emperor in Vienna.

Instructions: *CSPF, 1566-8,* no. 333.
Correspondence: *CSPF, 1566-8.*

E71.

RADCLIFFE, Thomas, 3rd Earl of Sussex (1526?-1583)*
NORTH, Roger, 2nd Baron North (1531-1600)*

20 May 1567[b] - 14 Mar. 1568[a]   [Special Ambassadors]
Audience: *c*.15 Aug. 1567   £6/d (Sussex)
Investment: 4 Jan. 1568

They were sent to Vienna in part to invest the Emperor with the Order of the
Garter. They visited various German princes as well as the Regent in the Low
Countries (qq.v.) on the journey to Vienna.

Instructions: *CSPF, 1566-8,* no. 1327.
Correspondence: BL, Cotton, Galba B.xi, Faust. C.ii, Titus B.ii; Bodl., Tanner
Mss. 50 (a diary of the mission); *CSPF, 1566-8.*

E72.
COBHAM alias BROOKE, Henry (later Sir Henry; 1538-1592)*

19 Aug. 1570[a] - 9 Dec. 1570[a]   [Special Ambassador]
Audience: 12 Sept. 1570   40s/d

He visited the Emperor at Speyer, and had in addition diplomatic responsibilities in the Low Countries (q.v.).

Instructions: *CSPF, 1569-71*, no. 1129.
Correspondence: *CSPF, 1569-71*.

E73.
SIDNEY, Philip (later Sir Philip; 1554-1586)*

7 Feb. 1577[a] - 8 June 1577[a]   [Special Ambassador]
                                          53s 4d/d

He visited Emperor Rudolph II at Prague; and also various German princes (q.v.). He visited the Prince of Orange and Don Juan in the Low Countries (q.v.) as well.

Instructions: BL, Sloane 2442, f. 38-9, Eg. 2790, f. 218, Lansd. 155, ff. 187-9; HMC *2nd Report*, p. 97.
Correspondence: *CSPF, 1575-7*.

E74.
ROGERS, Daniel (*c.*1538-1591)*

7 Sept. 1580[c] - *c.*Jan. 1585[h]   [Special Ambassador]

He was sent to the Emperor and also the Lutheran bishops (German States, q.v.). In fact, he was captured at the outset of this mission and spent the next four years imprisoned.

Instructions: BL, Sloane 2442, f. 69; *CSPF, 1579-80*, no. 441.
Correspondence: BL, Cotton, Galba C.vii, Harl. 285; *CSPF, 1579-80, 1581-2, 1582, 1583, 1583-4, 1584-5*.

E75.
GILPIN, George (1514-1602)*

4 June 1582[h] - *c.*25 Oct. 1582[h]   [Agent]

While secretary to the Merchant Adventurers at Antwerp, he was apparently directed to undertake a diplomatic assignment to the Emperor and the Imperial Diet at Augsburg.

Correspondence: *CSPF, 1582*.

E76.
WAAD, William (later Sir William; 1546-1623)*

Late Apr. 1583[h] - July? 1583[h]   [Special Ambassador]
Audience: *c.*7 June 1583

He visited the Emperor at Vienna.

Correspondence: *CSPF, 1583*.

E77.
PARKINS, Dr. Christopher (later Sir Christopher; *c*.1543-1622)*

20 Apr. 1593*ᵃ* - early Sept. 1593*ᵉ*	[Special Ambassador]
Audience: 27 June 1593	40*s*/d

He also visited various German states (q.v.).

Instructions: Inferred from PRO, SP/75/2, ff. 128-33, SP/80/1, ff. 140-2, 146-51; *L&A, 1591-2*, no. 889.
Correspondence: PRO, SP/80/1, SP/81/7; BL, Cotton, Nero B.ix; *L&A, 1592-3*.

E78.
WROTH, John (*d*. after 1616)*

26 Dec. 1597*ᵃ* - 22 June 1598*ᵃ*	[Special Ambassador]
Audience: *c*.Apr. 1598	20*s*/d

Wroth, in conjunction with Stephen Lesieur, visited various German princes and Hanse towns (qq.v.). Lesieur then apparently returned to England and Wroth contacted the Emperor.

Instructions: Inferred from PRO, SP/81/8, ff. 46-52.
Correspondence: PRO, SP/81/8; HMC *Salisb.*, xii.

E79.
LESIEUR, Stephen (later Sir Stephen; *d*.1627)*

1 June 1603*ᵃ* - 21 Jan. 1604*ᵇ*	[Special Ambassador]
	40*s*/d

Besides the Emperor, he visited the Duke of Saxony and other German princes (q.v.).

Instructions: Rymer, *Foedera*, xvi, p. 518; suggested in BL, Cotton, Galba E.i, ff. 69-74.
Correspondence: PRO, SP/80/1-2; BL, Cotton, Galba E.i.

E80.
KEITH, Sir Andrew (*fl*.1600s-1610s)

13 Feb. 1605*ᵇ* - n.d.	[Special Ambassador]

Correspondence: PRO, SP/80/2.

E81.
LESIEUR, Sir Stephen (*d*.1627)*

1 June 1610*ᵃ* - 9 Apr. 1611*ᵃ*	[Special Ambassador]
Audience: *c*.2 Aug. 1610	40*s*/d

He made contact with the Emperor in Prague.

Instructions: Inferred from HMC Buccleuch, i, pp. 94-5.
Correspondence: PRO, SP/80/2.

E82.
CECIL, William, Baron Roos (1590-1618)*

1 June 1612[b] - 3 July 1612[f]   [Special Ambassador]
Audience: 21 June 1612

Apparently while in Frankfurt upon other business, Lord Roos received the
King's commission to meet with the Emperor on diplomatic affairs. Lord
Roos completed his official responsibilities around 3 July 1612.

Correspondence: PRO, SP/80/2.

E83.
LESIEUR, Sir Stephen (*d.*1627)*

1 Aug. 1612[a] - 11 July 1614[a]   [Special Ambassador]
Audience: 5 Jan. 1613   £4/d

On this peripatetic trip, he visited a variety of German Protestant princes (q.v.)
as well as the Emperor in Vienna.

Instructions: PRO, SP/80/2, ff. 211-16.
Correspondence: PRO, SP/80/2-3.

E84.
HAY, James, 1st Viscount Doncaster (later Earl of Carlisle; *c.*1580- 1636)*

29 Apr. 1619[b] - 1 Jan. 1620[a]   Ambassador Extraordinary
Audience: *c.*mid-July 1619   £6/d
Secretary: Francis Nethersole (through
    Aug. 1619)

He found the Emperor, the principal object of his mission, at Salzburg. He also
visited various Protestant princes (German States, q.v.), the Archdukes
(Spanish Netherlands, q.v.), and the States General (Low Countries, q.v.).

Instructions: Gardiner, S. R. (ed.), *Letters and Other Documents Illustrating the
    Relations Between England and Germany...* Camden o.s., xc (1865), p. 64;
    inferred from PRO, SP/81/16, ff. 68-73, 249-50, 302-05.
Correspondence: PRO, SP/81/16; BL, Add. 3644, Eg. 2593, Stowe 743; HMC
    Westmoreland, Stewart...; Gardiner (ed.), *Letters and Other Documents...*;
    Birch, T. (ed.), *The Court and Times of James I...*(1849).

E85.
WOTTON, Sir Henry (1568-1639)*

3 Jun. 1620[b] - Mar. 1621[f]   Ambassador Extraordinary
Audience: 23 Aug. 1620   £5/d

He travelled to the Emperor at Vienna and various German princes (including
    the Prince Palatine) going from England to yet another assignment at Venice
    (q.v.).

Instructions: Inferred from PRO, SP/80/3, ff. 228-33.
Correspondence: PRO, SP/80/3, SP/81/18; Watson, C. (ed.), 'Letters from Sir
    Henry Wotton to King James I...,' *Archaeologia*, xl (1863), pp. 257-84;

Wotton, Sir H., *Letters and Dispatches from Sir Henry Wotton to James the First*...ed. G. Tomline (Roxburghe Club, 1850).

E86.
DIGBY, John, Baron Digby (later 1st Earl of Bristol; 1580-1653)*

7 May 1621[b] - 2 Nov. 1621[a]   Ambassador Extraordinary
Audience: 5 July 1621   £6/d
Secretary: Simon Digby

On his return from a mission to the Emperor Ferdinand II at Vienna, he visited, about mid-Oct. 1621, the Elector Palatine at Heidelberg (German States, q.v.), and the Archduke Albert, in late Oct., at Brussels (Spanish Netherlands, q.v.). Despite extensive discussion about it, he did not undertake a diplomatic mission to Spain at this time.

Instructions: PRO, SP/80/4, ff. 22-5; BL, Add. 36445, f. 53; Gardiner, S. R., *Prince Charles and the Spanish Marriage...* (1869), ii, p. 89.
Correspondence: PRO, SP/80/4.

E87.
DIGBY, Simon (*fl.*1620s-1640s)

28 May 1621[b] - 27 Dec. 1622[a]   Resident Ambassador
                                        40*s*/d

His diplomatic responsibilities overlapped those of Lord Digby, with whose mission he was joined, but he had arrived earlier, and remained at Vienna after Lord Digby left on 5 Sept. 1621.

Instructions: Comprised in part by PRO, SP/91/3, ff. 9-10.
Correspondence: PRO, SP/80/4-5.

E88.
ANSTRUTHER, Sir Robert (*fl.*1600-1640s)

While ambassador in Denmark (q.v.), he was seemingly commissioned to attend the Imperial Diet, spring 1627.

Instructions: PRO, SP/80/6, ff. 139-40.

E89.

29 June 1630[b] - c.2 Dec. 1630[a]   Ambassador Extraordinary
Audience: 25 Aug. 1630   40*s*/d (+ his regular diets)

He attended the Imperial Diet at Ratisbone and visited various German princes (q.v.) while under assignment as ambassador ordinary in Denmark (q.v.). He briefly returned to England before beginning his next assignment (immediately below).

Instructions: PRO, SP/80/6, ff. 207-10.
Correspondence: PRO, SP/80/6-7; Oxford, Mss. at All Souls Lib., ccxii; *CSPD, 1629-31*.

E90.

21 Mar. 1631[c] - 3 Dec. 1632[a]   Ambassador Extraordinary
Audience: 4 June 1631

Again, while serving as ambassador ordinary in Denmark (q.v.), he was
commissioned to the Emperor and the Imperial Diet at Ratisbone.

Instructions: PRO, SP/80/7, ff. 221-9.
Correspondence: PRO, SP/80/7-8; *CSPD, 1625-4, Add.*

E91.

3 Dec. 1632[a] - 28 July 1633[b]   [Ambassador Extraordinary]
                                          £4/d

Anstruther joined Thomas Howard, Earl of Arundel's entourage in the Low
Countries, was then dispatched to the Protestant conclave at Heilbronn,
visited the Emperor, and then returned to Denmark (q.v.) where he again
assumed the responsibilities of a resident ambassador.

Instructions: PRO, SP/80/7, ff. 221-9.
Correspondence: PRO, SP/80/7-8; Hervey, M. F., *The Life, Correspondence
and Collections of Thomas Howard, Earl of Arundel...*(1921).
Correspondence about: *CSPD, 1633-4.*

E92.

Apr. 1634[a] - Sept. 1634[b]   Ambassador Extraordinary
Secretary: Mr. Hurst

He was dispatched from Denmark (q.v.) to the Imperial Diet at Frankfurt
(seemingly accompanied by John Durie). He apparently returned to a
permanent residency at Hamburg.

Correspondence about: *CSPD, 1633-4, 1634-5.*

E93.
TAYLOR, John (1600?-1655)*

2 Aug. 1635[a] - c.10 May 1639[c]   Agent
Audience: c.30 Nov. 1635   40s/d

He was resident with the Emperor at Vienna. He may have returned to England
briefly in 1637. On his return to London in 1639, he seemingly stopped in
Brussels (Spanish Netherlands, q.v.).

Instructions: PRO, SP/80/9, ff. 34-47.
Correspondence: PRO, SP/80/9-10, SP/81/56; HMC *Denbigh*; Scrope, R, and
Monkhouse, T. (eds.), *State Papers Collected by Edward, Earl of
Clarendon...* (Oxford, 1767-86), i.

E94.

HOWARD, Thomas, 2nd Earl of Arundel and Surrey (later Earl of Norfolk; 1585-1646)*

1 Jan. 1636*ᵃ* - 30 Dec. 1636*ᵃ*   Ambassador Extraordinary
Audience: 6 June 1636   £6/d
Secretaries: Sir John Borough and
  John Taylor

Besides the Emperor at Vienna, he visited the States General of the Low Countries (q.v.).

Instructions: PRO, SP/80/9, ff. 105-16.
Correspondence: PRO, SP/80/9-10; BL, Add. 15970, 33596, Stowe 743; *Clarendon State Papers*; Hervey, *The Life...of Thomas Howard...*; Springell, F., *Connoisseur and Diplomat: The Earl of Arundel's Embassy to Germany in 1636...*(1963); Tierney, M., *The History and Antiquities of the Castle and Town of Arundel...*(1834).

E95.

AVERY, Joseph (*fl.*1630s-1660s)

While employed at Hamburg (Hanse, q.v.), he apparently attended the Imperial Diet at Lüneburg, Jan. 1636.

E96.

CURTIUS, William (later Sir William, Bart.; *fl.*1630s-1670s)

While serving as a royal agent to various German princes, he attended, in late 1639, the Imperial Diet at Nürnberg.

E97.

ROE, Sir Thomas (1581?-1644)*

1 Mar. 1641*ᵃ* - *c.*1 Sept. 1642*ᶜ*   [Special Ambassador]
Arrived (Vienna): early July 1641   £6/d

His principal mission was to the Diet at Ratisbone, and to the Emperor at Vienna. He also visited the Low Countries, Denmark and various German princes (qq.v.). He was joined in Vienna by William Curtius, who was the royal agent with the German princes (q.v.).

Correspondence: PRO, SP/80/10; *CSPD, 1640-1, 1641-3*; Mowat, R., 'The Mission of Sir Thomas Roe to Vienna, 1641-2,' *EHR*, xxv (Apr. 1910), pp. 264-75.

E98.

CURTIUS, William (later Sir William, Bart.; *fl.*1630s-1670s)

Again, while officially serving as the royal agent with various German princes (q.v.), he attended the Imperial Diet at Frankfurt in 1642 and at Nürnberg in 1649.

E99.
TAAFE, Theobald, 1st Earl of Carlingford (*d.*1677)*

22 Aug. 1665^c - *c.*10 Feb. 1667^c Envoy Extraordinary
Audience: 17 Jan. 1666
Secretary: William Loving

He visited the Spanish Netherlands and numerous German princes (qq.v.) on his journey to Vienna, where he found the Emperor Leopold.

Instructions: PRO, SP/104/174B, pp. 102-05; Bennet, Henry, Earl of Arlington, ...*the Earl of Arlington's Letters to Sir W. Temple...*(1701), i, pp. 21-9; [Taafe, Karl Graf], *Memoirs of the Family Taafe* (Vienna, 1856), pp. 31-6.
Correspondence: PRO, SP/80/11, SP/81/56-7; *CSPD, 1664-5*; Taafe, *Memoirs*.

E100.
GASCOIGNE, Sir Bernard (1614-1687)*

17 Feb. 1672^b - 29 Aug. 1673^a Envoy Extraordinary
Audience: *c.*5 June 1672   £5/d

He was apparently already on the continent when he undertook this mission. He had already visited the Grand Duke of Tuscany (Italy, q.v.) in pursuit of instructions.

Instructions: BL, Stowe 191, f. 28-33.
Correspondence: PRO, SP/80/12-13, SP/81/59-60; BL, Add. 21948, 34077; Brown, T., *Miscellanea Aulica...*(1702); Richards, S. (ed.), *Secret Writing...*(1974).

E101.
MORDAUNT, Henry, 2nd Earl of Peterborough (1624?-1697)*

25 Feb. 1673^a - 25 Nov. 1673^a [Ambassador Extraordinary]
Arrived: June 1673   £100/wk.
Secretaries: Sir Peter Wyche and
  John Dodington

Peterborough visited Paris (France, q.v.). He then went to Modena (Italian States, q.v.) to arrange the Duke of York's marriage and to Savoy (q.v.) after meeting with the Emperor.

Instructions: PRO, SP/104/88, f. 29.
Correspondence: PRO, SP/78/136-8, SP/85/11.

E102.
SKELTON, Bevil (*died c.*1692)*

29 Dec. 1675^a - 24 Jan. 1681^a Envoy Extraordinary
Audience: 3 July 1676   £4/d, £5/d (after 15 Nov. 1676)
Secretary: Réné Petit

He visited the Low Countries (q.v.) on his journey to Vienna.

Instructions: PRO, SP/80/13, ff. 251-3, 283, SP/104/56, pp. 87-92.

Correspondence: PRO, SP/80/14-16, SP/104/56-7, 193; BL, Add. 25119, Harl. 1515-16; Oxford, Mss. at All Souls Lib., cciii; *CSPD, 1675-6, 1677-8, 1679-80, 1680-1*.

E103.
MIDDLETON, Charles, 2nd Earl of Middleton (*c*.1650-1719)*

23 June 1680*a* - 21 June 1681*b*   Envoy Extraordinary
Audience: 8 Aug. 1680   £5/d

He visited the Low Countries (q.v.) on his journey to Vienna.

Instructions: PRO, SP/104/57, ff. 94-9; BL, Add. 41806, ff. 1-9; Oxford, Mss. at All Souls Lib., ccxli, ff. 442.

Correspondence: PRO, SP/80/16, SP/191/35; BL, Add. 18827, 25362, 35104, 37990; *CSPD, 1679-80, 1680-1*.

E104.
POLEY, Edmund (*fl*.1670s-1680s)

7 Feb. 1682*h* - 15 Apr. 1685*a*   [Resident Ambassador]
                              40*s*/d, 60*s*/d (after 17 Jan. 1683)

He came directly from an assignment in Brandenburg, and apparently became resident with the Reichstag at Regensburg. He was also in Ratisbone and Frankfurt, although his assignment seemed to encompass Germany (q.v.) as a whole.

Correspondence: PRO, SP/81/83-6, SP/104/58; BL, Add. 35104, 37986-7, 41834-5.

E105.
ETHEREGE, Sir George (1635-1691)*

30 Aug. 1685*a* - *c*.30 Jan. 1689*g*   Resident Ambassador
Arrival: mid-Nov. 1685   £3/d
Secretary: Hugh Hughes (after
   Mar. 1686)

He was resident with the Imperial Diet at Ratisbone.

Correspondence: PRO, SP/81/86; BL, Add. 11513 (letterbook), 41836-7, 41840-2; Rosenfeld, S. (ed.), *The Letterbook of Sir George Etherege* (1928); Rosenfeld, S., 'The Second Letterbook of Sir George Etherege,' *Review of English Studies*, n.s., iii, no. 9 (1952); Bracher, F. (ed.) *Letters of Sir George Etherege* (1974).

E106.
TAAFE, Nicholas, 2nd Earl of Carlingford (*d*.1691)*

15 Jan. 1688*d* - 1 May 1689*c*   [Envoy Extraordinary]

Instructions: PRO, SP/104/59, f. 64.

Correspondence: BL, Add. 41823; Oxford, Mss. at All Souls Lib., ccli.

FRANCE

F1.

DOCWRA, Sir Thomas (*d*.1527)*
WEST, Dr. Nicholas (later Bishop of Ely; 1461-1533)*

20 Jun. 1510[b] - *c*.1 Aug. 1510[g]   [Special Ambassadors]
Audience: 18 July 1510   40*s*/d (Docwra), 20*s*/d (West)

Instructions: *L&P*, i, 1, no. 519 (47).
Correspondence about: *L&P*, i, 1.

F2.

YOUNG, Dr. John (1467-1516)*

Early Aug. 1511[h] - *c*.2 Oct. 1511[c]   [Special Ambassador]
Audience: 23 Aug. 1511   20*s*/d

He travelled to the French King in company with the Spanish ambassador.

Instructions: Inferred from *L&P*, i, 1, nos. 850, 854, 858.
Correspondence about: *L&P*, i, 1.

F3.

SOMERSET, Charles, 1st Earl of Worcester (1460?-1526)*
DOCWRA, Sir Thomas (*d*.1527)*
WEST, Dr. Nicholas (later Bishop of Ely; 1461-1533)*

18 Aug. 1514[b] - *c*.30 Nov. 1514[e]   [Special Ambassadors]
Treaty confirmation: 14 Sept. 1514

They subsequently joined with the group led by Norfolk (immediately below).

Commission: BL, Add. 30600, f. 371; *L&P*, i, 2, no. 3226 (21).
Correspondence: BL, Cotton, Calig. D.vi; *L&P*, i, 2.

F4.

HOWARD, Thomas, 2nd Duke of Norfolk (1443-1524)*
GREY, Thomas, 2nd Marquis of Dorset (1477-1530)*
HOWARD, Thomas, Earl of Surrey (later 3rd Duke of Norfolk; 1473-1554)*

23 Sept. 1514[b] - mid-Oct. 1514[h]   [Special Ambassadors]
Marriage ceremony: 9 Oct. 1514

They accompanied Mary Tudor to her marriage with Louis XII of France. They
were joined by the foregoing ambassadors, led by Worcester. Norfolk
seemingly returned to England much sooner than the rest of the embassy,
which was involved in the later coronation and jousting activities.

Commission: *L&P*, i, 2, no. 3324 (33).
Correspondence: BL, Cotton, Calig. B.ii; *L&P*, i, 2.

F5.
BRANDON, Charles, Duke of Suffolk (*d*.1545)*

9 Oct. 1514[a] - *c*.30 Nov. 1514[h] [Special Ambassador]

While not at Queen Mary's marriage, he joined with Dorset and Worcester for
  her coronation.

Instructions: Inferred from *L&P*, i, 2, nos. 3476-7.
Correspondence: BL, Cotton, Calig. D.vi; *L&P*, i, 2.

F6.
BRANDON, Charles, Duke of Suffolk (*d*.1545)*
WINGFIELD, Sir Richard (1469?-1525)*
WEST, Dr. Nicholas (later Bishop of Ely; 1461-1533)*

14 Jan. 1515[c] - *c*.20 May 1515[e] [Special Ambassadors]
Audience: 1 Feb. 1515   66*s* 8*d*/d (Wingfield)

Suffolk of course married Queen Mary in mid-Feb. 1515, and returned to Dover
  with Mary, 2 May. Wingfield apparently returned to Calais to resume his
  duties in mid-Feb. West concluded the embassy and took his leave of Francis
  I, 8 May, and arrived in London on the date cited above.

Instructions: *L&P*, ii, 1, no. 24; inferred from no. 114.
Correspondence: BL, Cotton, Calig. D.vi, Vesp. F.xiii, Stowe 146; *L&P*, ii, 1.

F7.
SIDNEY, Sir William (1482?-1554)*

May 1515[c] - *c*.30 July 1515[d] [Special Ambassador]
Audience: *c*.6 July 1515

Instructions: *L&P*, ii, 1 no. 468.
Correspondence about: *L&P*, ii, 1.

F8.
WINGFIELD, Sir Richard (1469?-1525)*

Aug. 1515[c] - Sept. 1515[h] [Special Ambassador]

Although the documentation is extremely sketchy, he may have undertaken a
  brief mission to Paris, leaving from and returning to Calais, between these
  dates.

Instructions: *L&P*, ii, 1, no. 827.

F9.
SOMERSET, Charles, 1st Earl of Worcester (1460?-1526)*
WEST, Dr. Nicholas, Bishop of Ely (1461-1533)*
DOCWRA, Sir Thomas (*d.*1527)*
VAUX, Sir Nicholas (later 1st Baron Vaux; *d.*1523)*

9 Nov. 1518[c] - *c.*20 Feb. 1519[e]   Commissioners
Audience: 12 Dec. 1518   66*s* 8*d*/d (Worcester),
                                  53*s* 4*d*/d (West),
                                  40*s*/d (Docwra), 20*s*/d (Vaux)

This mission included the surrender of Tournai to France. They were joined at
Tournai by Sir Edward Belknap. West, on the other hand, had returned to
England *c.*10 Feb. 1519, and did not participate in the activities surrounding
the surrender of the town.

Commission: *L&P*, ii, 2, no. 4564.
Correspondence: BL, Cotton, Calig. D.vii; *L&P*, ii, 2, iii, 1.

F10.
BOLEYN, Sir Thomas (later Viscount Rochford, Earl of Wiltshire; 1477-
1539)*

Mid-Jan. 1519[h] - *c.*15 Mar. 1520[e]   [Resident Ambassador]
Audience: *c.*5 Feb. 1519   20*s*/d

Correspondence: BL, Cotton, Calig. D.vii; *L&P*, iii, 1.

F11.
WINGFIELD, Sir Richard (1469?-1525)*

31 Jan. 1520[a] - *c.*19 Aug. 1520[d]   [Resident Ambassador]
Audience: *c.*7 Mar. 1520   20*s*/d

Instructions: *L&P*, iii, 1, no. 629.
Correspondence: BL, Cotton, Calig. D.viii; *L&P*, iii, 1-2.

F12.
JERNINGHAM, Sir Richard (*d.*1525)

1 Aug. 1520[c] - *c.*21 Feb. 1521[d]   [Resident Ambassador]
Audience: early Aug. 1520   40*s*/d

Instructions: *L&P*, iii, 1, no. 936.
Correspondence: BL, Cotton, Calig., D.viii; *L&P*, iii, 1.

F13.
CAREW, Sir Nicholas (*c.*1496-1539)*

*c.*15 Dec. 1520[h] - *c.*15 Feb. 1521[h]   [Special Ambassador]
Audience: 31 Dec. 1520

Instructions: Implied in *L&P*, iii, 1, no. 1126.
Correspondence: BL, Cotton, Calig. D.viii; *L&P*, iii, 1.

F14.
FITZWILLIAM, Sir William (later Earl of Southampton; *c.*1490-1542)*

10 Jan. 1521*ᵃ* - *c.*21 Feb. 1522*ᵍ*   [Resident Ambassador]
Audience: 5 Feb. 1521   20*s*/d

Instructions: *L&P*, iii, 1, no. 1152.
Correspondence: BL, Cotton, Calig. D.viii; *L&P*, iii, 1-2.

F15.
JERNINGHAM, Sir Richard (*d.*1525)

*c.*5 May 1521*ᶜ* - *c.*10 Oct. 1521*ᵉ*   [Special Ambassador]
Audience: 20 May 1521

Instructions: *L&P*, iii, 1, nos. 1270, 1283.
Correspondence: BL, Cotton, Calig. D.viii, Galba D.vii; *L&P*, iii, 1-2.

F16.
SOMERSET, Charles, 1st Earl of Worcester (1460?-1526)*
WEST, Dr. Nicholas, Bishop of Ely (1461-1533)*

20 Oct. 1521*ᵈ* - *c.*1 Dec. 1521*ᵍ*   [Special Ambassadors]
Audience: 26 Oct. 1521

They joined with Fitzwilliam in France.

Instructions: BL, Cotton, Calig. D.viii, f. 121; *L&P*, iii, 2, no. 1696.
Correspondence: BL, Cotton, Calig. D.viii; *L&P*, iii, 2.

F17.
CHEYNE, Sir Thomas (1482/7-1558)*

*c.*15 Jan. 1522*ᶜ* - *c.*10 June 1522*ᵉ*   [Resident Ambassador]
Audience: 25 Jan. 1522

Instructions: BL, Cotton, Calig. D.viii, ff. 201-09; *L&P*, iii, 2, no. 1991.
Correspondence: BL, Cotton, Calig. D.viii; *L&P*, iii, 2.

F18.
PACE, Richard (later Sir Richard; 1482?-1536)*

During his mission to Rome and Venice (qq.v.), he visited the Duke of
   Bourbon's army, 13 June 1523.

F19.
RUSSELL, Sir John (later 1st Earl of Bedford; 1486?-1555)*

*c.*30 June 1523*ʰ* - 20 Sept. 1523*ᶜ*   [Special Ambassador]
Audience: late Aug. 1523

Instructions: *L&P*, iii, 2, no. 3217.
Correspondence: *L&P*, iii, 2; Wiffen, J., *Historical Memoirs of the House of
   Russell...*(1833), i.

F20.

Mid-Oct. 1523[h] - 5 Nov. 1525[a]   [Special Ambassador]
Contacted Bourbon: *c*.1 Nov. 1523   20*s*/d

He was sent specifically to the Duke of Bourbon and seemingly acted as a
    paymaster for the troops serving with Bourbon. He also had diplomatic
    responsibilities there, responsibilities which included travelling throughout
    the continent, and to Rome (q.v.).

Instructions: BL, Harl. 297, ff. 74-7; inferred from *L&P*, iii, 2, nos. 3399,
    3948-9, 3440.
Correspondence: BL, Cotton, Vitel. B.v; *L&P*, iii, 2 and iv, 1.

F21.
TAYLOR, Dr. John (*d*.1534)*
FITZWILLIAM, Sir William (later Earl of Southampton; *c*.1490-1542)*

15 Oct. 1525[e] - *c*.31 Jan. 1526[e]   [Special Ambassadors]
                    (Fitzwilliam)
Audience: *c*.24 Nov. 1525

Fitzwilliam departed France on 20 Jan. 1526, while Taylor remained as resident
    (see below). They visited Louise of Savoy (Savoy, q.v.) at Lyons in company
    with Clerk, Dec. 1525.

Instructions: *L&P*, iv, 1, no. 1705.
Correspondence: BL, Cotton, Calig. D.ix; *L&P*, iv, 1-2.

F22.
TAYLOR, Dr. John (*d*.1534)*

15 Oct. 1525[e] - *c*.1 Dec. 1526[g]   [Resident Ambassador]
Audience: *c*.24 Nov. 1525

Instructions: BL, Lansd. 121, no. 2; *L&P*, iv, 1, no. 1705.
Correspondence: BL, Cotton, Calig. D.ix, Titus B.vi, Lansd. 115; *L&P*, iv, 2.

F23.
TUNSTALL, Dr. Cuthbert, Bishop of London (later Bishop of Durham;
    1474-1559)*
SAMPSON, Dr. Richard (later Bishop of Coventry and Lichfield; *d*.1554)*

While returning from a mission to the Emperor (q.v.), they visited the captured
    French King at Madrid, 27 Jan. 1526.

Correspondence: *L&P*, iv, 1.

F24.
CHEYNE, Sir Thomas (1482/7-1558)*

20 Mar. 1526[c] - *c*.10 June 1526[e]   [Special Ambassador]
Audience: 9 Apr. 1526

He joined with Dr. Taylor, the resident, in Paris.

Instructions: BL, Cotton, Calig. D.ix, f. 164, Lansd. 115, no. 47(?), 121, no. 1(?); *L&P*, iv, 1, no. 2039.
Correspondence: BL, Cotton, Calig. D.ix; *L&P*, iv, 1-2.

F25.
CLERK, John, Bishop of Bath and Wells (*d*.1541)*

c.20 July 1526[f] - *c*.6 Sept. 1527[c]   [Special Ambassador]
Audience: 14 Aug. 1526

Instructions: Inferred from *L&P*, iv, 2, no. 2416.
Correspondence: BL, Cotton, Calig. D.ix-x, Harl. 283; *L&P*, iii, 2, iv, 1-2.

F26.
GHINUCCI, Jerome de, Bishop of Worcester (*fl.*1620s-1630s)

During a mission to the Emperor, he joined with Clerk and visited the French court (q.v.), with an audience 5 Dec. 1526.

F27.
FITZWILLIAM, Sir William (later Earl of Southampton; *c*.1490-1542)*

c.15 Dec. 1526[h] - *c*.20 Jan. 1527[d]   [Special Ambassador]
Audience: 23 Dec. 1526

He joined with Dr. Clerk.

Instructions: Suggested in *L&P*, iv, 2, no. 2728.
Correspondence: BL, Cotton, Calig. D.ix; *L&P*, iv, 2.

F28.
BOLEYN, Sir Thomas, Viscount Rochford (later Earl of Wiltshire; 1477-1539)*
BROWN, Sir Anthony (*c*.1500-1548)*

17 May 1527[b]- *c*.30 June 1527[g]   [Special Ambassadors]
            (Rochford)
            c.20 Nov. 1527[d]
            (Brown)
Audience: 8 June 1527
Administration of oath: 9 June 1527

On 30 May, they joined with John Clerk, the Bishop of Bath, in France.

Commission: BL, Add. 5712; *L&P*, iv, 2, no. 3124.
Correspondence: BL, Harl. 283; *L&P*, iv, 2 (including no. 3171, which is undoubtedly misattributed).

F29.
WOLSEY, Cardinal Thomas (1475?-1530)*

18 June 1527[b] - c.1 Oct. 1527[e]   [Special Ambassador]
Audience: 4 Aug. 1527

His retinue of over 900 horse included Cuthbert Tunstall, Bishop of London; Sir Henry Guildford; Lord Sandys; Sir Thomas More and others, but only Wolsey is listed in the commission.

Commission and Instructions: *L&P*, iv, 2, no. 3186.
Correspondence: *L&P*, iv, 2.

F30.
PLANTAGENET, Arthur, Viscount Lisle (1480?-1542)*
TAYLOR, Dr. John (*d*.1534)*
CAREW, Sir Nicholas (*c*.1496-1539)*
WRIOTHESLEY, Thomas (later Earl of Southampton; 1505-1550)*

22 Oct. 1527[b] - c.27 Nov. 1527[d]   [Special Ambassadors]
Investment: 10 Nov. 1527

They joined with Sir Anthony Browne, who was listed in the commission, and was already in France.

Commission: BL, Add. 5712; *L&P*, iv, 2, no. 3508.
Correspondence: *L&P*, iv, 2.

F31.
TAYLOR, Dr. John (*d*.1534)*

22 Oct. 1527[b] - 10 June 1529[b]   [Resident Ambassador]
Audience and Investment: 10 Nov.
   1527

He was joined with the ambassadors listed previously, and then remained as resident in France.

Commission: BL, Add. 5712, 25114; *L&P*, iv, 2, no. 3508; lost instructions referred to in *L&P*, iv, 2, no. 3574.
Correspondence: BL, Harl. 419; *L&P*, iv, 2-3.

F32.
GARDINER, Dr. Stephen (later Bishop of Winchester; 1483?-1555)*
FOX, Dr. Edward (later Bishop of Hereford; 1496?-1538)*

11 Feb. 1528[d] - late Feb. 1528[f]   [Special Ambassador]
Audience: 24 Feb. 1528

This mission was directed primarily to Rome (Italy, q.v.), but an important secondary purpose was contact with the French King during the dates given.

Commission: *L&P*, iv, 2, no. 3913 (for France specifically); HMC *Salisb.*, i, p. 6.
Correspondence: *L&P*, iv, 2; Gardiner, S., *Letters of Stephen Gardiner*, ed. J. Muller (New York, 1933); Pocock, N. (ed.), *Records of the Reformation...* (Oxford, 1870), i.

F33.
WALLOP, Sir John (*d.*1551)*

17 Feb. 1528*f* - early May 1528*g*   [Special Ambassador]
Audience: 28 Feb. 1528

Instructions: Implied in *L&P*, iv, 2, no. 3986-7.
Correspondence: *L&P*, iv, 2.

F34.
CLERK, Dr. John, Bishop of Bath and Wells (*d.*1541)*

*c.*20 Mar. 1528*h* - 4 Nov. 1528*g*   [Special Ambassador]
Arrived: *c.*10 Apr. 1528

Instructions: *L&P*, iv, 2, no. 4155 (follow-up instructions).
Correspondence: BL, Harl. 6989; *L&P*, iv, 2.

F35.
BRYAN, Sir Francis (*c.*1492-1550)*

21 Aug. 1528*c* - *c.*1 Nov. 1528*g*   [Special Ambassador]
Audience: 10 Sept. 1528

He joined with Clerk and Taylor.

Instructions: *L&P*, iv, 2, no. 4656.
Correspondence: *L&P*, iv, 2.

F36.
BRYAN, Sir Francis (*c.*1492-1550)*
VANNES, Peter (*d.*1563)*

On a mission to Rome (Italy, q.v.), they visited France, and had an audience
    with the King, *c.*12 Dec. 1528.

F37.
KNIGHT, Dr. William (later Bishop of Bath and Wells; 1476-1547)*
BENET, Dr. William (*d.*1533)*

4 Dec. 1528*b* - *c.*20 Mar. 1529*g*   [Special Ambassadors]
            (Benet)   40*s*/d (Knight)
            *c.*10 July 1529*h*
            (Knight)
Arrived: *c.*5 Jan. 1529

Besides the French court, they had specific instructions to make contact with
    Anne de Montmorency, the Grand Master of France.

Instructions: Inferred from *L&P*, iv, 3, nos. 5149-50.
Commission: *L&P*, iv, 2, no. 5023.
Correspondence: BL, Cotton, Vitel. B.xi; *L&P*, iv, 2-3.

F38.
BRANDON, Charles, Duke of Suffolk (*d.*1545)*
FITZWILLIAM, Sir William (later Earl of Southamption; *c.*1490-1542)*

12 May 1529[a] - *c.*10 July 1529[e]	[Special Ambassadors]
(Suffolk)　　　　　(Suffolk)	53*s* 4*d*/d (Fitzwilliam)
18 May 1529[a]　*c.*13 June 1529[e]	
(Fitzwilliam)　　(Fitzwilliam)	
Audience: *c.*1 June 1529	

They joined with Knight.

Instructions: Inferred from *L&P*, iv, 3, no. 5675.
Correspondence: *L&P*, iv, 3.

F39.
BRYAN, Sir Francis (*c.*1492-1550)*

14 July 1529[a] - *c.*1 Dec. 1529[g]	[Resident Ambassador]
Audience: 25 July 1529	26*s* 8*d*/d

Instructions: Inferred from *L&P*, iv, 3, nos. 5796, 5802.
Correspondence: *L&P*, iv, 3.

F40.
VANNES, Peter (*d.*1563)*

On his return from a mission to Rome (Italian States, q.v.), he stopped in Paris, Sept. 1529, to continue his efforts in behalf of the divorce with both the French King and with various churchmen.

F41.
BOLEYN, George, Viscount Rochford (*d.*1536)*
STOKESLEY, John (later Bishop of London; 1475?-1539)*

8 Oct. 1529[d] - late Feb. 1530[h]	[Special Ambassadors]
(Rochford)	40*s*/d (Rochford)
Audience: *c.*20 Jan. 1530	26*s* 8*d*/d (Stokesley)

Stokesley accompanied Rochford to France, but seemingly was more involved in soliciting scholarly opinion about the divorce than he was in diplomatic responsibilities. Boleyn apparently continued his journey directly from France, going into Italy generally and Venice specifically (qq.v.).

Instructions: *L&P*, iv, 3, no. 6073.
Correspondence: *L&P*, iv, 3.

F42.
BRYAN, Sir Francis (*c.*1492-1550)*

21 Feb. 1530[d] - *c.*1 Apr. 1530[c]	[Special Ambassador]
Arrived: 6 Mar. 1530	£170 (total)

Among his responsibilities was the conveyance to a Franco-Spanish conference of a jewel pledged to the French King by Henry VIII.

Instructions: Inferred from *L&P*, iv, 3, nos. 6227, 6255, 6257-8, 6265.
Correspondence about: *L&P*, iv, 3.

F43.
WELSBORNE, John (later Sir John; *c*.1498-1548)*

14 Mar. 1530*ᵃ* - 19 Dec. 1530*ᵇ*   [Special Ambassador]
                                        26*s* 8*d*/d

Correspondence: *L&P*, iv, 3.

F44.
BOLEYN, Thomas, Earl of Wiltshire (1477-1539)*
LEE, Dr. Edward (later Archbishop of York; 1482?-1544)*

While returning from a mission to the Emperor and the Pope (qq.v.), they
    visited the French King, with an audience *c*.1 May 1530.

F45.
FOX, Dr. Edward (later Bishop of Hereford; 1496?-1538)*

24 May 1530*ᵃ* - 20 July 1530*ᶜ*   [Special Ambassador]
                                        26*s* 8*d*/d

While the principal purpose of this mission was to secure learned foreign opinion
    about the divorce, he was both characterized as and paid as an ambassador.

Correspondence: BL, Harl. 296.
Correspondence about: *L&P*, iv, 3.

F46.
BRYAN, Sir Francis (*c*.1492-1550)*

13 Oct. 1530*ᵃ* - *c*.20 Dec. 1531*ᶜ*   [Resident Ambassador]
Audience: 11 Nov. 1530   40*s*/d

He was accompanied by one Richard Tate, whose status and role are unclear.

Instructions: Inferred from *L&P*, iv, 3, no. 6733.
Correspondence: BL, Add. 25114, 48044, Harl. 290; *L&P*, iv, 3 - v.

F47.
FOX, Dr. Edward (later Bishop of Hereford; 1496?-1538)*

4 May 1531*ᶠ* - *c*.20 Dec. 1531*ᶜ*   [Special Ambassador]
He joined with Bryan.

Instructions: Inferred from *L&P*, v, nos. 238, 251.
Correspondence: BL, Add. 25114, 48044(?); *L&P*, v.

F48.
GARDINER, Stephen, Bishop of Winchester (1483?-1555)*

29 Dec. 1531^f - 6 Mar. 1532^c [Special Ambassador]
Audience: *c*.2 Jan. 1531

Instructions: Inferred in *L&P*, v, nos. 711, 756; also Pocock, N., *Records of the Reformation...*, ii, pp. 157-65; Gardiner, S., *Letters of Stephen Gardiner*, p. 45.
Correspondence: *L&P*, v; Gardiner, *Letters*.

F49.
WALLOP, Sir John (*d*.1551)*

11 Sept. 1532^a - *c*.15 Mar. 1537^g [Resident Ambassador]
Arrived: by 1 Jan. 1533   26*s* 8*d*/d

Insofar as he was the lieutenant at Calais and since his correspondence is spasmodic, to say the least, it is assumed that this service must have been intermittent, with numerous and extended returns to either Calais or London.
Correspondence: BL, Lansd. 288; *L&P*, vi - xii; Merriman, R. B., *The Life and Letters of Thomas Cromwell* (1902).

F50.
CAREW, Sir Nicholas (*c*.1496-1539)*

2 Oct. 1532^f - *c*.24 Nov. 1532?^{h} [Special Ambassador]
He may have returned from France with Henry VIII.
Instructions: Implied from *L&P*, v, nos. 1377, 1429.

F51.
BOLEYN, George, Viscount Rochford (*d*.1536)*

13 Mar. 1533^f - 7 Apr. 1533^a [Special Ambassador]
Audience: *c*.16 Mar. 1533

Instructions: *L&P*, vi, no. 230.
Correspondence about: *L&P*, vi.

F52.
HOWARD, Thomas, 3rd Duke of Norfolk (1473-1554)*
BOLEYN, George, Viscount Rochford (*d*.1536)*
BRYAN, Sir Francis (*c*.1492-1550)*
PAULET, Sir William (later Baron of St. John, 1st Marquis of Winchester, Earl of Wiltshire; 1485?-1572)*
BROWNE, Sir Anthony (*c*.1500-1548)*

28 May 1533^e - 1 Sept. 1533^a [Special Ambassadors]
         (except Bryan)
Audience: 10 July 1533

They joined with Sir John Wallop. Apparently Drs. Goodrich, Aldrich and

Thirlby also accompanied the ambassadors. Sir Francis Bryan remained in France after the return of the embassy (see immediately below).

Instructions: In part in *L&P*, vi, no. 641.
Correspondence: *L&P*, vi.

F53.
BRYAN, Sir Francis (*c.*1492-1550)*

28 May 1533[e] - late Nov. 1533[g]   [Special Ambassador]
Audience: 10 July 1533

He remained after the main body of the Norfolk legation (above) returned.

Correspondence: *L&P*, vi.

F54.
GARDINER, Stephen, Bishop of Winchester (1483?-1555)*

2 Sept. 1533[f] - late Nov. 1533[g]   [Special Ambassador]
Audience: *c.*19 Sept. 1533

He joined with Bryan and Wallop, already in Paris. They also visited the Pope (Italian States q.v.) at Marseilles. Bryan and Gardiner apparently returned to England about the same time.

Instructions: Implied in *L&P*, vi, nos. 1071, 1572, 1164.
Correspondence: BL, Lansd. 288; *L&P*, vi.

F55.
BOLEYN, George, Viscount Rochford (*d.*1536)*
FITZWILLIAM, Sir William (later Earl of Southampton; *c.*1490-1542)*

14 Apr. 1534[e] - *c.*3 May 1534[c]   [Special Ambassadors]
Audience: 21 Apr. 1534

Instructions: *L&P*, vii, no. 470.
Correspondence: *L&P*, vii.

F56.
BOLEYN, George, Viscount Rochford (*d.*1536)*

9 July 1534[e] - *c.*25 July 1534[c]   [Special Ambassador]

Instructions: *L&P*, vii, no. 958.
Correspondence about: *L&P*, vii.

F57.
MOUNT, Christopher (later Dr. Christopher; 1497-1572)*
HEYNES, Dr. Simon (*d.*1552)*

1 Aug. 1535[a] - winter? 1535[h]   [Special Ambassadors]
            (Mount)
            *c.*1 Dec. 1535[h]
            (Heynes)

77

They first went to Paris, then Mount continued his mission alone to Wittenberg, Germany (q.v.), around 7 Sept. 1535.

Instructions: Inferred from *L&P*, ix, nos. 54, 180.
Correspondence: *L&P*, ix.

F58.
GARDINER, Stephen, Bishop of Winchester (1483?-1555)*

1 Oct. 1535[a] - 28 Sept. 1538[b]   [Resident Ambassador]
Audience: 25 Nov. 1535   56*s* 4*d*/d

Instructions: *L&P*, ix, no. 443.
Correspondence: BL, Add. 25114, Cotton, Vesp. C.xiv, Harl. 6989; *L&P*, ix - xiii; Gardiner, *Letters*; Merriman, *Letters of Cromwell*.

F59.
BRYAN, Sir Francis (*c*.1492-1550)*

12 Nov. 1535[f] - *c*.31 Dec. 1535[g]   [Special Ambassador]
Audience: *c*.10 Dec. 1535

Instructions: Inferred from *L&P*, ix, no. 947.
Correspondence: BL, Add. 48044, Cotton, Vesp. F.xiii; *L&P*, ix.

F60.
SADLER, Ralph (later Sir Ralph; 1507-1587)*

Although he went to France in mid-Mar. 1537, and delivered instructions to Gardiner, his primary purpose was to obtain an interview with the Scottish King (Scotland, q.v.), then in France.

F61.
KNYVETT, Sir Henry (*d*.1546)

c.30 July 1537[d] - *c*.20 Aug. 1537[c]   [Special Ambassador]
Audience: *c*.11 Aug. 1537

Instructions: *L&P*, xii, 1, no. 539.
Correspondence: *L&P*, *Add*. i, no. 1243.

F62.
HOBY, Philip (later Sir Philip; 1505-1558)*

c.28 Feb. 1538[c] - *c*.1 Apr. 1538[e]   [Special Ambassador]
                                               £46 13*s* 4*d* (total?)

He was accompanied on this mission by Hans Holbein, the artist, and his principal purpose seems to have been to make contact with the Regent's court at Brussels (Low Countries, q.v.) to view the Duchess of Milan. In France, they met with the Duchess of Lorraine to view one of her daughters, all for the English King's matrimonial purposes.

Instructions: *L&P*, xiii, 1, no. 380.
Correspondence about: *L&P*, xiii, 1.

F63.

BRYAN, Sir Francis (*c*.1492-1550)*

THIRLBY, Dr. Thomas (later Bishop of Westminster, Norwich, Ely; 1506?-1570)*

6 Apr. 1538*b* - *c*.15 Aug. 1538*g*   [Special Ambassadors]
Audience: *c*.27 Apr. 1538   53*s* 4*d*/d (Bryan),
                                                                40*s*/d (Thirlby)

They joined with Gardiner.

Instructions: Suggested in *L&P*, xiii, 1, nos. 900, 917, 1003.
Correspondence: *L&P*, xiii, 1-2.

F64.

BONNER, Edmund, Bishop of Hereford, and then London (1500?-1569)*

23 July 1538*d* - 16 Mar. 1540*a*   [Resident Ambassador]
Audience: End of Aug. 1538   40*s*/d, 53*s* 4*d*/d (after 1 Oct. 1538)

He went directly from a short mission to the Emperor (q.v.) in Spain to assuming the residency at Paris.

Instructions: BL, Add. 21564 (no folio no.); *L&P*, xiii, 1, no. 1441, xiii, 2, no. 143; Gardiner, *Letters*, pp. 82-91.
Correspondence: BL, Cotton, Calig. E.iv; *L&P*, xiii, 1 - xv.

F65.

BROWNE, Sir Anthony (*c*.1500-1548)*

Early Sept. 1538*h* - *c*.30 Oct. 1538*g*   [Special Ambassador]

He also visited Mary of Hungary in the Low Countries (q.v.), *c*.20 Oct. 1538. He apparently returned briefly to England in late Sept.

Correspondence: *L&P*, xiii, 2.

F66.

WYATT, Sir Thomas (1503-1542)*

15 Nov. 1539*a* - *c*.28 Apr. 1540*c*   [Special Ambassador]
Audience (with the French King):   53*s* 4*d*/d
   1 Dec. 1539

He joined with Bonner in France. He had audience with the Emperor (q.v.) at Paris and then accompanied him to Flanders.

Instructions: BL, Harl. 282, f. 78; *L&P*, xiv, 2, no. 524.
Correspondence: BL, Cotton, Vesp. C.xiv; *L&P*, xiv, 1 - xv; Nott, G. (ed.), *The Works of Henry Howard Earl of Surrey and Sir Thomas Wyatt the Elder* (1815-16).

F67.

WALLOP, Sir John (*d*.1551)*

2 Feb. 1540*c* - *c*.1 Mar. 1541*g*   [Resident Ambassador]
Audience: 23 Feb. 1540   40*s*/d

Instructions: Inferred from *L&P*, xv, no. 208; also inferred from Merriman, *Letters of Cromwell*, ii, pp. 250-3.
Correspondence: BL, Harl. 288; *L&P*, xv - xvi; Merriman, *Letters of Cromwell*, ii.

F68.
HOWARD, Thomas, 3rd Duke of Norfolk (1473-1554)*

14 Feb. 1540[f] - *c*.1 Mar. 1540[c]   [Special Ambassador]
Audience: 16 Feb. 1540

Instructions: *L&P*, xv, no. 145.
Correspondence: *L&P*, xv.

F69.
HOWARD, William, 1st Baron Howard of Effingham (1510?-1573)*

17 Jan. 1541[a] - *c*.5 Dec. 1541[e]   [Resident Ambassador]
Audience: 6 Feb. 1541   53*s* 4*d*/d

Instructions: *L&P*, xvi, 1, no. 464.
Correspondence: *L&P*, xvi.

F70.
PAGET, Sir William (later Lord Paget of Beaudesert; 1505-1563)*

24 Sept. 1541[c] - *c*.20 Apr. 1543[c]   [Resident Ambassador]
Audience: 20 Nov. 1541   40*s*/d

Instructions: *L&P*, xvi, no. 1198.
Correspondence: *L&P*, xvi - xviii.

F71.
DUDLEY, John, Viscount Lisle (later Duke of Northumberland; 1504/06-1553)*
PAGET, Sir William (later Lord Paget of Beaudesert; 1505-1563)
WOTTON, Dr. Nicholas (later Sir Nicholas; 1497?-1567)

17 Apr. 1546[b] - 14 June 1546[b]   [Peace Commissioners]
First meeting: 6 May 1546   53*s* 4*d*/d (Lisle)

The negotiations took place at Guines.

Instructions: BL, Eg. 2603, f. 31; *L&P*, xxi, 1, no. 610.
Correspondence: BL, Add. 5756, Harl. 283; *L&P*, xxi, 1.

F72.
CHEYNE, Sir Thomas (1482/7-1558)*

15 June 1546[a] - 19 July 1546[b]   [Special Ambassador]
Audience: 3 July 1546   66*s* 8*d*/d

Instructions: *L&P*, xxi, 1, nos. 1071, 1094.
Correspondence: *L&P*, xxi, 1.

F73.

KNYVETT, Sir Henry (*d.*1546)

2 July 1546[d] - *died c.*10 Aug. 1546   [Special Ambassador]
Audience: 15 July 1546

Credentials: *L&P*, xxi, 1, nos. 1257-59, 1295.
Correspondence: *L&P*, xxi, 1.

F74.

DUDLEY, John, Viscount Lisle (later Duke of Northumberland; 1504/06-1553)*
TUNSTALL, Cuthbert, Bishop of Durham (1474-1559)*
WOTTON, Dr. Nicholas (later Sir Nicholas; 1497?-1567)*

2 July 1546[b] - 12 Aug. 1546[c]   [Peace Commissioners]
Audience: 27 July 1546   30s/d (Tunstall);
Ratification: 1 Aug. 1546   £4/d (Lisle)

They joined Knyvett in Paris, who arrived just before this main diplomatic contingent. Wotton was to remain as resident (below).

Instructions: *L&P*, xxi, 1, nos. 1177, 1295.
Correspondence: *L&P*, xxi, 1.

F75.

WOTTON, Dr. Nicholas (later Sir Nicholas; 1497?-1567)*

2 July 1546[b] - late Aug. 1549[h]   [Resident Ambassador]
Audience (of presentation as   £56/mo.
    resident): 3 Aug. 1546

Wotton went to Paris with the above commissioners, and then remained as resident. He apparently returned temporarily to England in 1547.

Instructions: *L&P*, xxi, 1, no. 1177.
Correspondence: BL, Harl. 283; *L&P*, xxi, 1-2; *CSPF, 1547-53*; Richards, S. (ed.), *Secret Writing…*,(1974); Tytler, P. (ed.), *England Under the Reigns of Edward VI…*(1839).

F76.

MEWTAS, Sir Peter (*c.*1500-1562)

1 Feb. 1547[h] - *c.*5 Mar. 1547[c]   [Special Ambassador]

Instructions: *CSPF, 1547-53*, no. 4.
Correspondence about: *CSPS, 1547-9*.

F77.

RUSSELL, John, 1st Earl of Bedford (1486?-1555)*
PAGET, William, Baron Paget of Beaudesert (1505-1563)*
PETRE, Sir William (1505/06-1572)*
MASON, Sir John (1503-1566)*

1 Jan. 1550[b] - *c.*29 Mar. 1550[c]   [Peace Commissioners]
First meeting: 19 Feb. 1550
Secretary: Nicasius Yetswert

Instructions: PRO, SP/68/5, ff. 7-13; BL, Cotton, Calig. E.iv, ff. 201-03, 248-50, 284-6; Add. 4149, ff. 26-8.

Correspondence: BL, Cotton, Calig. E.iv, Lansd. 2; *APC, 1547-50*; Paget, W., *The Letters of William, Lord Paget...*, ed. Beer and Jack, Camden Misc., xxv (1974).

F78.

BROOKE, George, 6th Baron Cobham (*c*.1497-1558)*
PETRE, Sir William (1505/06-1572)*
MASON, Sir John (1503-1566)*

23 Apr. 1550*f* - *c*.20 May 1550*e*   [Commissioners]
Confirmation of treaty: 8 May 1550

Mason accompanied this ratification entourage, then remained as resident (see below).

Correspondence: PRO, SP/68/9; BL, Harl. 284.
Correspondence about: *CSPS, 1550-2*.

F79.

MASON, Sir John (1503-1566)*

23 Apr. 1550*f* - *c*.1 Aug. 1551*d*   Resident Ambassador
                                     37*s*/d

Correspondence: PRO, SP/68/9; BL, Cotton, Calig. E.iv, Add. 5498, 5935, Sloane 2442, Harl. 353; *CSPF, 1547-53*; Tytler, P., *History of Scotland* (Edinburgh, 1828-43), vi; Tytler, P., *England under the Reigns of Edward VI...*(1839), i.

F80.

PICKERING, Sir William (1516/17-1575)*

18 Feb. 1551*c* - *c*.15 Mar. 1551*e*   Special Ambassador
Audience: 3 Mar. 1551
Secretary: Thomas Dannet?

Instructions: BL, Add. 5935, ff. 96-100(?); Harl. 288, ff. 55-6, 353, ff. 86-94.
Correspondence: *CSPF, 1547-53*.

F81.

PARR, William, Earl of Essex and Marquis of Northampton (1513-1571)*
GOODRICH, Dr. Thomas, Bishop of Ely (*d*.1554)*
HOBY, Sir Philip (1505-1558)*
PICKERING, Sir William (1516/17-1575)*
SMITH, Sir Thomas (1513-1577)*
OLIVER, John (*fl*.1550s)

24 Apr. 1551*a* - 12 Aug. 1551*a*   [Special Ambassadors]
Audience: 19 June 1551   66*s* 8*d*/d (Northampton and
Secretary: John Dudley, Lord Lisle?   Hoby each)

This mission included a large entourage of various English noblemen, including the Earls of Rutland, Worcester and Ormond, and the Barons Fitzwalter, Bray and Eure. They joined with Mason, who was already in Paris. Pickering remained as resident (see below).

Instructions: BL, Add. 5498, ff. 16-21, 5935, ff. 100-07, Sloane 2442, f. 46-50, Harl. 353, ff. 110-11; *CSPF, 1547-53*, nos. 349-53.

Correspondence: BL, Add. 5498, 5935, Harl. 295 (report), 353; *CSPF, 1547-53*; Tytler, P. (ed.), *England under the Reigns of Edward VI...*(1839), i.

F82.
PICKERING, Sir William (1516/17-1575)*

21 Apr. 1551[a] - c.27 Aug. 1553[d]   [Resident Ambassador]
                                             £1100/an.

Pickering was joined with the above ambassadors, and then remained as resident.

Instructions: BL, Sloane 2442, f. 51, Harl. 353, f. 113b-15, Add. 5935, ff. 107-08; *CSPF, 1547-53*, nos. 318, 329, 396.

Correspondence: BL, Cotton, Calig. E.v, Harl. 1582; *CSPF, 1547-53, 1553-8*; *APC, 1550-2, 1552-4*; HMC *Salisb.*, i; Tytler, P. (ed.), *England under the Reigns of Edward VI...*(1839), i, ii.

F83.
CLINTON, Edward Fiennes de, 9th Baron Clinton and Saye (later 1st Earl of Lincoln; 1512-1585)

16 Nov. 1551[c] - c.20 Dec. 1551[h]   [Special Ambassador]
Audience: c.1 Dec. 1551

Instructions: *CSPF, 1547-53*, no. 485.

Correspondence: *CSPF, 1547-53*; *APC, 1550-2*; Tytler, P. (ed.), *England under the Reigns of Edward VI...*(1839), ii.

F84.
SIDNEY, Sir Henry (1529-1586)*

c.27 Dec. 1552[d] - c.4 Feb. 1553[a]   [Special Ambassador]

Instructions: BL, Sloane 2442, f. 52, Add. 5935, ff. 108-10, Harl. 353, ff. 127-9.

Correspondence about: *CSPF, 1547-53*.

F85.
WOTTON, Dr. Nicholas (later Sir Nicholas; 1497?-1567)*
CHALONER, Sir Thomas (1521-1565)*

2 Apr. 1553[d] - c.27 Aug. 1553[c]   [Special Ambassadors]
          (Chaloner)
Audience: 23 Apr. 1553

Chaloner and Wotton joined with Pickering in France. Wotton replaced Pickering as resident (see below).

Instructions: BL, Cotton, Calig. E.v, ff. 1-8; Add. 5935, ff. 110-14, Harl. 297, ff. 31-5; *CSPF, 1547-53*, no. 643.
Correspondence: *CSPF, 1547-53, 1553-8*; HMC *Salisb.*, i; Haynes, S. and Murdin, W. (eds.), *Collection of State Papers...Left by William Cecil, Lord Burghley...*(1740-59).

F86.
WOTTON, Dr. Nicholas (later Sir Nicholas; 1497?-1567)*

2 Apr. 1553[d] - *c.*26 June 1557[h]   [Resident Ambassador]
Audience (upon assuming the
  residency): *c.*16 Aug. 1553
Secretary: John Somers

He went with Chaloner, and then remained as resident.
Instructions: BL, Add. 5935, ff. 110-14.
Correspondence: BL, Add. 5935; *CSPF, 1547-53, 1553-8*; HMC *Salisb.*, i; *APC, 1554-6, 1556-8*; Haynes and Murdin, *Collection of State Papers*; Richards, S. (ed.), *Secret Writing...*(1974); Tytler, *England under the Reigns of Edward VI...*(1839), ii.

F87.
ST. LEGER, Sir Anthony (1496?-1559)*

*c.*8 Aug. 1553[h] - *c.*27 Aug. 1553[c]   [Special Ambassador]
Audience: 15 Aug. 1553

He joined with Wotton and Chaloner.

Instructions: Inferred from *CSPF, 1553-8*, nos. 9, 15.
Correspondence: *CSPF, 1553-8*.

F88.
CLINTON, Edward Fiennes de, 9th Baron Clinton and Saye (later 1st Earl of Lincoln; 1512-1585)*

*c.*8 Apr. 1556[h] - 3 May 1556[a]   [Special Ambassador]
Audience: 21 Apr. 1556

Instructions: Inferred from *CSPF, 1553-8*, no. 493.
Correspondence about: *CSPF, 1553-8*.

F89.
HOWARD, William, 1st Baron Howard of Effingham (1510?-1573)*
WOTTON, Dr. Nicholas (later Sir Nicholas; 1497?-1567)*
THROCKMORTON, Sir Nicholas (1515-1571)*

7 May 1559[b] - *c.*7 June 1559[c]   [Commissioners]
Audience: 24 May 1559
Ratification of treaty: 28 May 1559

They went to ratify the Treaty of Câteau-Cambrésis. Throckmorton was included in this commission, and then remained in France as resident ambassador (see below).

Instructions: *CSPF, 1558-9*, no. 619; *CSPScot, 1547-63*, no. 458; KL, i, pp. 323-5.

Correspondence: *CSPF, 1558-9*; plus others as cited in Weaver, F., 'Anglo-French Diplomatic Relations, 1558-1603,' *BIHR* (1926-9), iv, p. 77.

F90.

THROCKMORTON, Sir Nicholas (1515-1571)*

3 May 1559[a] - c.4 Feb. 1563[c]   Resident Ambassador
                                      66s 8d/d

Secretaries: Henry Killigrew, Robert
Jones, John Somers and Henry
Middlemore (at various times)

He was part of the commission immediately preceding, and remained after the departure of the other two commissioners. He returned to England from Nov. 1559 to Jan. 1560; he was captured by Huguenots Sept. 1562 on a return from Paris, and served briefly as Elizabeth's agent to the Huguenots, Sept. - Nov. 1562. He was subsequently captured by royalist French forces, and was released 13 Jan. 1563.

Instructions: *CSPF, 1558-9*, no. 621.

Correspondence: BL, Cotton, Calig. C.i, E.v, xii; Add. 4106, 4160, 5753, 5756, 35830, 35831, 35834, 35838, 32091, Lansd. 102; *CSPF, 1558-9, 1559-60, 1560-1, 1561-2, 1562, 1563*; KL, ii-iii; HMC *Salisb.*, i; plus others, as cited in Weaver, iv, p. 81.

F91.

HOWARD, Sir George (by 1519-1580)*

3 May 1559[c] - c.20 May 1559[c]   [Special Ambassador]
Audience: c.12 May 1559

Instructions: *CSPF, 1558-9*, no. 596; Forbes, P., *A Full View of the Public Transactions in the Reign of Elizabeth* (1740-1), i, p. 85.

Correspondence about: PRO, SP/70/4; *CSPF, 1558-9*.

F92.

HOWARD, Charles (later 2nd Baron Howard of Effingham and 1st Earl of Nottingham; 1536-1624)*

10 July 1559[c] - late July 1559[h]   [Special Ambassador]
Arrived: 13 July 1559

Instructions: *CSPF, 1558-9*, no. 967.

Correspondence about: *CSPF, 1558-9*.

F93.

MEWTAS, Sir Peter (c.1500-1562)

7 Aug. 1559[b] - c.15 Sept. 1559[e]   [Special Ambassador]
Audience: 27 Aug. 1559   53s 4d/d

Instructions: *CSPF, 1558-9*, no. 1153.

Correspondence about: *CSPF, 1558-9*.

F94.
KILLIGREW, Henry (later Sir Henry; *c*.1528-1603)*

11 Oct. 1559[b] - 29 Jan.1560[c]   Chargé d'Affaires
                                          ad hoc

With the aid of Robert Jones, he ran the embassy during Throckmorton's absence.

Instructions: *CSPF, 1559-60*, no. 63.
Correspondence: *CSPF, 1559-60*; Forbes, *A Full View...*, i.

F95.
MEWTAS, Sir Peter (*c*.1500-1562)

2 Sept. 1560[h] - mid-Jan. 1561[h]   [Special Ambassador]

Instructions: Inferred from Camden, W., *Annals...* (1635), pp. 34-5; Haynes and Murdin, *Collection of State Papers...* p. 751.

F96.
RUSSELL, Francis, 2nd Earl of Bedford (1527?-1585)*

21 Jan. 1561[b] - 9 Mar. 1561[c]   Ambassador Extraordinary
Audience: 16 Feb. 1561   £6/d

Instructions: *CSPF, 1560-1*, no. 898.
Correspondence: *CSPF, 1560-1*; HMC *5th Report*.

F97.
SOMERS, John (1527-1585)

6 May 1561[d] - mid-July 1561[h]   [Special Ambassador]
Audience: 23 May 1561

Instructions: Inferred from *CSPF, 1561-2*, no. 208.
Correspondence about: PRO, SP/70/26; *CSPF, 1561-2*.

F98.
SIDNEY, Sir Henry (1529-1586)*

28 Apr. 1562[c] - *c*.20 May 1562[c]   [Special Ambassador]
Audience: 5 May 1562

Instructions: *CSPF, 1561-2*, nos. 1063-4.
Correspondence: BL, Cotton, Titus B.xi; *CSPF, 1562*.

F99.
MEWTAS, Sir Peter (*c*.1500-1562)

c.20 July 1562[h] - *died c*.6 Sept. 1562   [Special Ambassador]
Audience: 29 July 1562

He apparently was also to contact Condé and/or Coligny, which he did not accomplish.

Instructions: Inferred from *CSPF, 1562*, nos. 372-3.
Correspondence: BL, Add. 35831, *CSPF, 1562*.

F100.
SMITH, Sir Thomas (1513-1577)*

31 Aug. 1562[b] - 1 June 1566[a]   Resident Ambassador
Audience: *c*.1 Nov. 1562   66*s* 8*d*/d
Secretary: Henry Middlemore

He joined with Throckmorton. In what was a distinct irritation to him, Smith's name, and thus his diplomatic status was placed second, after Throckmorton's, in their joint commission. Smith suffered arrest by the French between Aug. and Sept. 1563.

Instructions: *CSPF, 1562*, nos. 559, 654; Rymer, T., *Foedera...* (1704-32), ii, app. E, p. 48.
Correspondence: BL, Add. 4109, 4126, 4135-6, 35831, Cotton, Julius F.vi, Calig. C.iii, E.vi, Vesp. F.vi, Titus B.ii, Lansd. 8, 102, Stowe 541, Sloane 1710; *CSPF, 1562, 1563, 1564-5, 1566-8*; HMC *2nd Report*, p. 44; HMC *Pepys*; Forbes, *Full View*; Wright, T. (ed.), *Queen Elizabeth and Her Times* (1838), i; plus others as listed in Weaver, 'Anglo-French Diplomatic Relations,' v, pp. 14-15.

F101.
NORRIS, Sir William (1523-1591)*

Sept. 1562[h] - Oct. 1562[h]   Agent
Audience: *c*.12 Sept. 1562

Instructions: Inferred from *CSPF, 1562*, no. 620.

F102.
SOMERS, John (1527-1585)

24 Dec. 1562[c] - *c*.22 Jan. 1563[e]   [Special Ambassador]
Audience: 12 Jan. 1563

Instructions: *CSPF, 1562*, no. 1341.
Correspondence: *CSPF, 1562, 1563*.

F103.

25 Jan. 1563[c] - *c*.25 Feb. 1563[d]   [Special Ambassador]
Audience: 12 Feb. 1563

He was sent to join in negotiations with Sir Thomas Smith.

Instructions: *CSPF, 1563*, nos. 156-7.
Correspondence: *CSPF, 1563*.

F104.
MIDDLEMORE, Henry (1535-*c*.1597)

2 Feb. 1563[c] - *c*.25 Aug. 1563[c]   Agent
Audience: 18 Feb. 1563

He was resident with Sir Thomas Smith, when he was sent to Condé in the

Huguenot camp about this date. Apparently his responsibilities centered around that camp until approximately Aug., after which he returned to England. During his assignment, he travelled frequently between Smith, England and the Huguenots.

Instructions: *CSPF, 1563*, nos. 222, 275.
Correspondence: *CSPF, 1563*; HMC *Pepys*; Forbes, *Full View*.

F105.
THROCKMORTON, Sir Nicholas (1515-1571)*

11 Feb. 1563*b* - *c*.24 Mar. 1563*c*   [Special Ambassador]
Audience: 28 Feb. 1563   53*s* 4*d*/d

He was sent, among other reasons, to convey money to Admiral Coligny.

Instructions: *CSPF, 1563*, no. 285.
Correspondence: BL, Lansd. 102, Add. 5753; *CSPF, 1563*.

F106.
DANETT, Thomas (*c*.1525-1569)*

13 June 1563*c* - *c*.4 July 1563*c*   [Special Ambassador]
Audience: *c*.20 June 1563

He joined with Smith to demand the return of Calais.

Instructions: *CSPF, 1563*, nos. 879, 894, 895.
Correspondence: *CSPF, 1563*.

F107.
THROCKMORTON, Sir Nicholas (1515-1571)*

10 July 1563*b* - *c*.25 May 1564*e*   [Special Ambassador]
Audience: 9 Nov. 1563   66*s* 8*d*/d

He was sent to join with Smith in peace negotiations; he was arrested and made a prisoner-of-war, in Rouen (25 July) while on his way to the French court, then subsequently held as surety for the return of French prisoners. The French allowed him to assume a negotiating role (although they still kept him under restraint) about 1 Jan. 1564.

Instructions: *CSPF, 1563*, nos. 1030, 1348 and 1425.
Correspondence: *CSPF, 1563, 1564-5*, BL, Lansd. 102.

F108.
SOMERS, John (1527-1585)

26 Nov. 1563*c* - *c*.26 Dec. 1563*e*   [Special Ambassador]

He was joined with Smith and Throckmorton in negotiations, albeit in an apparently subordinate role.

Instructions (for all three diplomats): *CSPF, 1563*, no. 1425.
Correspondence: *CSPF, 1563*.

F109.

17 Mar. 1564*c* - *c*.21 Apr. 1564*e* [Special Ambassador]
Audience: *c*.1 Apr. 1564

Again he joined Throckmorton and Smith as a junior colleague, but with an essential part in negotiations.

Instructions: Inferred from *CSPF, 1564-5*, no. 258.
Correspondence: *CSPF, 1564-5*.

F110.
CAREY, Henry, 1st Baron Hunsdon (1526-1596)*

17 May 1564*b* - *c*.31 July 1564*c* Ambassador Extraordinary
Audience: 22 June 1564 £5/d
Investiture and ratification: 22 June
1564

He joined with Smith, and the Garter King of Arms, to invest the French King with the Order of the Garter and to receive the ratification of the Treaty of Troyes.

Instructions: *CSPF, 1564-5*, no. 433.
Correspondence: *CSPF, 1564-5*; BL, Add. 35831, Cotton, Titus B.ii.

F111.
SOMERS, John (1527-1585)

19 May 1565*b* - n.d [Special Ambassador]
Audience: 26 May 1565 £90 (plus expenses)

He was sent to join with Smith in giving answer to the French about an apparent marriage proposal between Elizabeth and a French prince.

Instructions: Inferred from *CSPF, 1564-5*, no. 1230.
Correspondence about: *CSPF, 1564-5*.

F112.
HOBY, Sir Thomas (1530-1566)*

1 Mar. 1566*a* - *d*.13 July 1566 Resident Ambassador
Audience: 8 May 1566 66*s* 8*d*/d
Secretary: Hugh Fitzwilliam

Instructions: *CSPF, 1566-8*, no. 188.
Correspondence: *CSPF, 1566-8*.

F113.
FITZWILLIAM, Hugh (*c*.1534-1577)*

13 July 1566*h* - 10 Jan. 1567*c* [Chargé d'Affaires]
10*s*/d

Correspondence: BL, Cotton, Galba D.ii, Titus B.iv; *CSPF, 1566-8*; *CSPD, 1566-79, Add.*

F114.
NORRIS, Sir Henry (later 1st Baron Norris of Rycote; *c*.1525-1601)*

26 Nov. 1566[b] - early Mar. 1571[c]   Resident Ambassador
Audience: 21 Jan. 1567   66*s* 8*d*/d
Secretaries: Thomas Barnaby, Daniel
  Rogers, Crispe and Mather (at
  various times)

Instructions: BL, Cotton, Calig. F.vi, f. 28; *CSPF, 1566-8*, no. 829.
Correspondence: BL, Cotton, Julius F.vi, Calig. C.i-ii, D.i-ii, E.vi, Stowe 147,
  541, Harl. 260, Lansd. 117, 177, Add. 4109, 4126, 4135, 4205; HMC
  Pepys; *CSPF, 1566-8, 1569-71*; *CSPScot, 1563-9, 1569-71*; HMC *1st
  Report*, p. 42; HMC *4th Report*, p. 252; HMC *5th Report*, p. 309; Wright,
  Elizabeth, i; plus others as listed in Weaver, 'Anglo-French Relations,' v, p. 21.

F115.
SMITH, Sir Thomas (1513-1577)*

13 Mar. 1567[b] - *c*.14 May 1567[e]   [Special Ambassador]
Audience (with French court):   66*s* 8*d*/d
  29 Apr. 1567

He was accredited along with William Wynter (see below) to demand the
  surrender of Calais from town authorities (they were heard at Calais 3 Apr.);
  and then accredited with resident Norris to demand the restitution of Calais
  from the French crown.

Instructions: BL, Calig. E.vi, ff. 1-9, 28; *CSPF, 1566-8*, nos. 141- 3.
Correspondence: BL, Julius F.vi, Calig. E.vi, Titus B.ii, iv, Lansd. 117, Stowe
  132, 541; *CSPF, 1566-8*.

F116.
WYNTER, William (later Sir William; *c*.1528-1589)*

22 Mar. 1567[h] - *c*.25 Apr. 1567[h]   [Special Ambassador]
Audience (with Calais authorities):   £40 (plus expenses)
  3 Apr. 1567

Accredited with Sir Thomas Smith (see above), he was sent to the town
  authorities specifically to take military possession.

Instructions: BL, Cotton, Calig. E.v, ff. 205-14; *CSPF, 1566-8*, no. 1037.
Correspondence: *CSPF, 1566-8*.

F117.
WALSINGHAM, Francis (later Sir Francis; *c*.1532-1590)*

11 Aug. 1570[a] - 29 Sept. 1570[a]   [Special Ambassador]
Audience: *c*.29 Aug. 1570   40*s*/d

Instructions: BL, Lansd. 155, ff. 405-08; *CSPF, 1569-71*, no. 1168.
Correspondence: BL, Lansd., 117, Add. 14028, Harl. 260; *CSPF, 1569-71*;
  Digges, D., *The Compleat Ambassador*...(1655).

F118.

17 Dec. 1570[a] - 10 May 1573[a]	Resident Ambassador
Audience: 25 Jan. 1571	66s 8d/d
Secretary: Henry Killigrew	

He was absent from his duties due to illness, 3 Nov. 1571 to 28 Feb. 1572.

Instructions: BL, Stowe, 147, f. 230; *CSPF, 1569-71*, no. 1441; Digges, *The Compleat Ambassador*, p. 18.

Correspondence: BL, Cotton, Calig. C.iii, E.vi, Vesp. F.vi, Julius F.vi, Titus F.iii, Stowe 143, 147, 162, Sloane 3199, Lansd. 13, 15, 117, 231, Harl. 36, 260, 283, 286, 4943, 6265, 6991, Add. 4103, 4160, 24671, 30156, 32091, 33531; *CSPF, 1569-71, 1572-4*; HMC *Salisb.*, ii; Martin, C. (ed.), *Journal of Sir Francis Walsingham...*, Camden o.s., cvi (1871); Digges, *The Compleat Ambassador*; *CSPScot, 1569-71, 1571-4*; plus others as listed in Weaver, 'Anglo-French Diplomatic Relations,' vi, pp. 2-3.

F119.

SACKVILLE, Thomas, Baron Buckhurst (later Earl of Dorset; 1535/6-1608)*

21 Jan. 1571[a] - *c.* 23 Mar. 1571[c]	[Special Ambassador]
Audience: 23 Feb. 1571	£4/d

Correspondence: *CSPF, 1569-71*; HMC Finch, i.

F120.

KILLIGREW, Henry (later Sir Henry; *c.*1528-1603)*

12 Oct. 1571[a] - 7 Mar. 1572[a]	[Chargé d'Affaires]
Audience: 30 Nov. 1571	40s/d

.Instructions: BL, Sloane 2442, f. 58, Eg. 2790, ff. 156-7, Lansd. 155, ff. 396b-8, Harl. 260, ff. 147-8; *CSPF, 1569-71*, no. 2069; HMC *2nd Report*, p. 96.

Correspondence: BL, Add. 4105, Harl. 260; *CSPF, 1569-71, 1572-4*.

F121.

SMITH, Sir Thomas (1513-1577)*

3 Dec. 1571[a] - 5 July 1572[a]	[Special Ambassador]
Audience: 4 Jan. 1572	66s 8d/d

He joined with Walsingham and was later joined by the Earl of Lincoln (see below).

Instructions: BL, Add. 4109, ff. 49-60, Cotton, Calig. E.vi, ff. 149-54, Vesp. F.vi, ff. 12-13, Julius F.vi, f. 168, Harl. 253, ff. 143-52.

Correspondence: BL, Cotton, Calig. C.iii, Vesp. F.vi, Harl. 260, Add. 24671, Sloane 3199; *CSPF, 1569-71, 1572-4*; *CSPScot, 1571-4*.

F122.

CLINTON, Edward Fiennes de, 1st Earl of Lincoln (1512-1585)*

18 May 1572[a] - *c.*5 July 1572[e]	Ambassador Extraordinary
Audience: late May 1572	£6/d

He joined with Smith and Walsingham for the ratification of the Treaty of Blois.

Instructions: BL, Cotton, Vesp. F.vi, f. 64; *CSPF, 1572-4*, no. 375- 8.

Correspondence: BL, Cotton, Vesp. F.vi, Lansd. 117, Add. 24671; *CSPF, 1572-4*.

F123.

SOMERSET, William, 3rd Earl of Worcester (1526-1589)*

15 Jan. 1573*a* - 27 Feb. 1573*e*	Ambassador Extraordinary
Audience: *c.*1 Feb. 1573	£6/d

Instructions: BL, Cotton, Vesp. F.vi, f. 247; Harl. 260, f. 406.

Correspondence: BL, Cotton, Vesp. F.vi, Harl. 260, Add. 20779; *CSPF, 1572-4*.

F124.

DALE, Dr. Valentine (by 1527-1589)*

19 Mar. 1573*b* - 24 Oct. 1576*a*	Resident Ambassador
Audience: 20 Apr. 1573	66*s* 8*d*/d
Secretary: Thomas Wilkes	

Instructions: HMC *9th Report*, p. 407-08.

Correspondence: BL, Cotton, Calig. E.vi, Vesp. F.vi, xii, Titus B.ii, Harl. 260, 286, 1582, 6991; Lansd. 18, Add. 4104; *CSPF, 1572-4, 1575-7*; HMC *Salisb.*, ii; Wright, *Elizabeth*, i; plus others as listed in Weaver, 'Anglo-French Diplomatic Relations,' vi, p. 5.

F125.

HORSEY, Edward (later Sir Edward; *d.*1583)*

18 June 1573*a* - *c.*20 July 1573*e*	[Special Ambassador]
Audience: *c.*1 July 1573	40*s*/d

Instructions: BL, Cotton, Calig. E.vi, f. 173; *CSPF, 1572-4*, no. 1069; HMC *Salisb.*, xiii, p. 143.

Correspondence: *CSPF, 1572-4*; HMC *Salisb.*, ii, xiii; plus others as listed in Weaver, 'Anglo-French Diplomatic Relations,' vi, p. 6.

F126.

RANDOLPH, Thomas (1523-1590)*

26 Oct. 1573*a* - 22 Dec. 1573*b*	[Special Ambassador]
Audience: 20 Nov. 1573	20*s*/d

Instructions: *CSPF, 1572-4*, no. 1206.

Correspondence: *CSPF, 1572-4*.

F127.

LEIGHTON, Thomas (later Sir Thomas; *c.*1535-1611)*

3 May 1574*b* - 30 June 1574*a*	[Special Ambassador]
Audience: 15 May 1574	*ad hoc*

Instructions: *CSPF, 1572-4*, no. 1414, and inferred from no. 1415.

Correspondence: BL, Add. 4104; *CSPF, 1572-4*.

F128.
NORTH, Roger, 2nd Baron North (1531-1600)*

3 Oct. 1574[a] - 6 Dec. 1574[b] [Special Ambassador]
Audience: *c*.1 Nov. 1574   £4/d

Instructions: *CSPF, 1572-4*, nos. 1573, 1576.
Correspondence of and about: BL, Cotton, Calig. E.vi; *CSPF, 1572-4*.

F129.
COBHAM alias BROOKE, Sir Henry (1538-1592)*

He had audience with the French king, *c*.7 Feb. 1575, on his way to Spain (q.v.).

F130.
WILKES, Thomas (later Sir Thomas; *c*.1541-1592)*

25 Nov. 1575[c] - *c*.13 June 1576[c] [English agent with the Huguenot army]

Wilkes, secretary to resident ambassador Valentine Dale, negotiated with the Elector Palatine (German States, q.v.) for German troops (to be combined with English money) to be sent to the French Huguenots. He also, about this date, joined the Huguenot army to represent English interests. He returned to England several times during this assignment.

Instructions: *CSPF, 1575-7*, no. 465.
Correspondence: BL, Add. 4104; *CSPF, 1575-7*.

F131.
RANDOLPH, Thomas (1523-1590)*

26 Mar. 1576[a] - 25 May 1576[b] [Special Ambassador]
Audience: 40*s*/d

Instructions: BL, Sloane 2442, ff. 55b-57, Eg. 2790, f. 197; Add. 5935, ff. 187-9, Lansd. 155, ff. 157b-60; *CSPF, 1575-7*, no. 719; HMC *2nd Report*, p. 97.
Correspondence: BL, Add. 4104, Cotton, Vesp. F.vi; *CSPF, 1575-7*.

F132.
PAULET, Sir Amias (*c*.1533-1588)*

7 Sept. 1576[a] - 11 Dec. 1579[b] Resident Ambassador
Audience: 7 Oct. 1576   66*s* 8*d*/d
Secretary: William Waad

Instructions: BL, Cotton, Calig. E.vii, ff. 13-49, Sloane 2442, ff. 59b-60, Harl. 36, f. 259, Lansd. 155, f. 169-71, Eg. 2790, f. 206; *CSPF, 1575-7*, no. 933; HMC *2nd Report*, p. 97.
Correspondence: BL, Cotton, Calig. E.vi, vii, Julius F.vi, Add. 15891, Harl. 285, 787, 1582, 4993; *CSPF, 1575-7, 1577-8, 1578-9*; HMC *Salisb.*, ii; plus others as listed in Weaver, 'Anglo-French Diplomatic Relations,' vi, p. 9.

F133.
SMITH, Sir John (1531-1607)*
On his way to Spain (q.v.), he had audience with the French King, 15 Dec. 1576.

F134.
STAFFORD, Edward (later Sir Edward; 1552-1605)*
15 May 1578^a - c.15 June 1578e   [Special Ambassador]
Audience: 25 May 1578   20s/d
Instructions: *CSPF, 1577-8*, no. 870.
Correspondence: *CSPF, 1577-8.*

F135.
COBHAM alias BROOKE, Sir Henry (1538-1592)*
15 Oct. 1579^a - c.15 Nov. 1583^c Resident Ambassador
Audience: 17 Nov. 1579   66s 8d/d
Instructions: BL, Sloane 2442, ff. 61-2, Stowe 132, f. 110; also inferred from
    CSPF, 1579-80, no. 85.
Correspondence: BL, Add. 15891, Cotton, Calig. C.v-viii, E.vii, Galba E.vi,
    Otho E.iv (letterbook), Lansd. 33, 146, Eg. 3048, Harl. 6265; *CSPF, 1579-*
    80, 1581-2, 1582, 1583; *CSPScot, 1574-81, 1581-3*; HMC *Salisb.*, ii, xiii;
    plus others as listed in Weaver, 'Anglo-French Diplomatic Relations,' vi,
    p. 8-9.

F136.
STAFFORD, Edward (later Sir Edward; 1552-1605)*
31 Oct. 1579^b - c.6 Jan. 1580^e [Special Ambassador]
Audience (with the Duke of Anjou):   *ad hoc*
    before 8 Dec. 1579
Audience (with French King and Queen
    Mother): 25 Dec. 1579
On this mission, he spent some time with Monsieur, the Duke of Anjou and
    Alençon.
Correspondence about: *CSPF, 1579-80.*

F137.
12 Jan. 1580^b - 18 Feb. 1580^e [Special Ambassador]
Audience: 8 Feb. 1580
Again, he spent substantial time during the mission with Anjou.
Correspondence: BL, Cotton, Calig. E.vii, Vesp. F.xii; Wright, *Elizabeth*, ii.

F138.
22 Jun. 1580^a - 11 Aug. 1580^a [Special Ambassador]
Audience (with Anjou): c.1 July 1580   £3/d
He was sent to the Duke of Anjou specifically.
Correspondence: *CSPF, 1579-80*; HMC *Salisb.*, ii, xiii.

F139.

6 Oct. 1580^a - 26 Dec. 1580^a   [Special Ambassador]

He was sent to the Duke of Anjou, the French court and the King of Navarre.

Instructions: BL, Cotton, Galba C.vii, ff. 180-5; inferred in part from *CSPF, 1579-80*, no. 479.
Correspondence: *CSPF, 1579-80*.

F140.
SOMERS, John (1527-1585)

20 June 1581^c - *c.*20 Sept. 1581^e   [Special Ambassador]
Audience (French King): 2 July 1581
Audience (Duke of Anjou): 17 Aug.
   1581

He joined with Cobham. He may have returned briefly to England early in September.

Instructions: *CSPF, 1581-2*, no. 225, *1583-4*, no. 741.
Correspondence: BL, Cotton, Galba E.vi, Add. 15891, Harl. 6265, Lansd. 33; *CSPF, 1581-2*; HMC *Salisb.*, ii, xiii.

F141.
WALSINGHAM, Sir Francis (*c.*1532-1590)*

22 July 1581^a - 21 Sept. 1581^a   [Special Ambassador]
Audience: 10 Aug. 1581   80s/d

Instructions: BL, Cotton, Galba E.vi, ff. 60, 65b, Harl. 6265, ff. 287, 289; *CSPF, 1581-2*, nos. 276-7.
Correspondence: BL, Cotton, Titus B.ii, vii, Add. 4103, 1582, 15891, Harl. 6265, Lansd. 33, Stowe 143; *CSPF, 1581-2*; HMC *Salisb.*, ii, xiii; plus others as listed in Weaver, 'Anglo-French Diplomatic Relations,' vi, p. 3.

F142.
STAFFORD, Sir Edward (1552-1605)*

15 Sept. 1583^a - 15 Apr. 1589^a   Resident Ambassador
Audience: 13 Oct. 1583   66s 8d/d
Secretaries: Edward Grimston, Thomas
   Bodley, Thomas Edmondes, Richard
   Hakluyt, and William Lyly (at
   various times)

Instructions: *CSPF, 1583-4*, no. 137.
Correspondence: BL, Cotton, Calig. C.viii, E.vii, Nero B.vi, Galba D.iii, E.vi, Harl. 286-8, 1582, 6993, Lansd. 103, 144, Eg. 2074, Add. 4128, 4160, 35834-6, 35841; *CSPF, 1583-4, 1584-5, 1585-6, 1586-8, 1588* (vol. 22), *1589*; *CSPScot, 1584-5, 1585-6, 1586-9*; *CSPD, 1581-90, Add. 1580-1625*; HMC *Salisb.*, iii, xiii; HMC *Ancaster*; Wright, *Elizabeth*, ii; plus others as listed in Weaver, 'Anglo-French Diplomatic Relations,' vii, p. 14.

F143.
SIDNEY, Sir Philip (1554-1586)*

8 July 1584[c] - by 17 July 1584[h]   [Special Ambassador]

The mission was stopped at Gravesend by the French King's 'temporary' refusal to receive the envoy.

Instructions: BL, Cotton, Galba E.vi, f. 241; *CSPF, 1583-4*, no. 738.
Correspondence about: *CSPF, 1583-4, 1584-5.*

F144.
STANLEY, Henry, 4th Earl of Derby (1531-1593)*

17 Jan. 1585[a] - *c*.15 Mar. 1585[c]   Ambassador Extraordinary
Audience: 14 Feb. 1585   £4/d
Investiture: 18 Feb. 1585

Instructions: Bodl., Tanner Mss. 78, ff. 32-3; *CSPF, 1584-5*, p. 265-6.
Correspondence: BL, Cotton, Calig. E.vii; Bodl., Tanner Mss. 78, 79; *CSPF, 1584-5*; HMC *Salisb.*, xiii.

F145.
WAAD, William (later Sir William; 1546-1623)*

10 Mar. 1585[c] - 17 Apr. 1585[a]   [Special Ambassador]
Audience: 23 Mar. 1585

Instructions: BL, Sloane 2442, f. 63; *CSPF, 1584-5*, pp. 337-9.
Correspondence: *CSPF, 1584-5.*

F146.
CHAMPERNOWN, Arthur (later Sir Arthur; *fl.*1580s-1610s)

1 Apr. 1585[c] - *c*.20 July 1585[g]   [Special Ambassador]
Audience: 23 May 1585

He was sent to Henry of Navarre.

Instructions: *CSPF, 1584-5*, p. 394.
Correspondence: *CSPF, 1584-5.*

F147.
LEIGHTON, Sir Thomas (*c*.1535-1611)*

1 Apr. 1585[c] - June? 1585[h]   [Special Ambassador]
Audience: *c*.10 May 1585

Instructions: *CSPF, 1584-5*, p. 393-4.
Correspondence about: *CSPF, 1584-5*; HMC *Salisb.*, iii.

F148.
WOTTON, Edward (later 1st Baron Wotton of Marley; 1548-1628)*

25 Sept. 1586[a] - 2 Dec. 1586[a]   [Special Ambassador]
Audience: by 7 Nov. 1586   40s/d

Instructions: BL, Cotton, Galba E.vi, f. 302; *CSPF, 1586-8*, pp. 96-8.
Correspondence: BL, Lansd. 50; *CSPF, 1586-8.*

F149.
WAAD, William (later Sir William; 1546-1623)*

16 Jan. 1587[a] - c.20 June 1587[c]   [Special Ambassador]
Audience: 29 Jan. 1587   40s/d

Instructions: BL, Sloane 2442, ff. 64-66b, Harl. 36, f. 357, 168, f. 65; *CSPF, 1586-8*, pp. 189-90.
Correspondence: BL, Harl. 288; *CSPF, 1586-8*.

F150.
BODLEY, Thomas (later Sir Thomas; 1545-1613)*

10 May 1588[b] - late May 1588[h]   [Agent]
Audience: c.20 May 1588

Instructions: Inferred from Bodley, T., *The Life of Sir Thomas Bodley*; *CSPF, 1586-8*, pp. 611, 629, 637.
Correspondence: *CSPF, 1586-8*.

F151.
LEIGHTON, Sir Thomas (c.1535-1611)*

Late May 1588[c] - c.1 July 1588[e]   [Special Ambassador]
Audience: c.9 June 1588

Instructions: *CSPF, 1586-8*, p. 633.
Correspondence: *CSPF, 1586-8*.

F152.
LYLY, William (*fl.*1580s-1590s)

26 Mar. 1589[h] - 21 Aug. 1590[c]   [Chargé d'Affaires]

He assumed responsibility for the mission after Stafford left in April (see above).

Correspondence: PRO, SP/78/19-21; BL, Lansd. 64; *CSPF, 1589*; *L&A, 1589-90, 1590-1*; *APC, 1589-90*.

F153.
STAFFORD, Sir Edward (1552-1605)*

c.1 Sept. 1589[h] - c.10 Oct. 1589[h]   [Special Ambassador]
Audience: c.10 Sept. 1589   [66s 8d/d]

It was during this mission that Peregrine Bertie, Lord Willoughby, recently the English military commander in the Low Countries, was sent with an English force to aid Henry IV in France. Although not strictly a diplomat, he had, along with Stafford, negotiating responsibilities about the use of the English force (Commission and instructions, PRO, SP/78/20, ff. 52, 56-60).

Instructions: *APC, 1589-90*, p. 86.
Correspondence: PRO, SP/78/20; *L&A, 1589-90*; *APC, 1589-90*.

F154.

13 July 1590^a - Dec. 1590^e Resident Ambassador
Audience: 21 Aug. 1590   66s 8d/d

Credentials: PRO, SP/78/21, f. 257; *L&A, 1590-1*, no. 423.
Correspondence: PRO, SP/78/21-2; *L&A, 1590-1*; HMC *Ancaster*.

F155.
PALAVICINO, Sir Horatio (*d.*1600)*

13 July 1590^a - *c.*26 Oct. 1590^e [Special] Ambassador
                                     53s 4d/d

He joined Stafford in negotiating with Henry IV.

Instructions: PRO, SP/78/21, ff. 292-5, SP/81/6, f. 46; *L&A, 1590-1*, nos. 424-6.
Correspondence: PRO, SP/78/21-2, SP/81/6; *L&A, 1590-1*.

F156.
GRIMSTON, Edward (*d.*1610)*

Late Oct. 1590^h - 25 Nov. 1591^a [Chargé d'Affaires]
                                     20s/d

Correspondence: PRO, SP/78/22-6; BL, Cotton, Calig. E.viii, Add. 4109, 38137; HMC *Salisb.*, iv; Lambeth Mss. 647-8.

F157.
YORKE, Edmund (*fl.*1590s)

29 Jan. 1591^b - *c.*14 Mar. 1591e [Special Ambassador]
Audience: *c.*20 Feb. 1591
Secretary: Edward Grimston

Instructions: PRO, SP/78/23 f. 48-59; BL, Cotton, Calig. E.viii, f. 139; *L&A, 1590-1*, nos. 490-3; Rymer, *Foedera...*, xvi, pp. 89- 92.
Correspondence: PRO, SP/78/23; *L&A, 1590-1*.

F158.
UNTON, Sir Henry (*c.*1558-1596)*

22 July 1591^a - 17 June 1592^a Resident Ambassador
Audience: 22 Oct. 1591   66s 8d/d
Secretary: Thomas Edmondes

Instructions: PRO, SP/78/25, ff. 81-8; BL, Add. 38137, f. 1, Cotton, Calig. E.viii, ff. 69-74, 194-7; *L&A, 1591-2*, nos. 549-50.
Correspondence: PRO, SP/78/25-8; BL, Add. 38137, Cotton, Calig. E.vii-viii, Titus B.ii, Lansd. 68; Lambeth Mss. 651; *L&A, 1591-2, 1592-3*; *APC, 1591-2*; HMC *Salisb.*, iv; Unton, Sir Henry, *Unton Correspondence...*, ed. J. Stevenson (Roxburghe Club, 1847); plus others as listed in Weaver, 'Anglo-French Diplomatic Relations,' vii, p. 20.

F159.
WILKES, Sir Thomas (*c.*1541-1598)*

8 Mar. 1592*ᵃ* - 15 Apr. 1592*ᵇ*   [Special Ambassador]
Audience: 2 Apr. 1592   40*s*/d

He was knighted by the French King, Henry IV, on this mission.

Instructions: PRO, SP/78/27, ff. 215-16, 230-1, 248-58, SP/84/41, f. 167;
   L&A, 1591-2, nos. 654-8.
Correspondence: PRO, SP/78/27; *L&A, 1591-2*; Unton, *Unton Correspondence*.

F160.
EDMONDES, Thomas (later Sir Thomas; *c.*1563-1639)*

1 Jun. 1592*ᵃ* - 14 Apr. 1596*ᵈ*   [Chargé d'Affaires]
                                      20*s*/d, 30*s*/d (after 1 Apr. 1594)

He returned to England Jan. - May 1594; and reverted to secretarial status
   during Unton's second embassy.

Instructions: BL, Stowe 166, f. 17.
Correspondence: PRO, SP/78/28-36; BL, Cotton, Calig. E.ix, Add. 4113-4,
   Stowe 166; Butler, G. (ed.), *The Edmondes Papers* (1939); *APC, 1592*;
   HMC *Salisb.*, iv-v, xiii; plus others as listed in Weaver, 'Anglo-French
   Diplomatic Relations,' vii, p. 21.

F161.
WILKES, Sir Thomas (*c.*1541-1598)*

18 July 1593*ᵃ* - 2 Sept. 1593*ᵃ*   [Special Ambassador]
Arrived: 10 Aug. 1593   40*s*/d

Instructions: PRO, SP/78/31, f. 242-51; BL, Cotton, Calig. E.ix, ff. 35, 134.
Correspondence: PRO, SP/78/32.

F162.
SIDNEY, Sir Robert (later Viscount Lisle, 1st Earl of Leicester; 1563-1626)*

21 Nov. 1593*ᵃ* - early Apr. 1594*ᶜ*   [Special Ambassador]
Audience: 21 Jan. 1594

Instructions: PRO, SP/78/32, ff. 258-64; BL, Cotton, Calig. E.ix, f. 93b-5.
Correspondence: PRO, SP/78/32-3; BL, Cotton, Calig. E.ix.

F163.
WILLIAMS, Sir Roger (1540?-1595)

1 Sept. 1595*ᶜ* - mid-Oct. 1595*ᵈ*   [Special Ambassador]
Audience: *c.*25 Sept. 1595

Instructions: PRO, SP/78/36, ff. 1-4; BL, Stowe 132, f. 112.
Correspondence: HMC *Salisb.*, v.
Correspondence about: *CSPD, 1595-7*.

F164.
UNTON, Sir Henry (*c*.1558-1596)

30 Nov. 1595[a] - *d*.23 Mar. 1596	Resident Ambassador
Audience: 13 Feb. 1596	66*s* 8*d*/d
Secretary: Thomas Edmondes	

Instructions: PRO, SP/78/35, ff. 119-26; BL, Cotton, Calig. E.ix, f. 251-8.
Correspondence: PRO, SP/78/37; HMC *Salisb*., vi; BL, Cotton, Calig. E.ix, Add. 4114-7, Stowe 166; Murdin and Haynes, *Collection of State Papers*...; plus others as listed in Weaver, 'Anglo-French Diplomatic Relations,' vii, p. 20.

F165.
TALBOT, Gilbert, 7th Earl of Shrewsbury (1553-1616)*
MILDMAY, Sir Anthony (*c*.1549-1617)*

27 Aug. 1596[a] - 22 Oct. 1596[e]	Ambassador Extraordinary
Audience: 9 Oct. 1596	£6/d

Sir Anthony Mildmay accompanied Shrewsbury and then remained as resident (see below).

Instructions: PRO, SP/78/37, f. 261, SP/78/38, ff. 61-81; BL, Stowe 132, f. 139; HMC *6th Report*, p. 457.
Correspondence: PRO, SP/78/38; BL, Add. 4121, 28098; HMC *Salisb*., vi; Lodge, E. (ed.), *Illustrations of British History*...(1838), ii.

F166.
MILDMAY, Sir Anthony (*c*.1549-1617)*

27 Aug. 1596[a] - *c*.15 Aug. 1597[e]	Resident Ambassador
Audience: 9 Oct. 1596	66*s* 8*d*/d
Secretary: John Phillips	

Instructions: PRO, SP/78/37, ff. 288-96, SP/78/38, ff. 61-81; BL, Cotton, Calig. E.xii, ff. 13-14.
Correspondence: PRO, SP/78/38-40; BL, Cotton, Calig. E.ix, Add. 4117-8, 4123; *APC, 1596-7, 1597*; HMC *Salisb*., vi-vii; plus others as listed in Weaver, 'Anglo-French Diplomatic Relations,' vii, p. 24.

F167.
EDMONDES, Thomas (later Sir Thomas; *c*.1563-1639)*

27 Mar. 1597[a] - *c*.1 Jun. 1597[e]	[Special Ambassador]
	40*s*/d

This in fact constituted two missions under one privy seal, with a brief return to England in late Apr. to early May.

Instructions: PRO, SP/78/39, ff. 237-39.
Correspondence: PRO, SP/78/39.

F168.

6 May 1597[d] - late July 1597[c]   [Special Ambassador]
                                       40s/d

Correspondence: HMC *Salisb.*, vii.

F169.
PHILLIPS, John (*fl.*1590s)

8 Aug. 1597[a] - 22 Nov. 1597[b]   [Chargé d'Affaires]
                                       20s/d

Correspondence: PRO, SP/78/40.

F170.
EDMONDES, Thomas (later Sir Thomas; *c.*1563-1639)*

12 Sept. 1597[a] - 15 June 1599[b]   Agent (and Chargé d'Affaires)
Audience: early Oct. 1597   40s/d
Secretary: Jean Beaulieu

He returned to England, May 1598, and again in June. He then assumed duties as a chargé d'affaires from late May 1598, until Neville's arrival in 1599. He did of course facilitate the Cecil embassy (see next entry).

Instructions (as chargé): BL, Lansd. 103, no. 87.
Correspondence: PRO, SP/78/40-3; Butler, *Edmondes Papers*; *APC, 1597-8, 1598-9*, HMC *Salisb.*, viii-ix, xiv; BL, Stowe, 167; plus others as listed in Weaver, 'Anglo-French Diplomatic Relations,' vii, p. 22.

F171.
CECIL, Sir Robert (later Earl of Salisbury; 1563-1612)*
HERBERT, Dr. John (later Sir John; *c.*1540-1617)*
WILKES, Sir Thomas (*c.*1541-1598)*

20 Jan. 1598[a] - 30 Apr. 1598[a]   Ambassadors Extraordinary
Audience: 23 Mar. 1598   £4/d (Cecil), 50s/d (Herbert and
                                Wilkes each)

Wilkes died on this mission, 1 Mar. 1598.

Instructions: PRO, SP/78/41, ff. 48-89, 236-42; BL, Cotton, Julius F.vi, ff. 94-8, Calig. E.ix, ff. 454-61, 484-91; Bodl., Tanner Mss. 77, ff. 123-8; HMC *Salisb.*, xxiii, pp. 10-20.
Correspondence: PRO, SP/78/41-2; BL, Add. 4108, 4125, 18654, 25416 (including a journal), 36444, 45140 (report), Cotton, Calig. E.ix, Stowe 167, Harl. 36; *CSPD, 1598-1601*; *APC, 1597-8*; HMC *Salisb.*, viii, xxiii, pp. 10-74 (a report on the mission).

F172.
NEVILLE, Sir Henry (1562-1615)*

15 Feb. 1599[a] - 31 July 1601[b]   Resident Ambassador
Audience: 13 May 1599   66s 8d/d
Secretary: Ralph Winwood

He returned to England 6 Aug. 1600, where he was caught up in the Essex conspiracy, was arrested (in the process of returning to France) and never resumed his duties in Paris. He continued to be paid, however, through 31 July 1601, and had served as one of the four English commissioners treating with the Spanish at Boulogne (Conferences, q.v.).

Instructions: PRO, SP/78/43, ff. 25-60.

Correspondence: PRO, SP/78/43-4; BL, Cotton, Calig. E.ix-x, Vesp. F.x, Lansd. 148, Harl. 1579, Add. 4715, 5664; *CSPD, 1598-1600*; *APC, 1599-1600*; HMC *8th Report*, pt. 1; HMC *Buccleuch*, i; Sawyer, E. (ed.), *Memorials of Affairs of State...of Sir Ralph Winwood...*(1725), i; plus others as listed in Weaver, 'Anglo-French Diplomatic Relations,' vii, p. 25.

F173.
WINWOOD, Sir Ralph (1563?-1617)*

10 May 1600[a] - 18 Feb. 1603[b]   [Chargé d'Affaires], Agent
Audience: late Aug. 1600   20s/d, 30s/d (by 1 Aug. 1601)
Secretary: Dudley Carleton

Correspondence: PRO, SP/78/44-7; BL, Cotton, Calig. E.x, Titus C.vii, Stowe 167; *CSPD, 1601-03*; Sawyer, *Winwood State Papers*, i; HMC *Buccleuch*, i.

F174.
EDMONDES, Thomas (later Sir Thomas; *c*.1563-1639)*

12 June 1601[a] - *c*.10 Aug. 1601[e]   [Special Ambassador]
     40s/d

Instructions: PRO, SP/78/45, ff. 132-3; BL, Cotton, Calig. E.ix, f. 514, Add. 5664, f. 154.
Correspondence: PRO, SP/78/45.

F175.

22 Aug. 1601[d] - *c*.1 Sept. 1601[h]   [Special Ambassador]
The French King was at Calais.

Instructions: Sawyer, *Winwood State Papers*, ii, p. 539; summarized in *CSPV, 1592-1603*, p. 469.
Correspondence: PRO, SP/78/45.

F176.
PARRY, Sir Thomas (1544-1616)*

6 Jan. 1602[a] - 18 Mar. 1606[b]   Resident Ambassador
Audience: *c*.14 Aug. 1602   66s 8d/d
Secretaries: St. Sauveur and Dudley
  Carleton

Instructions: PRO, SP/78/46, ff. 120-22.
Correspondence: PRO, SP/78/46-53; BL, Add. 38138, Cotton, Calig. D.ii, E.xi-xii, Vesp. C.ix, F.x, Titus C.vii, Harl. 4232, Sloane 1786, Stowe 145,

167-8; *CSPD, 1601-03*; HMC *Salisb.*, xv; Birch, T. (comp.), *The Court and Times of James I...*(1849); Sawyer, *Winwood State Papers*, i-ii; Magdalene College Library, Cambridge, Pepys Mss; *CSPD, 1601-03*; *1603-10*; plus others as listed in Weaver, 'Anglo-French Diplomatic Relations,' vii, p. 26.

F177.
EDMONDES, Thomas (later Sir Thomas; *c.*1563-1639)*

25 June 1602[b] - *c.*15 Aug. 1602[c]   [Special Ambassador]
                                               40s/d

F178.
HAY, Sir James (later Baron Hay, 1st Viscount Doncaster, Earl of Carlisle; *c.*1580-1636)*

5 Feb. 1604[c] - *c.*1 Apr. 1604[c]   [Special Ambassador]
Audience: 20 Mar. 1604   £300

Instructions: Suggested in *CSPV, 1603-07*, p. 203.
Correspondence about: PRO, SP/78/51.

F179.
CAREW, Sir George (*d.*1612)*

1 May 1605[a] - by 15 Oct. 1609[d]   Resident Ambassador
Audience: 28 Dec. 1605   £4/d
Secretary: William Beecher

Instructions: PRO, SP/78/52, ff. 394-5.
Correspondence: PRO, SP/78/52-55; BL, Add. 4466, 6178, 12497, 12503, 12506, 28571, 35846, Eg. 921, Harl. 1579, 1875, Lansd. 89, Stowe 168-71; Birch, T. (ed.), *An Historical View of the Negotiations...*(1749), incl. pp. 415-528 (Carew's narration of the embassy); HMC *Salisb.* xix; HMC *2nd Report*, App., p. 43; Sawyer, *Memorials*, ii.

F180.
STUART, Ludovick, Duke of Richmond and 2nd Duke of Lennox (1574-1624)*

27 Nov. 1604[b] - *c.*8 Mar. 1605[c]   [Special Ambassador]
Audience: 29 Jan. 1605   £3000 (total)

Instructions: PRO, SP/78/51, ff. 328-35.
Correspondence: PRO, SP/78/52.

F181.
GODOLPHIN, Sir William (*died c.*1613)*

10 June 1606[b] - July? 1606[h]   [Special Ambassador]
                                          £200

Instructions: Inferred from HMC *Salisb.*, xviii, p. 172.
Correspondence: HMC *Salisb.*, xviii.

F182.
BEECHER, William (*fl.*1600s-1620s)

1 Oct. 1609[a] - 24 May 1610[c]   [Chargé d'Affaires]
                             20s/d

He was in France prior to Oct. 1609. His responsibilities as chargé d'affaires presumably terminated upon Edmondes' arrival to assume the duties of resident, although Beecher remained in France until Oct. 1611, possibly as a consular agent.

Correspondence: PRO, SP/78/55-58; BL, Cotton, Julius C.v; Sawyer, *Memorials*, iii.

F183.
EDMONDES, Sir Thomas (*c.*1563-1639)*

25 Apr. 1610[b] - *c.*15 Nov. 1617[a]   Ambassador Ordinary, then
Arrived: *c.*24 May 1610   Ambassador Extraordinary
Secretary: Jean Beaulieu and   £4/d
John Woodford

He returned to England at least from Feb. to June 1614, and again from Dec. 1616 to May 1617. The Venetian ambassador saw the second return as indeed a second discrete mission, and it is the case that Edmondes did return with an increase in representational status, but the authorizing privy seal remained the same.

Instructions: PRO, SP/78/56, ff. 101-14; BL, Stowe 171, ff. 202-18; 178, ff. 22.
Correspondence: PRO, SP/78/56-67; BL, Add. 12504, 21406, 29550, Burney 367, Eg. 2592, Stowe 166-77; *CSPD, 1611-18*; *CSPC/EI, 1513-1616*; Sawyer, *Memorials*, iii; Birch, *Negotiations*; Birch, *Court and Times*; HMC *Salisb.*, xviii (letterbook); HMC *8th Report*, p. 10; HMC *Eglinton, Maxwell*...

F184.
WOTTON, Edward, 1st Baron Wotton of Marley (1548-1628)*

1 July 1610[b] - 7 Oct. 1610[c]   Ambassador Extraordinary
Audience: 2 Sept. 1610   £6/d

Instructions: PRO, SP/78/56, ff. 235-54; BL, Stowe 177, ff. 131-6.
Correspondence: PRO, SP/78/56; BL, Stowe 171.

F185.
WOTTON, Sir Henry (1568-1639)*

He visited Paris and had an audience with the French royals upon his return from Venice (q.v.), early Feb. 1611.

F186.

HAY, James, Baron Hay (later Viscount Doncaster, Earl of Carlisle; *c*.1580-1636)*

1 Mar. 1616*a* - 9 Oct. 1616*a*	Ambassador Extraordinary
Audience: *c*.21 Aug. 1616	£6/d

He stopped at the Hague (Low Countries, q.v.) on his way to Paris.

Instructions: PRO, SP/78/66, ff. 38-46 (This is a second set, sent after his arrival in France. The original instructions have not been found).

Correspondence: PRO, SP/78/66; BL, Eg. 2592, Sloane 856, Stowe 176, 743; Birch, *Negotiations*, p. 398

F187.

BEECHER, William (*fl*.1600s-1620s)

6 Oct. 1617*b* - 31 Jan. 1619*b*	Agent [and Chargé d'Affaires]
	40*s*/d

He was paid through Jan., but he had actually returned to England by 21 Nov. 1618.

Correspondence: PRO, SP/78/67-8; BL, Harl. 1580.

F188.

WAKE, Sir Isaac (1580-1632)*

He made a negotiating stop in Paris on his trip from Savoy (q.v.) to England in mid-Dec. 1618.

F189.

HERBERT, Sir Edward (later 1st Baron Herbert of Cherbury; 1583-1648)*

1 Feb. 1619*a* - *c*.7 Sept. 1621*c*	[Resident Ambassador]
Audience: Last of June 1619	£4/d

F190.

24 June 1622*b* - *c*.16 July 1624*c*	[Resident Ambassador]
Arrived: *c*.17 Jan. 1623	£4/d
Secretaries: Thomas Carew, then	
William Boswell	

The hiatus in his mission occurred when he had a dispute with the Duke of Luynes. He returned to England but his diets as ambassador continued. A new privy seal was issued June 1622, upon his commanded return to France. He visited England again in summer 1623.

Instructions: Partially in PRO, SP/78/68, ff. 243-4; Powys-Land Club, *Collections*, vi, p. 417; Herbert, Edward Lord, *Autobiography...* ed. Sidney Lee (1906), p. 332.

Correspondence: PRO, SP/78/68-72; BL, Harl. 4593, 1581, Eg. 2593-5, 2598, Add. 7082 (letterbook), 32092; Gardiner, S. (ed.), *...Relations between England Germany...*, Camden o.s., xcviii (1868), pp. 12-85; Smith, W. J., *Herbert Correspondence* (Cardiff, 1963); Herbert, *Autobiography*.

F191.

HAY, James, 1st Viscount Doncaster (later Earl of Carlisle; *c*.1580- 1636)*

18 July 1621^b - by 16 Feb. 1622^c Ambassador Extraordinary
Audience: *c*.mid Oct. 1621   £6/d? [*c*.£20,000 total]
Secretary: John Woodford

His audience was delayed by his serious illness once he arrived in France.

Instructions: Inferred from PRO, SP/78/69, ff. 142-7.
Correspondence: PRO, SP/78/69-70; BL, Add. 36445-6, Eg. 2594, Stowe 176.

F192.

28 Mar. 1622^b - 26 July 1622^c Ambassador Extraordinary
Audience: 1 May 1622   £6/d

Correspondence: PRO, SP/78/70; BL, Eg. 2595.

F193.

22 Feb. 1623^f - 15 May 1623^c Ambassador Extraordinary
Audience in France: mid-Mar. 1623

He was sent specifically to avert any ill consequences to Prince Charles in his
journey through France to Madrid. He continued in company with the Prince
and Buckingham to Spain.

Instructions: Verbal (he was dispatched in haste), but the gist is inferred in
CSPV, 1621-3, p. 585.
Correspondence: PRO, SP/78/71; BL, Eg. 2595, Harl. 1580.

F194.

RICH, Henry, 1st Earl of Holland (1590-1649)*

c. 30 Jan. 1624^h - mid-June 1625^c Ambassador Extraordinary
Audience: *c*.20 Feb. 1624   £6/d, £8/d (after 16 Sept.)
Secretary: Thomas Lorkin

He returned to England June - Aug. 1624. He began the mission as Baron
Kensington but was designated Earl of Holland during it. He was joined with
the Earl of Carlisle (see immediately below).

Instructions: BL, Add. 35832, f. 183; inferred from PRO, SP/78/72, ff. 94-112,
214-44, 271-4.
Correspondence: PRO, SP/78/72-5; BL, Add. 4164, 31999, 35832, 36447, Eg.
2596, Harl. 1580-1, Royal, King's 134; Oxford, Mss. at All Souls Lib.,
ccxii, ccxviii; *CSPD, 1623-5*; *Cabala*, pp. 286-94; *Clarendon State Papers*,
vol. ii, app. ii-xxiv; *Hardwicke State Papers*, i, pp. 523-70.

F195.

HAY, James, Earl of Carlisle (*c*.1580-1636)*

19 Feb. 1624^b - *c*.10 June 1625^c Ambassador Extraordinary
Audience: 1 June 1624   £8/d
Secretary: John Woodford, William
  Boswell, Thomas Lorkin

He departed England 18 May 1624 and was accredited conjointly with the Earl of Holland. Carlisle returned to England briefly, Dec. 1624 - Jan. 1625.

Instructions and Correspondence: See immediately above, under Henry Rich, Earl of Holland.

F196.
GORING, Sir George (later Baron Goring, Earl of Norwich; 1583?- 1663)*
1 Sept. 1624*ᶠ* - early Oct. 1624*ʰ*   [Agent?]
Instructions: Summarized in *CSPV, 1623-5*, p. 435.
Correspondence: PRO, SP/78/73.

F197.
*c.*20 Jan. 1625*ʰ* - 2 Apr. 1625*ᶜ*   [Agent]
Instructions: Summarized in *CSPV, 1623-5*, p. 568.
Correspondence: PRO, SP/78/74-5.

F198.
VILLIERS, George, 1st Duke of Buckingham (1592-1628)*
10 May 1625*ᵉ* - *c.*10 June 1625*ᶜ*   Ambassador Extraordinary
Audience: 14 May 1625

His purpose was to convey England's future queen, Henrietta Maria, to England, but he did have negotiating responsibilities. He was accompanied, in some capacity, by Secretary of State Sir Albert Morton.

Instructions: Suggested in *CSPV, 1625-6*, p. 62.
Correspondence: PRO, SP/78/75; BL, Add. 12528; *Memoires du Cardinal Richelieu* (1912-27), iii-viii.

F199.
[BARRETT, Sir Edward, Baron Newburgh (1581-1645)*
1625 - 1627   Resident Ambassador
                 £4/d

Instructions: PRO, SP/78/78, ff. 247-52.

Despite extensive documentation indicating a mission—including repeated warrants for pay—it is clear that Barrett did not actually undertake this or any other diplomatic assignment.]

F200.
LORKIN, Thomas (*d.*1625)
1 June 1625*ᵃ* - *d.*29 Sept. 1625   Agent
                         20s/d

He was in France dealing with the Duke of Mansfeldt in Jan., but seemingly assumed more official responsibilities in France in June 1625.

Correspondence: PRO, SP/76/75, SP/104/167; BL, Add. 34727, Eg. 2596, Harl. 1581.

F201.
RICH, Henry, 1st Earl of Holland (1590-1649)*
CARLETON, Sir Dudley (later Baron Carleton of Imbercourt, Viscount Dorchester; 1573-1632)*

28 Dec. 1625*a* - *c*.14 Apr. 1626*c*	Ambassadors Extraordinary
Audience: *c*.13 Jan. 1626	£8/d (Holland),
Secretary to Rich: John Hawkins?	£6/d (Carleton)

Instructions: PRO, SP/78/76, ff. 267-75; Rymer, T., *Foedera...*, xviii, p. 256.
Correspondence: PRO, SP/78/77-8; BL, Add. 31999, 35832, 36447, Harl. 1579; Oxford, Mss. at All Souls Lib., ccxxii; *CSPD, 1625-6*; HMC *Cowper*, i.

F202.
LEWIS, William (later Bart.; 1592-1667)*

28 Mar. 1626*a* - 12 Sept. 1626*a*	Agent
	20*s*/d

Correspondence: PRO, SP/78/78-80.

F203.
HAWKINS, John (*fl.*1620s)

22 May 1626*a* - *c*.20 May 1627*c*	[Chargé d'Affaires]
	20*s*/d

The Earl of Holland left him as chargé.
Instructions: PRO, SP/78/79, ff. 115-16.
Correspondence: PRO, SP/78/78-81 & 83.
Correspondence about: CSPD, 1625-6.

F204.
CARLETON, Dudley, Baron Carleton of Imbercourt (later Viscount Dorchester; 1573-1632)*

24 July 1626*c* - *c*.1 Oct. 1626*c*	Ambassador Extraordinary
Arrived: 2 Aug. 1626	£6/d

Instructions: PRO, SP/78/79, ff. 147-53, 297; Oxford, Mss. at All Souls Lib., ccxii, f. 149b.
Correspondence: PRO, SP/78/79-80; Oxford, Mss. at All Souls Lib., ccxxii.

F205.
MONTAGU, Walter (1603?-1677)*

c.21 Aug. 1626*h* - 11 Sept. 1626*c*	[Special Ambassador]

Instructions: Implied in *CSPV, 1625-6*, p. 527.

F206.
LEWIS, William (1592-1667)*

19 Dec. 1626*a* - 6 Mar. 1627*a*	Agent
Arrived: *c*.8 Feb. 1626	20*s*/d

Correspondence: PRO, SP/78/81.

F207.
MONTAGU, Walter (1603?-1677)*

15 Mar. 1627*f* - 18 Apr. 1628*c*   [Special Ambassador]

He was arrested in France in Nov. while on a 1627 mission to Savoy (q.v.). He
   was detained approximately six months, and then released to participate in
   negotiations in France late in 1628.

Instructions: PRO, SP/92/13, f. 34; *CSPV, 1626-8*, p. 209.
Correspondence: PRO, SP/92/13.

*F208.***HAY, James, Earl of Carlisle** (*c.*1580-1636)*

1 Jan. 1628*a* - 28 Jan. 1629*c*   Ambassador Extraordinary
Audience (Lorraine): *c.*7 June 1628
Secretary: William Boswell

On this extended embassy, he visited Savoy, Venice, Switzerland, Flanders and
   the Low Countries (qq.v.). In France, his only stop was at the court of
   Lorraine in June, which is not surprising, given the anti-Richelieu tenor of his
   mission.

Instructions: PRO, SP/92/13, ff. 70, 202, SP/92/14, f. 246.
Correspondence: PRO, SP/77/19, SP/104/169; *CSPD, 1628-9*.

F209.
MONTAGU, Walter (1603?-1677)*

5 Oct. 1628*h* - 15 Oct. 1628*b*   [Special Ambassador]

On this mission, he went twice (the second time on 14 Oct.) into France from the
   English fleet for negotiations, and then quickly returned to that fleet.

Instructions: Summarized in *CSPV, 1628-9*, p. 351.

F210.
EDMONDES, Sir Thomas (*c.*1563-1639)*

27 May 1629*b* - 21 Mar. 1630*a*   Ambassador Extraordinary
Swearing of peace: 6 July 1629   £6/d
Secretary: Henry de Vic, Robert
   Kirkham

Instructions: PRO, SP/78/84, ff. 100-13, 128-49, 162-7.
Correspondence: PRO, SP/78/84-6; BL, Stowe 176; HMC *Cowper*, ii.

F211.
AUGIER, Réné (*fl.*1620s-1660s)

23 Feb. 1629*b* - *c.*25 July 1640*c*   Agent, Chargé d'Affaires
                                               20*s*/d, 40*s*/d (after 1 Jan. 1637)

He was employed as an agent along with de Vic (below). He was specifically
   utilized as a secretary to the Earl of Leicester (below) and as chargé in

Leicester's absences. He returned to England in July of 1632, and also Jan. - Feb. 1637, among other times.

Instructions: Implied in *CSPV, 1629-32*, p. 96.
Correspondence: PRO, SP/78/92-109; BL, Harl. 7001; *CSPD, 1635*.

F212.
DE VIC, Henry (later Sir Henry, Bart.; *d.*1671)

2 Jan. 1630[a] - 21 Oct. 1636[a]	Agent, Chargé d'Affaires
	20*s*/d

He was a special agent and intermittently secretary to extraordinary missions, such as that of Thomas Edmondes. He was chargé d'affaires at Paris in the absence of formal embassies and was paid continuously.

Correspondence: PRO, SP/78/86-102; BL, Add. 15857, 15918, Eg. 2553, 2597, Harl. 7001; *CSPD, 1635*.

F213.
MONTAGU, Walter (1603?-1677)*

9 June 1630[b] - *c.*20 July 1630[c]	[Special Ambassador]
	£700 (total)

Instructions: Inferred from *CSPV, 1629-32*, p. 349.
Correspondence: PRO, SP/78/86.

F214.

20 Oct. 1630[b] - *c.*28 Jan. 1631[c]	[Special Ambassador]
Audience: *c.*1 Nov.1630	

Correspondence: PRO, SP/78/87-8.

F215.

*c.*4 Mar. 1631[h] - 12 Apr. 1631[c]	[Special Ambassador]
	£1000?

Correspondence: PRO, SP/78/88.

F216.
WAKE, Sir Isaac (1580-1632)*

*c.*15 Mar. 1631[h] - *d.*31 May 1632	Ambassador Ordinary
Audience: *c.*10 May 1631	£4/d
Secretary: Richard Browne	

Correspondence: PRO, SP/78/88-91; BL, Eg. 2597; Rymer, *Foedera...*, xix, p. 302; HMC *3rd Report*, p. 120.

F217.
WESTON, Jerome (later 2nd Earl of Portland, 1605-1663)*

6 Dec. 1631[a] - 12 Mar. 1633[a]	Ambassador Extraordinary
Arrived: 13 Aug. 1632	£6/d
Audience: 16 Feb. 1633	

He also went to the courts of Savoy, Florence, and Venice (qq.v.).

Instructions: PRO, SP/78/91, ff. 382-405.

Correspondence: PRO, SP/78/92-3.

F218.

MURRAY, William (later 1st Earl of Dysart; 1600?-1651)*

Murray was directed, in Nov. 1632, to visit the French Queen Mother, resident in Flanders (Spanish Netherlands, q.v. for full entry)

F219.

FEILDING, Basil, Viscount Feilding (later 2nd Earl of Denbigh; *c.*1608-1674)*

Lord Feilding visited the French court on his journey to his assignment as resident in Venice (q.v.). Audience in France: 24 Oct. 1634.

F220.

SCUDAMORE, John, 1st Viscount Scudamore (1601-1671)*

23 Apr. 1635*ᵃ* - 3 Mar. 1639*ᵃ*   Ambassador Ordinary
Audience: *c.*15 Aug. 1635   £6/d
Secretary: Henry de Vic?

Instructions: PRO, SP/78/98, ff. 86-93; BL, Add. 11044, ff. 57-70.

Correspondence: PRO, SP/78/98-107; BL, Add. 11044, 35097 (letterbook), 45142 (letterbook), Harl. 7001; *CSPD, 1635, 1635-6, 1636-7, 1637, Add. 1625-49.*

F221.

SIDNEY, Robert, 2nd Earl of Leicester (1595-1677)*

29 Feb. 1636*ᵃ* - *c.*15 Sept. 1641*ᵉ*   Ambassador Extraordinary
Audience: 28 May 1636   £6/d
Secretary: Réné Augier, James Battier

He joined with Augier and de Vic for the initial audience. He returned to London May 1638; March to July 1639; and Apr. 1641. Augier was chargé d'affaires during Sidney's absences.

Instructions: PRO, SP/78/101, ff. 31-40; Collins, A. (ed.), *Letters and Memorials...Sydney State Papers* (1746), ii, p. 374.

Correspondence: PRO, SP/78/101-11, SP/104/170; *CSPD, 1638-9, 1639, 1639-40, 1640, 1640-1, Add. 1625-49*; Collins, *Sydney State Papers*, ii; HMC *De Lisle and Dudley*, vi.

F222.

WINDEBANK, Thomas (*c.*1612-n.d)*

24 Nov. 1639*ᵍ* - 24 Apr. 1640*ᵃ*   [Ambassador Extraordinary]
Audience: 17 Dec. 1639

Correspondence about: *CSPV, 1636-9, 1640-2.*

Correspondence: *CSPD, 1639-40.*

F223.
BROWNE, Richard (later Sir Richard, Bart., 1605-1683)*

20 July 1641[b] - Dec. 1650[g]   Agent
Audience: 2 Sept. 1641   40s/d (at least to begin)

Initially an agent for Charles I in Paris, he seemingly continued during much of the Interregnum as the representative at the French court for Charles II.

Instructions: PRO, SP/78/111, ff. 61-2; BL, Add. 15856, ff. 9-10.
Correspondence: PRO, SP/78/111, 113 & 115, SP/81/56; BL, Add. 11044, 12184-6, 15856-8, 15948, 34702, 34710, 37047, Eg. 2434, 2536, 2547; *CSPD, 1641-3, 1649-50*; Nicholas, D., *Mr. Secretary Nicholas...*(1955), i & iv.

F224.
KERR, William, 3rd Earl of Lothian (1605?-1675)*

10 Jan. 1642[b] - c.29 Sept. 1643[c]   Agent

He was commissioned independently on this mission by both the Scottish Privy Council and King Charles I. The Scots commissioned him 10 Dec. 1642. His return date is the date he arrived in Oxford (after returning to London the 27th), where he was imprisoned by royalists who were suspicious of his actions.

Instructions: BL, Add. 15856, f. 10b, Eg. 2533, ff. 365-7; Laing, D. (ed.), *Correspondence of Sir Robert Kerr...*, (Edinburgh, 1875), i, pp. 142-3.
Correspondence: Laing, *Correspondence of Sir Robert Kerr...*, i.

F225.
GORING, George, Baron Goring (later Earl of Norwich; 1583?-1663)*

28 Aug. 1643[c] - 30 Nov. 1644[c]   Ambassador Extraordinary
Audience: 13 Dec. 1643

He was sent by Charles I. While proceeding to France, he paused in the Low Countries (q.v.) to consult with the Prince of Orange. It was for this mission that the Long Parliament impeached Goring for high treason.

Instructions: BL, Add. 15856, f. 11v.
Correspondence: PRO, SP/78/111; BL, Add. 15856, 18980, Sloane 1519; *CSPD, 1644*; *Clarendon State Papers*, ii.

F226.
AUGIER, René (*fl.*1620s-1670s)

26 Oct. 1644[c] - 25 Mar. 1651[b]   Agent [later Resident
Audience (with Brienne only):   Ambassador]
c.5 Dec. 1644   £400/an.
Secretary: René Petit

Accredited by Parliament in 1644, his status was not formally recognized by the French until 1647.

Correspondence: Bodl., Tanner Mss. 59, 60; HMC *Portland*; Cary, H. (ed.), *Memorials of the Great Civil War* (1842), i; Sainsbury, W., *Original...Papers...of Sir Peter Paul Rubens...*(1859).

F227.
MORRELL, Hugh (*d.*1664?)*

1651^h - 1651^h Agent
Audience (with Duke of Vendôme):
10 Apr. 1651

Instructions: Inferred from Cary, H. (ed.), *Memorials of the Great Civil War* (1842), ii, pp. 264-7.
Correspondence: Cary, *Memorials of the Great Civil War...*, ii; HMC *Portland*, i; *ThSP*, ii-iv.

F228.
PETIT, Réné (*fl.*1640s-1650s)

25 Mar. 1651^a - 19 Jan. 1655^b [Agent]
10s/d

Correspondence: *ThSP*, i, iii.

F229.
AUGIER, Réné (*fl.*1620s-1670s)

*c.*20 Dec. 1655^h - May 1656^g Agent
Audience: 1 Jan. 1656

Instructions: Suggested in *ThSP*, iv, pp. 374-5.
Correspondence: *ThSP*, iv.

F230.
MORLAND, Sir Samuel (1625-1695)*

He visited the French court on his way to his assignment as resident ambassador to the Swiss cantons (q.v.) at Geneva. Audience in France: 1 June 1655.

F231.
DOWNING, Sir George (later 1st Bart.; 1623-1684)*

He visited the French court on his way to Switzerland (q.v.) in 1655, and again on his return, with audience on return 21 Aug. 1655. Despite discussion of it, he did not go to Savoy.

F232.
AUGIER, Réné (*fl.*1650s-1670s)

Jan. 1656^h - summer? 1656 Agent

Instructions: Suggested in *ThSP*, iv, pp. 374-5.
Correspondence: *ThSP*, iv.

F233.
LOCKHART, Sir William (1621-1675)*

9 Apr. 1656*a* - *c*.Oct. 1659*f*   Ambassador [Ordinary]
Audience: 8 May 1656   £120/mo.

He returned to England, Dec. 1656 to Jan. 1657, as well as in early Oct. 1657, and then repeatedly in the spring of 1658. He spent some time in military operations against Dunkirk in May/June of 1658, and thereafter became the Governor of Dunkirk. Although he was only spasmodically in contact with the French court after this date, it is reasonably clear that he was considered the formal diplomatic representative from England to France during the period. He was involved in the negotiations that led to the Treaty of the Pyrennes.

Instructions: PRO, SP/78/113, ff. 84-97; Firth, C., 'Cromwell's Instructions to Colonel Lockhart in 1656,' *EHR*, xxi (1906), pp. 742-6; Abbott, W., *The Writings...of Oliver Cromwell* (Cambridge, Mass., 1937-47), iv, pp. 138-41; *ThSP*, v, p. 41.
Correspondence: PRO, SP/78/113-115; BL, Add. 4106-07, 4157, 4197, Lansd. 821-3?, Sloane 3083; *CSPD, 1656-7, 1658-9, 1659-60*; Bodl., Rawlinson Mss. A.29, 39, 42, 43, 47, 53, 58; Abbott, *Cromwell*, iv; *ThSP*, i, v-vii; Vaughan, R. (ed.), *The Protectorate of Oliver Cromwell...*(1838), i, ii; Swaine, S., 'English Acquisition and Loss of Dunkirk,' *TRHS*, n.s., i (1884), pp. 93-118.

F234.
BELASYSE, Thomas, Viscount Fauconberg (later Earl of Fauconberg; 1627-1700)*

25 May 1658*c* - *c*.8 June 1658*c*   [Ambassador Extraordinary]
Audience: *c*.28 May 1658

He greeted Louis XIV at Calais.

Instructions: *CSPD, 1658-9*, p. 27; inferred from Swaine, 'Dunkirk...,' pp. 93-118; Abbott, *Cromwell*, iv, pp. 809-10, 818.
Correspondence about: *CSPD, 1658-9*; *CSPV, 1657-9*.

F235.
CROFTS, William, Baron Crofts of Saxham (*c*.1611-1677)*

7 June 1660*d* - *c*.2 Sept. 1660*a* Ambassador Extraordinary
Correspondence: BL, Add. 22065.

F236.
JERMYN, Henry, Earl of St. Albans (*c*.1600-1684)*

1 Nov. 1660*a* - *c*.30 Nov. 1661*a* Ambassador Extraordinary
Audience: 6 Mar. 1661   £400/mo.

This mission was preceded by various private voyages to France. Jermyn returned to England repeatedly during this assignment, including during the summer of 1661.

Instructions: PRO, SP/78/115, ff. 193-6; Oxford, Mss. at All Souls Lib., ccxlix
(no folio given).
Correspondence: PRO, SP/78/115; BL, Add. 22062; Bodl., Clarendon Mss.,
75; Oxford, Mss. at All Souls Lib., ccxix; Ady, J., *Madame...*, pp. 76, 120.

F237.
TUKE, Samuel (later Sir Samuel; *d*.1674)*

1 Mar. 1661[h] - Apr. 1661[h]   [Ambassador Extraordinary]

F238.
CROFTS, William, Baron Crofts of Saxham (*c*.1611-1677)*
HYDE, Lawrence (later Viscount Hyde of Kennilworth, Earl of Rochester;
1642-1711)*

31 Oct. 1661[d] - n.d.   [Special Ambassadors]
Audience: 18 Nov. 1661

They were accompanied by Sir Charles Berkeley representing James, Duke of
York.

Instructions: Suggested in *CSPV, 1661-4*, p. 66.

F239.
JERMYN, Henry, Earl of St. Albans (*c*.1600-1684)*

c.15 Apr. 1662[h] - 1 Aug. 1662[a]   [Ambassador Extraordinary]
Audience: *c*.8 June 1662

Correspondence about: *CSPV, 1661-2*.

F240.
MONTAGU, Ralph (later 1st Duke of Montagu; 1638-1709)*

26 Oct. 1662[c] - *c*.7 Feb. 1663[c]   [Agent?]
Secretary: René Petit

Correspondence about: Hartmann, C. H., *Charles II and Madame* (1934).

F241.
HOLLES, Denzil, 1st Baron Holles of Ifield (1599-1680)*

29 Apr. 1662[a] - 28 May 1666[a]   Ambassador Extraordinary
Audience: 21 Aug. 1663   £400/mo.

His duties ended in Dec. 1665, but due to illness he remained temporarily in
France. From France, he went directly to the peace conference at Breda
(q.v.).

Instructions: PRO, SP/78/117, ff. 113-16; BL, Stowe 191, ff. 3-5.
Correspondence: PRO, SP/78/117-21; BL, Add. 22919-20, 23124, Lansd.
7010, Sloane 3509, Stowe 199; HMC *Heathcote*; Lister, T., *Life and
Administration of Edward, First Earl of Clarendon...*(1837- 8), iii; Archives

des Affaires Etrangeres, *Angleterre*, vol. 82- 8; Fanshawe, Sir R., *Original Letters and Negotiations of...Sir Richard Fanshawe...*(1724), i.
Correspondence about: Hartmann, *Charles II and Madame*.

F242.

GERARD, Charles, 1st Baron Gerard of Brandon (later Earl of Macclesfield; *d*.1694)*

22 Nov. 1662[h] - *c*.10 Dec. 1662[g]   Envoy Extraordinary

Instructions: Suggested in *CSPV, 1661-4*, p. 219; Hartmann, *Charles II and Madame*, p. 62.
Correspondence about: PRO, SP/78/116; Hartmann, *Charles II and Madame*.

F243.

TREVOR, John (later Sir John; 1624-1672)*

17 Feb. 1663[c] - Apr. 1663?[g]   [Agent?]
                                       £300? (total)

Instructions: PRO, SP/78/117, ff. 32-3.
Correspondence: PRO, SP/78/117.

F244.

MONTAGU, Robert, Viscount Mandeville (later 3rd Earl of Manchester; 1634-1683)*

c.25 May 1663[d] - mid-June 1663[g]   [Ambassador Extraordinary]
Arrived: *c*.1 June 1663

He seemingly went to inquire into the health of the English Queen Mother, but he also met, in a diplomatic capacity, with various French political personalities, including Madame d'Orleans.

Instructions: Inferred from *CSPV, 1661-4*, p. 249.
Correspondence: *CSPD, 1663-4*.
Correspondence about: PRO, SP/78/117, ff. 82-5; *CSPV, 1661-4*.

F245.

BERKELEY, Charles, Viscount Fitzharding of Berehaven (later Earl of Falmouth; 1630-1665)*

6 Nov. 1664[a] - 22 Nov. 1664[a]   [Special Ambassador]
Audience: 11 Nov. 1664   *ad hoc*

Instructions: PRO, SP/78/119, ff. 151-3; HMC *Heathcote*, p. 171.
Correspondence: PRO, SP/78/119; BL, Add. 32094; Hartmann, C., *The King's Friend: A Life of Charles Berkeley...*(1951).

F246.

JERMYN, Henry, Earl of St. Albans (*c*.1600-1684)*

23 Mar. 1666[d] - *c*.10 Sept. 1666[c]   [Ambassador Extraordinary]
Arrived: 20 Apr. 1666

He seems, in the absence of a regularly accredited ambassador, to have been handling diplomatic responsibilities, in addition to his attendance on the Queen Mother.

Correspondence: PRO, SP/78/122-3

F247.

28 Jan. 1667^g - 10 Feb. 1668^c   Ambassador Extraordinary
Audience: 3 Feb. 1667

Instructions: Lister, *Clarendon*, iii, p. 443.
Correspondence: PRO, SP/78/123-4; Bennet, Henry, Earl of Arlington, ...*the Earl of Arlington's Letters to Sir William Temple...* (1701), pp. 117-48; Lister, *Clarendon*, ii, iii; Mignet, F., *Negociations Relatives a la Succession...*(Paris, 1835-42), i, ii; Archives des Affaires Etrangeres, *Angleterre*, vols. 88-9.

F248.
TREVOR, Sir John (1624-1672)*

4 Feb. 1668^a - 18 June 1668^b   Envoy Extraordinary
Audience: 18 Feb. 1668
Secretary: Peter du Moulin

Instructions: PRO, SP/78/124, ff. 16, 31-43, SP/104/174B, pp. 141-5, 169-70; BL, Add. 40795, f. 71; Bodl., Rawlinson Mss. A.255, ff. 47, 49, 51; HMC *4th Report*, App., p. 231.
Correspondence: PRO, SP/78/124; Bodl., Rawlinson Mss. A.293; Ady, *Madame*, i; Mignet, *Negociations*, ii.

F249.
MONTAGU, Ralph (later 1st Duke of Montagu; 1638-1709)*

1 Jan. 1669^a - 6 May 1672^b   Ambassador Extraordinary
Audience: 26 Apr. 1669   £100/wk.
Secretaries: Peter du Moulin, Francis
  Vernon, and William Perwich?

He returned to England for a time, summer 1671 through Jan. 1672.

Instructions: PRO, SP/78/126, ff. 40-8, SP/104/174B, pp. 187-9; BL, Add. 32094, f. 216; HMC *5th Report*, p. 316.
Correspondence: PRO, SP/78/126-33; BL, Add. 4201, 4205, 21947-8, 23894, Stowe 191; HMC *Buccleuch*, i; HMC *4th Report*, p. 245; Archives des Affaires Etrangeres, *Angleterre*, vols. 95, 96, 103; Metzger, E., *Ralph, First Duke of Montagu, 1638-1709* (Lewiston, N.Y., 1987).

F250.
ARUNDELL, Henry, 3rd Baron Arundell of Wardour (1608-1694)*
BELINGE, Sir Richard (*d.*1716)*

7 Mar. 1669^e - June 1669^c   [Special Ambassadors]

They had irregular diplomatic status at first. Their responsibilities apparently
included initiating negotiations that led to the secret Treaty of Dover.

Correspondence about: Hartmann, *Charles II and Madame*.

F251.
SACKVILLE, Charles, Baron Buckhurst (later Earl of Middlesex, 6th Earl of
Dorset; 1643-1706)*

c.1 July 1669[h] - c.10 Sept. 1669[c]   [Special Ambassador]
Audience: c.22 July 1669   £1000 (+? total)

This was a mission of compliment to the French King at Dunkirk; he was
accompanied by Henry Savile, who seemingly represented Prince James.

Instructions: Inferred from Thibaudeau, A. (ed.), *The Bulstrode Papers...*
(1897), p. 114.

F252.
JERMYN, Henry, Earl of St. Albans (1600-1684)*

28 July 1669[b] - 18 Sept. 1669[a]   [Special Ambassador]
                              £4000 (minimum total)

St. Albans was in France in attendance on the Queen Mother. He did, however,
have some role in maintaining diplomatic contact with the French court.

Correspondence: Mignet, *Negociations*, iii.

F253.
JERMYN, Henry, Earl of St. Albans (1600-1684)*
ARUNDELL, Henry, 3rd Baron Arundell of Wardour (1608-1694)*
JENKINS, Dr. Leoline (later Sir Leoline; c.1625-1685)*

27 Sept. 1669[c] - c.24 Dec. 1669[g]   [Diplomatic status
'Opening of commission in France':   indistinct]
  9 Oct. 1669   £400 (total—Arundel),
Secretaries: Sir Richard Belinge,   £200 (total—Jenkins)
Francis Vernon, et al

They went to France to inquire into the late Queen Dowager's estate upon her
death. There they joined the resident ambassador, Ralph Montagu, and the
Queen Dowager's chaplain, Walter Montagu. Their responsibilities (especially Arundell's) included negotiations with the French crown about a secret
agreement between England and France.

Instructions: PRO, SP/78/12, ff. 146-50; SP/104/17, ff. 1-3; *CSPD, 1668-9*,
pp. 503-04.
Correspondence: PRO, SP/78/127-8.

F254.
BELASYSE, Thomas, Viscount Fauconberg (later Earl of Fauconberg; 1627-
1700)*

On his journey to his assignment in Venice (q.v.), he visited the French Court,
having audience Feb. 1670.

F255.

GODOLPHIN, Sidney (later Baron Godolphin of Rialton, 1st Earl of Godolphin; 1645-1712)*

24 Mar. 1670[h] - 22 Apr. 1670[e]   [Special Ambassador]
Arrived: 31 Mar. 1670   £600 (total)

Correspondence: PRO, SP/78/129; HMC *Buccleuch*, i.

F256.

SACKVILLE, Charles, Baron Buckhurst (later Earl of Middlesex and 6th Earl of Dorset; 1643-1706)*

18 May 1670[f] - 22 May 1670[a]   [Special Ambassador]
Audience: *c.*20 May 1670   £1000 (total)

This was yet another mission of compliment to the French King at Dunkirk. He was accompanied by one Mr. Thynne (presumably Thomas Thynne, later 1st Viscount Weymouth), representing the Duke of York.

Instructions: Inferred from Thibaudeau, *Bulstrode Papers*, p. 139.

F257.

VILLIERS, George, 2nd Duke of Buckingham (1628-1687)*

*c.*27 July 1670[b] - 12 Sept. 1670[a]   Ambassador Extraordinary
Audience: *c.*3 Aug. 1670   *c.*£5050 (total)
Secretary: Réné Petit

Instructions: Suggested in *CSPD, 1670*, p. 350; *CSPV, 1669-70*, pp. 238-9.

Correspondence: HMC *Buccleuch*, i; Burghclere, W., *George Villiers, 2nd Duke of Buckingham, 1628-1687* (1903).

F258.

BELASYSE, John, 1st Baron Belasyse of Worlaby (1614-1689)*

25 Apr. 1671[b] - 10 May 1671[a]   [Special Ambassador]

Accompanied by Mr. Vaughan, who represented Prince James, they paid compliments to the French King at Dunkirk.

Instructions: Suggested in Thibaudeau, *Bulstrode Papers*, p. 186.

F259.

GODOLPHIN, Sidney (later Baron Godolphin of Rialton, 1st Earl of Godolphin; 1645-1712)*

*c.*21 Nov. 1671[h] - *c.*17 Dec. 1671[c]   [Special Ambassador]

He apparently accompanied the Earl of Sunderland to Paris (next entry, q.v.).

Instructions: Inferred from Thibaudeau, *Bulstrode Papers*, p. 212; *CSPV, 1671-2*, p. 134.

F260.

SPENCER, Robert, 2nd Earl of Sunderland (1640-1702)*

He contacted the French court, 1 Dec. 1671, on his journey to Spain (q.v.). He later came directly from Spain to assume the residency in Paris (see below).

F261.
BELASYSE, Thomas, Viscount Fauconberg (later Earl Fauconberg; 1627-1700)*

On his return journey from his assignment in Venice (q.v.), he visited the French Court, having audience 14 Feb. 1672.

F262.
SIDNEY, Henry (later Viscount Sidney of Sheppey, Earl of Romney; 1641-1704)*

4 Mar. 1672[b] - c.15 Apr. 1672[e]   Envoy
Audience: 24 Mar. 1672

Mr. Vaughan, representing Prince James, accompanied him on this mission of condolence.

Instructions: Suggested in Thibaudeau, *The Bulstrode Papers*, p. 225.

F263.
LOCKHART, Sir William (1621-1675)*

On his journey to an assignment with various German states (q.v.), he had audience in France together with Henry Sidney, 24 Mar. 1672.

F264.
GODOLPHIN, Sidney (later Baron Godolphin of Rialton, 1st Earl of Godolphin; 1645-1712)*

2 Apr. 1672[a] - early Nov. 1672[e]   Envoy Extraordinary
Audience: 12 Apr. 1672   £5/d

Godolphin was assigned to accompany the French King during the campaign season. He took leave of the French King 13 Aug. but illness precluded his return to England before early Nov.

Instructions: BL, Stowe 191, ff. 34-5.
Correspondence: PRO, SP/78/133-4; Coventry Papers at Longleat, ii, lxxxii; *CSPD, 1671-2*; HMC *4th Report*, p. 246; HMC *Buccleuch*, i.

F265.
PERWICH, William (*fl.*1660s-1670s)

1 May 1672[a] - at least 29 Sept. 1677[a]   Agent [and Chargé
                                             d'Affaires in the absence of regular
                                             ambassadors]
                                             £1/d, £2/d (after Aug. 1673)

Beginning in 1669, he was at various times, and often simultaneously the maritime agent in France and the secretary to English legations. He also served as chargé when no ambassador was on site.

Correspondence: PRO, SP/78/126-42, SP/104/18; BL, Add. 23894, 34331; Curran, M. B. (ed.), *The Dispatches of William Perwich...*, Camden 3rd ser., v (1903).

F266.
VILLIERS, George, 2nd Duke of Buckingham (1628-1687)*
BENNET, Henry, Earl of Arlington (1618-1685)*
SAVILE, George, Viscount Halifax (later Earl of Halifax; 1633-1695)*

14 June 1672^c - 21 July 1672^a [Envoys Extraordinary]
First session: 26 June 1672   £4754 (shared jointly by
Secretary: Sir Joseph Williamson   Arlington and Buckingham); £1000
    (Halifax)

They were accredited to the French King, who was campaigning in the Low Countries, and they participated in the Franco-Dutch peace negotiations (Conferences, q.v.). They also contacted the Prince of Orange (Low Countries, q.v.). James Scott, Duke of Monmouth, the commander of the English forces in the Low Countries, was added to the commission 22 June 1672.

Instructions: PRO, SP/78/134, f. 82, SP/104/64, ff. 25-6, SP/105/101, ff. 6-7; *CSPD, 1672*, p. 226-8; Foxcroft, H., *The Life and Letters of Sir George Savile...*(1898), i, pp. 72-5.
Correspondence: PRO, SP/78/134, SP/84/189-90, SP/105/101; Foxcroft, *Savile*, i.

F267.
SAVILE, Henry (1642-1687)*

21 Sept. 1672^g - c.2 Nov. 1672^e Ambassador Extraordinary
Audience: 4 Oct. 1672   £5/d

Instructions: Suggested in *CSPV, 1671-2*, p. 305.
Correspondence: PRO, SP/78/135; BL, Add. 21948; HMC *4th Report*, p. 237; Cooper, W. (ed.), *Savile Correspondence*, Camden o.s., vii (1858).

F268.
BUTLER, Thomas, Earl of Ossory (1634-1680)*

8 Nov. 1672^b - c.4 Dec. 1672^c Envoy Extraordinary
    £200 (total)

Instructions: Inferred from *CSPV, 1671-2*, p. 318.
Correspondence about: *CSPD, 1672-3*.

F269.
SPENCER, Robert, 2nd Earl of Sunderland (1640-1702)*

13 Nov. 1672^b - 3 Sept. 1673^b Ambassador Extraordinary
Audience: 5 Nov. 1672   £100/wk.
Secretary: Thomas Chudleigh

He came directly from Spain to France to assume resident diplomatic duties. He arrived in Paris c.22 June but did not have a formal audience until early Nov., and was paid only under the privy seal designating him as the ambassador to France from 13 Nov. 1672.

Correspondence: PRO, SP/78/134-8; BL, Add. 25122, 32094; HMC *4th Report*, p. 244.

F270.

SPRAGGE, Sir Edward (*d*.1673)*

11 Jan. 1673[b] - *c*.9 Mar. 1673[c]	Ambassador Extraordinary
Audience: *c*.12 Feb. 1673	£300 (total?)

Instructions: PRO, SP/78/136, ff. 60-5, SP/104/64, ff. 29-30.
Correspondence: PRO, SP/78/136.

F271.

LOCKHART, Sir William (1621-1675)*

1 April 1673[a] - *d*.28 May 1675	Envoy Extraordinary, then Ambassador Ordinary £5/d (as Extraordinary), £100/wk. (as Ordinary)

He was appointed to follow the military campaign of 1673, and then, 20 Oct. 1673, he was appointed to remain as ambassador ordinary (resident). He returned briefly to England, Oct. 1673 to Jan. 1674.

Instructions: PRO, SP/78/136, ff. 179-81; as ordinary: PRO, SP/104/17, ff. 32-4.

Correspondence: PRO, SP/78/136-40, SP/104/18, 56, BL, Eg. 3354, Stowe 197; *CSPD, 1673-5, 1675-6*; HMC *4th Report*, pp. 237-42; Archives des Affaires Etrangeres, *Angleterre*, vols. 112, 114-115.

F272.

MORDAUNT, Henry, 2nd Earl of Peterborough (1624?-1697)*

He made diplomatic contact in France, Apr. 1673, on his way to the Emperor (q.v.).

F273.

SKELTON, Bevil (*died c*.1692)

3 Aug. 1674[h] - Nov. 1674[h]	[Special Ambassador]

This consisted of a secret mission for the King.

F274.

BERKELEY, John, 1st Baron Berkeley of Stratton (1606?-1678)*

7 Oct. 1675[a] - 6 Oct. 1676[f]	Ambassador Extraordinary
Audience: *c*.1 Dec. 1675	£100/wk.

Secretary: Ellis Leighton

He went directly from France to Nimwegen (Conferences, q.v.) to serve as a plenipotentiary at negotiations there.

Instructions: PRO, SP/104/239, ff. 1-6.
Correspondence: PRO, SP/78/141-2, SP/104/18, 185; BL, Add. 15948, 22548, 25119, Eg. 3326; HMC *4th Report*, pp. 244-5.

F275.
MONTAGU, Ralph (later 1st Duke of Montagu; 1638-1709)*

1 Sept. 1676*ᵃ* - 12 July 1678*ᵉ*   Ambassador Extraordinary
Audience: *c*.20 Dec. 1676   £100/wk.
Secretary: John Brisbane

He left his post without permission—12 July represents the date upon which his
   successor was appointed to assume the Paris residency. He had returned
   briefly to England, autumn 1677.

Instructions: PRO, SP/104/239, ff. 9-13; Bodl., Rawlinson Mss. A.255,
   ff. 265-6; BL, Add. 25119, f. 13; HMC *4th Report*, p. 232.
Correspondence: PRO, SP/78/142, SP/104/18 & 185-6; BL, Add. 25119,
   28054, 32680, 38849B, 39757, Harl. 1516, 1523, Eg. 2540, 3326, Stowe
   191; HMC *Buccleuch*, i; Oxford, Mss. in All Souls Lib., clxix, ccliii; HMC
   4th Report, p. 245; Browning, A., T*homas Osborne, Earl of Danby* ...
   (Glasgow, 1944-51), ii.

F276.
BRISBANE, John (*fl*.1670s)

19 Sept. 1676*ᵃ* - 15 July 1679*ᵃ*   Agent [and Chargé
Audience: 30 Oct. 1678   d'Affaires]
                                              £2/d, £4/d (after 19 Dec. 1677)

He served as chargé in the absence of regularly accredited ambassadors, i.e.,
   upon Montagu's departure (beginning 24 June 1678*ᵃ*) and he served as
   secretary to the legation and maritime agent when there were fully accredited
   ambassadors present. His responsibilities included travelling as an accredited
   envoy to the Spanish Netherlands (q.v.), early 1678. He returned to England,
   Aug. - Dec. 1678.

Instructions: (As maritime agent, 1676) Bodl., Rawlinson Mss. A.255, ff. 269,
   271; HMC *4th Report*, p. 242.
Correspondence: PRO, SP/78/142, SP/104/18, 185-6, 239; BL, Add. 28054,
   Eg. 3326; Bodl., Rawlinson Mss. A.268; *CSPD, 1679-80*; HMC *4th Report*,
   pp. 242-4; Browning, A., *Thomas Osborne, Earl of Danby*...(Glasgow,
   1944-51), ii.

F277.
DURAS, Louis, 2nd Earl of Feversham (1640?-1709)*

20 Oct. 1677*ʰ* - 2 Dec. 1677*ᵃ*   [Special Ambassador]
Audience: *c*.18 Nov. 1677

Instructions: BL, Add. 25119, ff. 6-12.
Correspondence: PRO, SP/104/180; BL, Add. 10115.

F278.
SPENCER, Robert, 2nd Earl of Sunderland (1640-1702)*

12 July 1678[a] - 10 Feb. 1679[b]   Ambassador Extraordinary
Audience: 22 July 1678   £100/wk.
Secretary: James Vernon? and John
  Brisbane

He returned briefly to England, Sept. - Oct. 1678.

Instructions: PRO, SP/104/239, ff. 34-5; Bodl., Rawlinson Mss. A.256, ff. 132-4.
Correspondence: PRO, SP/78/142; BL, Add. 28049, 28053, Eg. 3326; HMC *4th Report*, p. 245; Browning, A., *Danby*, ii.

F279.
SAVILE, Henry (1642-1687)*

27 Feb. 1679[a] - 1 Apr. 1682[a]   Envoy Extraordinary
French secretary: M. Godet   £5/d

He returned briefly to England, July 1680, and again in Aug. 1680.

Instructions: PRO, SP/104/239, ff. 38-42.
Correspondence: PRO, SP/78/143-4, SP/104/19 & 187-8; BL, Add. 23249, 24900, 28569, 32680, Eg. 3678; Oxford, Mss. at All Souls Lib., ccxiii; Cooper, (ed.), *Savile Correspondence*; HMC *4th Report*, p. 238; Sidney, A., *Letters of the Honourable Algernon Sidney to the Honourable Henry Savile, ambassador in France...*(1742); Sidney, H., Earl of Romney, *Diary of the Times of Charles the Second...*ed. R. Blencowe, (1843).

F280.
GRAHAM, Richard, Viscount Preston (1648-1695)*

31 Mar. 1682[a] - *c.*13 Sept. 1685[d]   Envoy Extraordinary
Audience: 7 June 1682   £5/d
Secretary: Richard Tempest

He made a brief return to England, May - June 1683.

Instructions: PRO, SP/78/145, ff. 177-9; HMC *7th Report*, App. 1, p. 262; Oxford, Mss. at All Souls Lib., cclv, f. 129.
Correspondence: PRO, SP/78/144-8, SP/104/19, 193; BL, Add. 28896, 34517; Oxford, Mss. at All Souls Lib., ccxii, ccxl; *CSPD, 1682*; HMC *7th Report*, pp. 261-428; Foxcroft, H., *The Life and Letters of Sir George Savile ...* (1898), i.

F281.
DURAS, Louis, 2nd Earl of Feversham (1640?-1709)*

10 Aug. 1682[b] - *c.*15 Sept. 1682[c]   Ambassador Extraordinary
Audience: 14 Aug. 1682   £1000 (total)

Instructions: Suggested in HMC *6th Report*, App., p. 321.

F282.

DOUGLAS, George, 1st Earl of Dumbarton (1636?-1692)*

11 July 1683[b] - c.1 Oct. 1683[e]   [Special Ambassador]
Audience: 31 Aug. 1683   £500 (total?)

He was accompanied by one Capt. Nicolls, who represented the Duke of York.

Instructions: Suggested in *CSPD, 1683*, p. 215; *CTB*, vii, 1, p. 891.
Correspondence: PRO, SP/78/146.

F283.

DOUGLAS, James, Earl of Arran (later 4th Duke of Hamilton; 1658- 1712)*

31 Dec. 1683[d] - Feb. 1684[c]   Ambassador Extraordinary

This was a brief mission of compliment to congratulate the King on the birth of
  the Duke of Anjou.

Correspondence about: *CSPD, 1683-4*.

F284.

CHURCHILL, John, Baron Churchill of Eyemouth (later 1st Duke of
  Marlborough; 1650-1722)*

c.17 Feb. 1685[h] - Apr. 1685[h]   Ambassador Extraordinary

F285.

TRUMBULL, Sir William (1639-1716)*

2 Sept. 1685[a] - 12 Oct. 1686[a]   Ambassador Extraordinary
Audience: 1 Dec. 1685   £5/d
Secretary: Jacques Dayrolle

Instructions: Bodl., Rawlinson Mss. A.257, f. 190.
Correspondence: PRO, SP/78/148-50, SP/104/19; BL, Add. 34799; *CSPD,
  1685, 1686-7*.

F286.

SKELTON, Bevil (*died c.1692*)*

17 Oct. 1686[a] - 16 Oct. 1688[b]   Envoy Extraordinary
Audience: 9 Jan. 1687   £5/d

Instructions: PRO, SP/104/19, 7 Nov. 1688 (no foliation); BL, Lansd. 1152,
  vol. ii, no. 25.
Correspondence: PRO, SP/78/150-1, SP/104/19; BL, Add. 22910, 28896,
  38847-8, 38493, Stowe 241, 291; Bodl., Rawlinson Mss. A.139.

F287.

WALDEGRAVE, Henry, 1st Baron Waldegrave of Chewton (1661-1689)*

23 Oct. 1688[b] - d.14 Jan. 1689   Envoy Extraordinary
Audience: 22 Dec. 1688   £5/d

Instructions: SP/104/19 (no foliation).

GERMAN STATES AND CENTRAL EUROPE
(Not including the Hanse Towns)

Because envoys, especially during the sixteenth century, were sent to a variety of the German princes during a single mission, and because the nature of the Empire was so fluid, the area of central Europe will be treated as a single entity, with careful geographical distinctions given under each mission.

G1.
PACE, Richard (later Sir Richard; 1482?-1536)*

11 May 1519ª - 10 Aug. 1519ª   [Special Ambassador]
Arrived (Frankfurt): *c.*10 June 1519

Instructed to attend the imperial elections at Frankfurt, he also spent extensive time with various German rulers and with Margaret of Savoy, Regent (Low Countries, q.v.) as well.

Instructions: BL, Cotton, Vitel. B.xx, f. 111; and in part in *L&P*, iii, 1, nos. 239-41.
Correspondence: BL, Vitel. B.xx; *L&P*, iii, 1.

G2.
PARKER, Henry, 8th Baron Morley (1476-1556)*
HUSSEY, Sir William (1473-1531?)*
LEE, Dr. Edward (later Archbishop of York; 1482?-1544)*

26 Aug. 1523ᶜ - early Jan. 1524ᵍ   [Special Ambassadors]
Investiture: 8 Dec. 1523

They bestowed the Order of the Garter on Archduke Ferdinand of Austria, who was at Nürnberg. They also visited the Regent in the Low Countries (q.v.). Sir Thomas Wriothesley was Garter King-at-Arms, and accompanied the mission.

Instructions: *L&P*, iii, 2, no. 3275.
Correspondence: BL, Cotton, Vitel. B.xx; *L&P*, iii, 2.

G3.
WALLOP, Sir John (*d.*1551)*

*c.*1 Sept. 1526ʰ - Sept.? 1527ʰ   [Special Ambassador]
Audience (Cologne): *c.*1 Oct. 1526
Audience (Archduke Ferdinand): 5 Feb.
  1527
Audience (Duke George of Saxony):
  mid-May 1527

He was sent in response to the Turkish threat to Central Europe after the Battle of Mohács and was apparently first to attend the King of Hungary. In light of the death of that prince, he saw instead the Archduke Ferdinand, King of Bohemia, at Prague. His visit also encompassed consultations with Margaret of Austria, Regent in the Low Countries; and the King of Poland (qq.v.).

Instructions: Inferred from *L&P*, iv, 2, no. 2530; Jasnowski, J., 'England and Poland in the 16th and 17th Centuries,' *Polish Science and Learning*, vii (1948), pp. 1-5.

Correspondence: BL, Cotton, Vesp. F.i, Vitel. B.xxi; *L&P*, iv, 2.

G4.
PAGET, William (later 1st Baron Paget of Beaudesert; 1505-1563)*

Aug. 1531[h] - 8 Feb. 1532[a]   [Special Ambassador]
Audience (Hesse): Sept. 1531

He was sent to the Duke of Saxony and the Landgrave of Hesse.

Correspondence about: *L&P*, v - vi; BL, Add. 25114.

G5.
CRANMER, Dr. Thomas (later Archbishop of Canterbury; 1489-1556)*

25 Jan. 1532[h] - c.1 Jan. 1533[e]   [Resident Ambassador]
Audience: 14 July 1532   20s/d?

He visited John Frederick of Saxony. He also visited the Emperor (q.v.) and may have gone to Italy.

Correspondence: *L&P*, v; Cranmer, Thomas, *Works*, ed. J. Cox, (Parker Society, 1844-6).

G6.
PAGET, William (later 1st Baron Paget of Beaudesert; 1505-1563)*

Late Feb. 1532[c] - 2 Nov. 1532[a]   [Special Ambassador]
Audience (John of Saxony): early Aug.
   1532

He was instructed to visit John Frederick, Duke of Saxony, Philip, Landgrave of Hesse, William and Lewis, Dukes of Bavaria, Ernest Duke of Lüneburg, Philip Duke of Brunswick and Wolfgang, Prince of Hainaut.

Instructions: BL, Cotton, Vitel. B.xxi, ff. 152-5; *L&P*, *Add.*, 1, no. 767.
Correspondence about: *L&P*, v.

G7.
MOUNT, Christopher (later Dr. Christopher; 1497-1572)*

28 July 1533[e] - summer 1534[h]   [Special Ambassador]
Audience (Duke of Bavaria):   10s/d
   c.1 Sept. 1533

He began his mission in company with Vaughan (see below), and they proceeded together to Nürnberg. They separated soon thereafter, however, and Mount continued to the Duke of Bavaria at Munich. Mount remained with the Duke the entire period.

Instructions: Suggested in *L&P*, vi, nos. 1039-40.
Correspondence: *L&P*, vi - vii.

G8.
VAUGHAN, Stephen (by 1502-1549)*

28 July 1533^e - *c*.1 Dec. 1533^c [Special Ambassador]
Audience (Duke of Saxony):   10*s*/d
  6 Sept. 1533

He began this journey in company with Christopher Mount, and together they arrived at Nürnberg, 22 Aug. 1533. Vaughan then proceeded alone to the Duke of Saxony's court.

Instructions: Inferred from *L&P*, vi, nos. 918, 1079, 1082.
Correspondence: *L&P*, vi.

G9.
PAGET, William (later 1st Baron Paget of Beaudesert; 1505-1563)*

Dec. 1533^h - early June 1534^g [Special Ambassador]

He visited Lüneburg, Mecklenburg and Prussia among the German states. He also visited Poland (q.v.).

Instructions: BL, Add. 29547, f. 1; *L&P*, vii, nos. 21, 148.
Correspondence: *L&P*, vii.

G10.
HEATH, Dr. Nicholas (later Bishop of Rochester, Worcester and Archbishop of York; 1501?-1578)*

c.5 Jan. 1534^c - n.d.   [Special Ambassador]
Audience (Munich, Bavaria): *c*.15 Mar.
  1534

He was to join with Christopher Mount, already in Germany, but apparently the connection was never made. He was instructed to visit the Duke of Bavaria, the Elector Palatine, the Duke of Saxony, the Landgrave of Hesse and the Archbishops of Cologne, Treves and Magdeburg(?).

Instructions: *L&P*, vii, no. 21.
Correspondence: *L&P*, vii.

G11.
BONNER, Dr. Edmund (later Bishop of Hereford, London; 1500?-1569)*
CAVENDISH, Richard (*fl.*1530s)

20 July 1535^b - 27 Apr. 1536^a [Special Ambassador]
Audience (Duke of Holstein—   13*s* 4*d*/d
  Cavendish only): 2 Oct. 1535

For the greater part of this mission of 1535-6, Cavendish accompanied Edmund

Bonner. Cavendish, however, visited the Duke of Holstein alone. Besides the Duke of Holstein, they visited the courts of Denmark, Sweden, and some of the Hanse towns (qq.v.).

Instructions: Suggested in *L&P*, x, nos. 24, 303.
Correspondence: BL, Add. 48036, Cotton, Vitel. B.xxi, Nero B.iii; *L&P*, viii - x; Merriman, R., *The Life and Letters of Thomas Cromwell* (1902).

G12.
MOUNT, Christopher (later Dr. Christopher; 1497-1572)*

1 Aug. 1535[a] - winter? 1535[h]   [Special Ambassador]

He first went to France (q.v.) in company with Dr. Simon Heynes, then continued his mission to Wittenberg, Germany, around 7 Sept. 1535.

Instructions: Inferred from *L&P*, ix, no. 54, 180.
Correspondence: *L&P*, ix.

G13.
FOX, Dr. Edward, Bishop of Hereford (1496?-1538)*
HEATH, Dr. Nicholas (later Bishop of Rochester, Worcester and Archbishop of York; 1501?-1578)*

31 Aug. 1535[d] - 4 July 1536[c]   [Special Ambassadors]
Audience (Saxony): Dec. 1535

Apparently Dr. Robert Barnes, already in Germany making contact with the Lutherans and soliciting opinions about the divorce, joined with the ambassadors.

Instructions: *L&P*, ix, no. 23.
Correspondence and correspondence about: *L&P*, ix, x.

G14.
MOUNT, Christopher (later Dr. Christopher; 1497-1572)*

28 Feb. 1538[e] - c.10 May 1538[c]   Special Ambassador
                                            20s/d

He went to the Duke of Saxony and the Landgrave of Hesse, and he also attended the Diet at Brunswick.

Instructions: BL, Cotton, Vitel. B.xxi, ff. 158-60; *L&P*, xiii, 1, no. 367.
Correspondence: *L&P*, xiii, 1.

G15.
MOUNT, Christopher (later Dr. Christopher; 1497-1572)*
PAYNELL, Thomas (*fl.*1520s-1560s)*

c.20 Jan. 1539[c] - 23 Apr. 1539[a]   Special Ambassador
Audience (Saxony): c.4 Feb. 1539

They visited the Duke of Saxony and the Landgrave of Hesse, and attended the Frankfurt Diet of the Evangelical League.

Instructions: *L&P*, xiv, 1, no. 103; Merriman, R. B., *Life and Letters of Thomas Cromwell* (1902), pp. 174-6.

Correspondence: BL, Cotton, Vitel. B.xxi; *L&P*, xiv, 1; Merriman, *Life and Letters*.

G16.
WOTTON, Dr. Nicholas (later Sir Nicholas; 1497?-1567)*
BERDE, Richard (*fl.*1530s)

11 Mar. 1539[a] - mid-June 1539	[Special Ambassadors]
(Berde)	20*s*/d (Wotton),
c.1 Jan. 1540[c]	10*s*/d (Berde)
(Wotton)	

Both men went to Cleves. Wotton then went alone to Saxony, a mission for which he received new credentials, 25 Oct. 1539, and Berde seemingly returned briefly to England. Wotton went back to Cleves and apparently came to England in the train of Anne of Cleves, the English Queen designate.

Instructions (for Wotton as sole ambassador): Implied in HMC *4th Report*, pp. 412-13.

Correspondence: BL, Cotton, Vitel. B.xxi; *L&P*, xiv, 1-2; Merriman, R. B., *The Life and Letters of Cromwell*.

G17.
BERDE, Richard (*fl.*1530s)

July 1539[h] - c.late Aug. 1539[h]	[Agent?]
	10*s*/d?

He again went to Cleves, with Hans Holbein as a part of his company.

Correspondence about: *L&P*, xiv, 1.

G18.
MOUNT, Christopher (later Dr. Christopher; 1497-1572)*

4 Aug. 1539[b] - 15 Oct. 1539[b]	[Special Ambassador]
	20*s*/d

He went to Saxony.

Correspondence about: *L&P*, xiv, 2.

G19.
HOBY, Philip (later Sir Philip; 1505-1558)*

c.8 Nov. 1539[d] - c.25 Nov. 1539[g]	[Special Ambassador]

He went to Cleves.

Instructions: Implied in *L&P*, xiv, 2, no. 480.
Correspondence about: *L&P*, xiv.

G20.
WOTTON, Dr. Nicholas (later Sir Nicholas; 1497?-1567)*

25 Jan. 1540[e] - c.15 July 1541[g]   [Special Ambassador]
Audience (Cleves): 12 Feb. 1540

He went to Cleves and other parts of the Empire.

Instructions: Inferred in *L&P*, xv, 1, no. 243.
Correspondence: BL, Cotton, Vitel. B.xxi; *L&P*, xv-xvi.

G21.
MOUNT, Christopher (later Dr. Christopher; 1497-1572)*
PAYNELL, Thomas (*fl.*1520s-1560s)*

Feb. 1540[a] - Aug.? 1540[h]   [Special Ambassadors]
                                      13s 4d/d (Mount)

They went to the Frankfort Assembly, Cleves, and the Diet being held at
  Hagenow during the course of this poorly documented mission.

Instructions: BL, Cotton, Vitel. B.xxi, p. 133.
Correspondence: BL, Cotton, Vitel. B.xxi, f. 133; *L&P*, xv.

G22.
CLERK, Dr. John, Bishop of Bath and Wells (*d.*1541)*

22 June 1540[b] - d.3 Jan. 1541   [Special Ambassador]
Audience: 5 Aug. 1540   53s 4d/d

He joined with Wotton, who was already at Cleves.

Instructions: Suggested in *L&P*, xv, no. 970.
Correspondence: *L&P*, xv.

G23.
MOUNT, Dr. Christopher (1497-1572)*

Early 1542[h] - 1553[h]   [Resident Agent]
                                 13s 4d/d

He seems to have been permanently resident in various parts of Germany after
  Jan. 1542. He apparently had no official responsibilities during the reign of
  Mary Tudor.

Correspondence: BL, Cotton, Galba B.xi, Harl. 353; *L&P*, xvii - xxi; *CSPF*,
  1547-53; Tytler, P., *England under the Reigns of Edward VI ...* (1839), ii.

G24.
BUCLER, Walter (*fl.*1540s)

20 Apr. 1545[a] - 19 Dec. 1545[a]   [Special Ambassador]
                                           26s 8d/d

He joined with Christopher Mount in a visit to Hesse.

Instructions: *L&P*, xx, 1, no. 91.
Correspondence: *L&P*, xx. 1.

G25.
MORISON, Richard (later Sir Richard; *c*.1514-1556)*

23 Dec. 1546[b] - early Mar.? 1547[h]   [Special Ambassador]
Secretary: Jacques Granada?   26*s* 8*d*/d

Besides a number of the German princes, he also visited the Hanse towns (q.v.).
   Additionally, he served as Henry VIII's delegate to a peace conference
   between the Duke of Holstein and King Christian of Denmark, held in
   Holstein.

Instructions: *L&P*, xxi, 2, no. 647 (50).
Correspondence: *L&P*, xxi, 2; *CSPF, 1547-53*.

G26.
BORTHWICK, Sir John (*fl.*1540s-1550s)

1548[h] - 1553?[h]   [Agent]

Documentation is exceptionally poor, but he seems to have been an agent
   residing between these dates in northern Germany or perhaps in the Hanse
   towns. From his post, he undertook periodic contact with Denmark (q.v.).

Correspondence: *APC, 1550-2*.

G27.
SHERS, John (*fl.*1540s-1560s)

10 May 1553[c] - *c*.1 Nov. 1553[c]   [Special Ambassador]
                                               20*s*/d

At Vienna he visited Ferdinand I, King of the Romans, and Maximilian II, King
   of Bohemia.

Instructions: *CSPF, 1547-53*, no. 676.
Correspondence about: *CSPF, 1547-53, 1553-8*.

G28.
SHELLEY, Richard (later Sir Richard; 1513/14-1587)*

c.21 Dec. 1553[h] - *c*.1 Mar. 1554[c]   [Special Ambassador]
Audience: 24 Jan. 1554

He went to Ferdinand I, King of the Romans at Vienna.

Instructions: Inferred from *CSPF, 1553-8*, no. 137. The following instructions
   seem quite clearly to apply to this mission although they are variously, and
   presumably mistakenly, dated 1557 or 1558: BL, Sloane 2442, f. 116, Eg.
   2790, f. 141b, Add. 5935, f. 144, Harl. 289, f. 162, 353, f. 190; *CSPF,
   1558-9*, no. 74; HMC *2nd Report*, p. 96.
Correspondence: *CSPF, 1553-8*.

G29.
FITZALAN, Henry, Baron Maltravers (1538-1556)*

May 1556[n] - *d*.30 June 1556   [Special Ambassador?]

He visited Maximilian II, the King of Bohemia, at Brussels.

Instructions: Suggested in *CSPS, 1554-8*, p. 271.
Correspondence about: *CSPF, 1553-6*.

G30.
MOUNT, Dr. Christopher (1497-1572)*

14 Dec. 1558[b] - *d.*Oct.? 1572   Agent

He was formally the English agent in Germany, based in Strasbourg, during the
early years of Elizabeth's reign. His responsibilities involved periodic
assignments to all parts of the Empire, among them:

Spring 1559 - attendance at the Diet at Augsburg

Dec. 1559 - visits to the Elector Palatine and the Duke of Württemburg

Early 1561 - attendance at an assembly of Protestant princes at Naumburg plus
various princely courts including the Margrave of Baden

Spring 1562 - another visit to the Duke of Württemburg and the Elector Palatine

Sept. 1562 - he accompanied Henry Knollys (see below) on his mission to
various Protestant princes and to the Emperor (q.v.)

Late 1563 - he again undertook a visit to the Duke of Württemburg

1566 - he attended the Diet at Augsburg which included contact with the
Margrave of Brandenburg

Spring 1569 - he accompanied Henry Killigrew to various parts of Germany.

Correspondence: BL, Cotton, Galba B.xi, Nero B.ix, Lansd. 14; *CSPF* (all
vols. from 1558-1572); HMC *Salisb.*, i, xiii; KL, v - vi.

G31.
WAAD, Armigal (by 1518-1568)*

15 Apr. 1559[c] - *c.*20 Aug. 1559[e]   [Special Ambassador]
Audience: *c.*1 July 1559

He was sent to the Duke of Holstein.

Instructions: BL, Add. 5935, ff. 199-200, Sloane 2442, f. 70, Harl. 36, f. 75;
CSPF, 1558-9, no. 541.
Correspondence about: *CSPF, 1558-9*.

G32.
BRIGANTINE, John (*fl.*1560s)

26 Feb. 1560[g] - 1 Aug. 1561[b]   [Agent]
Audience (Countess of Emden):
*c.*15 Mar. 1560

He was primarily at Emden, but his responsibilities included contact with the
Bishop of Osnabrück.

Accreditation: BL, Royal 13.B.1, ff. 30-1.
Correspondence: BL, Add. 34837, Cotton, Calig. B.ix; *CSPF, 1559-60,
1560-1*.

G33.
KNOLLYS, Henry (*c*.1515-1582)*

25 Sept. 1562[d] - *c*.4 Feb. 1563[c]   [Special Ambassador]
Audience (Count Palatine):
  30 Aug. 1562
Audience (Landgrave of Hesse—by
  proxy): 14 Sept. 1562
Audience (Duke of Saxony):
  30 Sept. 1562
Audience (Duke of Zweibrücken):
  31 Sept. 1562
Audience (Duke of Württemburg):
  18 Oct. 1562
Audience (King of Bohemia):
  18 Nov. 1562

He was accompanied by Christopher Mount. They also visited the Emperor at Frankfurt (q.v.).

Instructions: Inferred from *CSPF, 1562*, no. 434; Wright, T. (ed.), *Queen Elizabeth and Her Times* ... (1838), i, p. 95.
Correspondence: *CSPF, 1562, 1562-3.*

G34.
RADCLIFFE, Thomas, 3rd Earl of Sussex (1526?-1583)*
NORTH, Roger, 2nd Baron North (1531-1600)*

On their journey to the Emperor at Vienna (q.v.), they also visited the Duke of Württemburg at Stuttgart, with an audience 20 July 1567.

G35.
KILLIGREW, Henry (later Sir Henry; *c*.1528-1603)*

26 Jan. 1569[b] - 22 Sept. 1569[b]   [Special Ambassador]
Audience (Hamburg): 6 Mar. 1569   40*s*/d
Audience (Heidelburg—Elector
  Palatine): 1 Apr. 1569
Audience (Cassel—Landgrave of
  Hesse): *c*.20 Mar. 1569

He visited a number of the princes of the Empire, especially the Elector Palatine. He was accompanied by Mount.

Instructions: BL, Eg. 2790, f. 153b, Sloane 2442, ff. 20-1, Add. 5935, ff. 167-9, Lansd. 155, ff. 392b-5, Harl. 289, no. 65; HMC *2nd Report*, p. 96.
Correspondence: BL, Cotton, Galba B.xi, Nero, B.ix; Cambridge, Magdalene College, Pepys Mss., ii; *CSPF, 1569-71*; HMC *Pepys*; HMC *Salisb.*, i.

G36.
WILKES, Thomas (later Sir Thomas; *c*.1541-1598)*

16 Feb. 1575[c] - *c*.10 Nov. 1575[e]   Agent

He was sent to Frederick III, the Elector Palatine, and he was sent also to secure soldiers from Germany for the Huguenot army in France. He returned to Germany in early Dec. 1575, but went almost immediately to France (q.v.) with the Huguenot army. He had brief returns to England in Apr. 1575 and Oct. 1575.

Instructions: *CSPF, 1575-7*, no. 27.
Correspondence: *CSPF, 1575-7*; KL, vii.

G37.
ROGERS, Daniel (*c.*1538-1591)*

While in the Low Countries (q.v.) as an agent, he visited the Duke Casimir at Neustadt, with an audience on 18 Aug. 1576.

G38.
SIDNEY, Philip (later Sir Philip; 1554-1586)*

7 Feb. 1577[a] - 8 June 1577[a]	[Special Ambassador]
Audience (Elector Palatine):	53s 4d/d
c.1 May 1577	

He visited the Elector Palatine and various Protestant princes, as well as the Emperor Rudolph at Prague (q.v.). He also visited the Prince of Orange in the Low Countries (q.v.) on his return journey.

Instructions: BL, Sloane 2442, ff. 38-9, Eg. 2780, f. 218; HMC *2nd Report*, p. 97.
Correspondence: *CSPF, 1575-7*.

G39.
ALLEN, Richard (*d.*1602)

Early May 1577[h] - c.15 June 1577[e]	Special Ambassador
	£280 (total?)

He went to William, Landgrave of Hesse.

Instructions: Suggested in PRO, E/403/2559, f. 124; *CSPF, 1575-7*, nos. 1437, 1441.
Correspondence: *CSPF, 1575-7, 1577-8*.

G40.
BEALE, Robert (1541-1601)*

15 Aug. 1577[a] - 6 Feb. 1578[a]	[Special Ambassador]
Audience (Elector Palatine—	40s/d
Heidelburg): 27 Sept. 1577	
Audience (Duke Casimir—Neustadt):	
1 Oct. 1577	
Audience (Duke of Saxony): mid-Sept.	
1577?	

He joined with Daniel Rogers (see below). They were accredited to the Duke of Brunswick and Lüneburg, the Landgrave of Hesse, the Duke and Duchess of

Saxony, the Count Palatine, the Elector of Brandenburg, the Duke of Württemburg and Teck, the Marquis of Baden and the Duke Casimir.

Instructions: *CSPF, 1575-8*, nos. 131, 131A.
Correspondence: *CSPF, 1575-7*; HMC *9th Report*; KL, ix.

G41.
ROGERS, Daniel (*c.*1538-1591)*

While serving as an agent in the Low Countries (q.v.), he visited various German states. He had audience with the Elector Palatine, 1 Sept. 1577; and with the Landgrave of Hesse, 15 Sept. 1577. He also apparently visited Saxony.

Instructions: BL, Cotton, Galba C.v, pt. 1, ff. 3-4; *CSPF, 1575-7*, nos. 1486, 1492.
Correspondence: *CSPF, 1577-8*.

G42.

Again, while serving in the Low Countries, he visited the Duke Casimir at Kaiserslautern, 10 Apr. 1578.

G43.

5 Dec. 1578[d] - mid-Jan. 1579[c]

He went to the Duke Casimir and the Elector Palatine. He was also sent to the Low Countries (q.v.).

Instructions: *CSPF, 1578-9*, no. 439.
Correspondence: *CSPF, 1578-9*.

G44.

7 Sept. 1580[c] - *c.*Jan. 1585[h]   [Special Ambassador]

He was sent to the Emperor (q.v.) and also to the Lutheran bishops. In fact, he was captured at the outset of this mission and spent the next four years imprisoned.

Instructions: BL, Sloane 2442, f. 69; *CSPF, 1579-80*, no. 441.
Correspondence: BL, Cotton, Galba C.vii, Harl. 285, Lansd. 42; *CSPF, 1579-80, 1581-2, 1582, 1583, 1583-4, 1584-5*.

G45.
LESIEUR, Stephen (later Sir Stephen; *d.*1627)*

22 Apr. 1581[h] - *c.*30 Oct. 1582[c]   [Agent]
Audience (with Parma): 6 Mar. 1582

He went to various cities and princes, including the Duke of Cleves and the Prince of Parma at Tournai, to try to effect the release of Daniel Rogers. There was much travelling and returning to his base of operations at Antwerp during this period.

Correspondence: *CSPF, 1581-2, 1582*.

G46.
HERBERT, John (later Sir John; *c*.1540-1617)*

16 May 1583[b] - *c*.1 Sept. 1585[e]   [Special Ambassador]
Audience (Prussia): *c*.Apr. 1585

He left Denmark (q.v.) in autumn 1583 and went, both before and after Prussia, to Poland and to the Hanse towns (qq.v.).

Instructions: PRO, SP/88/1, no. 26.
Correspondence: BL, Cotton, Galba D.xiii; *CSPF, 1583*; Talbot, *Res Polonicae*.

G47.
LESIEUR, Stephen (later Sir Stephen; *d*.1627)*

1 Mar. 1584[a] - 26 Dec. 1584[b]   [Special Ambassador]
                                   ad hoc

He was sent from Antwerp to the Duke of Cleves to further the release of Daniel Rogers. As with previous negotiations in this matter, this mission was conducted intermittently, with considerable travel back and forth.

Correspondence: *CSPF, 1583-4*.

G48.
BODLEY, Thomas (later Sir Thomas; 1545-1613)*

27 Apr. 1585[b] - *c*.15 Aug. 1585[g]   [Special Ambassador]
Audience (Brunswick): 13 May 1585

Besides the Duke of Brunswick, whose council he saw (but not the Duke, because of that prince's illness), he also went to Denmark (q.v.).

Instructions: BL, Cotton, Nero B.iii, ff. 271-4; *CSPF, 1584-5*, pp. 415-16.
Correspondence: PRO, SP/82/3; BL, Cotton, Galba C.viii, ix, D.ix, xiii, Vesp. F.iii; *CSPF, 1584-5*.

G49.
BERTIE, Peregrine, Baron Willoughby d'Eresby (1555-1601)*

28 Jun. 1585[b] - *c*.1 Mar. 1586[h]   [Special Ambassador]
Audience: 26 Sept. 1585   £4/d

He also visited Denmark (q.v.).

Instructions: BL, Cotton, Julius F.vi, f. 184b, Nero B.iii, ff. 244- 6; inferred from *CSPF, 1585-6*, pp. 255-7; HMC *Ancaster*, p. 17.
Correspondence: BL, Cotton, Nero B.iii, Titus C.vii, ff. 226-35 (a summary of the mission by Willoughby); *CSPF, 1585-6*; HMC *Ancaster*.

G50.
PALAVICINO, Sir Horatio (*d*.1600)*

12 Feb. 1590[a] - *c*.26 Jun. 1590[c]   Special Ambassador
Audience (Dresden—Elector of Saxony:
  17 Feb. 1590
Arrived (Frankfurt): 22 Apr. 1590   53*s* 4*d*/d

Instructions: PRO, SP/81/5, f. 104, SP/81/6, f. 101; *L&A, 1589-90*, nos. 725-8.
Correspondence: PRO, SP/81/6; *L&A, 1589-90*.

G51.

28 Nov. 1590[a] - early Aug. 1591[h]   [Special Ambassador]

Arrived (at Torgau Conference): end   53*s* 4*d*/d
   Feb. 1591

He went to Germany with Henri de la Tour d'Auvergne, Viscount de Turenne, an ambassador of France's Henry IV. They also went to the Low Countries (q.v.).

Instructions: PRO, SP/81/6, ff. 86-95, 110-11; *L&A, 1590-1*, nos. 753-6; PRO, 'Report on the Royal Archives of Denmark,' *Reports of the Deputy Keeper*, xlv (1884) app. ii, p. 31.
Correspondence: PRO, SP/81/6-7; HMC *De Lisle and Dudley*, ii; *L&A, 1590-1, 1591-2*; PRO, 'Report on the Royal Archives of Denmark,' *Reports of the Deputy Keeper*, xlv (1884) app. ii.

G52.
PARKINS, Dr. Christopher (later Sir Christopher; *c*.1543-1622)*

9 May 1590[b] - *c*.26 July 1591[c]   [Special Ambassador]
Audience (Ansbach): 8 Oct. 1590

He met with the Duke of Prussia at Ansbach. This mission also included various Hanse towns, Poland and Denmark (qq.v.).

Instructions: Inferred from PRO, SP/75/2, ff. 128-33.
Correspondence: PRO, SP/103/31; *L&A, 1589-90, 1590-1*.

G53.

20 Apr. 1593[a] - early Sept. 1593[e]   Special Ambassador
Audience (Prague): 27 June 1593   40*s*/d

His primary objective was the Emperor (q.v.), but he visited the Duke of Brunswick, the Duke of Hamburg, the Elector Palatine, the Marquis of Baden, the Bishop of Metz, the Marquis of Ansbach, the Duke of Holstein, the Duke of Mecklenburg, the Duke of Lüneburg, the Landgrave of Hesse and other German princes.

Instructions: Inferred from PRO, SP/75/2, ff. 128-33, SP/80/1, ff. 140-2, 146-51; *L&A, 1591-2*, no. 889.
Correspondence: PRO, SP/80/1, SP/81/7.

G54.
CLINTON, Henry Fiennes de, Earl of Lincoln (*d*.1616)*

30 June 1596[a] - Sept. 1596[h]   [Special Ambassador]
Audience (Landgrave of Hesse):   £5/d
   mid-Aug. 1596
Secretary: John Wroth

John Wroth may well have been a secretary on this mission to the Landgrave of Hesse, but he then went independently to visit the Palatinate and other German principalities in late 1596 and early 1597 (see below).

Correspondence: PRO, SP/81/7-8; HMC *Salisb.*, vii.

G55.
WROTH, John (*d.* after 1616)*

30 June 1596^a - early 1597^h [Special Ambassador]
                                            £70 (total?)

Beginning as an attendant to the Earl of Lincoln (above), he subsequently was instructed to go independently to the Palatinate and other German principalities.

Correspondence: HMC *Salisb.*, vi.
Correspondence about: PRO, E/403/2560, f. 115

G56.
LESIEUR, Stephen (later Sir Stephen; *d.*1627)*
WROTH, John (*d.* after 1616)*

26 Dec. 1597^a - 22 Apr. 1598^a [Special Ambassador]
       (Lesieur)   20*s*/d (each)
       22 June 1598^b
       (Wroth)
Audience (Archbishop of Bremen):
  1 Feb. 1598
Audience (Duke of Brunswick at
  Hamburg): 6 Feb. 1598
Audience (Duke of Mecklenburg):
  13 Feb. 1598
Audience (Elector of Brandenburg):
  21 Feb. 1598
Audience (Prince of Anhalt):
  25 Feb. 1598
Audience (Duke of Brunswick—again):
  2 Mar. 1598

They also visited various Hanse towns (q.v.). In addition, Wroth apparently went to the Emperor (q.v.).

Instructions: Inferred from PRO, SP/81/8, ff. 46-52.
Correspondence: PRO, SP/81/8; HMC *Salisb.* xii.

G57.
CAREW, George (later Sir George; *d.*1612)*

20 May 1598^a - 21 Dec. 1598^b [Special Ambassador]
Audience (Brunswick): 23 July 1598   40*s*/d

Besides northern German and Hanse (q.v.) areas, this mission included stops in Denmark and Poland (qq.v.).

Instructions: PRO, SP/88/2, ff. 48-58.
Correspondence: PRO, SP/81/8.
Correspondence about: HMC *Salisb.*, viii.

G58.
LESIEUR, Stephen (later Sir Stephen; *d.*1627)*

11 Jan. 1599*ª* - 9 Sept. 1599*ᵇ*   Agent
Arrived (Frankfurt): 25 Feb. 1599   20*s*/d
Arrived (Speyer): *c.*1 Mar. 1599

He was sent to attend the Imperial Diet at Speyer.

Correspondence: PRO, SP/81/8; HMC *Salisb.*, ix.

G59.

1 June 1603*ª* - 21 Jan. 1604*ᵇ*   [Special Ambassador]
                                          40*s*/d

Besides the Emperor (q.v.), he visited the Duke of Saxony and other German
    princes.

Instructions: Rymer, T., *Foedera...*, xvi, p. 518.
Correspondence: PRO, SP/80/1-2, SP/81/9.

G60.
SPENCER, Robert, Baron Spencer of Wormleighton (1570-1627)*

6 Sept. 1603*ª* - 24 Dec. 1603*ᵇ*   [Special Ambassador]
Investment: 6 Nov. 1603   £4/d

He travelled to the court of Württemburg to invest the Duke with the Garter.

Commission: BL, Add. 41613, f. 19b.
Correspondence: BL, Add. 25079, 34079; Cotton, Calig. E.x.

G61.
WINWOOD, Sir Ralph (1563?-1617)*

24 June 1610*ª* - 2 Nov. 1610*ᵇ*   [Special Ambassador]
Audience (Cleves): 30 June 1610   30*s*/d (in addition to regular
                                              66*s* 8*d*/d)

He undertook this mission while regularly assigned as resident in the Low
    Countries (q.v.). He visited the duchies of Jülich and Cleves.

Instructions: Sawyer, E. (ed.), *Memorials of Affairs of State* ... (1725), iii,
    p. 112.
Correspondence: PRO, SP/81/10, SP/84/67-8, SP/105/93; BL, Stowe 171- 2;
    CSPD, 1603-10.

G62.
DICKENSON, John (*fl.*1610s)

15 Nov. 1610*ª* - 12 Jan. 1615*ᵇ*   Agent
Audience: 14 Dec. 1610   20*s*/d

He remained at the court of the Duke of Cleves in Düsseldorf. He travelled to the court of Brandenburg in late winter, 1613.

Correspondence: PRO, SP/81/10-13; BL, Stowe 172.

G63.
WINWOOD, Sir Ralph (1563?-1617)*

Mar. 1612[h] - May 1612[h]   [Special Ambassador]

Again during his residency in the Low Countries, he undertook a mission into Germany, this time to the Protestant princes at Wesel.

G64.
LESIEUR, Sir Stephen (*d.*1627)*

1 Aug. 1612[a] - 11 July 1614[b]   [Special Ambassador]
Audience (Düsseldorf): early Nov.   £4/d
  1612

He was resident at Vienna (Emperor, q.v.); and visited a variety of the Protestant princes during that assignment.

Instructions: PRO, SP/80/2, f. 206.
Correspondence: PRO, SP/80/2-3, SP/81/13.

G65.
WOTTON, Sir Henry (1568-1639)*

While on a mission to the Low Countries, he visited the German courts of Brandenburg, Neuburg and Brunswick, *c.*16 Sept. 1614 to late Nov. 1614.

Correspondence: PRO, SP/81/13; BL, Stowe 175.

G66.
CALVERT, George (later 1st Baron Baltimore; 1580?-1632)*

25 Mar. 1615[a] - *c.*1 July 1615[h]   [Special Ambassador]
                                             53*s* 4*d*/d

He visited the Elector Palatine.

G67.
WOTTON, Sir Henry (1568-1639)*

Wotton visited at least the Elector Palatine and perhaps other German princes on his trip to assume his residency at Venice (q.v.), late Apr. 1616.

G68.
MORTON, Sir Albert (1584?-1625)*

30 Oct. 1617[b] - *c.*11 Mar. 1621[c]   Agent
                                               £165/an.

He was assigned as the agent with the Protestant Princes of the Union. He returned to London repeatedly during this assignment.

Correspondence: PRO, SP/81/15, 19-20.

G69.
WAKE, Sir Isaac (1580-1632)*

He undertook an assignment to Germany in Apr. 1619, while he was resident at Savoy (q.v.). He returned to Turin late May 1619 after having apparently visited only the Palatinate.

Correspondence: PRO, SP/81/16.

G70.
HAY, James, 1st Viscount Doncaster (later Earl of Carlisle; *c.*1580- 1636)*

29 Apr. 1619[b] - 1 Jan. 1620[a]   Ambassador Extraordinary
Secretary: Francis Nethersole   £6/d (through Aug. 1617)

He visited both the Imperial Court (q.v.) and various German princes including the Princes of the Union. On his journey to the Emperor at Munich, he visited the Archdukes in the Spanish Netherlands (q.v.) and upon his return, he visited the States General of the Low Countries (q.v.).

Instructions: Gardiner, S. R. (ed.), *Letters...Illustrating the Relations Between England and Germany 1618-1620*, Camden o.s., xc (1865), p. 64; also summarized in PRO, SP/81/16, ff. 68-73, 249-50, 302-05.
Correspondence: PRO, SP/81/16; BL, Eg. 2593; Bodl., Tanner Mss. 74; HMC *Westmoreland, Stewart...*; Gardiner (ed.), *Letters ... 1618-1620*; Birch, T., *The Court and Times of James I ...* (1849).

G71.
WOTTON, Sir Henry (1568-1639)*

While returning home from his residency at Venice (q.v.), he visited, in June-July of 1619, the Elector Palatine and other Princes of the Union.

Instructions: PRO, SP/81/16, f. 10; Gardiner, S. R. (ed.), *Letters...Illustrating the Relations between England and Germany... 1618-20*, Camden o.s., xc (1865), p. 87.

G72.
NETHERSOLE, Sir Francis (1587-1659)*

23 Sept. 1619[a] - *c.*June 1633[b]   Agent
Audience: 5 Aug. 1620   £165/an.

He apparently served as an intermittent agent to the Protestant Princes of the Union simultaneously with his chores as secretary to Princess Elizabeth at Heidelberg. He had numerous and extended returns to England during this period.

Correspondence: PRO, SP/80/3, SP/81/17-41; BL, Eg. 2593, Add. 5950; *CSPD, 1619-23, 1623-5, 1625-6*; Boyd, D., 'Sir Francis Nethersole: His Life and Letters,' (Unpub. Ph.D. dissertation, Temple University, 1972).

G73.
WOTTON, Sir Henry (1568-1639)*

3 Jun. 1620*ᵇ* - Mar. 1621*ᶠ*   Ambassador Extraordinary
                                       £5/d

He was sent to the Emperor (q.v.) at Vienna and to various other princes of the
   Empire (including the Prince Palatine, the Princes of the Union and the
   Archbishop of Treves) on his return to Venice (q.v.).

Accreditation: PRO, SP/81/17, ff. 87-91.
Correspondence: PRO, SP/81/18, SP/80/3; Watson, C. (ed.), 'Letters from Sir
   Henry Wotton to King James I...,' *Archaeologia*, xl, pp. 257-84; Wotton, Sir
   H., *Letters and Dispatches from Sir Henry Wotton to James the First in the
   years MDCXVII-XX* ...ed. G. Tomline (Roxburghe Club, 1850).

G74.
WESTON, Sir Richard (later 1st Earl of Portland; 1577-1635)*
CONWAY, Sir Edward (later Viscount Conway; *d.*1631)*

1 June 1620*ᵃ* - *c.*9 Mar. 1621*ᶜ*   Ambassadors Extraordinary
Assistant: John Dickenson   £4/d (Conway)

In Germany they visited Mainz, Saxony, Treves and Noviberge. They also
   stopped in the Spanish Netherlands and in the Low Countries (qq.v.).

Instructions: BL, Add. 35832, f. 11.
Correspondence: PRO, SP/81/17-20; BL, Add. 35832, Eg. 2593.

G75.
VILLIERS, Sir Edward (1585?-1626)*

1 Jan. 1621*ᵍ* - *c.*10 Apr. 1621*ᶜ*   [Special Ambassador]
He was sent to the Elector Palatine (the King of Bohemia).
Correspondence: PRO, SP/81/19-20.

G76.
TRUMBULL, William (*d.*1635)*

While an agent in the Spanish Netherlands (q.v.), he undertook a mission to the
   Princes of the Union, *c.*Apr. 1621 through mid- summer 1621.

G77.
DIGBY, John, Baron Digby (later 1st Earl of Bristol; 1580-1653)*

7 May 1621*ᵇ* - 1 Nov. 1621*ᶜ*   [Special Ambassador]
Audience (Heidelberg): mid-Oct. 1621

Besides the Palatinate, he also visited the Emperor and the Spanish Netherlands
   (qq.v.).

Instructions: PRO, SP/80/4, ff. 22-3; BL, Add. 35897, f. 54b.

G78.
VILLIERS, Sir Edward (1585?-1626)*

*c.*1 Sept. 1621*ᶜ* - *c.*10 Oct. 1621*ᵉ*   [Special Ambassador]
Audience (Palatinate): 2 Oct. 1621
Instructions: Inferred from *CSPV, 1621-3*, pp. 130-1.

G79.
CHICHESTER, Arthur, Baron Chichester of Belfast (1563-1625)*

18 Feb. 1622*ᵇ* - 5 Nov. 1622*ᵃ*   Ambassador Extraordinary
Audience (Heidelberg): 1 June 1622   £6/d
Secretary: William Beecher

He visited the Elector Palatine, but, despite extensive discussion about it, he
  never went, after all, to the Imperial Court. He also visited the Low Countries
  (q.v.) on his way to the Palatinate.

Correspondence: PRO, SP/81/24-7; Oxford, Mss. at All Souls Lib., clxxx.

G80.
BEECHER, William (later Sir William; *d.*1651)

1 Nov. 1624*ᵃ* - 27 Mar. 1625*ᵇ*   Agent
                                         £3/d

He apparently returned to England from this assignment in the early part of
  1625, and there he prepared for a return to the Count of Mansfeld, a mission
  to be undertaken under the same privy seal. This mission was cancelled upon
  James I's death, which terminated Beecher's privy seal and pay.

Correspondence: PRO, SP/81/31-2; *CSPD, 1623-5*.

G81.
ANSTRUTHER, Sir Robert (*fl.*1600s-1640s)

While serving as ambassador to Denmark (q.v.), he visited Saxony, Oct. to
  Nov. 1624.

Instructions: Inferred from *CSPV, 1623-5*, pp. 487-90.

G82.

Again, while ambassador in Denmark (q.v.), he visited Brandenburg, and
  perhaps the Imperial Diet, summer 1627.

Instructions: PRO, SP/80/6, ff. 139-40.

G83.
VANE, Sir Henry (1589-1655)*

While on a mission to the Low Countries (q.v.), he visited the Palatine royals at
  Rhenen, Apr. 1629.

G84.
ROE, Sir Thomas (1581?-1644)*

On his way to the peace negotiations betwen Sweden and Poland (qq.v.), he had
  audience with the Prince Palatine, 7 July 1629, and at Brandenburg, 18 Aug.
  1629.

G85.
BELL, Capt. Henry (*fl.*1620s-1630s)

23 May 1629[b] - n.d.   [Special Ambassador]

He was sent to the Elector of Brandenburg and the Palsgrave of Neuburg.

G86.
ANSTRUTHER, Sir Robert (*fl.*1600s-1640s)

While ambassador to Denmark (q.v.), he attended the Imperial Diet at Ratisbone
(q.v.), June - Dec. 1630, and made contact as well with a variety of German
princes.

Correspondence: *CSPD, 1629-31.*

G87.
VANE, Sir Henry (1589-1655)*

Besides Sweden and Denmark (qq.v.) in his 1631-2 mission, he also visited the
Palatinate.

G88.
HOWARD, Thomas, 2nd Earl of Arundel and Surrey (later Earl of Norfolk;
1585-1646)*

10 Dec. 1632[a] - 4 Feb. 1633[a]   [Ambassador Extraordinary]
                                      £8/d

He visited Heidelberg, and the Low Countries (q.v.) as well.

Correspondence: Hervey, M., *The Life...of Thomas Howard, Earl of Arundel...*
(Cambridge, 1921); Tierney, M., *The History and Antiquities of the Castle
and Town of Arundel ...* (1834).

G89.
BOSWELL, Sir William (*d.*1649)*

While resident agent in the Low Countries (q.v.), he travelled, in early 1635, to
invest Prince Charles, Elector Palatine, with the Order of the Garter.

G90.
AVERY, Joseph (*fl.*1630s-1660s)

While agent with the Hanse towns and at Denmark (qq.v.), he visited Saxony
and Brandenburg, 1636-7.

G91.
FLEMING, Oliver (*fl.*1620s-1640s)

While ambassador to Switzerland (q.v.), he was sent to the Duke of Saxe-
Weimar in 1638.

G92.
CURTIUS, William (later Sir William, Bart.; *fl.*1630s-1670s)

17 Sept. 1639[a] - 1658[c]   Agent
                                  40s/d

He was sent as a representative of England to the several German princes by both Charles I and Charles II. He served late into the Commonwealth period. He appointment was episodic, but included assignments to the Imperial Diets (q.v.), such as in late 1639, and also in 1642 and 1649.

Instructions: PRO, SP/81/48, ff. 145.
Correspondence: PRO, SP/81/49-55; BL, Add. 15856, 37047, 38175, Eg. 2536, 2542; *CSPD, 1641-3*.

G93.
WAYTE, George (*fl.*1650s)

c.Dec. 1656[h] - n.d.   [Special Ambassador]

He visited Brandenburg.

Correspondence: PRO, SP/81/54, f. 171.

G94.
JEPHSON, Col. William (1615?-1659?)*

25 Aug. 1657[a] - *c*.15 Aug. 1658[c]   Ambassador Extraordinary
Audience: 20 Apr. 1658

He also went to Sweden and the Hanse towns (qq.v.).

Instructions: *ThSP*, vi, pp. 63, 471, 478-80.
Correspondence: *ThSP*, vi-vii; Jenks, E., 'Some Correspondence of Thurloe and Meadows,' *EHR*, vii (1892), pp. 720-42.

G95.
BETRIDGE, Col. Roger (*fl.*1660s)*

4 July 1664[b] - *c*.20 Sept. 1664[e]   [Special Ambassador]

He was sent to the Palatinate and Mainz.

Instructions: Inferred in part from PRO, SP/81/56, ff. 93-4.
Correspondence: PRO, SP/81/56.

G96.
CURTIUS, William (later Sir William, Bart.; *fl.*1630s-1670s)

5 Aug. 1664[b] - Sept. 1677[d]   [Resident Ambassador]

He was resident at Frankfurt am Main, and although he became less diplomatically active as time passed, he continued to send letters until his recredentialling in Sept. 1677. He seemingly visited the Palatinate in 1666.

Correspondence: PRO, SP/81/56-73, SP/104/56; BL, Add. 15857, 25122.

G97.
TEMPLE, Sir William (later 1st Bart.; 1628-1699)*

22 June 1665[c] - 8 Oct. 1665[f]   [Special Ambassador]
Audience: 5 July 1665

Temple's first assignment was as an envoy to Christopher Bernard von Ghalen,

Prince/Bishop of Münster, though he spent the majority of his time at Brussels during this assignment. He was eventually to become the resident ambassador in Brussels (q.v.).

Instructions: BL, Add. 9796, ff. 2-5; Courtenay, T., *Memoirs of...Sir William Temple* (1836), ii, App. B, pp. 377-80; Bennet, H., *...the Earl of Arlington's Letters to Sir William Temple...* (1701), i, pp. 9-13.

Correspondence: PRO, SP/77/33, SP/81/57; Courtenay, T., *Memoirs*, i; Bennet, H., *...the Earl of Arlington's Letters to Sir W. Temple...* (1701); Haley, K. H. D., *An English Diplomat in the Low Countries* (1986).

G98.

TAAFE, Theobald, 1st Earl of Carlingford (*d.*1677)*

22 Aug. 1665^c - *c.*10 Feb. 1667^c Envoy Extraordinary, later
Audience (Philip William of Neuburg): Ambassador Extraordinary
   21 Sept. 1665
Audience (Bishop of Münster):
   1 Oct. 1665
Audience (Princes of Brunswick-
   Lüneburg): 16 Oct. 1665
Audience (Elector of Brandenburg):
   1 Nov. 1665
Audience (Hesse-Cassel):
   *c.*15 Nov. 1665
Audience (Mainz): *c.*24 Nov. 1665
Secretary: William Loving, then John
   Martin

On his journey to the Emperor (q.v.), he visited the Spanish Netherlands (q.v.) and numerous German princes.

Instructions: Bennet, Henry, *...the Earl of Arlington's Letters to Sir W. Temple...*(1701), i, pp. 21-9; [Taafe, Karl Graf], *Memoirs of the Family Taafe* (Vienna, 1856), pp. 31-6.

Correspondence: PRO, SP/80/11, SP/81/56-7; [Taafe], *Memoirs*.

G99.

VANE, Sir Walter (*fl.*1660s-1670s)*

Late Nov. 1665^h - *c.*1 Mar. 1666^e [Special Ambassador]
Audience (Duke of Cleves): *c.*12 Dec.
   1665
Audience (Elector of Brandenburg): late
   Dec. 1665
Secretary: John Locke

He also visited the Spanish Netherlands (q.v.) on his journey into Germany.

Instructions: BL, Stowe 191, ff. 6-11; implied in BL, Add. 16272, f. 55.
Correspondence: PRO, SP/81/56-7; BL, Add. 16272 (letterbook).

G100.
THYNNE, Sir Thomas (later Viscount Weymouth; 1640-1714)*

In travelling home in Feb. 1669 from his residency in Sweden (q.v.), he visited the Dukes of Lüneburg and also Hamburg (Hanse, q.v.).

G101.
HOWARD, Charles, 1st Earl of Carlisle (1629-1685)*

On his journey from his embassy to Sweden (q.v.) in Sept.-Oct 1669, he visited the Dukes of Lüneburg.

G102.
HIGGONS, Sir Thomas (1624-1691)*

12 July 1668*ᵃ* - 31 May 1669*ᵃ*	Envoy Extraordinary
Investment: 18 Apr. 1669	£3/d

He invested the Elector of Saxony with the Order of the Garter. He was accompanied by Thomas St. George, Somerset Herald. He also visited Hamburg (Hanse, q.v.) on his journey to Saxony.

Instructions: PRO, SP/104/174B, ff. 175-6; BL, Stowe 191, ff. 16-17.
Correspondence: PRO, SP/81/58.

G103.
SILVIUS, Sir Gabriel (*fl.*1660s-1680s)

1 Feb. 1669*ᵃ* - 12 Sept. 1669*ᵃ*	Envoy Extraordinary
Audience (Lüneburg): *c.*13 Apr. 1669	£3/d
Audience (Brandenburg): 12 May 1669	

He was sent to Brandenburg, Brunswick, Hanover and Lüneburg. He also visited the Hague (Low Countries, q.v.).

Instructions: PRO, SP/104/174B, ff. 173-4; BL, Stowe 191, ff. 14-15.
Correspondence: PRO, SP/81/58.

G104.
BELASYSE, Thomas, Viscount Fauconberg (later Earl of Fauconberg; 1627-1700)*

On his journey to parts of Italy including, most importantly, Venice (qq.v.), he visited some principalities in Germany, including Treves, Dec. 1669. He also stopped in France and Savoy (qq.v.).

G105.
KEENE, William (*fl.*1670s)

26 Oct. 1670*ᶜ* - 1670*ʰ*	[Special Ambassador]

He was sent to the Palatinate.

Instructions: BL, Stowe 191, ff. 24-5.

G106.
SWANN, Sir William (*d.*1678)
While resident with the Hanse, he visited Hanover in 1671.
Correspondence: PRO, SP/81/80.

G107.
LOCKHART, Sir William (1621-1675)*

14 Mar. 1672[c] - 17 June 1672[a]   Envoy Extraordinary
Audience (Hesse): 12 Apr. 1672
Audience (Hanover): *c.*19 Apr. 1672
Audience (Brandenburg): 25 Apr. 1672

He was sent to Hesse, Hanover and Brandenburg. He also visited the French
    Court (q.v.) on his way to Germany, and in company with Sir Henry Sidney.
Instructions: PRO, SP/81/59, ff. 142-4, SP/104/64.
Correspondence: PRO, SP/81/59.

G108.
DODINGTON, John (*d.*1674)

He visited the Palatinate on his journey from his residency in Venice (q.v.),
    winter 1672-3.

G109.
SWANN, Sir William (*d.*1678)
While resident with the Hanse (q.v.), he visited Hanover in Feb. 1676.

G110.

Again while resident with the Hanse (q.v.), he visited the Elector of Saxony in
    Dresden from 11 Apr. to 12 May 1678. Audience in Dresden: 21 Apr. 1678.
    Similarly, he paid a visit of compliment to Duke Charles William of Anhalt,
    16 Apr. 1678.
Correspondence: PRO, SP/81/80; Oxford, Mss. at All Souls Lib., ccxl.

G111.
POLEY, Edmund (*fl.*1670s-1680s)

30 Oct. 1679[a] - 23 Jan. 1682[f]   Resident Ambassador
                                30*s*/d; 40*s*/d (after 30 Nov. 1681)

He was resident at Brandenburg. He went directly from Brandenburg to assume
    the residency at the Imperial Court (q.v.).
Instructions: PRO, SP/104/58, pp. 44-6.
Correspondence: PRO, SP/81/83-5, SP/104/58; BL, Add. 35104, 37986-7.

G112.
SOUTHWELL, Robert (1635-1702)*

1 Mar. 1680[a] - 14 Nov. 1680[a]   Envoy Extraordinary
Audience (Brandenburg): 14 Apr.   £5/d
    1680
Secretary: Edmund Poley

He was sent to Brandenburg, and also visited Brunswick/Lüneburg and Saxony. He also apparently visited the Prince of Orange (Low Countries, q.v.) on his way to Brandenburg.

Instructions: PRO, SP/81/82, ff. 15-18, 124-7, SP/104/57, ff. 38-50, 86-8; Oxford, Mss. at All Souls Lib., ccxli, f. 230.

Correspondence: PRO, SP/81/82-4, SP/105/49.

G113.
SILVIUS, Sir Gabriel (*fl.*1660s-1680s)

8 Mar. 1680[a] - 21 Oct. 1681[b]   Envoy Extraordinary
Audience (Münster): 2 May 1680   £5/d
Audience (Lüneburg): *c.*14 May, 1680
Audience (Hesse-Cassel): June 1680
Audience (Hanover): *c.*15 Jun. 1680

He was assigned to visit Hanover, the Bishop of Münster, the Landgrave of Hesse-Cassel, the Dukes of Brunswick and Lüneburg and the Duchy of Brandenburg. He also visited the Prince of Orange in the Low Countries on his journey (q.v.).

Instructions: PRO, SP/104/57, pp. 56-68; Oxford, Mss. at All Souls Lib., ccxlviii, pp. 29-33.

Correspondence: PRO, SP/81/82-4, SP/104/57, 189, 193; Bodl., Rawlinson Mss. C.727.

G114.
BERTIE, Charles (*c.*1641-1711)*

15 Oct. 1680[a] - 7 June 1681[b]   Envoy Extraordinary
Audience (Cologne): 13 Nov. 1680   £5/d
Audience (Trier): *c.*21 Jan. 1681
Audience (Mainz): *c.*30 Jan. 1681
Audience (Palatinate): *c.*Apr. 1681
Audience (Hesse-Cassel): 8 Apr. 1681

In this mission, he visited the electors of the Rhine.

Instructions: PRO, SP/104/57, pp. 100-110; Oxford, Mss. at All Souls Lib. 248, pp. 67, 106.

Correspondence: PRO, SP/81/84, SP/104/193; BL, Add. 27277, 35104.

G115.
LEGGE, Capt. William (*c.*1650-*c.*1697)*

19 Nov. 1680[b] - *c.*21 Jan. 1681[d]   Ambassador Extraordinary

He visited Hesse-Cassel, and also stopped in the Spanish Netherlands (q.v.).

Credentials: PRO, SP/104/57, p. 122.
Correspondence: PRO, SP/77/52.

G116.
SKELTON, Bevil (*died c.*1692)

14 Nov. 1681[a] - 3 Mar. 1685[b]   Envoy Extraordinary
Audience (Brunswick): 31 Jan. 1682   £5/d
Audience (Saxony): spring 1682

He was accredited to most German courts as a permanent, though roving ambassador. His credentials included the Hanse towns (q.v.), and in fact he was apparently stationed in Hamburg. He visited the Low Countries (q.v.) at least on his journey into Germany, and probably repeatedly during his tenure. He also visited Denmark (q.v.), Apr. - May 1684.

Instructions: PRO, SP/104/58, pp. 38-43.
Correspondence: PRO, SP/82/16, SP/104/190; BL, Add. 25119, 35104, 37983-4, 38847, 41824, Royal, King's 140; Oxford, Mss. at All Souls Lib., ccxlvii.

G117.
HOGIUS, Dr. Johann (*fl.*1680s)

Feb. 1686[d] - 1686[h]   Agent

He was designated agent at Cologne.

THE HANSE TOWNS

(Including, among other towns, Bremen, Brunswick, Danzig, Elbing, Emden, Hamburg, Stade and Lübeck)

H1.
KNIGHT, Dr. William (later Bishop of Bath and Wells; 1476-1547)*
SAMPSON, Dr. Richard (later Bishop of Coventry and Lichfield; d.1554)*
MORE, Thomas (later Sir Thomas; 1477/8-1535)*
WILTSHIRE, Sir John (*fl*.1520s)*

10 June 1520^b - Oct.? 1520^h [Special Ambassador]
First meeting: 13 Sept. 1520

They negotiated at Bruges over trade disputes with representatives of the Hanse towns.

Instructions: Inferred from *L&P*, iii, 1, nos. 868, 979.
Correspondence: *L&P*, iii, 1.

H2.
LEE, Dr. Thomas (later Sir Thomas; by 1511-1545)*

21 Dec. 1532^a - 28 Mar. 1533^a [Special Ambassador]
                                          20s/d

Instructions: Inferred from *L&P*, v, no. 1633.

H3.
BONNER, Dr. Edmund (later Bishop of Hereford, London; 1500?-1569)*
CAVENDISH, Richard (*fl*.1530s)

On their mission to Denmark, Sweden and Holstein (qq.v.), they visited, around Dec. 1535, both Hamburg and Lübeck.

Correspondence: BL, Cotton, Vitel. B.xxi.

H4.
MORISON, Richard (later Sir Richard; *c*.1514-1556)*

23 Dec. 1546^b - early Mar.? 1547^h [Special Ambassador]
Arrived (Hamburg): late Jan. 1547   26s 8d/d
Secretary: Jacques Granada?

He visited several of the Hanse towns, and also Denmark (q.v.).

Instructions: *L&P*, xxi, 2, no. 647.
Correspondence: *L&P*, xxi, 2; *CSPF, 1547-53*.

H5.
BRENDE, John alias William Watson (by 1515-1559)*

11 Dec. 1547^c - mid-Feb. 1548^h Special Ambassador
Audience (Bremen): 24 July 1548

He went to Bremen, Hamburg, and Lübeck.

Instructions: *CSPF, 1547-53*, no. 64.
Correspondence: *CSPF, 1547-53*.

H6.
BORTHWICK, Sir John (*fl.*1540s-1550s)

Although seemingly an agent somewhere in northern Germany, 1548-1553, he
  apparently maintained close contact with the Hanse.

H7.
ROGERS, Dr. John (*c.*1538-1603)*

1 July 1577[a] - 28 Oct. 1577[a]   [Special Ambassador]

After meeting with Danish commissioners in Hamburg (Denmark, q.v.), Rogers
  went, without his colleague Anthony Jenkinson, to visit several Hanse towns
  and possibly parts of northern Germany (q.v.).

Instructions: BL, Sloane 2442, p. 97; *CSPF, 1577-8*, nos. 28-30; HMC *2nd
  Report*, p. 97.
Correspondence: *CSPF, 1577-8*.

H8.

*c.*6 Aug. 1580[h] - autumn 1581[h]   [Special Ambassador]
Audience (Elbing): mid-Sept. 1580

He was accompanied by William Salkins, a merchant. This mission included
  visits to the courts of Denmark, Poland and Sweden (qq.v.).

Instructions: PRO, SP/88/1, no. 9; BL, Sloane 2442, ff. 41-3, Harl. 36, f. 319.
Correspondence: PRO, SP/88/1; Talbot, C. (ed.), *Res Polonicae Elisabetha I*
  (Rome, 1961).

H9.
HERBERT, John (later Sir John; *c.*1540-1617)*

16 May 1583[b] - *c.*1 Sept. 1585[e]   [Special Ambassador]
Audience (Elbing): 5 Aug. 1583

He also visited Prussia (German States), Poland, and Denmark (qq.v.). He was
  joined by the merchant, William Salkins, who served as a diplomatic adjunct.

Instructions: Implied from PRO, SP/88/1, no. 26; *CSPF, 1583-4*, pp. 62, 141.
Correspondence: BL, Cotton, Galba D.xiii, Vesp. F.xii; *CSPF, 1583, 1583-4,
  1584-5*; Talbot, *Res Polonicae*.

H10.
FLETCHER, Dr. Giles (1546-1611)*

May 1587[h] - Oct. 1587[g]   Agent
Audience (Hamburg): 7 June 1587
Audience (Stade): 19 June 1587

He apparently joined with the Governor of the Merchant Adventurers, Richard Saltonstall, to negotiate on behalf of English merchants.

Instructions: BL, Cotton, Nero B.iii, f. 333(?); inferred from *CSPF, 1586-8*, pp. 313-15, 398-9, *1595-7*, p. 123.

Correspondence: PRO, SP/82/2; *CSPF, 1586-8*; Berry, L. (ed.), *The English Works of Giles Fletcher* ... (Madison, Wisc., 1964).

H11.
HARBORNE, William (1552-1617)*

On his return to England from the Ottoman Porte (Turkey, q.v.), he visited several Hanse towns, with audience in Elbing, 12 Oct. 1588; Danzig, 27 Oct. 1588; Hamburg, 19 Nov. 1588; and Stade, 9 Dec. 1588.

H12.
PARKINS, Dr. Christopher (later Sir Christopher; *c.*1543-1622)*

9 May 1590^b - *c.*26 July 1591^c	[Special Ambassador]
Audience (Lübeck): 30 June 1590	£300 (total)
Audience (Danzig): 22 July 1590	
Audience (Elbing): 3 Aug. 1590	

He also visited Prussia (German States), Denmark, and Poland (qq.v.), with a great deal of travelling back and forth between these areas.

Instructions: Inferred from PRO, SP/75/2, ff. 128-33; *L&A, 1591-2*, nos. 887, 890.

Correspondence: PRO, SP/75/2, SP/103/31, SP/82/3; *L&A, 1589-90, 1590-1*; Talbot, *Res Polonicae.*

H13.

20 Apr. 1593^a - early Sept. 1593^e	Special Ambassador
Arrived (Stade): 22 May 1593	40*s*/d

His primary objective was to meet with the Emperor, but he also visited various German princes (qq.v.) and at least one Hanse town.

Instructions: Inferred from PRO, SP/80/1, ff. 140-2, 146-51.
Correspondence: PRO, SP/80/1, SP/81/7.

H14.
LESIEUR, Stephen (later Sir Stephen; *d.*1627)*
WROTH, John (*d.* after 1616)*

26 Dec. 1597^a - 22 Apr. 1598^a	[Special Ambassador]
(Lesieur)	20s/d (each)
22 June 1598^b	
(Wroth)	

Audience (Duke of Brunswick at Hamburg): 6 Feb. 1598
Arrived (Lübeck): 8 Aug. 1598

They apparently visited Hamburg and Lübeck, and perhaps other Hanse towns.

They also contacted various German princes, and Wroth continued with a visit to the Emperor (qq.v.).

Instructions: Inferred from PRO, SP/81/8, ff. 46-52.
Correspondence: PRO, SP/81/8; HMC *Salisb.*, xii.

H15.
CAREW, George (later Sir George; *d.*1612)*

20 May 1598[a] - 21 Dec. 1598[b]   [Special Ambassador]
Audience (Danzig): 7 Aug. 1598   40*s*/d

In the Hanse, he visited at least Elbing and Danzig. Additionally, his mission encompassed Sweden, Denmark and Poland (qq.v.).

Instructions: PRO, SP/88/2, ff. 48-58; BL, Cotton, Nero B.ii, f. 286; Talbot, *Res Polonicae*, pp. 212-16.
Correspondence: PRO, SP/81/8, SP/88/2; BL, Nero B.ii; Talbot, *Res Polonicae*.
Correspondence about: HMC *Salisb.*, viii.

H16.
LESIEUR, Stephen (later Sir Stephen; *d.*1627)*

On his mission to Denmark (q.v.), he had an audience in Stade, 12 May 1602.

H17.
ANSTRUTHER, Robert (later Sir Robert; *fl.*1600s-1640s)

1 Mar. 1625[a] - 26 Apr. 1635[a]   Ambassador Ordinary
Secretaries: Joseph Avery and   £4/d
    Mr. Hurst (after 1628)

He seems to have relocated to Hamburg from Denmark (q.v.) for the latter part of this embassy, Nov. 1627 through 1635. He returned to England briefly at least in Dec. 1628, and also late Nov. to early Dec. 1632.

Instructions: PRO, SP/75/6, f. 72; BL, Add. 35832, f. 179.
Correspondence: PRO, SP/75/6-13, SP/104/167, 169; BL, Add. 4474, 35832, 38669, Eg. 1820, 2553, Harl. 1583, Stowe 176; *CSPD, 1625-6, 1628-9, 1629-31, 1625-49 Add.*

H18.
GORDON, Francis (*fl.*1620s-1640s)

11 July 1626[a] - mid-Dec. 1641[h]   Agent
    £150/an., £300/an. (after Aug. 1632)

He was stationed at Danzig, it would seem, but his responsibilities were primarily oriented toward Poland (q.v.). His residency saw numerous trips to other principalities in northern Europe, including a 1627 trip to Denmark (q.v.). He also returned frequently to England, such as in 1636.

Instructions: PRO, SP/88/4, ff. 122-5.
Correspondence: PRO, SP/88/4-10.

H19.
ROE, Sir Thomas (1581?-1644)*

2 Apr. 1629*ª* - 4 July 1630*ª*   Ambassador Extraodinary

In this tour of Baltic areas, including Sweden, Poland, Denmark and various German princes (qq.v.), he visited Danzig.

Instructions: PRO, SP/104/170, pp. 31-40; HMC *3rd Report*, p. 190.
Correspondence: PRO, SP/88/5, SP/104/170; *CSPD, 1629-31*.

H20.
AVERY, Joseph (*fl*.1620s-1660s)

23 Sept. 1631*ª* - 1649*ʰ*   Agent

He had previously been chargé d'affaires during Anstruther's absence. As the agent to the Hanse towns, he was stationed predominately at Hamburg and undertook several missions during this time to the court of Denmark (q.v.). He also attended the courts of Brandenburg and Saxony in 1637? and the Imperial Diet at Lüneburg, 1636 (qq.v.). Henry de Vic, ambassador to Denmark (q.v.) from late 1637 to June 1638, joined him. After his service ended, he may have stayed for a time in his alternative role as deputy to the Merchant Adventurers.

Instructions: PRO, SP/75/12, ff. 232-5.
Correspondence: PRO, SP/75/12 & 14, SP/81/56, SP/95/4; BL, Harl. 7001; Bodl., Tanner Mss. 62.

H21.
SIDNEY, Robert, 2nd Earl of Leicester (1595-1677)*

He had audience in Hamburg, 27 Oct. 1632, upon his return from a mission to Denmark (q.v.).

H22.
ROE, Sir Thomas (1581?-1644)*

While attending the peace negotiations at Hamburg, 8 Apr. 1638 - 2 Jun. 1640 (Conferences, q.v.), he also carried out resident functions with the Hanse.

H23.
BRADSHAW, Richard (*fl*.1650s)*

30 Jan. 1650*ª* - *c*.15 Aug. 1658*ᶜ* [Resident Agent]
Secretary: Elias Strauss (until 1658) £200/qtr.

He was resident at Hamburg. He went to Denmark (q.v.) in Nov. 1652 and Feb. 1653. He also went to Russia (q.v.) Apr. 1657 to Apr. 1658. He returned to England from autumn 1651 through spring 1652.

Instructions: *CSPD, 1650*, pp. 68-9.
Correspondence: BL, Add. 4157; *ThSP*, i-vii; *CSPD, 1649-1660*.
Correspondence about: *CSPD, 1651-2* through *CSPD, 1659-60*; HMC *6th Report*.

H24.
JEPHSON, William (1615?-1659?)*

While on a mission that encompassed Sweden and Brandenburg (German States, q.v.), he stopped in Hamburg, *c*.15 Sept. 1657.

H25.
AVERY, Joseph (*fl*.1630s-1660s)

27 Aug. 1660[h] - 1663[h]   [Agent]

H26.
SWANN, Sir William (*d*.1678)

25 Mar. 1662[a] - *died c*.19 July 1678   Resident Ambassador
Secretary: David Eger?   20*s*/d, 40*s*/d (in 1669), 60*s*/d (in
                                       1672)

He was stationed principally at Hamburg. During his tenure, he had a number of missions into various German States (q.v.), including visits to Hanover in 1671 and Feb. 1676; and a visit to the Elector of Saxony at Dresden Apr. - May 1678. He returned to England for a long interlude, spring - summer, 1675.

Instructions: PRO, SP/82/10, f. 18; *CSPD, 1661-2*, p. 478.
Correspondence: PRO, SP/81/80, SP/82/10-16, SP/104/56; Oxford, Mss. at All Souls Lib., ccxl; [Taafe, Karl Graf], *Memoirs of the Family Taafe* (Vienna, 1856); Christie, W. D. (ed.), *Letters Addressed to...Sir Joseph Williamson*, Camden n.s., viii-ix (1874).

H27.
HIGGONS, Sir Thomas (1624-1691)*

On his way to invest the Elector of Saxony with the Garter, he stopped in Hamburg, with audience *c*.29 Apr. 1669.

H28.
THYNNE, Sir Thomas (later 1st Viscount Weymouth; 1640-1714)*

During his journey home from his residency in Sweden (q.v.) in Feb. 1669, he visited Hamburg, and also the Dukes of Lüneburg (German States, q.v.).

H29.
HOWARD, Charles, 1st Earl of Carlisle (1629-1685)*

On his return from his embassy to Sweden (q.v.) in 1669, he visited Hamburg.

H30.
BERTIE, Charles (*c*.1641-1711)*

On his way to Denmark (q.v.), he visited Hamburg, arriving in that city 7 May 1671.

H31.
WYCHE, Sir Peter (1628-1699?)*

29 Oct. 1678[a] - 31 Jan. 1682[a]	Resident Ambassador
Presentation of credentials: 16 Dec. 1678	£3/d

He was resident at Hamburg. He visited Denmark (q.v.) in 1679.

Instructions: PRO, SP/104/56, pp. 363-4.
Correspondence: PRO, SP/82/16, SP/104/56 & 193; BL, Add. 37982; *CSPD, 1680-1.*

H32.
SKELTON, Bevil (*died c.*1692)*

14 Nov. 1681[a] - 3 Mar. 1685[a]	Envoy Extraordinary
Audience (Hamburg): 9 Feb. 1682	£5/d
Audience (Lübeck): 1 Mar. 1682	

He was designated ambassador to the Hanse, but also to several of the German States (q.v.). which he visited on a regular basis. He went to Denmark (q.v.) Apr. - May 1684; and visited the Low Countries (q.v.) at least on his journey to his post, and probably repeatedly during his tenure.

Instructions: PRO, SP/104/58.
Correspondence: PRO, SP/82/16, SP/104/190; BL, Add. 25119, 35104, 37981, 37983-4, 38847, 41824, Royal, King's 140; Oxford, Mss. at All Souls Lib., ccxlvii; *CSPD, 1680-1.*

H33.
WYCHE, Sir Peter (1628-1699?)*

13 Apr. 1685[a] - May 1689[h]	Resident Ambassador
Audience: 27 May 1685	£3/d

He was resident at Hamburg.

Instructions: PRO, SP/104/58, p. 411.
Correspondence: PRO, SP/104/58; BL, Add. 41825-41827.

ITALIAN STATES

(Including Rome but excluding Venice)

Ambassadors were often sent to the Italian Peninsula to visit a variety of Italian courts, so this area will be handled geographically as one unit, with careful distinctions provided about precisely where each diplomat went.

IT1.
BAINBRIDGE, Christopher Cardinal, Archbishop of York (1464?-1514)*

*c.*30 Sept. 1509[h] - *d.*14 July 1514   [Resident Ambassador]

He was at Rome.

Audience: 24 Nov. 1509

Correspondence: BL, Cotton, Vitel. B.ii, Galba B.iii-iv, Harl. 3462; *L&P*, i, 1-2.

IT2.
GIGLIS, Silvestro, Bishop of Worcester (1463-1521)*

4 Feb. 1512[b] - *d.*18 Apr. 1521   Resident Ambassador
Arrived (Rome): Oct. 1512

Commission: *L&P*, i, 1048, 1083 (v), 1170 (i).
Correspondence: *L&P*, i, 2 - iii, 1.

IT3.
WINGFIELD, Sir Robert (*c.*1470-1539)*

While resident ambassador with the Emperor (q.v.), he was commissioned, 1 Apr. 1512, to visit Rome. It is not clear that he went. If he undertook the assignment, he may have joined with Silvestro Giglis, the Bishop of Worcester, who returned to Rome at this time.

Commission: *L&P*, i, 1, no. 1170 (i).

IT4.
CLERK, Dr. John (later Bishop of Bath and Wells; *d.*1541)*

June 1519[h] - n.d.   [Special Ambassador]

He went to Rome and apparently also to Louise of Savoy (Savoy, q.v.).

Instructions: *L&P*, iii, 1, no. 344.

IT5.

25 Feb. 1521[a] - *c.*15 Sept. 1522[e]   [Special Ambassador]
Arrived: 20 Apr. 1521   20s/d

He visited France on this journey to Rome.

Correspondence: BL, Cotton, Vitel. B.iv-v; *L&P*, iii, 1-2.

IT6.
PACE, Richard (1482?-1536)

c.15 Dec. 1521[h] - *c*.17 Nov. 1525[c]   [Resident] Ambassador
Arrived Rome: 27 Jan. 1522

Pace had a variety of diplomatic responsibilities on this extended mission. Besides Rome, he visited Venice (q.v.) several times, then later joined Bourbon's army (13 June 1523, France, q.v.). From Apr. through June 1524, he accompanied the Emperor's forces in Northern Italy.

Instructions: BL, Add. 48045, ff. 312-24, Cotton, Nero B.vii; HMC *3rd Report*, p. 194.

Correspondence: BL, Add. 5860, 48045, Harl. 282-3, 6260, Stowe 147; *L&P*, iii, 2 - iv; *CSPS, 1509-25*.

IT7.
HANNIBAL, Thomas (*d*.1531)*

9 Mar. 1522[b] - *c*.2 Sept. 1524[a]   [Resident Ambassador]
Arrived (Spain): 27 Apr. 1522
Audience (with the Pope at Zaragoza):
9 May 1522

Although his commission was to the Emperor (q.v.), it is not clear whether he visited that monarch. He had audience with the Pope at Zaragoza in Spain, and then followed the Pontiff to Rome where he served as resident. He returned to England as the Pope's ambassador to Henry VIII.

Commission: *L&P*, iii, 2, no. 2098.

Correspondence: BL, Add. 48045, Arundel 26, Cotton, Vitel. B.v-vi, Eg. 763, Harl. 297, 6260, Sloane 3839, 5860, Stowe 147; *L&P*, iii, 2 - iv, 1; *CSPS, 1509-25*.

IT8.
CLERK, Dr. John, Bishop of Bath and Wells (*d*.1541)*

12 Mar. 1523[b] - *c*.30 Dec. 1525[d]   [Resident Ambassador]
Audience: 5 June 1523

He joined with Hannibal and Pace in Rome. He also visited Louise of Savoy (Savoy, q.v.) at Lyons on his journey home.

Correspondence: BL, Add. 5860, 48045, Cotton, Calig. D.ix, Vitel. B.v-vii, Sloane 3839, Stowe 147, Harl. 297; *L&P*, iii, 2 - iv, 1; *CSPS, 1509-25*.

IT9.
GHINUCCI, Jerome de, Bishop of Worcester (*fl*.1520s-1530s)
CASALE, Sir Gregory da (*fl*.1520s-1530s)

20 Sept. 1525[d] - *c*.15 Nov. 1526[e]   [Special] Ambassadors
            (Worcester)
Audience (Rome): 31 Oct. 1525

Casale was dispatched from England, travelled by way of Lyons where he consulted with Margaret of Savoy (Savoy, q.v.), and joined with the Bishop of Worcester in Rome. Casale seemingly went to Venice *c.*23 Sept. 1526, where he apparently functioned for a time as a correspondent, while Worcester went to London.

Correspondence: BL, Cotton, Vitel. E.viii; *L&P*, iv, 1-2.

IT10.
RUSSELL, Sir John (later 1st Earl of Bedford; 1486?-1555)*

Part of his responsibilities, during his mission to France (q.v.), included a stop in Rome, where he apparently visited with the Pope. He arrived 8 Oct. 1524, and remained until late Jan. 1525.

Correspondence: *L&P*, iv, 1.

IT11.

2 Jan. 1527*d* - mid-June 1527*e*   [Special Ambassador]
Audience: 8 Feb. 1527

He was sent to the Pope.

Instructions: Implied from *L&P*, iv, 2, nos. 2769, 2870, 2875.
Correspondence: PRO, SP/1/48; BL, Cotton, Nero B.vi, Vitel. B.ix; *L&P*, iv, 2; Wiffen, J., *Historical Memoirs of the House of Russell...*(1833), i.

IT12.
CASALE, Sir Gregory da (*fl.*1520s-1530s)

27 Aug. 1527*d* - 1540?*h*   [Resident] Ambassador,
Audience (Ferrara): 15 Nov. 1527   Orator
Arrived (Florence): 18 Dec. 1527   40*s*/d
Audience (Pope at Orvieto): 20 Dec.
  1527

Previous to Aug. 1527, he seems to have been an English correspondent from the Italian peninsula. After this date, he apparently became, upon Wolsey's commission, an ambassador in Italy, whose responsibilities encompassed the entire area, but whose principal duties revolved around the Pope at Rome. He was especially involved, expectedly, with the divorce case. By *c.*1532, his importance seems to have become less critical and he is more frequently styled 'orator' rather than 'ambassador,' although his diets remain the same until there is no further record of them after 1539.

Correspondence: BL, Add. 28584, 33376, Cotton, Nero B.vi, Vitel. B.ix-xi, xii-xiv; *L&P*, iv, 2 - xii, 2.

IT13.
KNIGHT, Dr. William (later Bishop of Bath and Wells; 1476-1547)*

*c.*1 Sept. 1527*h* - early May 1528*g*   [Special Ambassador]
Audience: *c.*2 Dec. 1527

He went to the imprisoned Pope at Rome.

Instructions: Inferred from *L&P*, iv, 2, nos. 3400, 3420, 3422.
Correspondence: BL, Cotton, Vitel. B.x; *L&P*, iv, 2.

IT14.
GARDINER, Dr. Stephen (later Bishop of Winchester; 1483?-1555)*
FOX, Dr. Edward (later Bishop of Hereford; 1496?-1538)*

11 Feb. 1528^d - 3 May 1528^a [Special Ambassadors]
  (Fox)
  c.30 Aug. 1528^c
  (Gardiner)
Audience: 23 Mar. 1528

They went to Rome, stopping by Paris (France, q.v.) on the journey. In Rome they joined with Sir Gregory da Casale. Dr. Fox seemingly returned to England early.

Instructions: HMC *Salisb.*, i, p. 6; also suggested in *L&P*, iv, 2, nos. 3900-13.

Correspondence: BL, Harl. 283, 296, 419; *L&P*, iv, 2; Gardiner, S., *Letters of Stephen Gardiner*, ed. J. Muller (New York, 1933); Pocock, N., *Records of the Reformation* (Oxford, 1870), i.

IT15.
BRYAN, Sir Francis (c.1492-1550)*
VANNES, Peter (d.1563)*

26 Nov. 1528^b - 22 June 1529^c [Special Ambassadors]
(Vannes)   (Bryan)   26s 8d/d (each)
27 Nov.1528^b c.15 Oct. 1529^d
(Bryan)   (Vannes)
Arrived (Rome): c.25 Jan. 1529
Audience (Pope): 1 Apr. 1529

They stopped in Paris on the journey to Rome, and Vannes seemingly came by way of Paris on his return as well (France, q.v.). Their audience with the Pope was delayed due to the Pontiff's illness.

Instructions: BL, Cotton, Vitel. B.x, f. 197; *L&P*, iv, 2, nos. 4977, 4979, 5014.

Correspondence: BL, Arundel 151; Cotton, Vitel. B.x-xi, Harl. 283, 296, 353; *L&P*, iv, 3.

IT16.
GARDINER, Dr. Stephen (later Bishop of Winchester; 1483?-1555)*

14 Jan. 1529^a - 22 June 1529^c [Special Ambassador]
Audience: 1 Apr. 1529   26s 8d/d

Gardiner joined with the above ambassadors, already at Rome.

Commission: *L&P*, iv, 3, no. 5183.

Instructions: Implied in BL, Arundel 151, f. 46b, *L&P*, iv, 3, nos. 5210, 5476; later instructions in *L&P* iv, 3, nos. 5270, 5272.

Correspondence: BL, Cotton, Vitel. B.xi; *L&P*, iv, 3; Gardiner, S., *Letters of Stephen Gardiner*, ed. J. Muller (New York, 1933).

IT17.
BENET, Dr. William (*d.*1533)*

22 May 1529*ᵃ* - *c.*20 Dec. 1531*ᶜ*   [Resident Ambassador]
Audience: 21 June 1529   26*s* 8*d*/d

He was resident with the Pope.

Instructions: *L&P*, iv, 3, no. 5575.
Correspondence: BL, Add. 48044; *L&P*, iv, 3 - v.

IT18.
CAREW, Sir Nicholas (*c.*1496-1539)*
SAMPSON, Dr. Richard (later Bishop of Chichester, *d.*1554)*

8 Oct. 1529*ᵇ* - *c.*1 May 1530*ᵈ*   [Special Ambassadors]
                                                          26*s* 8*d*/d (each)

The principal object of this mission was the Emperor (q.v.) at Bologna, but they
    also saw the Pope.

Instructions: Implied in *L&P*, iv, 3, no. 6069, iv, 3, App., nos. 240, 253.
Correspondence: *L&P*, iv, 3 & iv, 3, App.; BL, Eg. 3315, Add. 35838.

IT19.
STOKESLEY, Dr. John, Bishop of London (1475?-1539)*

8 Oct. 1529*ᵈ* - *c.*6 Oct. 1530*ᵍ*   [Special Ambassador]
Audience (Pope at Bologna):   26*s* 8*d*/d
7 June 1530?

  He began this mission in conjunction with George Boleyn, Lord Rochford,
    when they went to France (q.v.). Stokesley's responsibilities seemed as much
    to collect the opinions of universities throughout Italy (especially at Bologna),
    and France about the divorce, as it was his duty to negotiate. However, he did
    have an audience with the Pope, and also a diplomatic audience in Venice
    (q.v.).

Instructions (for dealing with the Pope): Suggested in *L&P*, iv, 3, no. 6324.
Correspondence: *L&P*, iv, 3.

IT20.
BOLEYN, Thomas, Earl of Wiltshire (1477-1539)*
LEE, Dr. Edward (later Archbishop of York; 1482?-1544)*

20 Jan. 1530*ᵃ* - 3 Aug. 1530*ᵃ*   [Special Ambassadors]
Audience: *c.*15 Mar. 1530   £5/d (Wiltshire),
                                                          26*s* 8*d*/d (Lee)

They visited the Emperor (q.v.) and the Pope at Bologna, where they also joined
    with Dr. Benet. Thomas Cranmer was an unaccredited member of this
    legation. On their return journey, the embassy visited the French King (q.v.).

Instructions: *L&P*, iv, 3, no. 6111.
Correspondence: *L&P*, iv, 3.

IT21.
BENET, Dr. William (*d*.1533)*

1 Jan. 1532*ᵉ* - *d*.26 Sept. 1533   [Special] Ambassador
Audience: *c*.10 Feb. 1532

After only the briefest of pauses in England, he returned to the Pope. There is
some evidence that this mission may in fact have been an extension of the
1528-1531 mission. He acted much of the time in concert with Sir Gregory da
Casale. They were joined in spring 1532, by Drs. Bonner and Carne, who
handled the legal aspects of the divorce with the papal Consistory.

Instructions: BL, Add. 25114, ff. 56-9; *L&P*, v, no. 611.
Correspondence: BL, Cotton, Vitel. B.xiii; *L&P*, v-vi.

IT22.
GARDINER, Dr. Stephen, Bishop of Winchester (1483?-1555)*

While ambassador to France (q.v.), he had audience with the Pope at Marseilles,
c.16 Oct. 1533.

IT23.
VANNES, Peter (*d*.1563)*

While resident in Venice (q.v.), he visited Lucca, with an audience in Nov.
1551.

IT24.
THIRLBY, Thomas, Bishop of Ely (1506?-1570)*
BROWNE, Anthony, Viscount Montague (1528-1592)*
CARNE, Dr. Edward (1495/6-1561)*

16 Feb. 1555*ᶜ* - 24 Aug. 1555*ᶜ*   [Special Ambassadors]
Audience: 10 June 1555

They went to the Pope, where Carne remained as resident (see below).

Instructions: *CSPS, 1554-8*, p. 140.
Correspondence: BL, Harl. 252.
Correspondence about: *CSPF, 1553-8*.

IT25.
CARNE, Dr. Edward (1495/6-1561)*

12 Feb. 1555*ᵃ* - *c*.1 Apr. 1559*ᶜ*   Resident Ambassador
Audience: 10 June 1555   53*s* 4*d*/d

Carne was recalled from Rome when Queen Elizabeth ascended the throne, but
he feigned papal restraint, a deceit sanctioned by the Pope, and he remained
in Rome until his death. His responsibilities as an English minister obviously
had ceased by Apr. 1559.

Instructions (first recorded): *CSPF, 1553-8*, no. 366.
Correspondence: *CSPF, 1553-8, 1558-9*; BL, Cotton, Nero B.vi, Calig. E.v;
APC, 1554-6; HMC *Salisb.*, i; Tytler, P. (ed.), *England Under the Reigns of
Edward VI...*(1839).

IT26.
BRYSKETT, Ludovick (*fl*.1570s-1610s)*

c.29 Oct. 1600[h] - 1601[h]	[Special Ambassador]
Audience: early 1601	£100 (plus expenses)

He went to Florence.

Instructions: Crino, A., *Fatti e Figure del Seicento Anglo-Toscano*...(Florence, 1957) pp. 63-5.

IT27.
STANDEN, Sir Anthony (*fl*.1580s-1610s)

1 June 1603[a] - 22 Jan. 1604[b]	[Special Ambassador]
Audience (Florence): Oct.? 1603	40s/d

Besides Florence, he also went to Venice (q.v.).

Correspondence: Crino, A., *Fatti e Figure del Seicento Anglo-Toscano*...(Florence, 1957).

IT28.
BALFOUR, Sir Michael (later 1st Baron Balfour of Burleigh; 1567- 1619)*

25 Jan. 1604[b] - 5 Aug. 1604[a]	[Special Ambassador]
Audience: late Apr. 1604	£400 (total?)

He visited Florence.

Instructions: PRO, SP/98/2, f. 87; suggested in *CSPV, 1604-07*, p. 133.
Correspondence: Mackie, J., *Negotiations between King James VI and Ferdinand I, Grand Duke of Tuscany*...(1927)

IT29.
LESIEUR, Sir Stephen (*d*.1627)*

20 Feb. 1608[a] - *c*.2 Jan. 1609[c]	[Special Ambassador]
	50s/d

He went to Florence.

Correspondence about: *CSPD, 1603-10*.

IT30.
GAGE, George (*c*.1582-1638)*

May 1621[h] - 29 Aug. 1622[a]	[Agent]
Audience (Rome): 28 June 1621	

IT31.

30 Sept. 1622[d] - 30 Aug. 1623[b]	[Agent]
Audience (Rome): *c*.31 Jan. 1623	

Besides Rome, where he engaged in secret negotiations, he visited Florence, Parma, Savoy and Spain (qq.v.).

Instructions: Suggested in *CSPD, 1619-23*, pp. 451, 457.

IT32.
WESTON, Jerome (later 2nd Earl of Portland; 1605-1663)*

6 Dec. 1631[a] - 12 Mar. 1633[a]   Ambassador Extraordinary
Audience (Florence): Jan. 1633

Besides the Duke of Tuscany at Florence, he visited Savoy, Venice and France
(qq.v.).

Instructions: PRO, SP/78/91, ff. 382-45, SP/92/19, f. 200.
Correspondence: PRO, SP/78/92-3, SP/92/19.

IT33.
DIGBY, Sir Kenelm (1603-1665)*

Feb. 1645[h] - Feb. 1646[h]   [Special Ambassador]
Audience: c.28 May 1645

He visited the Pope in search for support for Charles I.

Correspondence: BL, Add. 15857; Digby, G., *The Lord George Digby's
Cabinet...* (1646).

IT34.
FEILDING, Basil, Viscount Feilding (later 2nd Earl of Denbigh; c.1608-
1674)*

In the midst of his service at Venice and at Savoy (qq.v.), he visited Mantua in
1638.

IT35.
KENT, Joseph (*fl.*1650s-1660s)

28 Jan. 1659[h] - c.8 Mar. 1664[g]   [Agent]
He was stationed at Florence.

Correspondence: PRO, SP/85/8-10; *CSPD, 1660-1.*

IT36.
DIGBY, George, 2nd Earl of Bristol (1612-1677)*

c.17 Feb. 1661[f] - 8 May 1661[a]   [Special Ambassador]
Audience (Milan): late Mar. 1661
Audience (Parma): c.1 Apr. 1661
Audience (Genoa): 12 Apr. 1661

He also visited the Spanish Netherlands (q.v.).

Instructions: Suggested in *CSPV, 1659-61*, pp. 248, 262.

IT37.
FINCH, Sir John (1626-1682)

31 Mar. 1665[b] - c.15 Aug. 1671[c]   [Resident Ambassador]
Audience: 6 July 1665   £1000/an.
Secretary: Bernard Gascoigne

While travelling to Venice and the surrounding area, he was made resident with the Grand Duke of Tuscany at Florence.

Instructions: PRO, SP/98/5 (12 Apr. 1665), SP/104/174B, pp. 61-4.

Correspondence: PRO, SP/98/5-13, SP/99/46; Bodl., Rawlinson Mss. A.477, 478; *CSPD, 1667-8, 1670*.

IT38.

BELASYSE, Thomas, Viscount Fauconberg (later Earl Fauconberg; 1627-1700)*

18 Nov. 1669[a] - 14 Nov. 1670[a]   Ambassador Extraordinary
Audience (Genoa): *c*.2 May 1670   £10/d
Audience (Florence): 29 May 1670
Secretary: John Dodington, Dr.
   Yerburgh

Italy, especially Venice (q.v.), seemed to have been the main object of his visit. Besides Genoa and Florence, he visited France, Savoy, and various German States, including Treves (qq.v.).

Instructions: PRO, SP/99/46, ff. 318-25, SP/104/88, ff. 3-6.

Correspondence: PRO, SP/88/11, SP/92/24, SP/99/47-8, SP/104/88; Bodl., Rawlinson Mss. A.477; *CSPD, 1670*; Ramsey, R., *Studies in Cromwell's Family Circle*...(1930).

IT39.

COTTERELL, Clement *(fl.*1670s)*

12 Mar. 1670[h] - Autumn 1670[h]   [Special Ambassador]
Audience (Florence): late May 1670
Audience (Rome): *c*.12 Aug. 1670

He went to Rome and to Florence.

Correspondence: PRO, SP/85/10.

IT40.

HAMILTON, James *(fl.*1670s)

21 June 1670[b] - 22 Oct. 1670[a]   Envoy Extraordinary
Audience: 2 Aug. 1670

He was accompanied to Florence by Henry Savile who represented Prince James.

Instructions: Suggested in Thibadeau, A., *The Bulstrode Papers* (1897), p. 143.
Correspondence: PRO, SP/98/11.

IT41.

GASCOIGNE, Sir Bernard (1614-1687)*

Although his mission to the Emperor and Germany (qq.v.) officially began in Feb. 1672, he apparently visited the Grand Duke of Tuscany Jan. 1672 pursuant to his instructions on that mission.

IT42.
MORDAUNT, Henry, 2nd Earl of Peterborough (1624?-1697)*

25 Feb. 1673*ᵃ* - 25 Nov. 1673*ᵃ*   Ambassador Extraordinary
Secretary: John Dodington   £100/wk.

He went to Modena regarding the Duke of York's marriage, and also to Savoy
and the Emperor (qq.v.).

Instructions: PRO, SP/104/88, f. 29.
Correspondence: PRO, SP/78/138, SP/85/11.

IT43.
FINCH, Sir John (1626-1682)

On his journey to assume the residency at Constantinople (Turkey, q.v.), he
stopped at Genoa, where he spent some time (July through Oct. 1673), and at
Florence, which he left 26 Oct. 1673.

IT44.
GRANVILLE, Bernard (1631-1701)*

While on a mission of condolence in the autumn of 1675 to Savoy (q.v.,
accompanied by Mr. Churchill), he apparently continued to Florence and
then Genoa in an official capacity and then to Venice for personal reasons.

IT45.
PLOTT, Thomas (*fl.*1670s-1680s)

6 Mar. 1678*ᵃ* - 22 Dec. 1678*ᵃ*   Agent
                                         20*s*/d

He was resident at Florence with the Grand Duke of Tuscany.

IT46.
HOWARD, Philip Thomas Cardinal (1629-1694)*

*c.*15 Mar. 1680*ʰ* - 1689?*ʰ*   [Cardinal Protector]
He became Cardinal Protector of England at Rome around this date.
Correspondence: BL, Add. 4274, 15908, 23720, 28225.

IT47.
DEREHAM, Sir Thomas (*fl.*1670s-1680s)

1 Sept. 1681*ᵃ* - 1 Feb. 1685*ᵃ*   Resident Envoy
                                         £1000/an.

He apparently went from being consul at Florence with the Grand Duke of
Tuscany to being a fully accredited minister.

Correspondence: PRO, SP/98/16-17, SP/104/188; BL, Royal, King's 40;
Oxford, Mss. at All Souls Lib., ccviii.

IT48.

PALMER, Roger, 1st Earl of Castlemaine (1634-1705)*

4 Jan. 1686^a - 12 Aug. 1687^a	Ambassador Extraordinary
Arrived: *c*.27 Aug. 1686	£100/wk.
Audience: 8 Jan. 1687	
Secretary: Sir John Litcott	

He was sent to Rome.

Correspondence about: *CSPD, 1686-7.*

IT49.

LITCOTT, Sir John (*fl.*1680s)

25 Feb. 1687^a - 16 Oct. 1688^g	Agent
	£3/d

He was resident with the Pope.

Instructions: BL, Lansd. 1152, vol. ii, no. 41.
Correspondence: PRO, SP/85/12, SP/98/17.

IT50.

DEREHAM, Sir Thomas (*fl.*1670s-1680s)

14 Mar. 1687^a - *c*.2 June 1689^h Agent

Again he was resident at Florence.

Correspondence: BL, Add. 41842.

IT51.

HOWARD, Thomas, Baron Howard of Norfolk (*fl.*1680s)*

8 June 1688^d - Nov. 1688^h Ambassador Extraordinary

He was sent to Rome.

Instructions: BL, Lansd. 1152, vol. ii, no. 23.
Correspondence: BL, Add. 41804, 41842.

LOW COUNTRIES

When an early sixteenth century ambassador went to the Low Countries on a mission to the emperor [the emperor being in residence at Brussels, Malines, etc.], that ambassador also frequently visited the imperial regent in the area. Since the emperor was the principal focus of the mission, the mission will typically be listed only under 'Emperor and Imperial Diets'.

(Missions to Charles V, while he was Prince of Castile but resident in the Low Countries, will be listed both under Spain as well as here.)

LC1.
SPINELLY, Thomas (*d.*1522)

22 Apr. 1509*a* - *c*.17 June 1517*e*   Agent, Ambassador
                                           £100/an.

He was resident agent with the Imperial Regent in the Low Countries. His designation seemingly was upgraded to the status of ambassador in 1515. He returned to England frequently.

Correspondence: *L&P*, i, 1-2, ii, 1-2.

LC2.
WINGFIELD, Sir Robert (*c*.1470-1539)*

On his journey to the Emperor (q.v.) in 1510, he visited the Regent in the Low Countries, *c*.7 June.

LC3.
KNYVETT, Christopher (*fl*.1510s)

Oct. 1512*h* - n.d.   [Special Ambassador]

He went to Margaret of Savoy.

LC4.
YOUNG, Dr. John (1467-1516)*
BOLEYN, Sir Thomas (later Viscount Rochford, Earl of Wiltshire; 1477-1539)*
WINGFIELD, Sir Richard (1469?-1525)*
POYNINGS, Sir Edward (1459-1521)*

8 Jan. 1513*a* - *c*.25 May 1513*c*   [Special Ambassadors]
(Wingfield   (Poynings, Young
and Poynings)   and Boleyn)
                  24 June 1513*b*
                  (Wingfield)

All four were commissioned, 20 Dec. 1512, to treat for the formation of a Holy League with: the Pope (or his representative in the Low Countries, Italy,

170

q.v.); the Emperor elect, Maximilian (q.v.); Margaret of Savoy; Charles Prince of Castile; and the King of Aragon who also negotiated on behalf of Castile (Spain, q.v.). Young and Boleyn were already in residence with the Emperor.

Instructions: Inferred from *L&P*, i, 1, nos. 1524 (39), 1680, 1745.
Correspondence: BL, Cotton, Galba B.iii; *L&P*, i, 1-2; *CSPS, 1509-25* (summary of negotiations and treaty).

LC5.
WINGFIELD, Sir Richard (1469?-1525)*
KNIGHT, Dr. William (later Bishop of Bath and Wells; 1476-1547)*

19 Feb. 1514[a] - 21 Nov. 1514[b]   [Commissioners]
     (Wingfield)   20s/d
Audience: *c*.21 Mar. 1514

They joined with Spinelly at Mechlin, and were specifically accredited to the Regent. From the Low Countries, Knight proceeded to Switzerland (q.v.).

Instructions: *L&P*, i, 2, nos. 2656, 2684.
Correspondence: BL, Cotton, Galba B.iii; *L&P*, i, 2.

LC6.
SAMPSON, Dr. Richard (later Bishop of Coventry and Lichfield; *d*.1554)*

c.1 Sept. 1514[g] - *c*.30 Mar. 1515[f]   [Resident Ambassador]
                                  20s/d

He was resident with Lady Margaret at Brussels. He later joined with the Tunstall commission (see below). In Oct. 1514, he undertook a mission to Paris, but seemingly in a private capacity for Wolsey.

Correspondence: *L&P*, i, 2.

LC7.
POYNINGS, Sir Edward (1459-1521)*

12 Feb. 1515[h] - Mar. 1515[h]   [Special Ambassador]
He left on his mission from Tournai, where he was captain of the town.

Instructions: Inferred from *L&P*, ii, 1, no. 149.
Correspondence: *L&P*, ii, 1.

LC8.
TUNSTALL, Dr. Cuthbert (later Bishop of London, Durham; 1474-1559)*
SAMPSON, Dr. Richard (later Bishop of Coventry and Lichfield; *d*.1554)*
MORE, Thomas (later Sir Thomas; 1477/8-1535)*
CLIFFORD, John (*fl*.1510s)

7 May 1515[b] - *c*.7 Feb. 1516[e]   [Special] Ambassadors
Audience: *c*.19 May 1515   20s/d (Tunstall and Sampson),
                                  13s 4d/d (More)

They negotiated about commercial treaties with Prince Charles of Castile (later

Emperor Charles V) in Brussels and Bruges (Spain, q.v.). Spinelly, already resident in the Low Countries with Lady Margaret, was accredited with and joined with them. Sampson returned periodically to his responsibilities at Tournai during this period.

Instructions: *L&P*, ii, 1, no. 422.
Correspondence: BL, Cotton, Galba B.iii-iv; *L&P*, ii, 1.

LC9.
POYNINGS, Sir Edward (1459-1521)*
KNIGHT, Dr. William (later Bishop of Bath and Wells; 1476-1547)*

7 May 1515[b] - c.21 Sept. 1515[e] (Poynings)	Special Ambassadors 20s/d (Knight)
Audience (Charles of Castile): 30 May 1515	
Audience (Margaret of Savoy): 30 May 1515	

They were accredited to negotiate with Charles of Castile. They joined briefly with Tunstall in early summer. Poynings returned to England and Knight was accredited with Tunstall to the Prince of Castile (see immediately below).

Instructions: *L&P*, ii, 1, no. 423.
Correspondence: BL, Cotton, Galba B.iii; *L&P*, ii, 1.

LC10.
TUNSTALL, Dr. Cuthbert (later Bishop of London, Durham; 1474-1559)*
KNIGHT, Dr. William (later Bishop of Bath and Wells; 1476-1547)*

1 Oct. 1515[b] - c.7 Feb. 1516[e] (Tunstall, More, etc.) c.1 Mar. 1516[g] (Knight)	Special Ambassadors

Treaty concluded: 24 Jan. 1516

Both were already in the Low Countries, as was Spinelly, who joined with them in the conclusion of a treaty with Charles of Castile. On 2 Oct. 1515, they and Spinelly, Sampson, More and Clifford, associated with Tunstall in his earlier commission, were accredited to continue trade negotiations.

Commission: *L&P*, ii, 1, no. 976, 986.
Correspondence: BL, Cotton, Galba B.iv; *L&P*, ii, 1.

LC11.
PACE, Richard (1482?-1536)*

He had audience, c.27 Oct. 1515, with the Regent Margaret at Antwerp on his journey to the Emperor and Switzerland (qq.v.).

LC12.
POYNINGS, Sir Edward (1459-1521)*
TUNSTALL, Dr. Cuthbert (later Bishop of London, Durham; 1474-1559)*

21 Feb. 1516[b] - *c.*15 May 1516[g]   [Special Ambassador]
Audience: 9 Mar. 1516   66*s* 8*d*/d (Poynings)

The went to Charles of Castile at Brussels, a mission which included conveying
  condolences on the death of Ferdinand of Aragon.

Commission: *L&P*, ii, 1, no. 1574.
Correspondence: BL, Cotton, Galba B.iv, vi, Vitel. B.xx; *L&P*, ii, 1.

LC13.
TUNSTALL, Dr. Cuthbert (later Bishop of London, Durham; 1474-1559)*
WINGFIELD, Sir Richard (1469?-1525)*

*c.*1 June 1516[h] - *c.*2 Sept. 1517[f]   [Special Ambassadors]
              (Wingfield)
        *c.*15 Sept. 1517[e]
              (Tunstall)
Audience (with Charles of Castile):
  4 June 1516

They joined with the Earl of Worcester and William Knight in negotiations with
  the Emperor (q.v.), Jan. 1517.

Instructions: Inferred in *L&P*, ii, 1, nos. 2006, 2176.
Correspondence: BL, Cotton, Galba B.v; *L&P*, ii, 1-2.

LC14.
KNIGHT, Dr. William (later Bishop of Bath and Wells; 1476-1547)*

*c.*30 Dec. 1516[c] - *c.*10 Mar. 1517[e]   [Special Ambassador]
Audience (with Charles of Castile):
  22 Jan. 1517

He was part of the Earl of Worcester's embassy to the Emperor (q.v.), and was
  accredited specifically to Lady Margaret, the Regent at Mechlin.

Instructions: *L&P*, ii, 1, no. 2713.
Correspondence: BL, Cotton, Galba B.v; *L&P*, ii, 1-2.

LC15.
PACE, Richard (1482?-1536)*

He had audience, May 1517, with the Regent Margaret at Antwerp on his return
  from the Emperor and Switzerland (qq.v.).

LC16.
KNIGHT, Dr. William (later Bishop of Bath and Wells; 1476-1547)*

*c.*29 Jan. 1518[h] - mid-Jan. 1519[h]   Special Ambassador
Audience (with regency Council):   20*s*/d
  21 Mar. 1518

He resided with the Lady Margaret at Mechlin and Brussels.

Instructions: Inferred from *L&P*, ii, 2, no. 3907.
Correspondence: BL, Cotton, Galba B.vi, Lansd. 1236; *L&P*, ii, 2 - iii, 1.

LC17.
PACE, Richard (1482?-1536)*

*c.*11 May 1519[a] - 10 Aug. 1519[a]   [Special Ambassador]
Audience (Margaret of Austria):
  *c.*19 May 1519

From Brussels, he proceeded to the imperial elections at Frankfurt (q.v.), his
  principal objective. He also visited various German princes (q.v.).

Instructions: In part in *L&P*, iii, 1, nos. 239-41.
Correspondence: *L&P*, iii, 1.

LC18.
TUNSTALL, Dr. Cuthbert (later Bishop of London, Durham; 1474-1559)*

On his mission to the Emperor (q.v.), he had audience with the Regent,
  Margaret of Savoy, *c.*22 Sept. 1519.

Correspondence: BL, Cotton, Galba B.iii; *L&P*, iii, 1.

LC19.
WINGFIELD, Sir Richard (1469?-1525)*

He visited the Regent in the Low Countries on his way to the Emperor in
  Germany (q.v.). Audience: *c.*13 May 1521.

LC20.
WINGFIELD, Sir Robert (*c.*1470-1539)*

20 Aug. 1522[c] - 15 Apr. 1523[c]   [Special Ambassador]
Audience: 1 Sept. 1522   20s/d

He visited Margaret of Savoy, Regent at Brussels. He returned to Calais at the
  end of his assignment.

Instructions: *L&P*, iii, 2, no. 2455; summarized in Wingfield, J. (ed.), *Some
  Records of the Wingfield Family* (1925), pp. 81-2.
Correspondence: BL, Cotton, Galba B.vii; *L&P*, iii, 2.

LC21.
KNIGHT, Dr. William (later Bishop of Bath and Wells; 1476-1547)*

Mar.? 1523[h] - *c.*11 May 1525[e]   Resident Ambassador
Audience: 9 Apr. 1523

He was resident with the Regent.

Instructions: BL, Add. 3839, ff. 119-29, Stowe 147, f. 119.
Correspondence: BL, Add. 48045, Cotton, Galba B.vi, viii; *L&P*, iii, 1 - iv, 1.

LC22.
PARKER, Henry, 8th Baron Morley (1476-1556)*
HUSSEY, Sir William (1473-1531?)*
LEE, Dr. Edward (later Archbishop of York; 1482?-1544)*
WRIOTHESLEY, Thomas (later Earl of Southampton; 1505-1550)*

On their way to invest the Archduke Ferdinand with the Garter, they had
audience *c*.23 Sept. 1523, with the Regent, Lady Margaret at Mechlin.

LC23.
JERNINGHAM, Sir Richard (*d*.1525)

31 Aug. 1524*e* - *c*.2 Dec. 1524*e*   [Special Ambassador]
Audience: 8 Sept. 1524

He went to Margaret of Savoy, the Regent, and there joined with Knight.

Instructions: Implied in BL, Add. 48045, ff. 235-70; *L&P*, iv, 1, nos. 615, 653.
Correspondence: BL, Cotton, Galba B.viii; *L&P*, iv, 1.

LC24.
FITZWILLIAM, Sir William (later Earl of Southampton; *c*.1490-1542)*
WINGFIELD, Sir Robert (*c*.1470-1539)*

c.20 Mar. 1525*h* - *c*.25 May 1526*f*   Special Ambassadors
Audience: 27 Apr. 1525   20*s*/d (Wingfield)

They joined with Knight and had audience with the Regent at Mechlin.

Instructions: BL, Cotton, Galba B.viii, f. 140; *L&P*, iv, 1, no. 1301; inferred
from Wingfield, *Records*, p. 88.
Correspondence: BL, Cotton, Galba B.viii; *L&P*, iv, 1.

LC25.
HACKETT, John (later Sir John; *d*.1534)

18 Apr. 1526*c* - 1 Feb. 1531*f*   [Resident Ambassador]
Audience: 6 May 1526   £100/an., £200/an. (beginning 1528)

He was resident with Mary of Hungary, the Regent, and he intermittently
returned to Calais. Upon the termination of this mission, he went to Calais,
and was immediately appointed resident with the Emperor (q.v.).

Correspondence: BL, Cotton, Galba B.vi, ix; *L&P*, iv-v, 1-3; Rogers, E. (ed.),
The Letters of Sir John Hackett, 1526-1534 (Morgantown, West Virginia,
1971).

LC26.
WALLOP, Sir John (*d*.1551)*

c.1 Sept. 1526*h* - Sept.? 1527*h*   [Special Ambassador]
Audience: 16 Sept. 1526

He was sent in response to the Turkish threat to Central Europe after the Battle
of Mohács and consulted with the Regent, Margaret of Austria. He also went
to the Polish King (q.v.) and to Archduke Ferdinand at Prague as well as to
various German princes (q.v.).

Instructions: Inferred from *L&P*, iv, 2, no. 2530; Jasnowski, J., 'England and Poland in the 16th and 17th Centuries,' *Polish Science and Learning*, vii, pp. 1-5.

Correspondence: *L&P*, iv, 2.

LC27.

HACKETT, Sir John (*d*.1534)

19 Apr. 1532*c* - *died c*.27 Oct. 1534   [Resident Ambassador]

He was resident with Mary of Hungary.

Instructions: *L&P*, v, no. 946; Rogers, *Letters*, pp. 107-112.

Correspondence: *L&P*, v - vii; Rogers, *Letters*.

LC28.

HUTTON, John (*d*.1538)

5 Apr. 1537*a* - *d*.5 Sept. 1538   [Resident Ambassador]

Audience: 9 Apr. 1537   20*s*/d

Instructions: *L&P*, xii, 1, no. 866.

Correspondence: BL, Cotton, Galba B.x; *L&P*, xii-xiii.

LC29.

HOBY, Philip (later Sir Philip; 1505-1558)*

c.28 Feb. 1538*c* - *c*.1 Apr. 1538*e*   [Special Ambassador]

Audience: *c*.11 Mar. 1538   £46 13*s* 4*d* (total?)

He was accompanied on this mission by Hans Holbein, the artist, and the principal purpose seems to have been to make contact with the Regent's court at Brussels and view the Duchess of Milan. He also apparently went to the Duchess of Lorraine (France, q.v.), to view her daughters, all for the English King's matrimonial purposes.

Instructions: *L&P*, xiii, 1, no. 380.

Correspondence: *L&P*, xiii, 1.

LC30.

VAUGHAN, Stephen (by 1502-1549)*

17 Sept. 1538*a* - 10 Feb. 1540*e*   Resident Agent

    20*s*/d

He resided with the Regent.

Instructions: *L&P*, xiii, 2, no. 419.

Correspondence: BL, Harl. 283?; *L&P*, xiii, 2 - xv.

LC31.

WRIOTHESLEY, Sir Thomas (later Earl of Southampton; 1505-1550)*

28 Sept. 1538*g* - *c*.27 Mar. 1539*e*   [Special Ambassador]

Audience: 6 Oct. 1538

He went to the Regent Mary of Hungary, where he joined with Vaughan.

Instructions: *L&P*, xiii, 2, no. 419.

Correspondence: *L&P*, xiii, 2 - xiv, i.

LC32.
CARNE, Dr. Edward (later Sir Edward; 1495/6-1561)*

12 Oct. 1538[c] - *c*.27 Mar. 1539[e]   [Special Ambassador]
Audience: 9 Nov. 1538   20*s*/d?

He joined with Wriothesley and Vaughan, who were already there.

Instructions: Inferred from *L&P*, xiii, 2, no. 880.
Correspondence: *L&P*, xiii, 2 - xiv, 1.

LC33.
BROWNE, Sir Anthony (*c*.1500-1548)*

Early Sept. 1538[h] - *c*.30 Oct. 1538[g]   [Special Ambassador]
Audience: *c*.20 Oct. 1538

He visited Mary of Hungary and he also went to the French Court (q.v.),
    seemingly equally an object of this mission. He apparently returned briefly to
    England in late Sept.

Correspondence: *L&P*, xiii, 2.

LC34.
ST. LEGER, Sir Anthony (1496?-1559)*

30 Oct. 1539[d] - *c*.15 Nov. 1539[e]   [Special Ambassador]
                                          40*s*/d

He went to Mary of Hungary to secure a safe conduct through Flanders for Anne
    of Cleves.

Instructions: Suggested in *CSPS, 1538-42*, pp. 200-01.
Correspondence: *L&P*, xiv, 2.

LC35.
CARNE, Dr. Edward (later Sir Edward; 1495/6-1561)*
VAUGHAN, Stephen (by 1502-1549)*

17 June 1541[a] - late Dec. 1541[g]   [Resident Agents]
                                        20*s*/d (each)

Instructions: *L&P*, xvi, no. 906.
Correspondence: *L&P*, xvi.

LC36.
SEYMOUR, Sir Thomas (later Baron Seymour of Sudeley, 1508?-1549)*
WOTTON, Dr. Nicholas (later Sir Nicholas; 1497?-1567)*

30 Apr. 1543[a] - *c*.15 July 1543[f]   [Resident Ambassadors]
        (Seymour)   40*s*/d (Seymour); 26*s* 8*d*/d,
        1 Dec. 1543[f]   40*s*/d (after 24 June
        (Wotton)   1543—Wotton)

They went to the Regent, Mary of Hungary in Brussels, but then Wotton was
    accredited in November to the Emperor (q.v.).

Instructions: *L&P*, xviii, 1, no. 473.
Correspondence: *L&P*, xviii, 1-2.

LC37.
LAYTON, Dr. Richard (1500?-1544)*

24 Nov. 1543[h] - *died c.*9 June 1544 Resident Ambassador
Audience: 13 Dec. 1543

He resided with Mary of Hungary.

Instructions: Suggested in *L&P*, xviii, 2, no. 420.
Correspondence: *L&P*, xviii, 2 - xix, 1.

LC38.
PAGET, Sir William (later 1st Baron Paget of Beaudesert; 1505-1563)*

On a mission to the Emperor (q.v.), he had audience of the Regent *c.*21 May 1544.

LC39.
CARNE, Dr. Edward (later Sir Edward; 1495/6-1561)*

June 1544[h] - July 1548[g] Resident Ambassador
Audience: 15 July 1544

Correspondence: BL, Add. 25114; *L&P*, xix, 1 - xxi, 2; *CSPF, 1547-53*;
 Tytler, P. (ed.), *England under the Reigns of Edward VI...*(1839), i.

LC40.
PAGET, Sir William (later 1st Baron Paget of Beaudesert; 1505-1563)*

15 Feb. 1545[b] - 10 Apr. 1545[a] [Special Ambassador]
Audience: 2 Mar. 1545

He also visited the Emperor who was in the Low Countries (q.v.).

Instructions: *L&P*, xx, 1, no. 227.
Correspondence: *L&P*, xx, 1.

LC41.
GARDINER, Dr. Stephen, Bishop of Winchester (1483?-1555)*

While on a mission to the Emperor (q.v.) who was in the Low Countries, he also
 had audience of the Regent, 6 Nov. 1545.

LC42.
BELLINGHAM, Sir Edward (by 1507-1550)*

1 Feb. 1547[c] - *c.*5 Mar. 1547[c] [Special Ambassador]
Audience: *c.*7 Feb. 1547

Sent to announce the death of Henry VIII and the accession of Edward VI, he
 was accredited equally to the Emperor (q.v.) and to the Regent.

Instructions: *CSPF, 1547-53*, no. 5.
Correspondence: *CSPF, 1547-53*.

LC43.

SMITH, Sir Thomas (1513-1577)*

15 June 1548^d - early Aug. 1548^h [Special Ambassador]
Audience: 8 July 1548

He went to the Regent in the Low Countries. He was joined by the resident
   Carne and the governor of the Merchant Adventurers, Thomas Chamberlain.

Instructions: Inferred from *CSPF, 1547-53*, nos. 101-02.
Correspondence: BL, Cotton, Galba B.xii; *CSPF, 1547-53*.

LC44.

CHAMBERLAIN, Sir Thomas (*c.*1504-1580)*

20 June 1550^c - *c.*1 Sept. 1553^e Resident Ambassador
Audience: *c.*10 July 1550

Instructions: BL, Sloane 2442, f. 67, Add. 5935, f. 86, Harl. 353, ff. 105-06.
Correspondence: BL, Cotton, Galba B.xii, C.x, Eg. 3048, Harl. 353; *CSPF,
   1547-53*; HMC *Salisb.*, i; Tytler, *England under the Reigns of Edward VI...
   i-ii.*

LC45.

WOTTON, Dr. Nicholas (later Sir; 1497?-1567)*

On his way to the Emperor (q.v.) at Augsburg in 1551, Wotton visited the
   Regent, with an audience 20 May 1551.

LC46.

HOBY, Sir Philip (1505-1558)*

13 Feb. 1552^c - *c.*5 Mar. 1552^d [Special Ambassador]
Audience: *c.*27 Feb. 1552

Instructions: BL, Cotton, Galba B.xii, ff. 154-5, Add. 5498, ff. 29-35, Harl.
   353, ff. 116-19; *CSPS, 1550-2*, p. 451.
Correspondence: *CSPF, 1547-53*; *CSPS, 1550-2*; HMC *Salisb.*, i.

LC47.

DUDLEY, Sir Andrew (*c.*1507-1559)*

While on a mission to the Emperor (q.v.) in Luxembourg, he visited the Regent
   at Brussels, with an audience on 8 Jan. 1553.

LC48.

CHEYNE, Sir Thomas (1482/7-1558)*

8 Aug. 1553^d - *c.*1 Sept. 1553^d [Special Ambassador]
Audience: 21 Aug. 1553

He was accredited equally to the Emperor (q.v.) and to the Regent, both in
   Brussels at the time. Cheyne announced the death of Edward VI and the
   accession of Mary.

Instructions: Implied in *CSPF, 1553-8*, nos. 18, 22.
Correspondence: *CSPF, 1553-8*.

LC49.
THIRLBY, Dr. Thomas, Bishop of Norwich (later Bishop of Ely; 1506?-
1570)*
HOBY, Sir Philip (1505-1558)*

2 Apr. 1553[d] - *c.*15 Aug. 1553[c]   Resident Ambassador
Audience (Regent): 7 May 1553   66*s* 8*d*/d (Thirlby)

They joined with Morison, who was with the Emperor (their principal objective,
q.v.) at Brussels. Hoby remained in Brussels as resident with the Regent (see
below) who, in light of the Emperor's illness, they all had visited extensively.
Thirlby remained as the resident with the Emperor.

Instructions: BL, Add. 5498, f. 61; *CSPF, 1547-53*, no. 646.
Correspondence: BL, Harl. 523; *CSPF, 1547-53, 1553-8*; *APC, 1552-4*; Tytler,
England under the Reigns of Edward VI..., ii.

LC50.
HOBY, Sir Philip (1505-1558)*

2 Apr. 1553[d] - *c.*1 Sept. 1553[d]   [Resident Ambassador]
Audience (to establish resident status):
18 May 1553

He went originally with Thirlby to the Emperor (q.v.), where they joined with
Morison (see above). Hoby was credentialled to remain as resident with the
Regent.

Instructions: BL, Add. 5498, f. 61.
Correspondence: BL, Add. 5498; *CSPF, 1547-53, 1553-8*; HMC *Salisb.*, i.

LC51.
PAGET, William, 1st Baron Paget of Beaudesert (1505-1563)*

*c.*6 May 1555[h] - 14 June 1555[c]   [Peace Commissioner]
First meeting: 20 May 1555

This peace conference was at Marcq, near Calais.

Commission: BL, Cotton, Calig. E.v, ff. 17-20.
Correspondence: PRO, SP/69/5; BL, Cotton, Titus B.v, Calig. E.v; Paget,
W.,*The Letters of William Lord Paget...*, ed. Beer and Jack, Camden Misc.,
xxv (1974); Tytler, *England under the Reigns of Edward VI...*, ii.

LC52.
BROOKE, William, 7th Baron Cobham (1527-1597)*

23 Nov. 1558[h] - *c.*7 Jan. 1559[c]   [Special Ambassador]
Audience: 9 Dec. 1558

He was sent specifically to Philip II in Brussels to announce Queen Mary's
death. He also briefly joined the English peace commissioners at Cercamp
and Brussels. He was joined by Wotton (see below).

Instructions: BL, Cotton, Galba C.i, f. 28; *CSPF, 1558-9*, no. 27; KL, i,
pp. 304.
Correspondence: BL, Cotton, Galba C.i; *CSPF, 1558-9*; KL, i.

LC53.
WOTTON, Dr. Nicholas (later Sir Nicholas; 1497?-1567)*
HOWARD, William, 1st Baron Howard of Effingham (1510?-1573)*

Late Dec. 1558[c] - late Jan. 1559[f]   [Special Ambassador]
Audience: 8 Jan. 1559

Although Lord Howard is mentioned along with Wotton in the instructions, Howard did not participate in this mission to Philip II at Brussels. Wotton joined with Cobham. Wotton returned to the negotiations at Câteau-Cambrésis in late Jan. 1559.

Instructions: *CSPF, 1558-9*, no. 176.
Correspondence: BL, Cotton, Galba C.i; *CSPF, 1558-9*; KL, i.

LC54.
CHALONER, Sir Thomas (1521-1565)*

5 July 1559[b] - c.15 Feb. 1560[e]   [Resident Ambassador]
Audience: 3 Aug. 1559   66s 8d/d

Accredited first to Philip II, Chaloner was then accredited (16 Aug. 1559) to the Duchess of Parma, Regent in the Low Countries, when Philip returned to Spain.

Instructions: BL, Cotton, Galba C.i, f. 44; *CSPF, 1558-9*, no. 1005; KL, i, pp. 565-8.
Correspondence: BL, Cotton, Galba C.i, B.xi, Calig. B.viii; *CSPF, 1558-9*, 1559-60; HMC *Salisb.*, i; KL, i-ii.

LC55.
GRESHAM, Sir Thomas (1519?-1579)*

5 Feb. 1560[h] - c.Apr. 1563[h]   Agent
Audience: 5 Feb. 1560
Secretary: George Gilpin

He had been employed in the Low Countries during this and the previous reigns, but usually for non-diplomatic purposes. During this mission, he returned to England intermittently. His formal diplomatic responsibilities were not clearly terminated (and his role of financial agent abroad for Elizabeth in fact continued), but his diplomatic responsibilities seem to have ceased by the date provided above. He certainly continued to provide an unofficial point of contact when he was in the Low Countries, even after Apr. 1563.

Correspondence: BL, Add. 5935, 35830-1, Eg. 2790; *CSPF, 1560-1, 1561-2*; KL, ii.

LC56.
DALE, Dr. Valentine (by 1527-1589)*

27 Dec. 1563[b] - early Mar. 1564[h]   [Special Ambassador]
Audience: 23 Jan. 1564   40s/d

Dale was sent to the Regent to protest the stoppage of English shipping into the region. He was joined in March 1564 by Shers (see below).

Instructions: *CSPF, 1563*, no. 1547; KL, iii, pp. 583-7.
Correspondence: BL, Cotton, Galba C.i; *CSPF, 1564-5*; KL, iii.

LC57.
SHERS, John (*fl.*1540s-1560s)

20 Feb. 1564[b] - mid-Apr. 1564[h]   [Special Ambassador]
Audience: 21 Mar. 1564   40*s*/d
Secretary: George Gilpin

Instructions: *CSPF, 1564-5*, no. 177.
Correspondence: HMC *Pepys*.

LC58.
RADCLIFFE, Thomas, 3rd Earl of Sussex (1526?-1583)*

On his mission to the Emperor (q.v.) at Vienna, he visited the Regent in the Low Countries. Audience: 5 July 1567.

LC59.
COBHAM alias Brooke, Henry (later Sir Henry; 1538-1592)*

19 Aug. 1570[a] - 9 Dec. 1570[a]   [Special Ambassador]
Audience (with Alva): 28 Aug. 1570   40*s*/d
Audience (with Queen of Spain):
     29 Aug. 1570

This was a mission of courtesy to the new Queen of Spain, who was briefly in the Low Countries; to the Emperor (q.v.) who was at Speyer; and to discover the destination of a Spanish fleet that was outfitting.

Instructions: *CSPF, 1569-71*, no. 1129; KL, v, pp. 689-91.
Correspondence: BL, Cotton, Galba C.iv; *CSPF, 1569-71*; KL, v.

LC60.
FITZWILLIAM, John (*d.*1571)

Dec. 1570[h] - *c.*4 Mar. 1571[e]   [Agent?]
Audience: 2 Jan. 1571

He was sent to discuss the mutual seizures of shipping that had occurred and the decline of Anglo-Spanish relations with the Duke of Alva.

Instructions: Inferred from *CSPF, 1569-71*, nos. 1460, 1486, 1509; and KL, vi, pp. 27-8.
Correspondence: BL, Cotton, Galba C.iv, Harl. 285; *CSPF, 1569-71*; KL, vi.

LC61.
WILSON, Dr. Thomas (1523-1581)*

5 Nov. 1574[a] - 30 Mar. 1575[a]   [Special Ambassador]
Audience: *c.*11 Dec. 1574   53*s* 4*d*/d
Secretary: Daniel Rogers?

He was accredited to the Governor of the Low Countries.

Instructions: BL, Harl. 6992, no. 30; *CSPF, 1572-4*, no. 1587; KL, vii, pp. 349-51.

Correspondence: BL, Harl. 6991; *CSPF, 1572-4, 1575-7*; KL, vii; HMC *Salisb.*, i.

LC62.
ROGERS, Daniel (*c.*1538-1591)*

8 June 1575*c* - late Oct. 1575*h*   Agent
He was sent to the Prince of Orange.

Instructions: BL, Cotton, Galba C.v, ff. 140-2, 145, 149, Sloane 2442, ff. 111-12, Eg. 2790, ff. 172-4, Lansd. 155, ff. 125-6; *CSPF, 1575-7*, no. 169; KL, vii, pp. 531-3; HMC *2nd Report*, p. 97.

Correspondence: BL, Cotton, Galba C.v; *CSPF, 1575-7*; KL, vii.

LC63.
HASTINGS, John (*c.*1525-1585)*

20 Oct. 1575*a* - 4 Jan. 1576*a*   [Special Ambassador]
Audience: 14 Nov. 1575   20*s*/d
He was sent to the Prince of Orange.

Instructions: BL, Cotton, Galba C.v, ff. 189-99, 204-07, Sloane 2442, ff. 108-10, Eg. 2790, ff. 189-93, Lansd. 155, ff. 147b-151, Harl. 285, ff. 22-4; *CSPF, 1575-7*, no. 425; KL, viii, pp. 10-15; HMC *2nd Report*, p. 97.

Correspondence: BL, Harl. 285; *CSPF, 1575-7*; KL, viii.

LC64.
CORBET, Robert (1542-1583)*

21 Oct. 1575*a* - 16 Jan. 1576*b*   [Special Ambassador]
Audience: *c.*15 Nov. 1575   20*s*/d

He was sent to Don Luis Requesens, Spanish governor of the Low Countries.

Instructions: BL, Cotton, Galba C.v, ff. 170-82, 200-03, Sloane 2442, f. 81, Harl. 285, f. 30, Eg. 2790, ff. 185-9, Add. 5935, ff. 178-83, Lansd. 155, ff. 141-6, Harl. 285, ff. 26-29; *CSPF, 1575-7*, nos. 412, 424; KL, viii, pp. 8-9; HMC *2nd Report*, p. 97.

Correspondence: BL, Cotton, Galba C.vi, Harl. 285; *CSPF, 1575-7*; KL, viii.

LC65.
ROGERS, Daniel (*c.*1538-1591)*

*c.*1 Mar. 1576*h* - May 1576*h*   Agent
He also visited the Duke of Casimir (German States, q.v.).

Correspondence: BL, Cotton, Galba C.v; *CSPF, 1575-7*; KL, viii.

LC66.
HERBERT, John (later Sir John; *c*.1540-1617)*

4 Mar. 1576[b] - 29 Mar. 1576[c]   [Special Ambassador]
Audience: *c*.20 Mar. 1576   £90 (total?)

His primary objective was to convey the wife of the Portuguese ambassador into England, but he also met with the Prince of Orange.

Instructions: Implied in PRO, E/403/2422, [f. 61].
Correspondence about: *CSPF, 1575-7.*

LC67.
DAVISON, William (*c*.1541-1608)*

26 Mar. 1576[a] - 20 May 1576[a]   [Agent]
Audience: *c*.3 Apr. 1576   20*s*/d

He was sent to the Spanish government in the Low Countries, and then to the Prince of Orange.

Instructions: BL, Cotton, Galba C.v, ff. 264-7, Eg. 2790, ff. 194-6, Sloane 2442, ff. 91-3, Add. 5935, ff. 183-6, Lansd. 155, ff. 152b-6; *CSPF, 1575-7,* no. 705; KL, viii, pp. 303-07; HMC *2nd Report,* p. 97.
Correspondence: BL, Cotton, Galba C.v; *CSPF, 1575-7;* KL, viii.

LC68.
BEALE, ROBERT (1541-1601)*

16 Apr. 1576[a] - 26 July 1576[a]   [Special Ambassador]
Audience: *c*.1 May 1576   40*s*/d

He was sent to the Prince of Orange. William Wynter joined him in June (see below).

Instructions: BL, Cotton, Galba C.v, ff. 271-2, Titus B.ii, f. 464; Sloane 2442, f. 113, Eg. 2790, f. 200, Lansd. 155, ff. 161b-2; *CSPF, 1575-7,* nos. 736, 747; KL, viii, pp. 339-40; HMC *2nd Report,* p. 97.
Correspondence: BL, Cotton, Galba C.v, Add. 5935, 14028, Eg. 1694; *CSPF, 1575-7.*

LC69.
WYNTER, Sir William (*c*.1528-1589)*

19 June 1576[a] - 26 July 1576[a]   [Special Ambassador]
          40*s*/d

He joined with Beale (see above).

Instructions: *CSPF, 1575-7,* no. 819; KL, viii, pp. 399-403.
Correspondence: BL, Cotton, Galba C.v.

LC70.
ROGERS, Daniel (*c*.1538-1591)*

22 June 1576[b] - 1 Feb. 1578[a]   [Agent]

He seems to have been in the Low Countries more or less continuously between these dates (with periodic returns to England, especially May - July 1577). He acted partly as an autonomous diplomatic agent; partly as an adjunct to other English envoys sent to the area in this period. He also visited the Elector Palatine, the Duke of Saxony, and the Landgrave of Hesse in mid-1577 (German States, q.v.).

Instructions (upon return in July 1577): PRO, SP/104/163, nos. 19, 21; *CSPF, 1575-7*, no. 1486.

Correspondence: PRO, SP/104/163; BL, Cotton, Galba C.vi, pt. 1; *CSPF, 1575-7, 1577-8*; KL, ix; HMC *Salisb.*, ii.

LC71.
WILSON, Dr. Thomas (1523-1581)*

20 Oct. 1576[a] - c.13 July 1577[a]   [Special Ambassador]
Audience (with the Duke of Arschot   53s 4d/d
and the Spanish Council): 12 Nov.
1576
Audience (with Don Juan): 6 Mar.
1577

He was accredited to Don Juan.

Instructions: BL, Cotton, Galba C.v, ff. 272b-5, Sloane 2442, ff. 94-5, Eg. 2790, ff. 208-10, Lansd. 155, ff. 172-4; *CSPF, 1575-7*, no. 1035; KL, viii, pp. 484-7; HMC *2nd Report*, p. 97.

Correspondence: BL, Cotton, Galba C.v, D.i, Harl. 6992; *CSPF, 1575- 7*; KL, ix.

LC72.
HORSEY, Sir Edward (*d.*1583)*

12 Dec. 1576[a] - 16 Jan. 1577[a]   [Special Ambassador]
Audience: c.28 Dec. 1576   53s 4d/d

He was sent to Don Juan. Richard Bingham accompanied him in an undisclosed capacity.

Instructions: BL, Add. 5935, f. 182b, Cotton, Titus B.ii, ff. 459- 61, Eg. 2790, ff. 214b-17, Sloane 2442, f. 96, Harl. 36, f. 287, 6992, no. 30, Lansd. 155, ff. 182b-6; *CSPF, 1575-7*, nos. 1067, 1069; KL, ix, pp. 90-1; HMC *2nd Report*, p. 97.

Correspondence: *CSPF, 1575-7*; KL, ix.

LC73.

15 Jan. 1577[a] - 9 Feb. 1577[a]   [Special Ambassador]
    53s 4d/d

He was sent again 'suddenly' to Don Juan, and apparently to the Estates General as well.

Correspondence about: *CSPF, 1575-7*.

LC74.
DAVISON, William (*c*.1541-1608)*

18 Jan. 1577[h] - *c*.15 Feb. 1577?[h]   [Special Ambassador]

He was sent to the Prince of Orange.

Correspondence about: *CSPF, 1575-7*, no. 1257.

LC75.
SIDNEY, Philip (later Sir Philip; 1554-1586)*

During his mission to the Emperor and various German princes (qq.v.) in 1577, he visited Don Juan in the Low Countries on the trip to Prague (Audience: 6 Mar. 1577) and the Prince of Orange on the return journey (Audience: *c*.1 June 1577).

Correspondence: KL, ix, p. 309 (a summary of his visit with Orange).

LC76.
DAVISON, William (*c*.1541-1608)*

1 Aug. 1577[a] - *c*.25 May 1579[d]   Resident Agent
Audience: 14 Aug. 1577   26*s* 8*d*/d

George Gilpin of the Merchant Adventurers was associated with him in a semi-official capacity. Davison briefly returned to London in May 1578.

Instructions: BL, Eg. 2790, f. 228, Lansd. 155, ff. 199-200, Harl. 285, ff. 44-5; *CSPF, 1577-8*, nos. 72-3; KL, ix, pp. 436-7, 444-5; HMC *2nd Report*, p. 97.
Correspondence: BL, Cotton, Galba C.vi, pts. 1&2, C.ix, Titus B.ii, B.vii, Harl. 285; KL, ix-xi; *CSPF, 1577-8, 1578-9*.

LC77.
LEIGHTON, Thomas (later Sir Thomas; *c*.1535-1611)*

20 Dec. 1577[b] - 5 Feb. 1578[a]   [Special Ambassador]
Audience: 5 Jan. 1578   40*s*/d

He was sent to both the Estates General of the Low Countries and the Spanish Governor Don Juan.

Instructions: Cotton, Galba, C.vi, pt. 1, ff. 25-9; *CSPF, 1577-8*, nos. 535-6; KL, x, pp. 174-8.
Correspondence: *CSPF, 1577-8*.

LC78.

7 Feb. 1578[a] - 24 Feb. 1578[a]   [Special Ambassador]
    40*s*/d

He went again to the Prince of Orange and the Estates General.

Instructions: *CSPF, 1577-8*, nos. 634, 635; KL, x, pp. 274-5.
Correspondence about: *CSPF, 1577-8*.

LC79.
ROGERS, Daniel (*c.*1538-1591)*

5 Mar. 1578[b] - mid-May 1578[g]   [Special Ambassador]

On this mission he also went into Germany (q.v.).

Instructions: PRO, SP/104/163, nos. 51-2; BL, Cotton, Galba, C.vi, pt. 2,
    ff. 152-4; *CSPF, 1577-8*, nos. 680, 688, 702; KL, x, pp. 319-21.
Correspondence: *CSPF, 1577-8*; KL, x-xi.

LC80.
WILKES, Thomas (later Sir Thomas; *c.*1541-1598)*

3 Apr. 1578[a] - 29 Apr. 1578[a]   [Special Agent]
Audience: 8 Apr. 1578   13*s* 4*d*/d

He was sent to Don Juan.

Instructions: PRO, SP/104/163, nos. 51-2; *CSPF, 1577-8*, nos. 771-3.
Correspondence: *CSPF, 1577-8*, no. 830 (report on mission).

LC81.
BROOKE, William, Baron Cobham (1527-1597)*
WALSINGHAM, Sir Francis (*c.*1532-1590)*

12 June 1578[a] - 7 Oct. 1578[a]   [Special Ambassadors]
(Walsingham)   £5/d (each)
7 June 1578[a]
(Cobham)
Secretary: John Somers?, Laurence
    Thompson

They were accredited to the Spanish Governor of the Low Countries.

Instructions: BL, Cotton, Galba C.vi, pt. 2, ff. 169-70, Vesp. F.xii, ff. 202-03,
    Sloane 2442, ff. 89-90; *CSPF, 1578-9*, nos. 17-18; KL, x, pp. 518-21.
Correspondence: BL, Cotton, Galba C.vi, pt. 2 (includes a report), Titus B.ii;
    CSPF, 1578-9; KL, x.

LC82.
ROGERS, Daniel (*c.*1538-1591)*

5 Dec. 1578[d] - mid-Jan. 1579[c]   [Agent?]

He also went to the Duke Casimir in Germany (q.v.).

Instructions: *CSPF, 1578-9*, no. 439.
Correspondence: *CSPF, 1578-9*.

Diplomatic contact was seemingly quite informal between 1579 and 1582. What
    relations there were, various merchants handled, especially George Gilpin
    (secretary to the Merchant Adventurers), Christopher Hoddesdon (governor
    of the Merchant Adventurers) and Leicester's agent William Herle, none of
    whom were formally accredited envoys on specific missions.

LC83.
WILKES, Thomas (later Sir Thomas; *c.*1541-1598)*

*c.*1 June 1582[h] - end June 1582[h]   Agent

He was sent to the Prince of Orange.

Correspondence: Van Prinsterer, G. Groen, *Archives ou Correspondance Inédite de la Maison D'Orange Nassau*, 1st ser., viii, pp. 105-11.

LC84.
GREVILLE, Fulke (later 1st Baron Brooke of Beauchamps Court; 1554-1628)*

Late Mar. 1582[h] - *c.*10 Apr. 1582[g]   [Special Ambassador]
Arrived: 1 Apr. 1582

Correspondence: *CSPF, 1581-2.*

LC85.
DARCY, Edward (later Sir Edward; 1543-1612)*

*c.*20 Jan. 1583[h] - 2 Mar. 1583[a]   [Special Ambassador]
Audience (Duke of Anjou): 31 Jan.
  1583
Audience (Prince of Orange): 3 Feb.
  1583

Instructions: Inferred from *CSPF, 1583*, no. 90.
Correspondence: *CSPF, 1583.*

LC86.
SOMERS, John (1527-1585)

15 Mar. 1583[a] - 20 Apr. 1583[a]   [Special Ambassador]
Audience (Duke of Anjou):   20s/d
  24 Mar. 1583
Audience (Estates General): 1 Apr.
  1583
Audience (Prince of Orange): 2 Apr.
  1583

He was sent primarily to Francis, Duke of Anjou and Alençon, who was in the Low Countries.

Instructions: Inferred from *CSPF, 1583*, nos. 204, 225.
Correspondence: *CSPF, 1583.*

LC87.
DYER, Edward (later Sir Edward; 1543-1607)*

Late Jan. 1584[h] - *c.*1 Mar. 1584[e]   [Special Ambassador]
Arrived: 31 Jan. 1584

He was sent to the Prince of Orange.

Instructions: *CSPF, 1583-4*, no. 793.
Correspondence: PRO, SP/84/21; BL, Cotton, Galba C.vii; *CSPF, 1583-4.*

LC88.
HERLE, William (*d.*1589)*

8 June 1584*d* - Oct. 1584*g*   [Special Ambassador]

He was sent to Count John of Emden.

Instructions: *CSPF, 1583-4*, no. 668.
Correspondence: BL, Harl. 286; Bodl., Rawlinson Mss. C.424; *CSPF, 1583-4*.

LC89.
DAVISON, William (*c.*1541-1608)*

20 Oct. 1584*a* - *c.*1 June 1585*e*   [Special Ambassador]
Audience: 27 Nov. 1584   40*s*/d

Instructions: *CSPF, 1584-5*, pp. 149-51.
Correspondence: BL, Cotton, Galba C.viii, Lansd. 150, Harl. 285, 6936;
  CSPF, 1584-5.

LC90.

25 Aug. 1585*a* - 13 Feb. 1586*a*   [English Councillor]
Audience: 12 Sept. 1585   40*s*/d

Instructions: *CSPF, 1585-6*, pp. 36, 42-3.
Correspondence: BL, Cotton, Galba C.viii, Lansd. 102, Harl. 285; *CSPF,
  1585-6*.

LC91.
KILLIGREW, Henry (later Sir Henry; *c.*1528-1603)*
CLERKE, Dr. Bartholmew (*c.*1537-1590)*

26 Nov. 1585*b* - *c.*10 Nov. 1586*h*   [English Councillors]
          (Clerke)   40*s*/d each
          *c.*20 Nov. 1586*h*
          (Killigrew)
Arrival: *c.*1 Jan. 1586 (Clerke)
          *c.*24 Jan. 1586 (Killigrew)

They both served on the Dutch Council of State for approximately one year.

Correspondence: BL, Add. 3299, Cotton, Galba C.x; *CSPF, 1585-6, 1586-7*.

LC92.
HENEAGE, Sir Thomas (by 1532-1595)*

*c.*14 Feb. 1586*h* - 9 June 1586*a*   [Special Ambassador]
Audience: 14 Mar. 1586

Instructions: BL, Cotton, Galba C.viii, ff. 24-8; inferred from *CSPF, 1585-6*,
  pp. 445-6; Dudley, R., Earl of Leicester, *Correspondence...1585 and 1586*,
  Camden o.s., xxvii (1844), pp. 105-10.
Correspondence: BL, Cotton, Galba C.ix, Titus B.vii; *CSPF, 1585-6*.

LC93.

HERLE, William (*d*.1589)*

c.1 Apr. 1586[h] - late Apr. 1586[h]   [Special Ambassador]

The Earl of Leicester, upon direction from the Privy Council, sent him to Count Edzard of Emden.

Instructions: CSPF, 1585-6, pp. 466, 702.
Correspondence: BL, Cotton, Galba D.ix, Lansd. 43, Sloane 3299.
Correspondence about: *CSPF, 1585-6.*

LC94.

WILKES, Thomas (later Sir Thomas; *c*.1541-1598)*

16 July 1586[a] - 15 Sept. 1586[c]   [Special Ambassador]
Audience: 7 Aug. 1586   40*s*/d

Instructions: BL, Add. 14028, f. 66, 48104, ff. 263-6.
Correspondence: *CSPF, 1586-7.*

LC95.

12 Oct. 1586[b] - early July 1587[d]   [English Councillor]
Arrived: *c*.24 Oct. 1586   40*s*/d

Instructions: BL, Cotton, Galba, C.x, ff. 79-82; *CSPF, 1586-7*, pp. 249-51; Dudley, *Correspondence*, pp. 432-7.
Correspondence: PRO, SP/105/91; BL, Cotton, Galba C.v, x, Titus B.ii, Add. 5935, 21506, Harl. 6994; *CSPF, 1586-7, 1587.*

LC96.

KILLIGREW, Henry (later Sir Henry; *c*.1528-1603)*

25 June 1587[c] - *c*.30 Jan. 1589[e]   [English Councillor]

He was appointed to the Dutch Council of State.

Correspondence: *CSPF, 1587, 1588*; BL, Cotton, Galba D.iii, Add. 5935, Eg. 1694, Harl. 287; HMC *Ancaster.*

LC97.

BEALE, Robert (1541-1601)*

26 June 1587[c] - *c*.28 Sept. 1587[e]   [English Councillor]
Arrived: *c*.10 July 1587

He joined with Killigrew on the Dutch Council of State.

Instructions: *CSPF, 1587*, pp. 129-30, 167.
Correspondence: BL, Cotton, Galba D.i-iv, Add. 5935, 48014; *CSPF, 1587, 1588* (xxi-4), 1588 (xxii), 1589.

LC98.

SACKVILLE, Thomas, Baron Buckhurst (later Earl of Dorset; 1535/6-1608)*

CLERKE, Dr. Bartholomew (*c.*1537-1590)*

4 Mar. 1587*ᵃ* - *c.*14 July 1587*ᶜ*   [Special Ambassadors]
Arrived: 24 Mar. 1587   £4/d (Buckhurst)

Instructions: *CSPF, 1586-7,* pp. 411-12.
Correspondence: BL, Cotton, Galba D.i (summary) - iii, Add. 5935, 48078; *CSPF, 1586-7, 1587.*

LC99.

ROGERS, Daniel (*c.*1538-1591)*

He apparently had audiences at the Hague both on his way to Denmark (q.v.) in late 1587 and on his return journey, mid-Jan. 1588.

LC100.

HERBERT, Dr. John (later Sir John; *c.*1540-1617)*

17 Oct. 1587*ᵃ* - *c.*4 Feb. 1588*ᵍ*   [Special Ambassador]
Arrived: 6 Nov. 1587   40*s*/d

Instructions: *CSPF, 1587,* pp. 365-7.
Correspondence: *CSPF, 1587, 1588* (xxi-4).

LC101.

DALE, Dr. Valentine (by 1527-1589)*

30 Nov. 1587*ᵇ* - 10 Aug. 1588*ᶜ*   [Special Ambassador]
                                 53*s* 4*d*/d

He later joined with the peace commissioners in the Low Countries (Conferences, q.v.)

Instructions: HMC *Salisb.,* iii, p. 341.
Correspondence: BL, Lansd. 58. For the pre-Armada peace negotiations, see under Conferences, Congresses.

LC102.

NORRIS, Sir John (*c.*1547-1597)*

9 Oct. 1588*ᵈ* - *c.*20 Dec. 1588*ʰ*   [Special Ambassador]
Audience: 26 Oct. 1588

He was sent to the Estates General.

Instructions: *CSPF, 1588* (xxii), pp. 221 and 247-50.
Correspondence: *CSPF, 1588* (xxii).

LC103.

BODLEY, Thomas (later Sir Thomas; 1545-1613)*

8 Nov. 1588*ᶜ* - *c.*10 June 1593*ᵉ*   English Councillor
Audience: 3 Jan. 1589   40*s*/d
Secretary: George Gilpin

He served on the Dutch Council of State.

Instructions: PRO, SP/84/63B, f. 380; *CSPF, 1588* (xxii), pp. 324-5, 333-4, 356.

Correspondence: PRO, SP/84/34-46, SP/103/34, SP/105/91; BL, Cotton, Galba D.iii-v, vii-ix, Titus B.ii, Harl. 287; *CSPF, 1588* (xxii), *1589; L&A, 1589-90, 1590-1; CSPD, 1591-4; APC, 1588-9* through *1592-3;* HMC *Salisb.,* iv; HMC *Ancaster.*

LC104.

WILKES, Thomas (later Sir Thomas; *c.*1541-1598)*

20 May 1590*ª* - *c.*26 Aug. 1590*ᵉ*   [Special Ambassador]
Audience: 13 June 1590   40*s*/d

He was sent to the States General in place of Thomas Sackville, Lord Buckhurst, who was originally scheduled for this mission. Wilkes joined with Bodley there.

Instructions: PRO, SP/84/37, ff. 176-81, 242-3; BL, Cotton, Galba D.vii, ff. 155-64, 167-9.

Correspondence: PRO, SP/84/37-8, SP/105/91; Cotton, Galba D.vii, Harl. 287; *APC, 1590;* HMC *De Lisle and Dudley,* i; Collins, A. (ed.), *Letters and Memorials of State...*(1746), i; Netherlands, U.P., Staaten General, *Resolutien der Staten Generall van 1576 tot 1609...*(S-Gravenhage, 1915-30), vii; HMC *Salisb.,* iv.

LC105.

PALAVICINO, Sir Horatio (*d.*1600)*

He and Turenne visited Middelburg *c.*8 Dec. 1590 on their way to Germany (q.v.).

LC106.

NORRIS, Sir John (*c.*1547-97)*

1 Jan. 1591*ᶜ* - *c.*20 Mar. 1591*ʰ*   [Special Ambassador]
Audience: 27 Jan. 1591

He was sent to the States General and there joined with Bodley. He returned to England briefly in early February. His mission did not conclude in England, but his diplomatic duties were superseded by military responsibilities, *c.*20 Mar 1591.

Instructions: PRO, SP/84/41, f. 3; BL, Cotton, Galba D.vii, pp. 15-18; *L&A, 1590-1,* no. 262.

Correspondence: PRO, SP/84/41-2; BL, Cotton, Galba D.vii, viii; *L&A, 1590-1.*

LC107.

GILPIN, George (1514-1602)*

*c.*30 June 1593*ʰ* - *d.*4 Sept. 1602   English Councillor

He began in Mar. 1586 as the English secretary to the Dutch Council of State, but he became a fully accredited councillor c.30 June 1593, replacing Bodley, and then continued in that role despite Bodley's return.

Correspondence: PRO, SP/84/46-61; BL, Cotton, Galba D.x, xii, Sloane 35, 4205, Stowe 166; *APC, 1592-3, 1594-5, 1595-6, 1596-7, 1597-8, 1598-9, 1600-01*; HMC *Salisb.*, iv-xii.

LC108.
BODLEY, Thomas (later Sir Thomas; 1545-1613)*

4 May 1594[a] - c.31 Dec. 1596[h]	[Special Ambassador and
Audience: 21 May 1594	English Councillor]
	40s/d

He was sent to the States General and Prince Maurice and remained to serve again on the Dutch Council of State. He returned briefly to England, at least in autumn 1594 and July 1595.

Instructions: PRO, SP/84/48, f. 185; BL, Cotton, Galba D.x, ff. 111-13, Galba D.xi, ff. 3-6.
Correspondence: PRO, SP/84/48-53; BL, Add. 15552, Cotton, Galba D.x- xii (f. 88b is a summary of negotiations); *CSPD, 1595-7*; *APC, 1595-6*; HMC *Salisb.*, v-vi, xiv.

LC109.
VERE, Sir Francis (c.1560-1609)*

3 Feb. 1596[c] - c.20 Apr. 1596[g]   [Special Ambassador]

This diplomatic assignment was apparently undertaken in the midst of his military responsibilities in the Low Countries.

Instructions: PRO, SP/84/52, ff. 82-3.
Correspondence: PRO, SP/84/52; HMC *Salisb.*, vi-vii.

LC110.
FLETCHER, Dr. Giles (1546-1611)*

May 1598[c] - late July 1598[c]   [Special Ambassador]

He went to the Hague, in company with five members of the Merchant Adventurers, to discuss commercial disputes and privileges. He seemingly had ambassadorial status, although this is unclear.

Instructions: PRO, SP/12/268, no. 5.
Correspondence: HMC *Salisb.*, viii; Berry, L. (ed.), *The English Works of Giles Fletcher*...(Madison, Wisc., 1964).

LC111.
VERE, Sir Francis (c.1560-1609)*

7 June 1598[c] - July? 1598[h]   [Special Ambassador]
Audience: 18 June 1598

He was accompanied by George Gilpin. He went directly from this diplomatic assignment to a command of English troops at Ostend.

Instructions: PRO, SP/84/56, f. 157; BL, Cotton, Galba D.xii, ff. 159-72; implied from *CSPV, 1592-1603*, pp. 356-60.

LC112.

c.1 Nov. 1598[h] - c.30 Dec. 1598[e]   [Special Ambassador]
Audience: c.3 Nov. 1598

Again Vere left his military responsibilities to negotiate alongside Gilpin at the Hague.

Correspondence: *APC, 1598-9*; HMC *Salisb.*, viii-ix.

LC113.
WINWOOD, Ralph (1563?-1617)*

1 Apr. 1603[a] - c.1 June 1607[c]   Agent
Audience: July 17 1603   40s/d

Instructions: Inferred from his maiden speech to the Dutch Assembly, PRO, SP/84/64, ff. 32-5.
Correspondence: PRO, SP/84/64-6; BL, Stowe 167-9, Add. 40837; HMC *Salisb.*, xvi, xvii, xix; Winwood Papers at Boughton House.

LC114.
VERE, Sir Francis (c.1560-1609)*

Late Nov. 1605[h]- June 1606[e]   [Special Ambassador]
Audience: c.14 Dec. 1605

Instructions: Inferred from HMC *Salisb.*, xvii, p. 553.
Correspondence: PRO, SP/84/65; HMC *Salisb.*, xvii-xviii; Markham, Sir C., *The Fighting Veres*...(1888).

LC115.
WINWOOD, Sir Ralph (1563?-1617)*
SPENCER, Sir Richard (1553-1624)*

17 June 1607[a] - 25 June 1609[a]   Commissioners
(Winwood)   £4/d (Spencer),
6 July 1607[a]   £2/d (Winwood)
(Spencer)
Audience: 28 Aug. 1607
Secretary: John Dickenson

Spencer returned on the date cited. Winwood, who was paid until this date, had returned approximately six weeks earlier. Winwood went back to the Low Countries almost immediately to assume the residency (see below).

Instructions: PRO, SP/84/66, f. 50, SP/105/92, ff. 5-20; Sawyer, *Winwood State Papers*, ii, p. 329.
Correspondence: PRO, SP/84/66, SP/105/92; BL, Stowe 170; HMC *Salisb.*, xix; Sawyer, *Winwood State Papers*, iii.

LC116.
DICKENSON, John (*fl.*1600s-1610s)

17 June 1609[a] - 1 Sept. 1609[b]   [Chargé d'Affaires]
Correspondence: PRO, SP/84/66.

LC117.
WINWOOD, Sir Ralph (1563?-1617)*

25 June 1609[a] - *c.*8 Sept. 1613[a]   Resident Ambassador
Audience: *c.*1 Sept. 1609   66*s* 8*d*/d
Secretary: John Dickenson

While resident at the Hague, he undertook separate missions to various German princes (q.v.), both in 1610 and 1612. He also had numerous returns to England, including Jun. - July 1612.

Instructions: Inferred from BL, Stowe 171, f. 111; Sawyer, *Winwood State Papers*, vi.
Correspondence: PRO, SP/84/66-9, SP/105/93; HMC *Salisb.*, xxi; Sawyer, *Winwood State Papers*.

LC118.
WOTTON, Sir Henry (later Sir; 1568-1639)*

1 June 1614[a] - *c.*14 Sept. 1615[c]   Ambassador Extraordinary
Audience: *c.*20 Aug. 1614   £4/d

Correspondence: PRO, SP/84/70-1; *CSPCol/EI, 1513-1616*; Watson, C. (ed.), 'Letters from Sir Henry Wotton to King James I...' *Archaeologia*, xl (1863).

LC119.
EDMONDES, Clement (later Sir Clement; 1564?-1622)*
MIDDLETON, Robert (*fl.*1610s)
ABBOT, Maurice (1565-1642)*

29 Dec. 1614[b] - *c.*5 May 1615[c]   Commissioners
Audience: 30 Jan. 1615   £300 (Edmondes); £200 (Abbot and
                                            Middleton each)

They were involved in commercial negotiations with the Dutch, and were joined with Ambassador Wotton.

Instructions: Referred to in Clark, G. and Eysinga, W., 'The Colonial Conferences between England and the Netherlands...,' *Bibliotheca Visseriana Dissertationum Jus Internationale*, xvii (1940-51), pp. 149-51; also inferred in *CSPCol/EI, 1513-1616*, nos. 853-5, 874.
Correspondence: PRO, SP/84/71-2; *CSPCol/EI, 1513-1616*; BL, Harl. 147; *CSPD, 1611-18*; Clark and Eysinga, 'The Colonial Conferences...', xv.

LC120.
CARLETON, Sir Dudley (later Baron Carleton of Imbercourt, Viscount Dorchester; 1573-1632)*

1 Dec. 1615*a* - 10 Dec. 1625*a* [Resident Ambassador]
Audience: 20 Mar. 1616 66s 8d/d, £4/d (on 13 Nov. 1622)
Secretary: Dudley Carleton (a nephew,
  served after *c.*1622)

He returned to London only once, that being in June 1618.

Instructions: PRO, SP/84/72, ff. 8-14; Carleton, Dudley, Viscount Dorchester, *Letters from and to Sir Dudley Carleton Knt. during his embassy in Holland, from January 1615/16 to December 1620*, ed. Philip Yorke (1757).

Correspondence: PRO, SP/84/72-130, SP/104/167; BL, Add. 4148, 4173- 5, 6394, 22867, 23103, 35832, 36444-7, 39288, 46188, Eg. 2592-6, Harl. 1580, Stowe 133, 176; *CSPD, 1611-18, 1619-23, 1623-5, 1625-6*; HMC *Salisb.*, xxii; Carleton, *Letters...*; Carleton, Dudley, Viscount Dorchester, *The Speech of Sir Dudley Carleton...[to] the Estates Generall of the United Provinces of the Low Countries...*(1618); Carleton, Dudley, Viscount Dorchester, *Lettres, Memoires et Negotiations du Chevalier Carleton...*(La Nave and Leide, 1759); Baker, L., *The Letters of Queen Elizabeth of Bohemia* (1953); Birch, T. (ed.), *The Court and Times of James the First...*(1849); Lee, M. (ed.), *Dudley Carleton to John Chamberlain, 1603-1624...(New Brunswick, N.J., 1972); Chamberlain, John, The Letters of John Chamberlain*, ed. McClure (Philadelphia, Pa., 1939).

LC121.
HAY, James, 1st Viscount Doncaster (later Earl of Carlisle; *c.*1580- 1636)*

On his return from the Emperor and various German States (qq.v.), he had audience with the States General, 18 Dec. 1619.

LC122.
ABBOT, Maurice (1565-1642)*
DIGGES, Sir Dudley (1583-1639)*

Mid-Nov. 1620*h* - *c.*10 Feb. 1621*e* Commissioners
Audience: *c.*18 Nov. 1620

Instructions: PRO, CO/77/1, f. 95; and inferred from *CSPV, 1619-21*, pp. 487-8, 502-03.
Correspondence: PRO, SP/84/98.

LC123.
CHICHESTER, Arthur, Baron Chichester of Belfast (1563-1625)*

On a mission to the Palatinate and the Emperor (qq.v.), he stopped at the Hague. He had audience 9 May 1622.

LC124.
ANSTRUTHER, Sir Robert (*fl.*1600s-1640s)

On his way to Denmark (q.v.), he stopped at the Hague, where he remained from 25 June 1624 through 5 July 1624.

LC125.
MORTON, Sir Albert (1584?-1625)

12 May 1625[a] - 24 Aug. 1625[a]	Ambassador Extraordinary
Audience: 1 July 1625	£6/d

Correspondence: PRO, SP/84/128.

LC126.
VILLIERS, George, 1st Duke of Buckingham (1592-1628)*
RICH, Henry, 1st Earl of Holland (1590-1649)*

1 Sept. 1625[a] - 7 Dec. 1625[c]	Ambassadors Extraordinary
Audience: 10 Nov. 1625	

They were sent to negotiate an Anglo – Dutch – Danish treaty of alliance, and also to raise money by pawning some of the royal jewels.

Instructions: PRO, SP/84/129, f. 188.
Correspondence: PRO, SP/84/129-30.

LC127.
ANSTRUTHER, Sir Robert (*fl.*1600s-1640s)

Again on his way to Denmark (q.v.), Anstruther had audience at the Hague, mid-Nov. 1625.

LC128.
SPENCE, Sir James (*fl.*1600s-1620s)

On his mission to Sweden (q.v.), Spence had audience with the Palatine royals in the Low Countries and also 'some of the states' of the United Provinces, *c.*1 Apr. 1625.

LC129.
CARLETON, Dudley (later Sir Dudley; *fl.*1620s-1630s)

26 Dec. 1625[h] - 9 Nov. 1632[a]	Chargé d'Affaires, then Agent, then Resident Ambassador
	20s/d, later 40s/d

He assumed responsibility for the legation when the Duke of Buckingham returned to England accompanied by the resident, his uncle Sir Dudley Carleton (later Baron Carleton and Viscount Dorchester). He was appointed resident agent *c.*23 Feb. 1628.

Correspondence: PRO, SP/84/137-45, SP/104/167, 170.

LC130.

CARLETON, Dudley, Baron Carleton of Imbercourt (later Viscount Dorchester; 1573-1632)*

1 Nov. 1626[a] - 2 June 1628[a]   [Resident Ambassador]
Audience: 14 June 1627   £6/d
Secretary: Dudley Carleton [nephew]

He was joined by the Earl of Carlisle, May 1628.

Instructions: PRO, SP/84/133, ff. 162, 186, 215; HMC *4th Report*, p. 372; Carleton, Dudley, *Viscount Dorchester; Sir Dudley Carleton's State Papers during his Embassy at the Hague, 1627*...ed. Thomas Phillipps (1841), pp. 5-15.

Correspondence: PRO, SP/84/133-7, SP/104/167, 169; BL, Add. 4106, 4148, 36778 (letterbook); *CSPD, 1627-8*; Carleton, *Carleton's State Papers*.

LC131.

HAY, James, Earl of Carlisle (*c.*1580-1636)*

1 Jan. 1628[a] - 28 Jan. 1629[c]   Ambassador Extraordinary
Audience: 1 May 1628   £8/d
Investment: 12 May 1628
Secretary: William Boswell, Thomas
Rowlandson

He joined Carleton, and invested Frederick Henry, Prince of Orange, with the Garter. He continued to Savoy, Venice, Switzerland and the Spanish Netherlands (qq.v.).

Instructions: PRO, SP/84/137, ff. 43-4, SP/92/13, ff. 70, 202, SP/92/14, f. 246.

Correspondence: PRO, SP/84/137, SP/104/169; *CSPD, 1628-9*.

LC132.

PORTER, Endymion (1587-1649)*

He visited the Hague on his way to the Spanish Netherlands and Spain (qq.v.), *c.*Sept. 1628.

LC133.

VANE, Sir Henry (1589-1655)*

6 Mar. 1629[a] - *c.*24 May 1629[c]   Ambassador Extraordinary
Audience: 20 Mar. 1629   £4/d

He also visited the Palatinate royals at Rhenen (German States, q.v.)

Instructions: PRO, SP/84/139, f. 60.

Correspondence: PRO, SP/84/139; *CSPD, 1628-9*; *Add. 1625-49*.

LC134.

ROE, Sir Thomas (1581?-1644)*

While on a mission to the peace negotiations between Sweden and Poland (qq.v.), he stopped in the Low Countries, and had audience at the Hague, 2 July 1629.

LC135.
VANE, Sir Henry (1589-1655)*

19 Sept. 1629[b] - 29 Apr. 1630[a]	Ambassador Extraordinary
Audience: 5 Nov. 1629	£4/d

Instructions: PRO, SP/84/140, f. 116, SP/104/170, pp. 42-8.
Correspondence: PRO, SP/84/140-1; *CSPD, 1629-31, Add. 1625-49.*

LC136.

1 May 1630[a] - 18 Jan. 1631[a]	Ambassador Extraordinary
Arrived: 29 July 1630	£6/d

On this mission, his objective was the Emperor in Vienna (q.v.) but he stopped for a substantial period (until Dec.) in the Hague.

Instructions (for Holland): PRO, SP/84/141, f. 284.
Correspondence: PRO, SP/84/141-2; BL, Harl. 7000; *CSPD, 1629-31, Add. 1625-49.*

LC137.
PRINGLE, James (*d.*1630)

30 July 1630[b] - *d.*Aug.? 1630[h]	[Special Ambassador]
£200 (total)	

Instructions: Inferred from PRO, E/403/2749, p. 226.

LC138.
BOSWELL, Sir William (*d.*1649)*

31 Jan. 1631[b] - *d.*June 1649	Resident Agent,
Audience: 28 Aug. 1632	[Resident] Ambassador
Secretary: Mr. Oudart, John Bouillon	(from *c.*July 1634)
	40*s*/d

He returned to England early in 1634, received a new privy seal (16 Mar. 1634, with the same diets but enhanced status), and again took up his responsibilities at the Hague that same month. He continued as resident until his death. Early in 1635, he travelled to Prince Charles, Elector Palatine (German States, q.v.), to invest him with the Garter. He also apparently returned for a visit to England in summer of 1640.

Instructions: PRO, SP/84/144, ff. 162-78.
Correspondence: PRO, SP/84/144-58; BL, Add. 4106, 6394-5, 15857, 34600, 37047, Harl. 374, 7001, Stowe 133; *ThSP*, i; *CSPD, 1631-44*; Hervey, M., *The Life, Correspondence and Collections of Thomas Howard ...* (Cambridge, 1921).

LC139.
HOWARD, Thomas, 2nd Earl of Arundel and Surrey (later Earl of Norfolk; 1585-1646)*
ANSTRUTHER, Robert (*fl*.1600s-1640s)

10 Dec. 1632*ᵃ* - 4 Feb. 1633*ᵃ*   [Ambassadors Extraordinary]
Audience: 4 Jan. 1633   £8/d (Arundel)

Accredited to the Prince of Orange and the States General, Arundel also went to the Queen of Bohemia. Anstruther, resident in Denmark, joined him the Low Countries, and then returned to Denmark (q.v.).

Instructions: PRO, SP/84/145, f. 198.
Correspondence: PRO, SP/84/145-6; Hervey, *The Life of Thomas Howard.*

LC140.
HOWARD, Thomas, 2nd Earl of Arundel and Surrey (later Earl of Suffolk; 1585-1646)

He stopped and counselled with the Prince of Orange and the Estates General of the Low Countries on his way to the German Emperor (q.v.) in 1636. Audience in Low Countries: 11 Apr. 1636. He also returned by way of the Hague, arriving there 17 Dec. 1636.

LC141.
ROE, Sir Thomas (1581?-1644)*

On a mission to the Emperor and various German States (qq.v.), he had audience in the Low Countries, mid-May 1641.

LC142.
STRICKLAND, Walter (*fl*.1640s-1660s)*

26 Aug. 1642*ᵍ* - *c*.2 Aug. 1650*ᶜ*   [Resident Ambassador]
Audience: *c*.31 Aug. 1642   £400/an.

He went to serve as resident for Parliament. He returned briefly to England at least in Oct. 1649 and Jan. 1650.

Instructions: Inferred from HMC *10th Report*, pp. 6, 87.
Correspondence: PRO, SP/84/157-8; Bodl., Tanner Mss. 56-9, 62; *CSPD, 1644, 1644-5, 1645-7, 1648-9, 1649-50, 1650*; *ThSP*, i; Cary, Henry (ed.), *Memorials of the Great Civil War...* (1842), i, ii.

LC143.
GORING, George, Baron Goring (later Earl of Norwich; 1583?-1663)*

On his journey to France (q.v.), he stopped in Holland *c*.10 Oct. 1643, to consult with the Prince of Orange.

LC144.
DORISLAUS, Dr. Isaac (1595-1649)*

1 Oct. 1648*ᶜ* - 1648*ʰ*   [Special Ambassador]

LC145.

20 Apr. 1649[d] - *d.*12 May 1649   [Resident Ambassador]
Arrived: 9 May 1649

Royalist agents assassinated this Parliamentary representative.

Instructions: *CSPD, 1649-50*, p. 103.
Correspondence about: *ThSP*, i.

LC146.
STRICKLAND, Walter *(fl.*1640-1660s)*
ST. JOHN, Oliver (1598?-1673)*

14 Feb. 1651[b] - 28 June 1651[a]   Ambassadors Extraordinary
Audience: 25 Mar. 1651
Secretary: John Thurloe

Instructions: *ThSP*, i, pp. 182-3; HMC *Portland*, i, pp. 557-8.
Correspondence: Bodl., Tanner Mss. 54, Rawlinson Mss. 2; *ThSP*, i; HMC
    Portland, i; Cary, *Memorials of the Great Civil War...*, ii.

LC147.
BONEL, Peter *(fl.*1650s)

6 May 1653d - n.d.   [Special Ambassador]
Audience: 13 May 1653

He was sent to the Estates General.

Instructions: *ThSP*, i, p. 244.

LC148.
DOWNING, Sir George, 1st Bart. (1623-1684)*

18 Dec. 1657[a] - *c.*1 Sept. 1665[e]   Envoy Extraordinary
Audience: *c.*10 Feb 1657   £1000/an.
Secretary: Included N. Greenham

He returned to England at the Restoration, and was re-accredited to the Hague,
    to which he returned, June 1661, with a new privy seal authorization. He
    visited England late 1662-1663, and June 1664. He returned to England at the
    end of his assignment *c.*Sept. 1665, but his pay continued for another three
    months because of his expenses in returning home.

Instructions: Inferred from *ThSP*, vi, pp. 637, 639, 676.
Correspondence: PRO, SP/84/162, 164-77; BL, Add. 4158, 4197, 22919, Eg.
    2537-8, 2618, Lansd. 1236, 7010; Bodl., Clarendon Mss. 104- 05, Carte
    Mss. 73, Rawlinson Mss. A.61-3; *ThSP*, vi-vii; *CSPD, 1658-9, 1659-60,
    1663-4*; Abbott, W., *The Writings and Speeches of Oliver Cromwell*
    (Cambridge, Mass., 1937-47), iv; Lister, T., *Life and Administration of
    Edward, First Earl of Clarendon...* (1837-8); Latham, R. and Matthews, W.,
    The Diary of Samuel Pepys (Berkeley, 1970).

LC149.
TEMPLE, Sir William, 1st Bart. (1628-1699)*

17 Dec. 1667[h] - 28 Dec. 1667[c]   [Special Ambassador]
Audience: *c.*20 Dec. 1667

Instructions: Courtenay, T., *Memoirs of the Life, Works and Correspondence of Sir William Temple...*(1836), ii, App. B, pp. 381-4.
Correspondence: PRO, SP/77/37; Temple, W., *The Works of Sir William Temple, Bart...*, ed. Jonathan Swift (1720), iii.

LC150.

3 Jan. 1668[f] - 13 Feb. 1668[f]   [Special Ambassador]
Audience: 9 Jan. 1668

Instructions: Courtenay, T., *Memoirs of the Life, Works and Correspondence of Sir William Temple...*(1836), ii, App. B, pp. 384-7.
Correspondence: Temple, W., *The Works of Sir William Temple, Bart...*, ed. Jonathan Swift (1720), iii.

LC151.

24 July 1668[a] - early Oct. 1670[c]   Ambassador Extraordinary
Audience: *c.*28 Aug. 1668   £7/d, £10/d (after 1 Jan.
Secretaries: Thomas Downton and   1669)
   William Balthwayt

He was not formally terminated until July 1671. In fact, his family remained in the Low Countries until long after Temple returned to England, on the date given above.

Instructions: PRO, SP/104/174B, ff. 165-8; Bennet, H., *...the Earl of Arlington's Letters to Sir W. Temple...*(1701), i, pp. 201-02; Courtenay, T., *Memoirs of the Life, Works and Correspondence of Sir William Temple...* (1836), i, pp. 384-8.
Correspondence: PRO, SP/84/183-6; BL, Add. 35852, 37988, 40795, Sloane 1003; Bodl., Rawlinson Mss. A.478; Bennet, *Arlington Letters*; Courtenay, *Memoirs*; Temple, W., *Letters Written By Sir William Temple...*ed. D. Jones (1699); Temple, W., *The Works of Sir William Temple, Bart.,...*, ed. Jonathan Swift (1720), iii.

LC152.
HOLLES, Denzil, 1st Baron Holles of Ifield (1599-1680)*
COVENTRY, Henry (*c.*1618-1686)*

For their participation in the Breda Conference, 1667, see Conferences, Congresses.

LC153.
SILVIUS, Sir Gabriel (*fl.*1660s-1670s)

On the return journey from his mission to various German States (q.v.), he stopped at the Hague, *c.*August 1669.

LC154.
BLATHWAYT, William (*c*.1649-1717)*

June 1671[h] - 15 Jan. 1672[c] [Chargé d'Affaires]
Correspondence: PRO, SP/84/186-8.

LC155.
DOWNING, Sir George, 1st Bart. (1623-1684)*

1 Dec. 1671[f] - 7 Feb. 1672[a] [Ambassador Extraordinary]
Audience: 30 Dec. 1671

He left his post without permission, for which he was imprisoned.

Instructions: PRO, SP/84/187, f. 222.
Correspondence: PRO, SP/84/187-8; BL, Add. 22920, Stowe 142.

LC156.
VILLIERS, George, 2nd Duke of Buckingham (1628-1687)*
BENNET, Henry, Earl of Arlington (1618-1685)*
SAVILE, George, Viscount Halifax (later Earl of Halifax; 1633-1695)*

14 June 1672[c] - 21 July 1672[a] [Envoys Extraordinary]
First session: 26 June 1672 £4754 (shared jointly by
Secretary: Sir Joseph Williamson Arlington and Buckingham),
£1000 (Halifax)

Although they were accredited to the French King, who was campaigning in the
Low Countries, and they participated in the Franco-Dutch peace negotiations
(Conferences, q.v.), they also had substantial contact with the Prince of
Orange. James Scott, Duke of Monmouth, the commander of the English
forces in the Low Countries, was added to the commission 22 June 1672.

Instructions: PRO, SP/78/134, f. 82, SP/104/64, ff. 25-6, SP/105/101, ff. 6-7;
   CSPD, 1672, p. 226-8; Foxcroft, H., *The Life and Letters of Sir George
   Savile...*(1898), i, pp. 72-5.
Correspondence: PRO, SP/78/134, SP/84/189-90, SP/105/101; Foxcroft,
   Savile, i.

LC157.
SILVIUS, Sir Gabriel (*fl*.1660s-1680s)

June? 1672[h] - *c*.28 July 1672[c] [Special Ambassador]
Audience: *c*.15 July 1672

Instructions: Suggested in *CSPV, 1671-2*, p. 266.
Correspondence about: *CSPD, 1672*; *CSPV, 1671-2*.

LC158.

10 Feb. 1674[a] - 13 Sept. 1674[a] Envoy Extraordinary
£5/d

Instructions: Inferred in *CSPD, 1673-5*, p. 147.
Correspondence: PRO, SP/84/196, SP/104/66.

LC159.
TEMPLE, Sir William, 1st Bart. (1628-1699)*

27 May 1674[b] - *c*.7 Mar. 1679[e]   Ambassador Extraordinary
Audience: *c*.17 July 1674
Secretary: Roger Meredith

This mission included several returns to England, and extensive involvement in the peace negotiations at Nimwegen (Conferences, q.v.). In Temple's several absences, Meredith served as chargé.

Instructions: PRO, SP/84/196, ff. 105-11; Courtenay, *Memoirs*, ii, pp. 405-10.
Correspondence: PRO, SP/84/196-205, SP/104/66; BL, Add. 25119, Eg. 3325, Harl. 1514-16, 1522-3, Stowe 205-09, 755; Oxford, Mss. at All Souls Lib., ccxxv; *CSPD, 1678*; Hyde, H., *The Correspondence of Henry Hyde, Earl of Clarendon*...ed. S. Singer, (1828); Browning, A., *Thomas Osborne, Earl of Danby*...(Glasgow, 1944- 51).

LC160.
JENKINS, Sir Leoline (*c*.1625-1685)*
WILLIAMSON, Sir Joseph (1633-1701)*

On their return journey from the Congress at Cologne (Conferences, q.v.), they stopped at the Hague, *c*.21 Apr. 1674.

LC161.
BENNET, Henry, Earl of Arlington (1618-1685)*
BUTLER, Thomas, Earl of Ossory (1634-1680)*
OSBORNE, Edward, Viscount Latimer (1654-1689)*

10 Nov. 1674[f] - 7 Jan. 1675[a]   [Special Ambassadors]
Audience: 14 Nov. 1674

Instructions: None written, but the nature of their verbal instructions is suggested in *CSPV, 1673-5*, p. 310.
Correspondence: PRO, SP/84/197; BL, Add. 32094.

LC162.
SILVIUS, Sir Gabriel (*fl*.1660s-1680s)

24 Dec. 1675[b] - *c*.20 Apr. 1676[c]   Envoy Extraordinary
Audience: Jan. 1676

He went to the Prince of Orange.

Correspondence: PRO, SP/84/200.

LC163.
SKELTON, Bevil (*died c*.1692)*

He delivered letters to the Prince of Orange 20 Jan. 1676, during his mission to the Emperor (q.v.).

Correspondence: *CSPD, 1675-6*.

LC164.

HYDE, Laurence (later Viscount Hyde of Kenilworth, Earl of Rochester; 1642-1711)*

He had audience with the Prince of Orange, 4 Jan. 1677, on his return from a mission to Poland (q.v.).

Correspondence: BL, Add. 15892 (diary).

LC165.

MEREDITH, Roger (*fl.*1670s)

25 May 1678[a] - 14 Oct. 1679[b]   Chargé d'Affaires
                                          20s/d, 40s/d (by 1679)

He returned to England briefly July - Aug. 1678.

Instructions: PRO, SP/104/66, f. 154.
Correspondence: PRO, SP/84/206-08, 215, SP/104/56.

LC166.

GODOLPHIN, Sidney (later Baron Godolphin of Rialton, 1st Earl of Godolphin; 1645-1712)*

4 Mar. 1678[a] - 12 July 1678[a]   Envoy Extraordinary
Audience: 12 Apr. 1678   £4/d

He returned to England briefly from *c.*21 Mar. through 16 Apr. 1678.

Instructions: BL, Add. 25119, f. 21; Bodl., Firth Mss. B I/I; Browning, A., *Thomas Osborne, Earl of Danby*...(Glasgow, 1944- 51), i, pp. 264-5, ii, pp. 598-601.
Correspondence: PRO, SP/78/129, SP/84/206, SP/104/11; Bodl., Firth Mss., B.I/I; Coventry Papers at Longleat, xli; Browning, *Thomas Osborne*; Osborne, T., *Letters Written to and from the Earl of Danby*...(1710).

LC167.

SIDNEY, Henry (later Viscount Sidney of Sheppey, Earl of Romney; 1641-1704)*

*c.*1 June 1679[b] - 6 July 1681[b]   Envoy Extraordinary
Audience: 29 July 1679   £5/d

He returned to England briefly June to July 1679, and late 1679 to early 1680.

Instructions: Suggested in *CSPD, 1679-80*, p. 284.
Correspondence: PRO, SP/84/215-16, SP/104/68; BL, Add. 35104; Sidney, H., *Diary of the Times of Charles the Second*...(1843); Foxcroft, H., *The Life and Letters of Sir George Savile*... (1898).

LC168.

MIDDLETON, Charles, 2nd Earl of Middleton (*c.*1650-1719)*

He visited the Low Countries on his way to the Imperial Court (q.v.), with an audience at the Hague, 14 July 1680.

LC169.
SOUTHWELL, Sir Robert (1635-1702)*

On his journey to the Elector of Brandenburg (German States, q.v.), he visited
the Prince of Orange, Mar. 1680.

LC170.
PLOTT, Thomas (*fl.*1670s-1680s)

*c.*5 Feb. 1681[h] - 5 Feb. 1682[g]   [Agent]

Correspondence: BL, Add. 37979; Middlebush, F. A., *The Dispatches of
Thomas Plott 1681-1682 and Thomas Chudleigh 1682-1685*...(The Hague,
1926).

LC171.
SKELTON, Bevil (*died c.*1692)*

He visited the Prince of Orange on his way to various German States (q.v.) late
1681, and probably he visited the Low Countries repeatedly while stationed
in Hamburg as the envoy to the Hanse and northern Germany (qq.v.),
1681-5.

LC172.
CHUDLEIGH, Thomas (1650?-*c.*1700)*

15 Dec. 1681[a] - 5 Apr. 1685[a]   Envoy Extraordinary
Audience: 5 Feb. 1682   £5/d
Secretary: Mr. Constable

He returned to England briefly in the summer of 1682.

Instructions: BL, Add. 35104; Bodl., Rawlinson Mss. A.256, I, 287.
Correspondence: PRO, SP/84/217-18, SP/104/68, 189; BL, Add. 34339-40,
35104, 36988, 37980, 41809-11, 41823; *CSPD, 1689*; Oxford, Mss. at All
Souls Lib., ccxxii; Middlebush, F. A., *The Dispatches of Thomas Plott 1681-
1682 and Thomas Chudleigh 1682-1685*...(The Hague, 1926).

LC173.
SKELTON, Bevil (*died c.*1692)*

16 Mar. 1685[a] - 17 Oct. 1686[a]   Ambassador Extraordinary
Audience: 1 Apr. 1685   £5/d

Correspondence: PRO, SP/84/220; BL, Add. 15892, 36988, 41817-20, 41823,
Sloane 1983; *CSPD, 1685*; Oxford, Mss. at All Souls Lib., ccix, ccxxii.

LC174.
WHITE, Ignatius, Marquis d'Albeville (*d.*1694)*

7 Nov. 1686[a] - 1689[g]   Envoy Extraordinary
Audience: 14 Feb. 1687   £5/d

He returned to England briefly Nov. - Dec. 1687.

Instructions: Partially inferred in *CSPD, 1686-7*, no. 1320.
Correspondence: PRO, SP/77/55; BL, Add. 25374, 41815-16, 41820-1, 41823;
CSPD, 1687-9.

NORTH AFRICA

Diplomatic contact with various parts of North Africa followed in the wake of the opening of commercial activities. At first, such contacts were made principally by merchants, but by the seventeenth century, except for a few special cases, most negotiations were handled in conjunction with naval actions in the area. Only those naval men who had substantial negotiating responsibilities are actually listed here (the distinction between naval responsibilities and diplomatic functions is often obscure at best).

NA1.
HOGAN, Edmund (*d*.1607)

6 May 1577[g] - late Aug. 1577[h] [Agent]
Audience: 1 June 1577

He was sent to the King of Morocco.

Instructions: BL, Burney 2790, f. 200b, Cotton, Nero B.viii, ff. 62-5, Eg. 2790, f. 220, Lansd. 155, no. 71, Sloane 2442, f. 107; HMC *2nd Report*, p. 97.
Correspondence: BL, Cotton, Nero B.xi (report); *CSPF, 1575-7, 1577-8*.

NA2.
PRYNNE, Edward (*fl*.1590s)

Feb. 1590[d] - Mar. 1591[c] [Special Ambassador]
Audience: 9 April 1590

He went to Morocco.

Instructions: Summarized in *L&A, 1589-90*, no. 815.
Correspondence: PRO, SP/71/12; *L&A, 1589-90, 1590-1*.

NA3.
MANSELL, Sir Robert (*c*.1569-1656)*

20 July 1620[b] - July 1621[h] Admiral/Envoy
Arrived (Algiers): *c*.27 Nov. 1620

Instructions: BL, Add. 36445, f. 15; inferred from PRO, SP/77/1, ff. 21-4.
Correspondence: PRO, SP/77/1; BL, Add. 36444-5, Eg. 2584, Lansd. 1581; *CSPD, 1619-23*.

NA4.
HARRISON, John (*fl*.1590s-1630s)*

Spring 1625[h] - *c*.1 June 1626[a] Agent
Audience: 8 June 1625 40*s*/d

He went to the Barbary States.

Correspondence: PRO, SP/71/12; BL, Harl. 1581.

NA5.

13 Sept. 1626[b] - 28 Sept. 1630[a]   Agent
                                        40s/d

He served, probably intermittently, in the Barbary States and in the town of
    Sallee. He was, for instance, in London in June 1627 - 1628, but continued to
    be paid.

Instructions and commission: BL, Add. 21993, ff. 281-4; inferred from PRO,
    SP/71/1, ff. 70-1.
Correspondence: PRO, SP/71/12.

NA6.
BRADSHAW, Capt. Edmund (*fl.*1630s)

Summer 1636[h] - mid-1637[h]   Captain/Envoy
Audience: 15 Sept. 1636

He went to Morocco.

Correspondence: PRO, SP/71/12-3.

NA7.
RAINBOROW, Capt. William (*d.*1642)*

17 Feb. 1637[c] - 13 Oct. 1637[c]   Captain/Envoy

Captain Rainborow had, as his principal task, a naval expedition to Sallee in
    Morocco to redeem English captives, but he carried the King's diplomatic
    commission and was involved, by the King's direction, in negotiations there.

Military instructions: *CSPD, 1636-7*, p. 449.
Correspondence: PRO, SP/71/13; *CSPD, 1636-7*, 1637 (including journal).
Correspondence about: *CSPV, 1636-9*.

NA8.
FINCH, Heneage, 2nd Earl of Winchilsea (1627/1628-1689)*

He negotiated, in Nov. 1660, with the Algerines on his voyage to his post at
    Constantinople (Turkey, q.v.). Those negotiations continued under the
    auspices of Consul Robert Brown after Winchilsea's departure.

Correspondence: PRO, SP/97/17.
Correspondence about: *CSPV, 1659-61*.

NA9.
MONTAGU, Edward, 1st Earl of Sandwich (1625-1672)*

13 June 1661[f] - 18 Feb. 1662[f]   Admiral/Envoy
                                        £10,248 (total)

He carried out negotiations in Algeria from late 1661 to early 1662 in his
    capacity as admiral of the fleet and while conducting naval exercises in the

Mediterranean. This voyage also encompassed diplomatic responsibilities in Portugal (q.v.).

Correspondence: *CSPD, 1661-2.*

NA10.
LAWSON, Sir John (*d.*1665)*

23 Oct. 1661[b] - late 1662[h]   Vice Admiral/Envoy
Audience: *c.*10 Oct. 1662

He went to Algeria primarily on naval affairs, but he also had negotiating responsibilities.

Commission: PRO, SP/71/25, ff. 13-15.
Correspondence: PRO, SP/71/25; BL, Add. 2755, Harl. 1595, Sloane 5752; *CSPD, 1661-2.*

NA11.
WARREN, Thomas (*fl.*1660s)

9 July 1665[b] - *c.*June 1666[h]   Agent

He was sent to Morocco.

Instructions: PRO, SP/104/174B, pp. 65-8; inferred from PRO, SP/71/13, ff. 149-50, 157.
Correspondence: PRO, SP/71/13.

NA12.
ROOTH, Richard (*fl.*1660s)

30 July 1668[d] - *c.*25 Jan. 1669[g]   Captain/Envoy
Audience: Nov.? 1668

He was sent to Morocco.

Instructions: Suggested in *CSPD, 1667-8* (6 Aug. 1668).
Commission: PRO, SP/71/13, f. 158.
Correspondence and correspondence about: *CSPD, 1667-8, 1668-9.*

NA13.
HOWARD, Henry, Baron Howard of Castle Rising (later Earl of Norwich, 6th Duke of Norfolk; 1628-1684)*

18 June 1669[a] - 5 Oct. 1670[a]   Ambassador Extraordinary
Secretary: Thomas Warren   £100/wk.

He was sent to Morocco.

Instructions: PRO, SP/71/13, ff. 301-04; BL, Add. 19872, f. 1b.
Correspondence: PRO, SP/71/13-14; BL, Add. 5750, 35100, 38015, Sloane 3513.

NA14.

SPRAGGE, Sir Edward (*d.*1673)*

Sept. 1671[d] - 11 Mar. 1672[c]   [Special Ambassador]

He was sent to Algeria in a military/diplomatic capacity.

Instructions: Implied from Thibaudeau, A., *The Bulstrode Papers...* (1897).

Correspondence: PRO, SP/71/2; Curran, M. B. (ed.), *The Dispatches of William Perwich...*, Camden 3rd ser., v (1903).

Correspondence about: *CSPD, 1671, 1671-2.*

NA15.

MIDDLETON, John, 1st Earl of Middleton (1619-1674)*

Summer 1672[h] - late 1672[h]   [Ambassador Extraordinary]

He was governor at Tangier and arranged a treaty with the Moorish King.

Correspondence: BL, Sloane 1958, 3299.

Correspondence about: *CSPV, 1671-2.*

NA16.

BRISBANE, John (*fl.*1670s)

19 Oct. 1674[c] - *c.*Feb. 1675[h]   [Agent?]

Audience: 9 Dec. 1674

He was involved in negotiations in Algeria with Admiral Sir John Narborough and Consul Martin.

Instructions: PRO, SP/71/2, ff. 38-40.

Correspondence: PRO, SP/71/2.

NA17.

LESLIE, Sir James (*fl.*1680s)

22 Nov. 1680[a] - 16 Jan. 1682[a]   Ambassador [Extraordinary]

He is called the ambassador in Fez.

Instructions: PRO, SP/104/188, no foliation.

NA18.

HERBERT, Sir Arthur (later Earl of Torrington; *c.*1648-1716)*

*c.*Sept. 1681[h] - May 1682[h]   Admiral/Envoy

He visited Algiers as an admiral, but he had diplomatic responsibilities.

Instructions: Oxford, Mss. at All Souls Lib., cclvii, f. 169.

Correspondence: PRO, SP/71/2; BL, Add. 46412, Eg. 2621; Oxford, Mss. at All Souls Lib., cclvii.

NA19.

SOAME, Sir William (*d.*1686)

On his voyage to Turkey (q.v.) to assume the residency there, he stopped at Algiers, Tripoli and Tunis, having audience at Algiers on 5 Apr. 1686.

Correspondence: PRO, SP/71/3.

NA20.
FITZROY, Henry, 1st Duke of Grafton (1663-1690)*

Aug.? 1687^h - Mar. 1688^h Captain/Envoy
Audience (Algiers): *c.*20 Sept. 1687
He visited Algiers, Tripoli and Tunis.
Correspondence: PRO, SP/71/3.

PER1.
ROE, Sir Thomas (1581?-1644)*

8 Jan. 1615*b* - 25 Sept. 1619*a*   Special Ambassador
Audience (Surat): *c*.12 Oct. 1615   £600/an.
Audience (Hindustan): 10 Jan. 1616

His primary objective was the court of Jehangir, the Mogul Emperor of
    Hindustan. He also visited the Governor of Surat and apparently stopped at
    the Persian court on his return trip.

Instructions: *CSPCol/EI..., 1513-1616*, no. 852; Roe, Sir T., *The Embassy of
    Sir Thomas Roe*...ed. W. Foster (Hakluyt Society, 1899), pp. 551-3.

Correspondence: BL, Add. 6115, Harl. 1576; *CSPD, 1611-18, 1619-23*;
    CSPCol/EI..., 1513-1616; Roe, *The Embassy*...; Carew, George Lord,
    *Letters from George Lord Carew to Sir Thomas Roe, Ambassador to the
    Court of the Great Mogul*...ed. J. Maclean, Camden o.s., lxxvi (1860).

PER2.
COTTON, Dodmore (*d*.1628)

15 Apr. 1626*c* - *d*.22 July 1628   [Ambassador Ordinary]
Audience: 25 May 1628   40*s*/d
Secretary: Robert Stodart

He went as an ambassador to the court of Persia.

Instructions: Oxford, Mss. at All Souls Lib., ccxii, f. 144b, ccxxii, f. 84;
    Stodart, R., *The Journal of Robert Stodart*...(1935), p. 17-20.

Correspondence: *CSPD, 1627-8*; Oxford, Mss. at All Souls Lib., ccxii; Stodart,
    Journal (a contemporary description of the mission).

POLAND

PL1.
WALLOP, Sir John (*d*.1551)*

c.1 Sept. 1526[h] - Sept.? 1527[h]   [Special Ambassador]
Audience: *c*.5 May 1527

This mission took him to the court of Margaret of Savoy, the Emperor, and various German princes (qq.v.).

Instructions: Inferred from Polish correspondence, and related in Jasnowski, J, 'England and Poland in the 16th and 17th Centuries,' *Polish Science and Learning*, vii (1948), p. 9.
Correspondence: *L&P*, iv, 2.

PL2.
PAGET, William (later 1st Baron Paget of Beaudesert; 1505-1563)*

Dec. 1533[h] - early June 1534[c]   [Special Ambassador]

He also went to Lüneburg, Mecklenburg and Prussia in Germany (q.v.).

Instructions: *L&P*, vii, no. 148; BL, Add. 2954, f. 1.
Correspondence: *L&P*, vii.

PL3.
ROGERS, Dr. John (*c*.1540-1603)*

c.6 Aug. 1580[h] - autumn 1581[h]   [Special Ambassador]
Audience: 10 Mar. 1581

This mission also included stops in Denmark, Sweden and the Hanse towns (qq.v.). The merchant William Salkins accompanied him.

Instructions: PRO, SP/88/1, no. 9; BL, Sloane 2442, ff. 41-3, Harl. 36, f. 319.
Correspondence: PRO, SP/88/1; *CSPF, 1583, Add*.

PL4.
HERBERT, John (later Sir John; *c*.1540-1617)*

16 May 1583[b] - *c*.1 Sept. 1585[e]   [Special Ambassador]
Audience: 28 July 1584

This mission began with a residency in Denmark (q.v.). He was instructed to proceed directly to the Hanse towns (q.v.) and Poland, which he did, 23 June 1584. The merchant, William Salkins seemingly joined him as a diplomatic adjunct.

Instructions: Inferred in PRO, SP/88/1, no. 26.
Correspondence: PRO, SP/91/1; BL, Cotton, Galba D.xiii; *CSPF, 1583, 1583-4, 1584-5*.

PL5.

HARBORNE, William (1552-1617)*

He passed through Poland, Oct. 1588, on his return from Turkey (q.v.), and had audience with the Grand Chancellor, 27 Sept. 1588.

PL6.

PARKINS, Dr. Christopher (later Sir Christopher; *c*.1543-1622)*

9 May 1590^b - *c*.26 July 1591^c [Special Ambassador]
Audience: 4 Sept. 1590   £300 (total)

This mission included a visit to Prussia (German States), Denmark, and the Hanse towns (qq.v.), and a great deal of travelling between these areas.

Instructions: Inferred from PRO, SP/75/2, ff. 128-33; *L&A, 1591-2*, no. 888-9.
Correspondence: PRO, SP/75/2, SP/88/1; Talbot, C., *Res Polonicae Elisabetha...* (Rome, 1961).

PL7.

29 Dec. 1594^a - *c*.June 1595^h [Special Ambassador]
Audience: 12 Mar. 1595   40s/d

Instructions: PRO, SP/88/1, ff. 215-16.
Correspondence: PRO, SP/88/1.

PL8.

CAREW, George (later Sir George; *d*.1612)*

20 May 1598^a - 21 Dec. 1598^b [Special Ambassador]
Audience with Polish King in   40s/d
Sweden: 12 Sept. 1598

He also went to Denmark, Brunswick (German States), and some of the Hanse towns (qq.v.).

Instructions: PRO, SP/88/2, ff. 48-58; BL, Cotton, Nero B.ii, ff. 291-2.
Correspondence: PRO, SP/88/2; BL, Cotton, Nero B.ii, Royal 18.B.1; Carew, G., 'A Relation of the State of Polonia and the United Provinces of the Crown anno 1598,' in Mews, G., *Deutschland und der Osten* (Leipzig, 1936) (a report on his mission).
Correspondence about: HMC *Salisb.*, viii.

PL9.

LYEL, Henry (*fl*.1600s-1610s)

2 Apr. 1603^d - *c*.8 Aug. 1603^h [Special Ambassador]

PL10.

BRUCE, Dr. William (*fl*.1600s-1610s)

20 Apr. 1604^a - 22 Mar. 1610^b [Resident Agent]
     £100/an.

He returned to England, 1605-06.
Correspondence: PRO, SP/88/2; HMC *Salisb.*, xviii-xx; Talbot, C., *Res Polonicae Iacobo I...*(Rome, 1962).

PL11.
SANDILANDS, James, 2nd Lord Torphichen (*c*.1574-1617)*

c.1 June 1609*h* - *c*.1 Oct. 1609*f*   [Ambassador Extraordinary]
Arrived: *c*.30 June 1609

Correspondence about: Talbot, *Res Polonicae Iacobo I.*

PL12.
GORDON, Patrick (later Sir Patrick; 1635-1699)*

1 May 1610*a* - mid-Dec. 1621*c*   [Resident] Agent
                                              6*s* 8*d*/d

He returned to England late in 1613 and remained through part of 1614, and he
    also returned 1615 - 1616, and 1619 - 1620. His pay was equally intermittent.

Instructions: PRO, SP/88/3, f. 48-9; inferred from *CSPV, 1613-15*, no. 203.
Correspondence: PRO, SP/88/3; BL, Add. 38597; Talbot, *Res Polonicae
    Iacobo I.*

PL13.
DICKENSON, John (*fl*.1610s)

1 July 1615*a* - 6 Jan. 1616*b*   [Special Ambassador]
Audience: 28 Sept. 1615   40*s*/d

Instructions: Kraushar, A., *Poselstwo Dickensona, Credentials from James I for
    J. Dickenson* (1909), p. 16.
Correspondence: Niemscewicz, J., *Zbior Pamietnikow*, ii.

PL14.
GORDON, Francis (*fl*.1620s-1640s)

11 July 1626*a* - mid-Dec. 1641*c*   Agent
                                              £150/an., £300/an. (after Aug. 1632)

He was likely stationed in Danzig (Hanse, q.v.), but his responsibilities were
    heavily oriented toward Poland. His residency saw numerous trips to other
    principalities in northern Europe, including a 1627 trip to Denmark (q.v.).
    He also returned frequently to England, such as in 1635, 1636 and summer
    1640.

Instructions: PRO, SP/88/4, ff. 122-5.
Correspondence: PRO, SP/88/4-10, SP/104/170.

PL15.
ROE, Sir Thomas (1581?-1644)*

2 Apr. 1629*a* - 4 July 1630*a*   Ambassador Extraordinary
Arrived (at peace negotiations):   £4/d
    29 Aug. 1629

This mission included visits to the courts of the United Provinces, the Palatinate,
    Denmark, Sweden, the towns of the Hanse and Prussia (qq.v.).

Instructions: PRO, SP/88/5, ff. 42-9, SP/104/170, pp. 31-40; Gardiner, S. R., *Letters Relating to the Mission of Sir Thomas Roe to Gustavus Adolphus, 1629-30*, Camden n.s., xiv (1875), pp. 10-21; HMC *3rd Report*, p. 190.

Correspondence: PRO, SP/88/5-6, SP/104/170; *CSPD, 1629-31*; HMC *Portland*, ii; Gardiner, *Letters Relating to the Mission of Roe*.

PL16.

DOUGLAS, Sir George (*d.*1636)

10 Nov. 1634[a] - *d.*15 Mar. 1636   Ambassador Extraordinary
Audience: Jan. 1635   40s/d
Secretary: John Fowler

Douglas came directly from serving as agent with Queen Elizabeth of Bohemia (in the Palatinate, German States, q.v.).

Instructions: PRO, SP/88/8, f. 201.

Correspondence: PRO, SP/88/8-9; Fowler, J., *The History of the Troubles of Suethland and Poland...with a briefe commemoration of the Life and Death of Sir George Douglas...*(1656) (detailed report on the embassy by his secretary).

PL17.

WYCHE, Sir Peter (1628-1699?)*

24 Nov. 1669[b] - 3 July 1670[a]   Ambassador Extraordinary
Audience: 2 Jan. 1670   £3/d
Secretary: Robert Yard

He came to Poland directly from Russia (q.v.) without any return to England. A new privy seal was issued for the Polish mission, which the above beginning date reflects. His diets were later increased by £1/d.

Correspondence: PRO, SP/88/12; BL, Sloane 1003.

PL18.

HYDE, Laurence (later Viscount Hyde of Kenilworth, then Earl of Rochester; 1642-1711)*

5 July 1676[a] - 13 Feb. 1677[a]   Ambassador Extraordinary
Audience: 8 Nov. 1676   £10/d
Latin Secretary: Dr. Robert South

He also visited the Low Countries (q.v.).

Instructions: PRO, SP/104/118, f. 19; suggested in *CSPD, 1676-7*, pp. 132, 220.

Correspondence: PRO, SP/88/14, SP/104/118; BL, Add. 15892 (journal), 25119, 29587, 32095, Stowe 305; *CSPD, 1678*; Singer, S. (ed.), *The Correspondence of Henry Hyde...and Laurence Hyde...*(1828).

PORTUGAL

POR1.
WILSON, Dr. Thomas (1523-1581)*

June 1567[c] - c.1 Nov. 1567[h]   [Agent?]
Audience: c.1 Sept. 1567

Instructions: BL, Cotton, Nero B.i, ff. 146-9.
Correspondence: BL, Cotton, Nero B.i.

POR2.
WOTTON, Edward (later 1st Baron Wotton of Marley; 1548-1628)*

16 May 1579[a] - 13 Oct. 1579[b]   [Special Ambassador]
Audience: late July 1579   40s/d

He did visit the Spanish court (q.v.) on his return to England.

Instructions: PRO, SP/70/148, ff. 14-16; and inferred from *CSPF, 1579-80*,
    no. 39.
Correspondence: *CSPF, 1579-80*.

POR3.
VANE, Charles (*fl.*1650s)*

30 Jan. 1650[a] - 4 July 1650[a]   [Special] Agent
Audience: 1 Apr. 1650   £800/an.

Instructions: In part in *CSPD, 1649-50*, p. 515.
Correspondence: *ThSP*, i.
Correspondence about: *CSPD, 1650*; *CSPV, 1647-52*.

POR4.
MEADOW, Philip (1626-1718)*

19 Feb. 1656[c] - c.6 Nov. 1656[c]   [Special] Agent
Audience: 7 Apr. 1656

Instructions: Suggested in *ThSP*, iv, pp. 588, 681-2, 758.
Correspondence: *ThSP*, iv.

POR5.
FINCH, Heneage, 2nd Earl of Winchilsea (1627/1628-1689)*

On the way to his assignment in Turkey (q.v.), Winchilsea stopped to pay his
    compliments at the Portuguese court. Audience: 7 Nov. 1660; departure:
    12 Nov. 1660.

POR6.

MONTAGU, Edward (*c.*1636-1665)*

Dec. 1660[h] - 6 May 1661[a]   [Special Ambassador]

He went with Richard Talbot, later the Earl of Tyrconnel, who represented the Duke of York.

Correspondence about: *CSPV, 1661-4.*

POR7.

MONTAGUE, Edward, 1st Earl of Sandwich (1625-1672)*

13 June 1661[f] - 13 May 1662[a]   Ambassador Extraordinary
Audience: 14 Mar. 1662   £10,248 (total)

He proceeded directly from Algeria (North Africa, q.v.), where he had naval as well as diplomatic responsibilities. He left Algeria for Portugal 18 Feb. 1662. His mission essentially was to convey Princess Katherine of Braganza to England for her marriage with Charles II. He had previously paid an unofficial visit at Lisbon on his way to Algeria, 1 Sept. - Oct. 1661.

Correspondence: *CSPD, 1661-2.*

POR8.

FANSHAWE, Sir Richard, 1st Bart. (1608-1666)*

1 Aug. 1661[a] - 1 Jan. 1662[a]   Envoy Extraordinary
Audience: *c.*20 Sept. 1661   £4/d
Secretary: John Price

Instructions: BL, Eg. 2453, f. 59; Bodl., Clarendon Mss. 78, ff. 160-1; HMC *Heathcote*, pp. 18-22.
Correspondence: PRO, SP/89/5, SP/44/1; BL, Add. 34329; *CSPD, 1663-4.*

POR9.

11 Feb. 1662[a] - 14 Sept. 1663[a]   [Ambassador Extraordinary]
Audience: *c.*15 Sept. 1662   £6/d

Letters of credence were not issued until 14 July 1662.

Instructions: PRO, SP/89/5, f. 103, SP/89/16, ff. 275-6; Bodl., Tanner Mss. 47, ff. 56-7.
Correspondence: PRO, SP/89/5-6; Bodl., Tanner Mss. 47-8; HMC *Heathcote.*

POR10.

SOUTHWELL, Sir Robert (1635-1702)*

25 Dec. 1665[a] - *c.*23 Feb. 1668[c]   [Resident Ambassador]
Audience: *c.*29 Jan. 1666   £100/mo.
Secretary: Francis Parry

He made a negotiating trip to Spain (q.v.), 26 Feb. 1666 - 22 June 1666 and Sept. 1666.

Instructions: PRO, SP/104/174B, ff. 152-7; BL, Add. 34336, ff. 5-10.
Correspondence: PRO, SP/89/7-9, SP/94/50-2; BL, Add. 34330-1, 34336-8,
   35099, Lansd. 7010; *CSPD, 1665-6, 1666-7*; Bennet, H., *The Right
   Honourable the Earl of Arlington's Letters to Sir William Temple*...(1701), i-
   ii; [Carte, T.], *The History of the Revolutions of Portugal...with letters of Sir
   Robert Southwell...(1740)*.

POR11.
FANSHAWE, Sir Richard, 1st Bart. (1608-1666)*

Fanshawe, who was resident at Madrid at this time (Spain, q.v.), left Madrid for
   Lisbon 6 Jan. 1666, was granted audience in Lisbon *c*.1 Feb. 1666, and
   returned to Madrid 26 Feb. 1666.

POR12.
MONTAGU, Edward, 1st Earl of Sandwich (1625-1672)*

He stopped in Lisbon Apr. - May 1666, on his way to his post as resident in
   Spain (q.v.). He also came to Lisbon Jan. - Mar. 1668, while resident in
   Spain.

POR13.
WYCHE, Sir Peter (1628-1699?)*

28 Nov. 1666[f] - *c*.20 Feb. 1667[c]   [Special Ambassador]
Secretary: Francis Parry

He was accompanied by a Mr. Roper, who represented the Queen.

Instructions: Suggested in *CSPD, 1666-7*, p. 299.
Correspondence: *CSPD, 1666-7*.
Correspondence about: PRO, SP/89/8.

POR14.
MONTAGU, Edward, 1st Earl of Sandwich (1625-1672)*

While resident in Spain (q.v.), he visited Lisbon Jan. - Mar. 1668.

POR15.
SOUTHWELL, Sir Robert (1635-1702)*

9 May 1668[b] - 15 Aug. 1669[a]   Ambassador Extraordinary
Audience: 14 July 1668   £3/d
Secretary: Francis Parry

Instructions: PRO, SP/89/9, ff. 68-72, SP/104/174B, ff. 158-61; BL, Add.
   34338, f. 95.
Correspondence: PRO, SP/89/9-10; BL, Add. 34331, 34337-8.

POR16.
PARRY, Francis (*fl*.1660s-1670s)

1 June 1669[b] - *c*.25 Nov. 1680[c]   [Chargé d'Affaires, then
Audience: *c*.20 Sept. 1670   Resident Ambassador]
                                             20*s*/d, then 40*s*/d, then 60*s*/d

He became resident ambassador 18 May 1672, at which point his pay became 40s/d. He returned to England, Sept. 1676 - Nov. 1677; diets after this trip were raised to 60s/d.

Instructions: PRO, SP/92/25, ff. 48-50, SP/104/239, ff. 25-8; Oxford, Mss. at All Souls Lib., ccliv, f. 346.

Correspondence: PRO, SP/89/10-14, SP/104/184, 186-7; BL, Add. 4292, 25120, 34332-4, 35099-101 (letterbooks); *CSPD, 1672, 1673*; Anonymous, *Letters from the Secretaries of State, ...to Francis Parry...*(1817).

POR17.
GODOLPHIN, Sir William (1635-1696)*

Godolphin, resident in Spain (q.v.), visited Portugal on his trip to Madrid, May - June, 1669. He had audience *c*.5 May 1669.

POR18.
FANSHAWE, Charles (later 4th Viscount Fanshawe of Dromore, 1643-1710)*

| 13 May 1680[b] - 12 May 1686[a] | Envoy Extraordinary |
| | £5/d |

His instructions are dated 12 Aug. 1680.

Instructions: PRO, SP/104/187, pp. 34-7.

Correspondence: PRO, SP/89/4-16, SP/104/187-8, 193; Oxford, Mss. at All Souls Lib., ccxviii, ccxxv.

POR19.
GRANVILLE, Charles, Viscount Granville of Lansdowne (1661-1701)*

He stopped in Lisbon in July 1685, on his way to his resident post in Spain (q.v.); and he departed Lisbon 1 Sept. 1685.

Correspondence: PRO, SP/89/16.

POR20.
SCARBOROUGH, Charles (*fl.*1680s)

| 15 June 1686[a] - Oct. 1688[d] | Envoy Extraordinary |
| Audience: 25 Feb. 1687 | £5/d |

Instructions: PRO, SP/104/187, pp. 230-6; BL, Lansd. 1152, vol. ii, no. 5.
Correspondence: PRO, SP/89/16, SP/104/187.

RUSSIA

The Hugh Willoughby/Richard Chancellor expedition established first contact with the Russian court at Moscow. It left Gravesend 18 May 1553. Chancellor arrived in Moscow in winter of 1553/54, and returned to England in 1554. Several trading voyages followed.

The first formal diplomatic contact with the Tsar at Moscow seems to have been:

R1.
JENKINSON, Anthony (1530?-1611)*

20 Apr. 1566^d - mid-Dec. 1567^c Agent (partially commercial,
Audience: 1 Sept. 1566   partially diplomatic)

He returned briefly to England in the winter of 1566, and arrived back in Moscow c.May 1567.

Instructions: Tolstoy, G., ...*England and Russia*...(1875), pp. 24-6; PRO, SP/70/147 ff. 269-70; BL, Royal 13.B.1, ff. 160-1.
Correspondence: PRO, SP/70/147; BL, Cotton Nero B.xi; Bodl., Tanner Mss. 50; Morgan and Coote, *Early Voyages...to Russia*...(1886);
Correspondence about: *CSPF, 1566-8.*

R2.
RANDOLPH, Thomas (1523-1590)*

16 June 1568^c - 27 Aug. 1569^c Special Ambassador
Audience: 20 Feb. 1569   £1526 17s (total)

Instructions: *CSPF, 1566-8*, no. 2272; Morgan and Coote, ii, pp. 240-3; Tolstoy, pp. 43-6.
Correspondence: BL, Lansd. 10-11, 111; Bodl., Tanner Mss. 50; *CSPF, 1566-8; 1569-71.*

R3.
JENKINSON, Anthony (1530?-1611)*

15 June 1571^d - c.10 Sept. 1572^h Special Ambassador
Audience: 23 Mar. 1572
Secretary: Daniel Sylvester

Instructions: Implied from: Huttenbach, H., '...Ambassador Jenkinson's Mission to Muscovy in 1571-72...,' *Canadian/American Slavic Studies*, vi, no. 3, App. B & D.
Correspondence: Tolstoy; Morgan and Coote, ii; *CSPF, 1569-71.*

R4.
SYLVESTER, Daniel (*d.*1577)

9 May 1575^c - Mar.? 1576^e Special Ambassador
Audience: 29 Nov. 1575

Instructions: BL, Sloane 2442, f. 118, Eg. 2790, f. 178-80, Cotton, Nero B.xi, ff. 349, 393, Lansd. 155, ff. 131-4, Harl. 36, ff. 186, 231-3; *CSPF, 1575-7*, no. 116; HMC *2nd Report*, p. 97; Tolstoy, pp. 160-5;
Correspondence: PRO, SP/70/137; BL, Cotton, Nero B.viii, xi, Harl. 36, 289; Tolstoy.

R5.

June 1576[h] - *d.*15 July 1577   [Special Ambassador]

He was sent back immediately by Elizabeth, and was killed by lightning in the city of Kholmogory, on his way to Moscow.

R6.
BOWES, Sir Jerome (*d.*1616)*

5 June 1583[b] - *c.*20 Sept. 1584[a]   Special Ambassador
Audience: Oct. 1583   £1882 (total)

Instructions: PRO, SP/91/1, ff. 10-15, 18; BL, Cotton, Nero B.viii, ff. 29-35; *CSPF, 1583*, nos. 340-1, 374; *1583-4*, no. 354; Tolstoy, pp. 201-06, 211-13, 215-21; Casimir, N., 'The English in Muscovy During the Sixteenth Century,' *TRHS*, vii, pp. 115-20.
Correspondence: PRO, SP/91/1; BL, Harl. 6993; *CSPD, 1580-1625, Add.*; *CSPF, 1583-4, 1584-5*; *L&A, 1589-90*; Tolstoy; Hakluyt, i, pp. 516-20.

R7.
HORSEY, Jerome (*c.*1550-1626)*

23 Mar. 1586[d] - *c.*4 Oct. 1587[h]   Agent
Audience: 5 June 1586

Correspondence: Tolstoy; see also *CSPF, 1586-8*, p. 231; BL, Cotton, Nero B.xi.

R8.
FLETCHER, Dr. Giles (1546-1611)*

6 June 1588[d] - *c.*1 Sept. 1589[h]   Special Ambassador
Audience: 19 Dec. 1588

Instructions: Inferred from Berry, L., ...*Works of Giles Fletcher* (Madison, Wisc., 1964), pp. 367-75; and drawn from Tolstoy, pp. 288-95.
Correspondence: BL, Cotton, Nero B.xi, Lansd. 60; Berry, L., ...*Works of Giles Fletcher* (Madison, Wisc., 1964).
Correspondence about: *CSPF, 1589*.

R9.
HORSEY, Jerome (*c.*1550-1626)

Mar. 1590[c] - Aug.? 1591[h]   Special Ambassador
                              40*s*/d

He arrived in Russia in early July 1590, but was never granted an audience. He travelled through and reported from the Hanse town of Hamburg, but seemingly had no diplomatic responsibilities.

Instructions: Suggested in Bond, E. A., *Russia at the Close of the Sixteenth Century*...(1856) pp. xcviii-cvii; Tolstoy, pp. 373-81.

Correspondence: PRO, SP/82/3, SP/91/1; BL, Cotton, Nero B.viii, f. 21; *L&A, 1589-90, 1590-1*; *CSPD, 1591-4*; Bond, *Russia at the Close*.

R10.

CHERRY, Francis (later Sir Francis; *fl.*1590s)

7 Apr. 1598*c* - 23 Mar. 1599*c* Special Ambassador
Audience: 11 July 1598

Instructions: PRO, SP/91/1, f. 105; BL, Lansd. 112, ff. 132-4.

Correspondence: PRO, SP/91/1; Collier, J. P., *The Egerton Papers*..., Camden o.s., xii (1840), pp. 292-301; HMC *Salisb.*, ix.

R11.

WILLIS, Timothy (*c.*1560-1615?)*

Mid-July 1599*h* - spring 1600*h*

He arrived in Moscow 4 Sept. 1599, and had no specific audience. He was expelled from Russia that same month.

Instructions: Suggested by HMC *Salisb.*, x, p. 237.

Correspondence: PRO, SP/91/1; BL, Cotton, Nero B.xi; HMC *Salisb.*, x.

R12.

LEE, Sir Richard (*c.*1548-1608)*

30 May 1600*b* - *c.*29 July 1601*c* Special Ambassador
Audience: Late Oct. 1600

He apparently visited Sweden (q.v.) on his return journey.

Instructions: PRO, SP/91/1, ff. 133-4, 137; BL, Cotton, Nero B.viii, f. 32; HMC *Salisb.*, x, pp. 169-72.

Correspondence: PRO, SP/91/1; BL, Eg. 2714; HMC *Salisb.*, x-xi.

R13.

MERRICK, John (later Sir John; *d.*1638)

29 Oct. 1601*c* - 5 Sept. 1602*a* Special Ambassador
Audience: 12 Feb. 1602

He also went to Sweden (q.v.).

Instructions: PRO, SP/91/1, ff. 177-81 & 189-90 (instructions on being sent to Duke Charles of Sweden).

Report on mission: BL, Cotton, Nero B.viii, f. 35; *Gents. Magazine*, no. 114, pt. 2, pp. 226-9; HMC *Salisb.*, xii.

R14.
SMITH, Sir Thomas (1558?-1625)*

10 June 1604[e] - mid-Sept. 1605[c]   Special Ambassador
Audience: 11 Oct. 1604

Instructions: PRO, SP/91/1, ff. 196-8; Wadmore, J., 'Sir Thomas Smythe...,' *Archaeologia Cantiana*, 1892, pp. 85-8.
Correspondence: PRO, SP/91/1; HMC *Salisb.*, xvii; Wadmore, J., 'Sir Thomas Smythe...'; Smith, Sir Thomas, *Sir Thomas Smithes Voiage and Entertainment in Rushia* (1605).

R15.
MERRICK, John (later Sir John; *d.*1638)
RUSSELL, William (*d.*1654)*

19 Apr. 1613[c] - autumn 1613[h]   Special Ambassadors

Instructions: *CSPD, 1611-18*, pp. 181-2; Rymer, *Foedera*...(1704-32), vii, pt. 2, p. 193.

R16.
MERRICK, Sir John (*d.*1638)

18 June 1614[d] - 4 Nov. 1617[a]   Ambassador Extraordinary
Audience: 1 Jan. 1615
Secretary: William Beecher

Assisted by Beecher, he also served at times as a Swedish representative at the Russian – Swedish peace negotiations at Novgorod and Narva, a peace which resulted in the Treaty of Stolbvo.

Instructions: Implied from letters referred to in Lubimenko, I., 'The Correspondence of the First Stuarts with the First Romanovs,' *TRHS*, 4th series, i (1918), pp. 80-1; and from treatment in Konovalov, 'Anglo-Russian Relations, 1617-18,' *Oxford Slavonic Papers*, i (1950), pp. 65-9, 83 passim.
Correspondence: PRO, SP/91/2; BL, Add. 35125.

R17.
DIGGES, Sir Dudley (1583-1639)*

*c.*1 April 1618[g] - 22 Oct. 1618[a]   Special Ambassador
Secretary: Thomas Leake   £1000 (upon return)

No audience was granted to Digges. He travelled as far as Archangel, then returned home, although his secretary, Thomas Leake, and his nephew, Thomas Finch did, under the auspices of the embassy, make their way to Moscow and have audience of the Tsar, 16 Mar. 1619.

Instructions: *APC, 1618-19*, pp. 101-03, 151-2, 156; Rymer, *Foedera*..., xvii, p. 257; also as implied in Lubimenko, I., 'The Correspondence of the First Stuarts ...,' p. 81.
Correspondence: Bodl., Tanner Mss. 74.
Correspondence about: *CSPD, 1611-18*.

R18.
MERRICK, Sir John (*d*.1638)

24 June 1620*ᵃ* - *c*.3 Oct. 1621*ᶜ*   [Special] Ambassador
Audience: 15 Dec. 1620

Instructions: PRO, SP/103/61, f. 26; inferred from SP/91/2, f. 69; Rymer, *Foedera...*, xvii, pp. 256-7.
Correspondence: Konovalov, 'Anglo-Russian Relations, 1620-4,' *Oxford Slavonic Papers*, iv, pp. 71-131.

R19.
COCKS, Christopher (*fl*.1620s)

Apr. 1623*ʰ* - late Oct. 1624*ʰ*   Agent
Audience: 16 Nov. 1623

Instructions: Inferred from PRO, SP/91/2, ff. 91-2; *APC, 1623-5*, p. 237.
Correspondence: *CSPD, 1623-5*; *APC, 1623-5*; Konovalov, 'Anglo-Russian Relations, 1620-4'.

R20.
SMITH, Fabian (*d*.1632)

1626?*ʰ* - *d*.spring 1632   Agent
Correspondence: PRO, SP/91/2.

R21.
WYCHE, Thomas (*fl*.1630s)

c.Jan. 1633*ʰ* - late 1633*ʰ*   Agent
Credentials: PRO, SP/91/2, f. 233.
Correspondence: PRO, SP/91/2.

R22.
SWIFT, Richard (*fl*.1630s)

Late 1633*ᵈ* - early 1635*ʰ*   Agent
Credentials: PRO, SP/91/2, f. 236.

R23.
DIGBY, Simon (*fl*.1620s-1640s)

c.18 Apr. 1635*ʰ* - *c*.1640*ʰ*   Agent
Audience: 3 Jan. 1636

Instructions: Inferred in part from PRO, SP/91/3, f. 9.
Correspondence: PRO, SP/91/3.

R24.
PRIDEAUX, William (*fl*.1650s)

16 Feb. 1655*ᵈ* - Aug.? 1656*ᵍ*   Special Ambassador
Audience: 16 Feb. 1656

Correspondence: *ThSP*, ii-iv.

R25.
BRADSHAW, Richard (*fl.*1650s)*

c.12 Apr. 1657^c - autumn 1657^f Special Ambassador
£1200 (upon return)

While resident at Hamburg (Hanse, q.v.), he travelled to Russia, and got as far as Mitau in Courland, but was refused entry into Russia.

Instructions: Inferred from material in Moscow as reported in: Lubimenko, I., 'Anglo-Russian Relations during the First English Revolution,' *TRHS*, 4th ser., xi (1928), pp. 53-4; *ThSP*, vi, p. 278.
Correspondence: *ThSP*, vi; Bodl., Rawlinson Mss. A.62.

R26.
HOWARD, Charles, 1st Earl of Carlisle (1629-1685)*

20 June 1663^b - 31 Jan. 1665^c Ambassador Extraordinary
Audience: 11 Feb. 1664   *ad hoc*
Secretaries: Andrew Marvel and Guy
de Miege

He also went to Denmark and Sweden (qq.v.).

Instructions: Suggested in Konovalov, S., 'England and Russia: Three Embassies,' *Oxford Slavonic Papers*, x (1962), p. 67.
Correspondence: PRO, SP/91/3; Bodl., Clarendon Mss. 80-1; Konovalov, 'England and Russia: Three Embassies,'; and a contemporary narrative in: [Miege, G. de], *A Relation of Three Embassies...*(1669).

R27.
HEBDON, Sir John (*d.*1670)

15 Mar. 1667^c - Sept. 1668^e Ambassador Extraordinary
Audience: 20 Sept. 1667

Instructions: PRO, SP/91/3, ff. 120-6; Konovalov, S., 'England and Russia: Two Missions, 1666-1668,' *Oxford Slavonic Papers*, xiii (1967), pp. 59-61.
Correspondence: PRO, SP/91/3; Konovalov, 'England and Russia: Two Missions.'

R28.
WYCHE, Sir Peter (1628-1699?)*

4 Feb. 1669^a - 24 Nov. 1669^a Envoy Extraordinary
Audience: 17 June 1669   £3/d, £4/d
Secretary: Robert Yard (midway into
the mission)

He went directly from Russia to Poland (q.v.), and was issued a new privy seal for the Polish mission on 24 Nov.

Correspondence: PRO, SP/91/3; BL, Sloane 1003.

R29.
HEBDON, John (*fl*.1670s)

16 Sept. 1676[a] - 15 July 1678[a]   Ambassador Extraordinary
Audience: 8 May 1677   50s/d

Instructions: PRO, SP/104/118, ff. 33-7; SP/91/3, ff. 210-12.
Correspondence: PRO, SP/91/3.

R30.
GORDON, Patrick (later Sir Patrick; 1635-1699)*

29 Nov. 1686[b] - *c*.1687[h]   Ambassador Extraordinary
                                            £4/d

The English government apparently credentialled him after he had arrived in
    Russia (in August), and in part to secure his release from Russian captivity.
    Released, he remained in a military capacity in the Tsar's service until his
    death in 1699, and thus it is not clear when his mission might be said to have
    expired.

Correspondence: BL, Add. 41823, 41842.

SAVOY

SAV1.
CLERK, Dr. John (later Bishop of Bath and Wells; *d.*1541)*
June 1519[h] - n.d.   [Special Ambassador]

Besides visiting Louise of Savoy during this poorly documented mission, he also
went to Rome (q.v.).

Instructions: *L&P*, iii, 1, no. 344.

SAV2.
CASALE, Sir Gregory da (*fl.*1520s-1530s)

On an embassy to Rome (Italian States, q.v.), he stopped for an audience with
Louise of Savoy at Lyons *c.*15 Oct. 1525.

SAV3.
CLERK, Dr. John, Bishop of Bath and Wells (*d.*1541)*

After serving as a resident at Rome, he visited Louise of Savoy at Lyons,
15 Dec. 1525, on his journey home. He joined in this visit with Sir William
Fitzwilliam and Dr. John Taylor, who were already in France (q.v.).

SAV4.
CLINTON, Edward Fiennes de, 9th Baron Clinton and Saye (later 1st Earl
of Lincoln; 1512-1585)*

17 Oct. 1554[c] - early Dec. 1554[g]   [Special Ambassador]
Investment: 6 Nov. 1554

He conveyed the Order of the Garter to the Duke of Savoy who was at Hesdin,
France. He also visited the Emperor (q.v.) at Brussels.

Instructions: Inferred from *CSPF, 1553-8*, nos. 276-7.
Correspondence: *CSPF, 1553-8.*

SAV5.
WOTTON, Sir Henry (1568-1639)*

5 Dec. 1611[a] - 31 Aug. 1612[b]   Ambassador Extraordinary
Audience: 4 May 1612   £5/d
Secretary: William Parkhurst

Instructions: HMC *Salisb.*, xxi, pp. 343-5.

SAV6.
PARKHURST, William (*fl.*1610s)

2 Jun. 1612[h] - *c.* 8 Jan. 1615[c]   [Chargé d'affaires]
Audience: 22 Jan. 1613?   then Agent

He had become an agent by Jan. 1613.

Instructions: Inferred from PRO, SP/92/1, ff. 84-7, SP/92/2, f. 138.
Correspondence: PRO, SP/92/1-2; Richards, S. (ed.), *Secret Writing*...(1974).

SAV7.
MORTON, Albert (later Sir Albert; 1584?-1625)*

1 July 1613[a] - 30 June 1615[b]   Agent
Audience (upon assuming residence   20s/d
  in Turin): *c*.15 Jan. 1615

Although accredited to Savoy, Morton travelled extensively on diplomatic
  business in France, Switzerland and the Italian States, including Venice
  (qq.v.) during this period. He was resident at Turin only in the late winter and
  spring of 1615.

Instructions: Inferred from *CSPV, 1613-15*, pp. 292-3, 321, 326.
Correspondence: PRO, SP/92/2-3.

SAV8.
CARLETON, Sir Dudley (later Baron Carleton of Imbercourt, Viscount
  Dorchester; 1573-1632)*

10 Oct. 1614[a] - 11 Oct. 1615[b]   [Resident Ambassador]
Audience: 20 Feb. 1615   40s/d (in addition to his
Secretary: Isaac Wake   regular 66s 8d/d for his Venetian
                                               assignment)

He moved from Venice (q.v.) to Savoy, and there remained as resident for
  approximately one year. He continued his diplomatic contacts with various
  Italian States, especially Rome (q.v).

Instructions: Inferred from PRO, SP/92/2, ff. 186-200.
Correspondence: PRO, SP/92/2-3; *CSPD, 1611-18*.

SAV9.
WAKE, Sir Isaac (1580-1632)*

1 Dec. 1614[a] - 24 Nov. 1624[f]   Agent
Audience: 11 June 1615   20s/d, 40s/d (after 16 Apr. 1619)
Secretaries: Thomas Rowlandson, John
  Jacob, Anthony Hales

He returned to London Apr. to July 1615 and late 1618 to spring 1619. He went
  to Germany (q.v.) on special assignment in May 1619. He returned to
  London in spring of 1624, then went on assignment to Venice, but went by
  way of Turin, where he completed his diplomatic assignment by Dec. 1624.

Instructions: Inferred from *CSPV, 1613-15*, pp. 460-2.
Correspondence: PRO, SP/92/3-12; BL, Add. 34310, Stowe 176; HMC *Bath*.

SAV10.
BIONDI, Sir Giovanni Francesco (1572-1644)*

Although his principal objective was the Calvinist assembly at Grenoble, he visited the Savoyard court at Turin in a diplomatic capacity upon his return, Oct. 1615.

SAV11.
WOTTON, Sir Henry (1568-1639)*

Wotton stopped in Turin on his way to his assignment in Venice (q.v.). Audience: 15 May 1616.

Credentials: PRO, SP/92/4, f. 79.

SAV12.
GAGE, George (c.1582-1638)*

He was employed as a secret envoy to Florence, Parma, and principally to Rome (qq.v.) as well as to Savoy (early 1623).

SAV13.
HALES, Anthony (fl.1620s-1630s)

c.24 Nov. 1624[h] - 19 April 1635[a]   Chargé d'Affaires
                                          20s/d

While secretary to Sir Isaac Wake, Hales' responsibilities increased so that by the above starting date, he began to function as a chargé during the frequent and extensive absences of Wake. Wake in fact assumed the residency in Venice at this date, but continued to spend substantial periods of time at Turin.

Correspondence: PRO, SP/92/12-20, SP/104/169; BL, Eg. 2597.

SAV14.
WAKE, Sir Isaac (1580-1632)*

While serving as resident at Venice (q.v.), he was accredited, c.June 1625, to Savoy and Switzerland (q.v.) and remained, principally at Turin, until late 1626.

Correspondence: PRO, SP/92/11-12; *CSPD, Add. 1625-49.*

SAV15.
MONTAGU, Walter (1603?-1677)*

15 Mar. 1627[f] - 18 Apr. 1628[c]   [Agent]
Audience: c.12 Apr. 1627

After a return to England, he resumed his diplomatic duties at Turin by 20 Aug. 1627. His mission included visits to various Italian States (q.v.) as well.

Instructions: Inferred in the first instance from PRO, SP/92/13, f. 34-40, and *CSPV, 1626-8*, p. 209; PRO, SP/92/13, ff. 81-4 (for the mid-summer return).
Correspondence: PRO, SP/92/13.

SAV16.
HAY, James, Earl of Carlisle (*c.*1580-1636)*

1 Jan. 1628[b] - 28 Jan. 1629[c]   Ambassador Extraordinary
Audience: 13 July 1628 and 9 Oct.   £8/d
  1628
Secretaries: William Boswell, Thomas
  Rowlandson

This embassy included a tour of Lorraine, Switzerland, the Spanish Netherlands, Venice and the Low Countries (qq.v.) as well as a stop in Turin both going to and returning from Venice.

Instructions: Inferred from PRO, SP/92/13, ff. 202, 246.
Correspondence: PRO, SP/92/13-14; *CSPD, 1628-9.*

SAV17.
WAKE, Sir Isaac (1580-1632)*

Oct. 1628[h] - *c.*1 Mar. 1631[f]   [Resident Ambassador]
Audience: 9 Oct. 1628   £4/d
Secretary: Anthony Hales

Although still formally ambassador to Venice, he seems to have assumed permanent representational responsibilities at Turin— after he travelled there with the Earl of Carlisle. He went directly from Savoy to an assignment in France (q.v.).

Correspondence: PRO, SP/92/14-18; *CSPD, 1628-9.*

SAV18.
DACRE, Edward (*fl.*1620s)

*c.*1 Feb. 1629[h] - *c.*15 Mar. 1629[e]   [Special Ambassador]
Audience: 5 May 1629

Instructions: PRO, SP/92/15, ff. 107-08; and inferred from *CSPV, 1628-9*, pp. 563-4.
Correspondence: PRO, SP/92/16.

SAV19.
WESTON, Jerome (later 2nd Earl of Portland; 1605-1663)*

6 Dec. 1631[a] - 12 Mar. 1633[a]   Ambassador Extraordinary
Audience: 4 Oct. 1632   £6/d

This embassy included stops in France, Venice and Florence (qq.v.).

Instructions: PRO, SP/78/91, ff. 382-5, SP/92/19, ff. 199-200.
Correspondence: PRO, SP/78/92-3, SP/92/19.

SAV20.
FEILDING, Basil, Viscount Feilding (later 2nd Earl of Denbigh; *c.*1608-
1674)*

On the way to his assignment in Venice, he stopped in Savoy, with audience
16 Dec. 1634.

Correspondence: PRO, SP/92/20.

SAV21.
MORTON, Peter (*fl.*1630s-1640s)

Feb. 1635[h] - after Jan. 1642[g]   Agent
                                 £40/qtr. (after Jan. 1639)

Morton, Lord Feilding's secretary and formerly of Wake's household, was left
at Turin by Lord Feilding, after that nobleman peremptorily dismissed Hales
(for Hales, see above).

Correspondence: PRO, SP/92/21-3; Richard, S. (ed.), *Secret Writing*...(1974).

SAV22.
FEILDING, Basil, Viscount Feilding (later 2nd Earl of Denbigh; *c.*1608-
1674)*

20 Nov. 1637[b] - early Jan. 1639[f]   Ambassador Extraordinary
Audience: 4 Apr. 1638   [£6/d]
Secretary: Peter Morton

He undertook this mission while accredited as the resident in Venice (q.v.). He
also visited other Italian courts (q.v.).

Instructions: HMC *6th Report*, p. 277.
Correspondence: PRO, SP/92/22-3; Bodl., Tanner Mss. 61; HMC *Denbigh*.

SAV23.
MORLAND, Sir Samuel (1625-1695)*

23 May 1655[c] - 18 Dec. 1656[c]   [Special Ambassador]
Audience: *c.*23 June 1655

Although accredited as the resident to Geneva (Switzerland, q.v.), he had
extensive contact with Savoy and France (q.v.).

Instructions: Inferred from Morland, S., *The History of the Evangelical
Churches*...(1658), pp. 563-5.
Correspondence: Vaughan, R. (ed.) *The Protectorate of Oliver
Cromwell*...(1838); Abbott, W. C., *The Writings and Speeches of Oliver
Cromwell* (1937-47); *ThSP*, iii.

SAV24.
ROPER, Francis (*fl.*1660s)

23 Apr. 1664[b] - n.d.   [Special Ambassador]

Instructions: Inferred in *CSPV, 1664-6*, p. 20.

SAV25.

BELASYSE, Thomas, Viscount Fauconberg (later Earl of Fauconberg; 1627-1700)*

On his 1669 mission to the Italian States, especially Venice (qq.v.), he had audience at Savoy 14 Apr. 1670.

SAV26.

FINCH, Sir John (1626-1682)

He stopped briefly at Turin in mid-June 1673 on his way to Turkey (q.v.).

Instructions: Inferred from PRO, SP/92/25. ff. 42-3.

Correspondence: PRO, SP/92/25.

SAV27.

MORDAUNT, Henry, 2nd Earl of Peterborough (1624?-1697)*

Peterborough apparently visited Savoy and Modena (Italian States, q.v.), in early fall 1673, after his mission to the Emperor.

SAV28.

GRANVILLE, Bernard (1631-1701)*

5 Aug. 1675[b] - Dec.? 1675[h]   Envoy Extraordinary
Audience: 15 Sept. 1675

He was accompanied by John Churchill, who represented Prince James on this embassy of condolence. He continued to Florence and Genoa (Italian States, q.v.). He also visited Venice, but the Venetian sojurn seems to have been undertaken solely for personal reasons.

Correspondence: PRO, SP/92/25.

SAV29.

SOAME, Sir William (*fl.*1670s)

28 Sept. 1677[b] - 6 Mar. 1681[a]   Envoy Extraordinary
Arrived: June 1678   £5/d

Instructions: PRO, SP/92/25, ff. 48-50, SP/104/239, ff. 29-30; Oxford, Mss. at All Souls Lib., ccliv, f. 346.

Correspondence: PRO, SP/92/25, SP/104/188.

SAV30.

BERKELEY, John, 3rd Baron Berkeley of Stratton (1663-1697)*

1 July 1684[b] - Jan. 1685[c]   [Special Ambassador]

Instructions: Suggested in *CTB*, vii, pt. 2, p. 1189.

SCOTLAND

The following are the discoverable formal missions to Scotland. It should be understood, however, that even in the absence of specific ambassadors, substantial contact with, and of course news gathering out of Scotland occurred through English officials at Berwick and other border towns. Secondly, numerous border conclaves took place on English soil, and thus are not detailed. Finally, there was also naturally a steady stream of messengers, heralds (who are not included unless they had identifiable diplomatic responsibilities), informants and spies making their way between the two kingdoms, so contact was far more consistent than even these entries would suggest.

SC1.
DRURY, Sir Robert (by 1456-1535)*
BATEMANSON, Dr. John (*fl.*1500s-1510s)
CONSTABLE, Sir Marmaduke (1455?-1518)*

7 Sept. 1509^b - early Dec. 1509^h Special Ambassadors
Ratification: 28 Nov. 1509

Instructions: *L&P*, i, 1, no. 161.
Correspondence about: *L&P*, i, 1.

SC2.
DRURY, Sir Robert (by 1456-1535)*
CONSTABLE, Sir Marmaduke (1455?-1518)*

1 June 1510^b - Nov.? 1510^h [Special Ambassadors]
Commission: *L&P*, i, 1, no. 519.1.

SC3.
WEST, Dr. Nicholas (later Bishop of Ely; 1461-1533)*

3 Nov. 1511^b - Dec.? 1511^h Special Ambassador
He was accompanied by one Christopher Walls, whose status is unclear.
Instructions: Inferred from *L&P*, i, 1, no. 880.
Commission: *L&P*, i, 1, no. 969.2.

SC4.
DACRE, Thomas, Baron Dacre of Greystoke (1467-1525)*
WEST, Dr. Nicholas (later Bishop of Ely; 1461-1533)*

15 Apr. 1512^b - *c.*22 July 1512^c [Special] Ambassadors
                                                £2/d (Dacre), 30*s*/d (West)

There is some evidence that Lord Dacre accompanied West to Edinburgh, and then returned immediately to Carlisle.

Instructions: Suggested in Lesley, J., *The History of Scotland* (1830), p. 85.
Commission: *L&P*, i, 1, nos. 1170.14-1170.15.
Correspondence about: *L&P*, i, 1.

SC5.

15 Feb. 1513b - c.15 Apr. 1513^c [Special] Ambassadors
Audience: 21 Mar. 1513   20s/d (West)

There is little evidence that Lord Dacre accompanied West other than in the earliest part of the mission, if even then.

Commission: *L&P*, i, 1, no. 1662.32.
Correspondence: *L&P*, i, 2.

SC6.
DRURY, Sir Robert (by 1456-1535)*

1 Feb. 1513^b - June? 1513^h [Special Ambassador]

He was commissioned with William Lord Conyers, whose responsibilities were apparently acquitted on the English side of the Scottish border. It is not even entirely clear that Drury went into Scotland, although the probability is strong.

Commission: *L&P*, i, 1, no. 1662.2.
Correspondence about: *L&P*, i, 1-2.

SC7.
MAGNUS, Dr. Thomas (*d*.1550)*

Mid-May 1519^h - n.d.   [Special Ambassador]

Instructions: Suggested in *L&P*, iii, 1, no. 269.
Correspondence about: *L&P*, iii, 1.

SC8.
MAGNUS, Dr. Thomas (*d*.1550)*
RADCLIFFE, Roger (*fl*.1520s)

24 Oct. 1524^c - 21 Dec. 1524^c [Special Ambassadors]
           (Radcliffe)
           12 Jan. 1526^c
           (Magnus)
Audience: 1 Nov. 1524

There were numerous returns to Berwick during this mission, including one in Dec. 1525. Radcliffe returned early to England. Upon his final return to Berwick, Magnus continued his diplomatic responsibilities from that post.

Instructions: *L&P*, iv, 1, no. 767.
Correspondence: *L&P*, iv, 1; BL, Cotton, Calig. B.vi.

SC9.
CLIFFORD, Thomas (*fl.*1510s)

*c.*late Nov. 1529[h] - mid-Dec. 1529[h]   [Special Ambassador]
Audience: *c.*1 Dec. 1529   20*s*/d

There is a possibility that he delivered messages from Henry VIII several times
    around this period to the Scottish King.

Correspondence about: *L&P*, iv, 3.

SC10.
HALLEY, Thomas (*d.*1557)*

15 Nov. 1531[c] - late Jan. 1532[g]   Herald

Instructions: *L&P*, v, nos. 536-7.
Correspondence about: *L&P*, v.

SC11.

1 Mar. 1532[c] - 27 May 1532[g]   Herald

Halley was Carlisle herald.

Instructions: *L&P*, v, nos. 844-5; BL, Add. 32646, f. 2; Bain, J. (ed.), *The
    Hamilton Papers...*, (Edinburgh, 1892) i, no. 1.
Correspondence: *L&P*, v.

SC12.

16 June 1532[e] - July? 1532[h]   Herald

SC13.

*c.*30 Sept. 1532[c] - n.d.   Herald

Instructions: *L&P*, v, no. 1367.

SC14.
MAGNUS, Dr. Thomas (*d.*1550)*
FRANKLYN, William (1480?-1556)*
WHITEHEAD, Hugh (*fl.*1530s)

26 May 1534[c] - *c.*9 July 1534[c]   [Special Ambassadors]
Treaty confirmation: 30 June 1534

Instructions: Suggested in *L&P*, vii, nos. 958, 963.
Correspondence: *L&P*, vii, 1; *The Hamilton Papers...*, i.

SC15.
HOWARD, William (later 1st Baron Howard of Effingham; 1510?-1573)*

23 Jan. 1535[a] - 20 Mar. 1535[a]   [Special Ambassador]
Investment: 21 Feb. 1535

Instructions: *L&P*, viii, no. 70.
Correspondence about: *L&P*, viii, p. 474.

SC16.
BARLOW, Dr. William (later Bishop of St. David's, St. Asaph, Bath and Wells, Chichester; *d.*1569)*
HOLCROFT, Thomas (later Sir Thomas; 1505/6-1558)*

3 Oct. 1535[c] - c.20 Dec. 1535[e]   [Special Ambassadors]
                                          20*s*/d (Barlow)

Instructions: BL, Add. 32646, ff. 26-37; *The Hamilton Papers...*, i, no. 22.
Correspondence: *L&P*, ix.

SC17.
HOWARD, William (later 1st Baron Howard of Effingham; 1510?-1573)*
BARLOW, Dr. William (later Bishop of St. David's, St. Asaph, Bath and Wells, Chichester; *d.*1569)*

16 Jan. 1536[c] - 30 May 1536[a]   [Special Ambassador]
        (Howard)
        c.1 Oct. 1536[h]
        (Barlow)
Audience: 14 Apr. 1536

Barlow made numerous returns to England during his tenure.

Instructions: BL, Add. 32646, ff. 69-70.
Correspondence: BL, Cotton, Vesp. C.xiii, Calig. B.iii; *L&P*, x; *The Hamilton Papers*, i.

SC18.
HOLCROFT, Thomas (later Sir Thomas; 1505/6-1558)*

27 Dec. 1536[h] - n.d.   [Special Ambassador]

Instructions: Inferred from *L&P*, xi, no. 1373.

SC19.
SADLER, Ralph (later Sir Ralph; 1507-1587)*

mid-Jan. 1537[f] - mid-Feb. 1537[h]   [Special Ambassador]
Audience: c.30 Jan. 1537

Instructions: *L&P*, xii, 1, no. 1313?
Correspondence: *L&P*, xii, 1.

SC20.

mid-Mar. 1537[h] - mid-Apr. 1537[g]   [Special Ambassador]
Audience: c.1 Apr. 1537

Sadler found the Scottish King at Rouen in France.

Instructions: *L&P*, xii, 1, no. 540.
Correspondence: *L&P*, xii, 1.

SC21.

Late May 1537[h] - *c*.29 June 1537[c]   [Special Ambassador]

Instructions: Suggested in *L&P*, xii, 2, no. 55.

SC22.

Late Jan. 1540[g] - early Mar. 1540[e]   [Special Ambassador]
Audience: 19 Feb. 1540

Instructions: *L&P*, xv, no. 136; Scott, W., *Sadler State Papers* (1809), pp. 3-13.
Correspondence: *L&P*, xv; *Sadler State Papers*.

SC23.

13 Mar. 1543[c] - 12 Dec. 1543[c]   [Resident Ambassador]
Audience: 17 Mar. 1543

Instructions: BL, Add. 32650, ff. 29-45, Eg. 2790, f. 130; *L&P*, xviii, 1, no. 271; *Sadler State Papers*, i, pp. 59-63; *Hamilton Papers*, i, no. 330.
Correspondence: BL, Add. 32640-56, Lansd. 155; *L&P*, xviii, 1-2; *Sadler State Papers*; *Hamilton Papers*, i-ii.

SC24.
CHALONER, Sir Thomas (1521-1565)*

10 May 1551[c] - Aug.? 1551[h]   [Special Ambassador]

Sir Robert Bowes and Sir Leonard Beckwith were joined with him in a commission to discuss with the Scots the issue of the debatable lands on this date, but only Chaloner seems to have carried negotiations into Scotland, *c*.mid-July.

Instructions: BL, Add. 5935, ff. 95-6, Sloane 2442, f. 53b; *CSPF, 1547-63*, no. 318; *CSPScot, 1547-63*, no. 371.
Correspondence: BL, Lansd. 2; *CSPScot, 1547-63*.

SC25.
DACRE, Sir Thomas (later Baron Dacre; *c*.1527-1566)*
MUSGRAVE, Sir Richard (1524-1555)*

Nov. 1552[c] - Dec.? 1552[h]   [Special Ambassadors]

Instructions: *CSPScot, 1547-1563*, no. 395.

SC26.
CHALONER, Sir Thomas (1521-1565)

Feb. 1556[c] - n.d.   [Special Ambassador]

Instructions: BL, Sloane 2442, p. 141, Eg. 2790, f. 139-41, Add. 5935, ff. 150-1, Lansd. 155, ff. 373-4; HMC *2nd Report*, p. 96; *CSPScot, 1547-63*, no. 410.

SC27.
PERCY, Thomas, 1st Earl of Northumberland (1528-1572)*
HENMER, Dr. Robert (*fl.*1550s)

21 Jan. 1558*[b]* - Feb.? 1558*[h]*   [Commissioners]

Instructions: Implied in *CSPScot, 1547-63*, nos. 427-9; *CSPF, 1553-8*, nos. 427-31.

Correspondence: *CSPScot, 1547-63*.

SC28.
RANDOLPH, Thomas (1523-1590)*

Sept. 1558*[h]* - 23 Sept. 1563*[c]*   Agent
                                         20*s*/d (begin 16 Sept. 1561)

At first he was the English intelligencer *cum* agent in Scotland with the Protestant faction. He had official although *ad hoc* pay. His role evolved, by 1561, into a more formal diplomatic role. He returned to London from Nov. 1559 to 25 Dec. 1559, and in June 1563, among other numerous returns to Berwick or London.

Correspondence: PRO, SP/52/6-8; BL, Sloane, 2442, Eg. 2790, Add. 5935, 6990, Harl. 6986, 6990; *CSPF, 1559-60, 1560-1, 1561-2, 1562, 1563; CSPScot, 1547-63, 1563-9*; HMC *Salisb.*, i.

SC29.
KILLIGREW, Henry (later Sir Henry; *c.*1528-1603)*

23 Mar. 1560*[a]* - 11 May 1560*[c]*   [Special Ambassador]
Arrived: 6 Apr. 1560   *ad hoc*

He was specifically designated to accompany the Bishop of Valence (accredited by Francis and Mary to the Earl of Arran) into Scotland.

Instructions: Inferred from *CSPF, 1559-60*, no. 892 & note; *CSPScot, 1547-63*, no. 717.

Correspondence: BL, Add. 33924, Lansd. 103; *CSPF, 1559-60, 1560-1; CSPScot, 1547-63*.

SC30.
CECIL, Sir William (later Baron Burghley; 1520/1-1598)*
WOTTON, Sir Nicholas (1497?-1567)*

27 May 1560*[a]* - 28 July 1560*[b]*   [Commissioners]
Treaty signed: 6 July 1560   £4/d (Cecil)

They were sent to negotiate the Treaty of Edinburgh, which was concluded after deliberations in Newcastle and Edinburgh.

Instructions: BL, Cotton, Calig. B.ix, ff. 118-21, 149-52; *CSPScot, 1547-63*, no. 803; *CSPF, 1560-1*, no. 134.

Correspondence: BL, Lansd. 103; *CSPF, 1560-1; CSPScot, 1547-63*; HMC *Salisb.*, i; Haynes, S. and Murdin, W. (eds.), *Collection of State Papers...Burghley...*(1740-59).

SC31.
MEWTAS, Sir Peter (*c.*1500-1562)

16 Sept. 1561[b] - *c.*11 Oct. 1561[c]   [Special Ambassador]

He went specifically to the Queen of Scots upon her arrival in Scotland.

Commission: *CSPF, 1561-2*, no. 506; *CSPScot, 1547-63*, no. 1019.
Correspondence about: *CSPF, 1561-2.*

SC32.
SIDNEY, Sir Henry (1529-1586)*

15 July 1562[a] - *c.*6 Aug. 1562[h]   [Special Ambassador]
Audience: 23 July 1562

He joined with Randolph, who was already there.

Instructions: *CSPScot, 1547-63*, no. 1120; HMC *Salisb.*, i, p. 267; Haynes and
   Murdin, *State Papers...*, p. 392.
Correspondence: *CSPF, 1562*; *CSPScot, 1547-63.*

SC33.
RANDOLPH, Thomas (1523-1590)*

20 Aug. 1563[c] - *c.*25 Sept. 1563[c]   [Agent]
Audience: 1 Sept. 1563

Instructions: BL, Sloane 2442, f. 142b, Eg. 2790, f. 143, Add. 5935, ff. 152-4,
   Lansd. 155, ff. 377b-378, Harl. 289, f. 163; *CSPF, 1563*, nos. 1162-3.
Correspondence: BL, Add. 5935; *CSPF, 1563.*

SC34.

16 Nov. 1563[c] - *c.*17 June 1564[c]   [Agent]
Audience: 11 Dec. 1563

Instructions: BL, Sloane 2442, f. 144, Eg., 2790, ff. 145-7, Lansd. 155,
   ff. 379b-81, Harl. 289, f. 163; HMC *2nd Report*, p. 96; *CSPScot, 1563-9*,
   no. 37.
Correspondence: *CSPF, 1563, 1564-5*; *CSPScot, 1563-9.*

SC35.

12 Oct. 1564[b] - *c.*15 June 1566[c]   Agent
Audience: 24 Oct. 1564

Instructions: BL, Cotton, Calig. B.x, f. 270, Sloane 2442, f. 146, Eg. 2790,
   ff. 147-9, Add. 5935, ff. 156-9, Lansd. 155, ff. 382b-5, Harl. 289, f. 165;
   CSPScot, 1563-9, no. 110.
Correspondence: BL, Add. 35125; *CSPF, 1564-5, 1566-8.*

SC36.
THROCKMORTON, Sir Nicholas (1515-1571)*

1 May 1565[b] - 24 May 1565[c]   [Special Ambassador]
Audience: 15 May 1565   66s 8d/d
Secretary: Henry Middlemore

Instructions: *CSPF, 1564-5*, no. 1118; *CSPScot, 1563-9*, no. 173.
Correspondence: BL, Lansd. 5; *CSPF, 1564-5*; *CSPScot, 1563-9*.

SC37.
TAMWORTH, John (c.1524-1569)*

30 July 1565[c] - c.1 Sept. 1565[c]   [Special Ambassador]
Audience: 7 Aug. 1565

Instructions: *CSPF, 1564-5*, no. 1333; *CSPScot, 1563-9*, no. 220.
Correspondence: *CSPF, 1564-5*; *CSPScot, 1563-9*.

SC38.
KILLIGREW, Henry (later Sir Henry; c.1528-1603)*

15 June 1566[b] - mid-July 1566[c]   [Special Ambassador]
Audience: 24 June 1566   20s/d
Secretary: William Davison

Instructions: PRO, SP/52/12, f. 72; BL, Sloane 2442, ff. 148-51, Eg. 2790,
    ff. 149-53, Add. 5935, ff. 159-64, Lansd. 155, ff. 386-91, Harl. 289,
    ff. 166b-8; HMC *2nd Report*, p. 96; *CSPF, 1566-8*, no. 491; *CSPScot,
    1563-9*, no. 397.
Correspondence: *CSPScot, 1563-9*.

SC39.
RUSSELL, Francis, 2nd Earl of Bedford (1527?-1585)*

c.1 Dec. 1566[h] - 9 Jan. 1567[c]   [Special Ambassador]
Arrived: 9 Dec. 1566

He went for the christening of Prince James.

Instructions: Inferred from *CSPF, 1566-8*, no. 825.
Correspondence: BL, Cotton, Calig. B.ix; *CSPF, 1566-8*; *CSPScot, 1563-9*;
    HMC *Salisb.*, i.

SC40.
KILLIGREW, Henry (later Sir Henry; c.1528-1603)*

c.1 Mar. 1567[h] - c.15 Mar. 1567[c]   [Special Ambassador]
Audience: 8 Mar. 1567

Instructions: BL, Cotton, Calig. B.x, ff. 384-6; inferred from *CSPF, 1566-8*,
    no. 997; *CSPScot, 1563-9*, no. 397.
Correspondence: BL, Cotton, Calig. B.x; *CSPF, 1566-8*; *CSPScot, 1563-9*.

SC41.

THROCKMORTON, Sir Nicholas (1515-1571)*

29 June 1567[b] - *c*.5 Sept. 1567[c] [Special Ambassador]
Audience (with Lords Atholl, Morton, 66*s* 8*d*/d
   et al): 15 July 1567
Secretary: Henry Middlemore

Throckmorton never saw the Queen of Scots, to whom he was sent.

Instructions: BL, Cotton, Calig. C.i, f. 3; *CSPF, 1566-8*, nos. 1364, 1378;
   CSPScot, 1563-9, nos. 538, 540, 542.
Correspondence: *CSPF, 1566-8*; *CSPScot, 1563-9*.

SC42.

MIDDLEMORE, Henry (1535-*c*.1597)

June 1568[c] - *c*.13 July 1568[c] [Special Ambassador]
Audience: 15 June 1568

Instructions: BL, Cotton, Calig. C.i, f. 88; *CSPF, 1566-8*, no. 2263; *CSPScot,
   1563-9*, nos. 689-90.
Correspondence: BL, Cotton, Calig. B.ix, C.i, Harl. 289; *CSPF, 1566-8*;
   CSPScot, 1563-9.

SC43.

CAREY, George (later 2nd Baron Hunsdon; 1547-1603)*

c.1 Oct. 1569[h] - *c*.13 Oct. 1569[c] [Special Ambassador]
He was sent to the Regent Murray.

Correspondence about: *CSPF, 1569-71*; *CSPScot, 1563-9*.

SC44.

22 Dec. 1569[c] - 27 Dec. 1569[c] [Special Ambassador]
Audience: 23 Dec. 1569

He was sent from Sussex, Hunsdon and Sadler, who were negotiating in the
   North, but he went upon Queen Elizabeth's authority.

Instructions: *CSPF, 1569-71*, no. 556; *CSPScot, 1569-71*, no. 59.
Correspondence: *CSPF, 1569-71*; *CSPScot, 1569-71*.

SC45.

DRURY, William (later Sir William; 1527-1579)*
GATES, Sir Henry (*c*.1515-1589)*

3 Jan. 1570[c] - 29 Jan. 1570[c] [Special Ambassadors]
Audience: 19 Jan. 1570

Drury may have left for Scotland in late Dec. 1569, with Gates following in
   early Jan. 1570.

Instructions: Drury—*CSPF, 1569-71*, no. 554; *CSPScot, 1569-71*, no. 58.
   Gates—*CSPF, 1569-71*, nos. 614-15; *CSPScot, 1569-71*, nos. 76 & 82.
Correspondence: BL, Cotton, Calig. C.i; *CSPF, 1569-71*; *CSPScot, 1569-71*.

SC46.
RANDOLPH, Thomas (1523-1590)*

29 Jan. 1570[a] - 20 Jan. 1571[a]   [Special Ambassador]
Arrived: 9 Feb. 1570   40s/d

This mission included numerous returns to England, including April - June 1570.

Instructions: Cotton, Calig. C.i, f. 375; *CSPF, 1569-71*, no. 650; *CSPScot, 1569-71*, nos. 100 & 115.

Correspondence: BL, Cotton, Calig. C.iii; *CSPF, 1569-71*; *CSPScot, 1569-71*.

SC47.
DRURY, Sir William (1527-1579)*

20 May 1571[c] - c.25 June 1571[c]   [Special Ambassador]

He made a return to Berwick from 31 May to c.5 June.

Instructions: Inferred from *CSPF, 1569-71*, no. 1715-16, 1776; *CSPScot, 1569-71*, no. 753.

Correspondence: BL, Cotton, Calig. C.iii; *CSPF, 1569-71*; *CSPScot, 1569-71*.

SC48.

31 Jan. 1572[b] - c.1 July 1572[c]   [Special Ambassador]
Arrived: c.15 Feb. 1572   40s/d
Secretary: Nicholas Errington?

In the first instance, Drury accompanied Randolph to Scotland (see below), came back to Berwick on Apr. 23, and then was ordered to accompany the French ambassador de Croc to Scotland, 30 Apr. 1572.

Instructions: BL, Cotton, Calig. C.iii, no. 275; *CSPF, 1572-4*, no. 315-16, 334; *CSPScot, 1571-4*, nos. 285-6.

Correspondence: *CSPF, 1572-4*; *CSPScot, 1571-4*; HMC *Salisb.*, ii; Haynes and Murdin, *State Papers...*

SC49.
RANDOLPH, Thomas (1523-1590)*

2 Feb. 1572[a] - 12 May 1572[a]   [Special Ambassador]
Arrived: c.15 Feb. 1572   40s/d

Randolph and Drury (see above) initially went on the mission together, but Drury's responsibilities extended far longer.

Instructions: Inferred from *CSPF, 1572-4*, no. 214; *CSPScot, 1571-4*, no. 138.

Correspondence: BL, Cotton, Calig., C.iii, Lansd. 15; *CSPF, 1572-4*; *CSPScot, 1571-4*.

SC50.
DRURY, Sir William (1527-1579)*

5 July 1572*b* - 1 Aug. 1572*c* [Special Ambassador]
Secretary: Nicholas Errington 40*s*/d

Instructions: Inferred from *CSPScot, 1571-4*, no. 384.
Correspondence: BL, Lansd. 15; *CSPF, 1572-4*; *CSPScot, 1571-4*.

SC51.
KILLIGREW, Henry (later Sir Henry; *c.*1528-1603)*

5 Sept. 1572*a* - 8 July 1573*b* [Special Ambassador]
Audience: *c.*13 Sept. 1572 40*s*/d
Secretary: Nicholas Errington?

He returned several times to Berwick.

Instructions: BL, Add. 4106, ff. 25-6, Eg. 2790, ff. 157-8, Harl. 289, f. 149, Lansd. 155, ff. 399-400, Sloane 2442, f. 152; HMC *2nd Report*, p. 97; HMC *Salisb.*, ii, p. 23; *CSPScot, 1571-4*, no. 427.
Correspondence: BL, Cotton, Calig. C.iii-iv; *CSPF, 1572-4*; *CSPScot, 1571-4*; Tytler, P., *History of Scotland* (Edinburgh, 1828-43), vii.

SC52.

24 May 1574*a* - 19 Sept. 1574*a* [Special Ambassador]
Arrived: 10 June 1574 40*s*/d
Secretary: William Davison

Instructions: BL, Sloane 2442, f. 154, Eg. 2790, f. 160, Harl. 289, f. 150, Lansd. 155, f. 401; HMC *2nd Report*, p. 97; *CSPScot, 1571-4*, no. 771; *CSPF, 1572-4*, no. 1421.
Correspondence: *CSPScot, 1571-4, 1574-81*; *CSPF, 1572-4*.

SC53.

12 June 1575*a* - 27 Sept. 1575*a* [Special Ambassador]
Arrived: 20 July 1575 40*s*/d
Secretary: William Davison

Instructions: BL, Sloane 2442, f. 154, Eg. 2790, f. 160, Lansd. 155, ff. 402-04, Harl. 289, f. 150b; *CSPScot, 1574-81*, no. 160; HMC *2nd Report*, p. 97.
Correspondence: *CSPScot, 1574-81*; *CSPF, 1575-7*.

SC54.
BOWES, Robert (1535?-1597)*

8 Sept. 1577*c* - *c.*8 Oct. 1577*c* [Special Ambassador]

Instructions: *CSPF, 1577-8*, no. 200-01.
Correspondence (immediately upon return): *CSPScot, 1574-81*.

SC55.

17 Nov. 1577*a* - *c.*Dec. 1579*h* Resident Agent
20*s*/d, 40*s*/d (by June 1578)

Instructions: Inferred from BL, Cotton, Calig. C.v, f. 88; *CSPScot, 1574-81*, no. 283.

Correspondence: BL, Add. 19401, 23109, 34208, Cotton, Julius F.vi, Calig. C.iii, v, Harl. 289, 6992; *CSPScot, 1574-81*; HMC *Salisb.*, ii; Bowes, R., *The Correspondence of Robert Bowes of Aske...*, ed. Stevenson, J. (1842); Tytler, P., *History of Scotland* (Edinburgh, 1828-43), viii.

SC56.
RANDOLPH, Thomas (1523-1590)*

28 Jan. 1578[a] - 13 Apr. 1578[c]   [Special Ambassador]
Audience: 26 Feb. 1578   40s/d

Instructions: BL, Cotton, Calig. C.v, f. 3, Harl. 6992, no. 45; *CSPScot, 1574-81*, nos. 295, 299.
Correspondence: BL, Cotton, Calig. C.v, Harl. 6992; *CSPScot, 1574-81*.

SC57.
ERRINGTON, Nicholas (*fl.*1570s-1580s)

16 Sept. 1579[c] - c.10 Oct. 1579[c]   [Special Ambassador]
Audience: c.25 Sept. 1579

Instructions: BL, Harl. 291, f. 14; *CSPScot, 1574-81*, no. 427.
Correspondence: *CSPScot, 1574-81*.

SC58.

5 Oct. 1579[c] - c.30 Dec. 1579[c]   [Special Ambassador]

Instructions: BL, Sloane 2442, ff. 156-9, Cotton, Calig. C.v, ff. 137-42, Harl. 289, f. 152; *CSPScot, 1547-81*, no. 437.
Correspondence: BL, Cotton, Calig. C.v; *CSPScot, 1574-81*.

SC59.

22 Feb. 1580[c] - c.15 Apr. 1580[c]   [Special Ambassador]

Instructions: *CSPScot, 1574-81*, no. 456.
Correspondence: BL, Cotton, Calig. C.vi; *CSPScot, 1574-81*.

SC60.
BOWES, Robert (1535?-1597)*

19 Apr. 1580[c] - 22 May 1580[c]   [Special Ambassador]
Audience: 29 May 1580

Instructions: BL, Cotton, Calig., C.vi, f. 12; *CSPScot, 1574-8*, no. 476; Bowes, *Correspondence*, pp. 26-7, 31-7.
Correspondence: BL, Cotton, Calig. B.viii, C.iii, vi, Harl. 6999; *CSPScot, 1574-81*; Bowes, *Correspondence*.

SC61.

31 Aug. 1580[c] - *c*.18 Oct. 1580[d]   [Special Ambassador]

Instructions: Inferred from *CSPScot, 1574-81*, nos. 581, 585; *CSPF, 1579-81*, no. 421.

Correspondence: BL, Cotton, Julius F.vi, Calig. C.vi; *CSPScot, 1574-81*; Bowes, *Correspondence*.

SC62.
RANDOLPH, Thomas (1523-1590)*

6 Jan. 1581[a] - 28 Mar. 1581[c]   [Special Ambassador]
Audience: 21 Jan. 1581   40*s*/d

Instructions: *CSPScot, 1574-81*, nos. 651-3.

Correspondence: BL, Harl. 6999, 7395 (summary of negotiations), Lansd. 30-2; *CSPScot, 1574-81*; Tytler, *History of Scotland*, viii.

SC63.
ERRINGTON, Nicholas (*fl.*1570s-1580s)

26 Oct. 1581[c] - n.d.   [Special Ambassador]

He was denied entrance into Scotland in early Nov.

Instructions: *CSPScot, 1581-3*, no. 72.

SC64.
CAREY, Sir George (later 2nd Baron Hunsdon; 1547-1603)*
BOWES, Sir Robert (1535?-1597)*

29 Aug. 1582[b] - 9 Oct. 1582[a]   [Special Ambassadors]
Audience: 12 Sept. 1582   40*s*/d

Carey was joined at Berwick by Sir Robert Bowes, who remained as resident (see below).

Instructions: BL, Cotton, Calig. B.v, ff. 228-31; *CSPScot, 1581-3*, no. 149; inferred from *CSPF, 1582*, no. 298.

Correspondence: BL, Add. 3199, 32092, Cotton, Calig. C.vii; Harl. 291; *CSPScot, 1581-3*.

SC65.
BOWES, Robert (1535?-1597)*

4 Sept. 1582[a] - *c*.5 Oct. 1583[c]   [Resident Ambassador]
    40*s*/d

Instructions: Inferred from HMC *Salisb.*, iii, p. 1.

Correspondence: BL, Add. 33531, Cotton, Calig. B.viii, C.vii, ix, Harl. 291, 6980; *CSPScot, 1581-3*; HMC *Salisb.*, iii; Bowes, *Correspondence*.

SC66.
DAVISON, William (*c.*1541-1608)*

10 Dec. 1582[a] - 12 Apr. 1583[a]   [Special Ambassador]
                                           20*s*/d

He joined with Bowes.

Instructions: BL, Cotton, Calig. C.ix, f. 31.
Correspondence: BL, Add. 33531, Cotton, Calig. C.vii; Harl. 286, 291, 6980; *CSPScot, 1581-3*; *CSPF, 1583-4*.

SC67.
WALSINGHAM, Sir Francis (*c.*1532-1590)*

13 Aug. 1583[a] - 21 Oct. 1583[c]   [Special Ambassador]
Audience: *c.*8 Sept. 1583   80*s*/d

Instructions: *CSPScot, 1581-3*, nos. 599, 660.
Correspondence: BL, Harl. 6993; *CSPF, 1583-4*; HMC *Salisb.*, iii; Tytler, *History of Scotland*, viii.

SC68.
DAVISON, William (*c.*1541-1608)*

24 Apr. 1584[b] - *c.*16 Sept. 1584[c]   [Special Ambassador]
Audience: 5 June 1584   40*s*/d

Instructions: BL, Cotton, Calig. C.ix, ff. 96-8, Harl. 291, ff. 118-20; *CSPScot, 1584-5*, nos. 73, 75; summarized in *CSPF, 1583-4*, no. 659.
Correspondence: BL, Calig. C.viii, Harl. 291; *CSPScot, 1584-5*; *CSPF, 1583-4*.

SC69.
WOTTON, Edward (later 1st Baron Wotton of Marley; 1548-1628)*

11 May 1585[a] - *c.*12 Oct. 1585[c]   [Special Ambassador]
Audience: 30 May 1585   40*s*/d

Instructions: BL, Cotton, Calig. C.viii, ff. 187-8; C.ix, ff. 131-3; *CSPScot, 1584-5*, no. 587.
Correspondence: BL, Add. 32657, Cotton, Calig. C.ix, Lansd. 45; *CSPScot, 1584-5, 1585-6*; HMC *Salisb.*, xiii; Cameron, A., *The Warrender Papers*...(Scottish Historical Society, 1931); *Hamilton Papers*, ii.

SC70.
KNOLLYS, William (later 1st Earl of Banbury; 1547-1632)*

Nov. 1585[h] - *c.*Dec. 1585[g]   [Special Ambassador]
Audience: 23 Nov. 1585

Instructions: Implied in *CSPScot, 1585-6*, nos. 205-06.
Correspondence: *CSPScot, 1585-6*.

SC71.
RANDOLPH, Thomas (1523-1590)*

28 Jan. 1586*a* - *c*.15 Aug. 1586*c*   [Special Ambassador]
Audience: 29 Feb. 1586   40*s*/d
Secretaries: Giles Fletcher?, Thomas
   Milles

He returned to Berwick several times in this mission, and in fact his letters are all
   dated from Berwick beginning in early July 1586.

Instructions: BL, Cotton, Calig. C.viii, ff. 282-4; *CSPScot, 1585-6*, nos. 258-9.
Correspondence: BL, Cotton, Calig. C.ix, Harl. 291, 6994, Lansd. 49;
   CSPScot, 1585-6, CSPF, 1585-6; HMC *Salisb.*, iii.

SC72.
CAREY, Robert (later Baron Carey of Leppington; 1st Earl of Monmouth;
   c.1560-1639)*

c.10 Feb. 1587*h* - n.d.   [Special Ambassador]

He was appointed to explain the execution of Mary, Queen of Scots to her son,
   James VI, but was refused permission to enter Scotland. A hiatus in relations
   resulted.

Correspondence about: *CSPScot, 1586-9*.

SC73.

12 May 1588*b* - n.d.   [Special Ambassador]

Carey apparently re-opened diplomatic contact with Scotland in this poorly
   documented mission.

Instructions: BL, Cotton, Calig. D.i, ff. 159-62?; HMC *Salisb.*, p. 329 (dated
   16 June 1588).
Correspondence about: *CSPScot, 1586-9*.

SC74.
ASHBY, William (*d*.1593)*

26 June 1588*a* - 21 Jan. 1590*c*   [Resident Ambassador]
Audience: 24 July 1588   30*s*/d

Instructions: Inferred from *CSPScot, 1586-9*, no. 476.
Correspondence: BL, Cotton, Calig. D.i, Titus B.ii, Eg. 2124, 2598, Add.
   22958, Harl. 4647; *CSPScot, 1586-9, 1589-93*.

SC75.
SIDNEY, Sir Robert (later Viscount Lisle, 1st Earl of Leicester; 1563-1626)*

14 Aug. 1588*a* - 16 Sept. 1588*a*   [Special Ambassador]
Audience: 1 Sept. 1588   40*s*/d

Instructions: *CSPScot, 1586-9*, no. 507.
Correspondence: BL, Cotton, Calig. D.i, Harl. 7004; *CSPScot, 1586-9*.

SC76.
BOWES, Robert (1535?-1597)*

1 Dec. 1589a - *d.*15 Nov. 1597   Resident Ambassador
Audience: *c.*1 Jan. 1590   40*s*/d
Secretary: George Nicholson

He was intermittently in Scotland and England. For instance, he was in England
   most of 1595. During these absences Nicholson acted as chargé d'affaires.

Instructions: *CSPScot, 1589-93*, no. 307.
Correspondence: BL, Add. 12503, Cotton, Calig. D.ii, x, Harl. 292, 851, 4647-
   8, Lansd. 103; *CSPScot, 1589-93, 1593-5, 1595-7*; *CSPScot, 1589-1603*
   (1858 ed.); *APC, 1590, 1591-2, 1592-3, 1595-6, 1596-7*; Tytler, *History of*
   Scotland, ix; HMC *Salisb.*, v-vii.

SC77.
SOMERSET, Edward, 4th Earl of Worcester (1553-1628)*

20 May 1590^a - *c.*29 June 1590^e [Special Ambassador]
Audience: 14 June 1590   £5/d

Instructions: Inferred from *CSPScot, 1587-93*, no. 426.
Correspondence: *CSPScot, 1589-93*.

SC78.
BURGH, Thomas, 5th Baron Burgh (1558?-1597)*

9 Feb. 1593^b - *c.*13 Apr. 1593^g [Special Ambassador]
Audience: 16 Mar. 1593

He joined with Bowes in Edinburgh.

Instructions: *CSPScot, 1593-5*, no. 26.
Correspondence: *CSPScot, 1593-5*.

SC79.
ZOUCHE, Edward la, 11th Baron Zouche of Harringworth (1556?-1625)*

18 Dec. 1593^a - *c.*13 Apr. 1594^c Ambassador Extraordinary
Audience: 13 Jan. 1594   £5/d

Instructions: *CSPScot, 1593-5*, nos. 181-4.
Correspondence: BL, Cotton, Calig. D.ii; *CSPScot, 1593-5*.

SC80.
RADCLIFFE, Robert, 5th Earl of Sussex (1569?-1629)*

*c.*1 Aug. 1594^c - *c.*21 Sept. 1594^c Ambassador Extraordinary
Audience: 29 Aug. 1594

He represented Queen Elizabeth at the christening of Prince Henry.

Instructions: *CSPScot, 1593-5*, no. 323.
Correspondence: *CSPScot, 1593-5*.

SC81.
BOWES, Sir William (*d.*1611)*

1 Apr. 1597*c* - early July 1597*c* [Special] Ambassador
Audience: 7 May 1597

He joined with Robert Bowes.

Instructions: BL, Harl. 292, ff. 83-4; *CSPScot, 1595-7*, no. 404.
Correspondence: BL, Cotton, Calig. D.ii, Harl. 292, 851; *CSPScot, 1595-7*;
  HMC *Salisb.*, vii.

SC82.
NICHOLSON, George (*fl.*1590s-1600s)

15 Nov. 1597*a* - 23 Mar. 1603*a* Resident Agent
  13*s* 4*d*/d

He had acted as chargé d'affaires during Robert Bowes' numerous absences
  prior to 1597.

Correspondence: BL, Cotton, Calig. D.ii; *CSPScot, 1589-1603* (1858 ed.);
  APC, 1598-9, 1599-1600, 1601-04; HMC *Salisb.*, ix-xii, xiv-xv.

SC83.
BOWES, Sir William (*d.*1611)*

Autumn 1597*h* - *c.*8 Feb. 1598*c* [Special Ambassador]
Audience: *c.*1 Feb. 1598 20*s*/d

Instructions: Suggested in *CSPScot, 1589-1603* (1858 ed.), p. 744.
Correspondence: *CSPScot, 1589-1603* (1858 ed.).
Correspondence about: *CSPD, 1598-1601*; *APC, 1597-8*.

SC84.

20 Apr. 1599*a* - 21 Aug. 1599*b* Resident Ambassador
  40*s*/d

Correspondence: BL, Cotton, Calig. D.ii; *CSPScot, 1589-1603* (1858 ed.);
  HMC *Salisb.*, ix.
Correspondence about: *CSPD, 1598-1601*.

SC85.
BROUNCKER, Sir Henry (*c.*1550-1607)*

21 Aug. 1600*d* - *c.*25 Sept. 1600*c* [Special Ambassador]
  £140 (total)

Instructions: Suggested in *CSPScot, 1589-1603* (1858 ed.), p. 786.
Correspondence: *CSPScot, 1589-1603* (1858 ed.).

SC86.

CAREY, Sir Robert (later Baron Carey of Leppington, 1st Earl of Monmouth; *c.*1560-1639)*

24 Mar. 1603[a] - Apr. 1603[h]   [Special Ambassador]
Audience: 27 Mar. 1603

He informed James VI of Queen Elizabeth's death. With the accession of the Scottish King, James VI, to the throne of England as James I, formal English representation in Scotland ceased.

SPAIN

There were numerous missions to Spain during the reign of Henry VIII, most of which are subsumed under the heading 'Emperor and Imperial Diets.'

SP1.
STILE, John (*fl.*1500s-1510s)

Apr. 1509[h] - 16 June 1518[b]   [Resident Ambassador]
                                        10*s*/d

He was resident with King Ferdinand.

Correspondence: *L&P*, i-ii; *CSPS, 1509-25*.

SP2.
KNIGHT, Dr. William (later Bishop of Bath and Wells; 1476-1547)*

3 June 1512[g] - *c*.1 Sept. 1513[g]   [Special Ambassador]
Arrived: 14 June 1512

He apparently accompanied the English army into Spain and then shifted to a fully diplomatic role, joining with Stile at the court of Aragon.

Correspondence: BL, Cotton, Vesp. C.i; *L&P*, i, 1-2; HMC *Salisb.*, i.

SP3.
YOUNG, Dr. John (1467-1516)*
BOLEYN, Sir Thomas (later Viscount Rochford, Earl of Wiltshire; 1477-1539)*
WINGFIELD, Sir Richard (1469?-1525)*
POYNINGS, Sir Edward (1459-1521)*

8 Jan. 1513[a] - *c*.25 May 1513[c]   [Special Ambassadors]
(Wingfield   (Poynings, Young
and Poynings)   and Boleyn)
                24 June 1513[b]
                (Wingfield)

All four were commissioned, 20 Dec. 1512, to treat for the formation of a Holy League with the Pope ([or his representative in the Low Countries] Italy, q.v.), the Emperor Elect, Maximillian (q.v.), Margaret of Savoy (Low Countries, q.v.), Charles Prince of Castile, and the King of Aragon, who also negotiated on behalf of Castile. The negotiations took place at Brussels and Mechlin. Young and Boleyn were already resident with the Emperor.

Instructions: Inferred from *L&P*, i, 1, nos. 1524.39, 1680, 1745.
Correspondence: BL, Cotton, Galba B.iii; *L&P*, i, 1-2; *CSPS, 1509-25* (summary of negotiations and treaty).

SP4.
TUNSTALL, Dr. Cuthbert (later Bishop of London, Durham; 1474-1559)*
MORE, Thomas (later Sir Thomas; 1477/8-1535)*
CLIFFORD, John (*fl.*1510s-1520s)

7 May 1515[b] - *c.*6 Oct. 1517[c]   [Special] Ambassadors
Audience: *c.*19 May 1515   20s/d (Tunstall),
          13s 4d/d (More)

They negotiated about commercial treaties with Prince Charles of Castile (later
    Emperor Charles V) in Brussels. Sampson and Spinelly, already resident in
    the Low Countries (q.v.) with Lady Margaret, joined them. Tunstall, at least,
    returned to England 2 - 20 Oct. 1515, 30 Jan. - mid-Feb. 1516, and May
    1516.

Instructions: *L&P*, ii, no. 422.
Correspondence: BL, Cotton, Galba B.iii-iv; *L&P*, ii.

SP5.
POYNINGS, Sir Edward (1459-1521)*
KNIGHT, Dr. William (later Bishop of Bath and Wells; 1476-1547)*

7 May 1515[b] - *c.*21 Sept. 1515[e]   Special Ambassadors
          (Poynings)   20s/d (Knight)
Audience (Charles of Castile): 30 May
    1515

They were accredited to negotiate with Charles of Castile. They joined briefly
    with Tunstall in early summer. Poynings returned to England and Knight was
    accredited with Tunstall to the Prince of Castile (see immediately below).

Instructions: *L&P*, ii, 1, no. 423.
Correspondence: BL, Lansd. 1236; *L&P*, ii, 1.

SP6.
TUNSTALL, Dr. Cuthbert (later Bishop of London, Durham; 1474-1559)*
KNIGHT, Dr. William (later Bishop of Bath and Wells; 1476-1547)*

1 Oct. 1515[b] - *c.*1 Mar. 1516[g]   Special Ambassadors
          (Knight)
Treaty concluded: 13 Feb. 1516

Both were already in the Low Countries, as was Spinelly, who joined with them
    in the conclusion of this treaty with Charles of Castile.

Commission: *L&P*, ii, 1, no. 976, 986.
Correspondence: *L&P*, ii, 1.

SP7.
POYNINGS, Sir Edward (1459-1521)*
TUNSTALL, Dr. Cuthbert (later Bishop of London, Durham; 1474-1559)*

21 Feb. 1516[b] - *c.*15 May 1516[g]   [Special Ambassadors]
Audience: 9 Mar. 1516   66s 8d/d

253

They went to Charles of Castile at Brussels, a mission which included conveying condolences on the death of Ferdinand of Aragon.

Commission: *L&P*, ii, 1, no. 1574.

Correspondence: BL, Cotton, Galba B.iv, Vitel. B.xx; *L&P*, ii, 1.

SP8.
SPINELLY, Sir Thomas (*d*.1522)

mid-July 1517*ᵈ* - *d*.26 Aug. 1522   Resident Ambassador
Audience: 3 Aug. 1517   20*s*/d

He was resident with Charles, King of Castile, beginning in 1517. He attended Charles in Brussels, and then moved with him to Spain. He accompanied Charles to Aachen when the King was crowned Emperor, 28 July 1519. Spinelly died at Valladolid not long after the Imperial Court returned to Spain.

Correspondence: *L&P*, ii, 2 - iii, 1-2.

SP9.
KITE, John, Archbishop of Armagh (later Bishop of Carlisle; *d*.1537)*
BOURCHIER, John, 2nd Baron Berners (1463-1533)*

c.28 Feb. 1518*ʰ* - *c*.1 Mar. 1519*ᵉ*   [Special Ambassadors]
Audience: 24 Apr. 1518

They visited Charles, King of Castile.

Instructions: *L&P*, ii, 2, no. 4160, iii, 1, no. 10.

Correspondence: BL, Harl. 295; *L&P*, ii, 2 - iii, 1.

SP10.
MASON, John (later Sir John; 1503-1566)*

26 Dec. 1540*ᵇ* - *c*.20 Jan. 1541*ᶜ*   [Special Ambassador]

He never arrived in Spain. Because of his association with Wyatt, he was recalled about halfway to his destination, and imprisoned.

Instructions: *L&P*, xvi, no. 354.

Correspondence about: *L&P*, xvi.

SP11.
RUSSELL, John, 1st Earl of Bedford (1486?-1555)*
RADCLIFFE, Thomas, Baron Fitzwalter (later 3rd Earl of Sussex; 1526?-1583)*

12 Mar. 1554*ᶜ* - 20 July 1554*ᶜ*   [Special Ambassadors]
Ratification: 28 Apr. 1554

They ratified the marriage treaty with Philip II and conveyed him to England.

Instructions: BL, Cotton, Vesp. C.vii, f. 198, Eg. 2790, ff. 136-9, Add. 5935, ff. 146-8, Sloane 2442, ff. 133-4, Lansd. 155, ff. 369b-72, Harl. 289, ff. 159; HMC *2nd Report*, p. 96.

Correspondence: *CSPF, 1553-8*; *APC, 1554-6*; Tytler, P. (ed.), *England under the Reigns of Edward VI...*(1839), ii.

SP12.
BROWNE, Anthony, Viscount Montagu (1528-1592)*
CHAMBERLAIN, Sir Thomas (*c.*1504-1580)*

12 Jan. 1560*b* - *c.*24 June 1560*e*   Special Ambassadors
Audience: *c.*18 Mar. 1560   £5/d (Montague), 60s/d
                                               (Chamberlain)

Chamberlain remained as resident (see below).

Instructions: *CSPF, 1559-60*, nos. 629-30; BL, Cotton, Galba C.i, ff. 30-8.,
    Vesp. C.vii, ff. 107-08.
Correspondence: BL, Add. 5752, Cotton, Galba C.i, Vesp. C.vii; *CSPF, 1559-
    60, 1560-1, 1561-2*; HMC *Salisb.*, i.

SP13.
CHAMBERLAIN, Sir Thomas (*c.*1504-1580)*

12 Jan. 1560*b* - mid-Apr. 1562*g*   Resident Ambassador
                                             60*s*/d

Instructions: BL, Cotton, Vesp. C.vii, f. 107; *CSPF, 1559-60*, nos. 629-30.
Correspondence: BL, Add. 35830, 39866 (letterbook), Royal 13.B.1, Cotton,
    Galba C.i, Vesp. C.vii; *CSPF, 1559-60, 1560-1, 1561-2, 1562*; HMC
    Salisb., i.

SP14.
CHALONER, Sir Thomas (1521-1565)*

30 Sept. 1561*b* - mid-May 1565*c*   Resident Ambassador
Audience: *c.*21 Jan. 1562   66*s* 8*d*/d

Correspondence: BL, Cotton, Vesp. C.vii, Galba C.i-ii, Add. 35830-1; *CSPF,
    1561-2, 1562, 1563, 1564-5*; HMC *Pepys*; HMC *Salisb.*, i.

SP15.
PHAYRE, William (*d.*1578?)

5 Mar. 1565*c* - 4 Apr. 1566*f*   [Chargé d'Affaires]
                                         ad hoc

Instructions: PRO, SP/70/77, f. 48; *CSPF, 1564-5*, no. 1025; with further
    elaboration in no. 1629.
Correspondence: *CSPF, 1564-5, 1566-8*.

SP16.
MAN, Dr. John (1512-1569)*

12 Jan. 1566*b* - 5 Oct. 1568*a*   Resident Ambassador
Audience: 25 Apr. 1566   66*s* 8*d*/d

He was exiled from the Spanish court 23 Apr. 1568, and recalled to England
    4 June 1568.

Instructions: BL, Cotton, Vesp. C.viii, f. 291; *CSPF, 1566-8*, nos. 112-13.
Correspondence: Cambridge University Library, Mss. Mm 3.8; BL, Cotton,
    Vesp. C.vii-viii, Galba C.ii-iii; HMC *Pepys*; *CSPF, 1566-8*.

SP17.
COBHAM alias BROOKE, Sir Henry (1538-1592)*

20 Mar. 1571*ᵃ* - 5 July 1571*ᵃ*   [Special Ambassador]
Audience: 1 May 1571   40*s*/d

Instructions: BL, Cotton, Galba C.iv, ff. 70-2; *CSPV, 1558-80*, no. 507.
Correspondence: BL, Cotton, Calig. E.vii, Galba C.iv, Eg. 2723; *CSPF, 1569-71.*

SP18.

20 June 1575*ᵃ* - 10 Jan. 1576*ᵃ*   [Special Ambassador]
Audience: 26 Oct. 1575   50*s*/d

He visited the French court (q.v.) on his way to Spain.

Instructions: BL, Lansd. 155, ff. 137-8, Cotton, Vesp. C.vii, ff. 328-41, Add. 5935, ff. 169-78, Eg. 2790, f. 180b, Sloane 2442, ff. 120-3, Harl. 288, ff. 142-5; *CSPF, 1575-7*, no. 199.
Correspondence: BL, Cotton, Galba C.v; *CSPF, 1575-7*; KL, viii.

SP19.
SMITH, Sir John (1531-1607)*

18 Nov. 1576*ᵃ* - 28 July 1577*ᵃ*   [Special Ambassador]
Audience: 24 Jan. 1577   50*s*/d

He stopped at the French court (q.v.) on his way to Spain.

Instructions: BL, Cotton, Vesp. C.vii, old f. 343; Titus B.ii, f. 482, Lansd. 155, ff. 175-81, Harl., 289, f. 159, 6992, no. 30; *CSPF, 1575-7*, no. 1024.
Correspondence: BL, Cotton, Titus C.vii, Vesp. C.vii; *CSPF, 1575-7.*

SP20.
WILKES, Thomas (later Sir Thomas; *c.*1541-1598)*

14 Dec. 1577*ᵃ* - 15 Feb. 1578*ᵃ*   [Special Ambassador]
Audience: Early Jan. 1578.   40*s*/d

Instructions: PRO, SP/194/163, ff. 88-94; *CSPF, 1577-8*, nos. 524, 538.
Correspondence: *CSPF, 1577-8.*

SP21.
WOTTON, Edward (later 1st Baron Wotton of Marley; 1548-1628)*

This was primarily a mission of observation on affairs in Portugal (q.v.), but he did visit the Spanish court, early Aug. 1579, on his return to England.

SP22.
WAAD, William (later Sir William; 1546-1623)*

14 Jan. 1584*ᵃ* - 13 Apr. 1584*ᵃ*   [Special Ambassador]
Arrived: *c.*1 Mar. 1584   50*s*/d
   (no audience was ever granted)

Instructions: Inferred from *CSPF, 1583-4*, no. 473.
Correspondence: *CSPF, 1583-4*; BL, Cotton, Vesp. C.vii.

THERE exists a substantial hiatus in relations during the war years of the 1580s and the 1590s.

SP23.
WILSON, Thomas (1560?-1629)*

7 Jan. 1605[b] - late July 1605[c]   [Agent]
                                          30*s*/d

Apparently he was the original point of contact in movements to re-establish Anglo-Spanish diplomatic relations.

Correspondence: PRO, SP/94/10-11.

SP24.
HOWARD, Charles, 1st Earl of Nottingham (1536-1624)*

2 Mar. 1605[a] - 4 July 1605[a]   Ambassador Extraordinary
Audience: 18 May 1605
Secretary: Robert Treswell?

This was the mission that ceremonially re-inaugurated diplomatic relations.

Instructions: PRO, SP/94/12, ff. 171 & 216; BL, Cotton, Vesp. C.ix, ff. 1-[5], Harl. 1875, ff. 1-4.

Correspondence: PRO, SP/94/11-12; BL, Stowe 168; HMC *Salisb.*, xvii; Treswell, R., *A Relation of...the Journey of...Charles Earle of Nottingham...* (1605).

SP25.
CORNWALLIS, Sir Charles (*d.*1629)*

1 Jan. 1605[a] - 31 Oct. 1609[b]   Resident Ambassador
Audience: 20 May 1605   £4/d
Secretaries: Francis Cottington, Walter
   Hawksworth

He went with the Nottingham mission, and remained to serve as resident ambassador.

Instructions: PRO, SP/94/12, f. 163; BL, Cotton, Vesp. C.ix, ff. [5- 9?], Harl. 1875, ff. 4b-9.

Correspondence: PRO, SP/94/11-16; BL, Add. 4149, 12507, 35837, 36444, 39853, 44848, Cotton, Vesp. C.ix, Eg. 2026, Harl. 295, 1875, Lansd. 90, 156, 255, Stowe 168-71, 424; Bodl., Tanner Mss. 75, 82, 265; HMC *Salisb.*, xvii-xviii, xix-xxi.

SP26.
COTTINGTON, Francis (later Baron Cottington of Hanworth; 1578?- 1652)*

*c.*15 Oct. 1609[h] - 31 Aug. 1611[b]   Agent
                                          20*s*/d

At the end of this mission, he became, after a brief return to England, the consul at Seville.

Instructions: PRO, SP/94/17, f. 264?

Correspondence: PRO, SP/94/16-18; BL, Add. 35847.

SP27.
DIGBY, Sir John (later Baron Digby, 1st Earl of Bristol; 1580-1653)*

1 Oct. 1610*a* - 10 July 1616*b*   [Resident Ambassador]
Audience: 13 Jun. 1611   £6/d
Secretary: Simon Digby

Instructions: PRO, SP/94/18, ff. 50-5; BL, Add. 36444, f. 62.
Correspondence: PRO, SP/94/18-22; BL, Add. 12507, 36444, Harl. 1580,
    Stowe 172-4; *CSPD, 1611-18*; Richards, S. (ed.), *Secret Writing...*(1974);
    HMC *Salisb.*, xxi; HMC *Eglinton, Maxwell...Digby...*

SP28.
COTTINGTON, Francis (later Baron Cottington of Hanworth; 1578?- 1652)*

29 Dec. 1615*b* - 4 Oct. 1622*a*   Agent [and Chargé d'Affaires]
Audience: *c.*23 Jan. 1616   40*s*/d

He served as chargé d'affaires during the absence of fully accredited residents,
    and as an agent during other periods.

Correspondence: PRO, SP/94/22-3; BL, Add. 35847, Harl. 1580; Bodl.,
    Tanner Mss. 73; *CSPD, 1611-18*.

SP29.
CECIL, William, Baron Roos (1590-1618)*

1 May 1616*a* - 28 Feb. 1617*b*   Ambassador Extraordinary
Audience: 12 Jan. 1617   £6/d

Instructions: A reference to them is contained in Devon, F., *Issues of the
    Exchequer...*(1836), p. 191; and they are implied in *CSPV, 1615-17*, pp. 314,
    316, 362.
Correspondence: Hervey, M. F. S., *The Life, Correspondence and Collections
    of Thomas Howard, Earl of Arundel...*(Cambridge, 1921), ch. ix; Cecil, W.,
    Lord Roos, *A Relation of...Lord Roos, His Majesties Embassadour
    Extraordinary to the King of Spaine...*(1617).

SP30.
DIGBY, Sir John (later Baron Digby, 1st Earl of Bristol; 1580-1653)*

1 May 1617*a* - 9 May 1618*b*   Ambassador Extraordinary
Audience: 17 Dec. 1617   £6/d

Instructions: PRO, SP/94/22, f. 120; Gardiner, S. R., *Prince Charles and the
    Spanish Marriage* (1869), i, p. 66.
Correspondence: PRO, SP/94/22-3; BL, Add. 4149; Bodl., Tanner Mss. 74.

SP31.
ASTON, Sir Walter (later Baron Aston of Forfar; 1584-1639)*

11 Nov. 1619*a* - *c.*25 Mar. 1625*c*   Ambassador Ordinary
Audience: late Mar. 1620   £6/d

Instructions: PRO, SP/94/24, f. 279.
Correspondence: PRO, SP/94/23-33; BL, Eg. 2542, 2595, Add. 20846, 29587, 35832, 36444-36447, 36449, 36451, 44848, Harl. 304, 1323, 1580, 4761; Bodl., Tanner Mss. 82; HMC *2nd Report*, p. 59.

SP32.
DIGBY, John, 1st Earl of Bristol (1580-1653)*

Feb. 1622[h] - 30 Apr. 1624[a]   Ambassador Extraordinary
Audience: 31 May 1622   £6/d
Secretaries: Simon Digby, Mr. Hole

Instructions: Inferred from *CSPV, 1621-3*, pp. 279-80.
Correspondence: PRO, SP/94/25-31; BL, Add. 18201, 29975, 45143, 44848, 48166 (letterbook), Eg. 2592, Harl. 1580, 2232, 4761, Stowe 145, 156; Bodl., Tanner Mss. 73, 82; HMC *8th Report*, p. 214.

SP33.
PORTER, Endymion (1587-1649)*

3 Oct. 1622[h] - 2 Jan. 1623[a]   [Special Ambassador]
Audience: c.20 Nov. 1622

Instructions: Summarized in *CSPV, 1621-3*, p. 475.
Correspondence: PRO, SP/94/30, f. 160? (report on mission); *CSPD, 1619-23*; Townshend, D., *Life and Letters of Mr. Endymion Porter...*(1897); De Fonblanque, E., *The Lives of the Lords Strangford...*(1877).

SP34.
GAGE, George (c.1582-1638)*

28 Oct. 1622[d] - c.30 Aug. 1623[b]   [Special Ambassador—'semi-
Audience: early Dec. 1622   legationus'] and secret envoy
          40s/d

He was employed to coordinate a papal dispensation for the marriage of Prince Charles with the Infanta. During this mission, he was ordered (Dec. 1622) to Rome (q.v.) once again. He also visited the Spanish Netherlands, Florence and Parma (qq.v.).

Report: Bodl., Rawlinson Mss. B.488, ff. 44-6.

SP35.
HAY, James, Earl of Carlisle (c.1580-1636)*

22 Feb. 1623[f] - 15 May 1623[c]   Ambassador Extraordinary
Audience: early April 1623

He was sent specifically to avert any ill consequences to Prince Charles on his journey through France to Madrid.

Instructions: Verbal (he was dispatched in haste) but implied in *CSPV, 1621-3*, p. 585.
Correspondence: PRO, SP/78/71; BL, Eg. 2595.

SP36.
WYCHE, Sir Peter (*d*.1643)*

1 Mar. 1625^a - 30 Apr. 1626^a [Agent]
                                        40*s*/d

Instructions: PRO, SP/94/33, f. 158.
Correspondence: PRO, SP/104/169.

SP37.
PORTER, Endymion (1587-1649)*

11 Aug. 1628^h - 5 Jan. 1629^a [Special Ambassador]
Audience: 14 Sept. 1628

He also went to Holland and the Spanish Netherlands (qq.v.) on this mission.

Instructions: Inferred from HMC *Skrine*, pp. 157-8.
Correspondence: PRO, SP/94/34; *CSPD, 1628-9*; Townshend, D., *Life and Letters of Mr. Endymion Porter...*(1897); De Fonblanque, *...Lords Strangford...*; Sainsbury, W., *...Life of Sir Peter Paul Rubens...*(1859).

SP38.
COTTINGTON, Sir Francis (later Baron Cottington of Hanforth; 1578?-1652)*

1 July 1629^a - 20 Mar. 1631^a Ambassador Extraordinary
Audience: 2 Jan. 1630   £6/d
Secretary: Arthur Hopton

He stopped in Portugal on his way to Spain (q.v.).

Correspondence: PRO, SP/94/34-5; BL, Add. 14004, 35847, 38091; *CSPD, 1629-31*; Richards, S. (ed.), *Secret Writing...*(1974); Sainsbury, W., *Unpublished Papers...of the Life of Sir Peter Paul Rubens...*(1859).

SP39.
HOPTON, Arthur (later Sir Arthur; 1588?-1650)*

18 Dec. 1630^a - 23 Apr. 1636^b Agent
                                        40*s*/d

Instructions: BL, Eg. 1820, f. 1.
Correspondence: PRO, SP/80/8, SP/94/35-7; BL, Add. 32093, 36448, 39288, Eg. 1820, 2597, Stowe 186; Knowler, W. (ed.), *The Earl of Strafford's Letters and Despatches...*(1739).

SP40.
TAYLOR, John (1600?-1655)*

13 July 1634^a - 24 May 1635^a [Agent]
                                        10*s*/d

Correspondence: PRO, SP/94/37.

SP41.

ASTON, Walter, Baron Aston of Forfar (1584-1639)*

26 Dec. 1634[a] - 31 July 1638[a]   Ambassador Ordinary
Audience: 9 Nov. 1635   £6/d
Secretary: Richard Fanshawe

Instructions: PRO, SP/94/37, f. 189-201.
Correspondence: PRO, SP/94/37-40; BL, Add. 36448, 36450; *CSPD, 1635, 1635-6, 1636-7, 1637*; HMC *Denbigh*.

SP42.

FANSHAWE, Richard (later Sir Richard, 1st Bart.; 1608-1666)*

Apr. 1638[h] - *c*.10 June 1638[c]   [Chargé d'Affaires]
Audience: 6 May 1638

Correspondence: PRO, SP/94/40.
Correspondence about: *CSPV, 1636-9*.

SP43.

HOPTON, Sir Arthur (1588?-1650)*

21 Mar. 1638[a] - Dec. 1645[h]   Ambassador Ordinary
Audience: *c*.10 July 1638   £6/d

Correspondence: PRO, SP/94/40-2, SP/104/170; BL, Add. 15856; *CSPD, 1640, Add. 1625-49*; Bodl., Tanner Mss. 65.

SP44.

ASCHAM, Anthony (*d*.1650)*

25 Jan. 1650[a] - *d*.27 May 1650   [Resident] Agent
Arrived: 26 May 1650   £800/an.
Secretary: George Fisher

He was the ambassador sent by Parliament. He was assassinated by Royalists.

Correspondence: PRO, SP/94/43.
Correspondence about: *ThSP*, i; *CSPD, 1650*.

SP45.

FISHER, George (*fl*.1650s)

27 May 1650[h] - 26 Sept. 1651[a]   Agent
Correspondence: PRO, SP/94/43; *ThSP*, i; *CSPD, 1651*.

SP46.

BENNET, Sir Henry (later Earl of Arlington; 1618-1685)*

c.Feb. 1657[h] - *c*.1 May 1661[c]   [Resident Ambassador]
Audience: 4 Apr. 1657

He first represented the exiled Charles II, and then continued as resident after the Restoration. His first audience with his new credentials: 1 Aug. 1660.

Instructions: *Clarendon State Papers*, iii, p. 222.
Correspondence: PRO, SP/94/44; BL, Eg. 2534-5, 2537, 2542; Bodl., Clarendon Mss., 72; *CSPD, 1660-1.*

SP47.
DIGBY, George, 2nd Earl of Bristol (1612-1677)*

c.20 Dec. 1659[h] - c.2 June 1660[c]   [Special Ambassador]
Secretary: Richard Fanshawe

Correspondence about: *CSPV, 1659-61.*

SP48.
FANSHAWE, Sir Richard, 1st Bart. (1608-1666)*

7 Dec. 1663[a] - d.16 June 1666   [Resident Ambassador]
Audience: 8 June 1664   £1000/qtr. (diets &
Secretary: Lionel Fanshawe   extraord.)

He left Madrid for a mission to Portugal (where he had previously been ambassador, q.v.) 6 Jan. - 26 Feb. 1666.

Instructions: PRO, SP/94/45, ff. 172-88, SP/94/46, ff. 11-12, SP/104/174B, pp. 1-2; Bennet, H., *...The Earl of Arlington's Letters to Sir W. Temple...*(1701), ii, pp. 4-12; Fanshawe, R., *Original Letters and Negotiations of...Sir Richard Fanshawe, the Earl of Sandwich, the Earl of Sunderland and Sir W. Godolphin...*(1724), pp. 1-21.
Correspondence: PRO, SP/89/6, SP/94/45-51; BL, Add. 22920, 34329, 34336-8, Harl. 7010, Stowe 1952, 3509; Fanshawe, *Original Letters of Fanshawe, et al*; Fanshawe, R., *Original Letters of...Sir Richard Fanshawe, during his Embassies in Spain and Portugal...*(1702); HMC *Heathcote*; *CSPD, 1663-4, 1664-5.*

SP49.
MONTAGU, Edward, 1st Earl of Sandwich (1625-1672)*

20 Feb. 1666[b] - 11 Oct. 1668[a]   Ambassador Extraordinary
Audience: 20 June 1666   £100/wk.
Secretaries: William Godolphin and
John Werden

From 26 Dec. 1667 - 22 Mar. 1668, he resided as ambassador in Portugal, (q.v.). He had also visited Lisbon on his original voyage to Madrid.

Instructions: Bodl., Carte Mss. 274, ff. 5 et seq., vol. 103, ff. 331-46.
Correspondence: PRO, SP/94/50-3; BL, Add. 38015, 34336-8, Sloane 3499, Stowe 139; Bodl., Clarendon Mss. 84; Fanshawe, R., *Original Letters of Fanshawe, et al.*, i-ii; Bennet, *Letters*; Anonymous, *Hispania Illustrata...* (1703); BL, Add. 34336-8, 38015.

SP50.
SOUTHWELL, Sir Robert (1635-1702)*

While resident in Portugal (q.v.), he visited Spain from 26 Feb. 1666 to 22 June 1666, and also Sept. 1666. He was granted an audience in Madrid 15 Mar. 1666.

SP51.
WERDEN, John (later Sir John, 1st Bart.; 1640-1716)*

10 July 1668[h] - 10 June 1669[c]   [Chargé d'Affaires]
                                 £100/mo.

He assumed chargé responsibilities upon Sandwich's departure, a role in which he had also functioned during Sandwich's absences in Portugal.

Correspondence: PRO, SP/89/9, SP/94/53-4.

SP52.
GODOLPHIN, Sir William (1635-1696)*

25 Feb. 1669[a] - Aug. 1678[g]   Envoy Extraordinary, then
Arrived: 20 Aug. 1669   Ambassador Ordinary
Secretary: Robert Yard   £5/d, then £10/d, then £100/wk.

Godolphin visited Portugal Apr. - June 1669, on his way to Madrid. His diets were further increased to £100/wk. beginning 20 May 1672.

Instructions: PRO, SP/104/174B, ff. 181-6; BL, Add. 40795, ff. 85-90.
Correspondence: PRO, SP/80/73, SP/94/54-65, SP/104/56, 184-6; BL, Add. 17018, 34331-2, 34077, 34331-3, 35079, 35099-101, 35838, 35875, 36807, 38197, 47899, Eg. 1509, Harl. 1515-6, 7010, Sloane 3512-3, Stowe 180, 210, 256; Bodl., Rawlinson Mss. A.478; Oxford, Mss. at All Souls Lib., cciii; *CSPD, 1668-9, 1673-5*; Fanshawe, *Original Letters of Fanshawe, et al*; Anonymous, *Hispania Illustrata...*; Bennet, *Letters*; Richards, S. (ed.), *Secret Writing...*(1974).

SP53.
SPENCER, Robert, 2nd Earl of Sunderland (1640-1702)*

21 Nov. 1671[a] - 20 May 1672[f]   Envoy Extraordinary
Audience: 6 Jan. 1672   £100/wk.
Secretary: Thomas Chudleigh

He left Spain, and proceeded directly to France (q.v.) to become a resident there.

Instructions: Suggested in *CSPV, 1671-2*, pp. 123, 132, 157.
Correspondence: PRO, SP/94/59; BL, Stowe 191; Anonymous, *Hispania Illustrata...*; Bennet, *Letters*.

SP54.
WHITE, Ignatius, Baron de Vic, Bart. (later Marquis d'Albeville; *d*.1694)

29 Jun. 1677*d* - Oct. 1677*h*   [Agent]

This was a secret mission from Charles II.

Correspondence: PRO, SP/94/64-5.

SP55.
GOODRICKE, Sir Henry, 2nd Bart. (1642-1705)*

12 June 1679*a* - 27 Mar. 1683*a*   Envoy Extraordinary
Secretary: Peter Levett (later in   £5/d
   mission)

Instructions: PRO, SP/104/239, ff. 44-6; Goodricke, C. A., (ed.), *History of the Goodricke Family* (1885), p. 25.
Correspondence: PRO, SP/94/67-69, SP/104/186-8, 193; BL, Add. 17017, 24023, 35101, 47899, Eg. 3682; Oxford, Mss. at All Souls Lib., ccxviii.

SP56.
LEVETT, Peter (*fl*.1680s)

10 Dec. 1682*h* - 16 Nov. 1685*c*   [Chargé d'Affaires]
Correspondence: PRO, SP/94/68-71, SP/104/193.

SP57.
GRANVILLE, Charles, Viscount Granville of Lansdowne (1661-1701)*

13 May 1685*a* - Dec.?, 1688*h*   Envoy Extraordinary
Arrived Madrid: 16 Nov. 1685   £5/d

He stopped in Lisbon, Portugal (q.v.), from July until 11 Sept. 1685.

Instructions: PRO, SP/104/187, p. 157.
Correspondence: PRO, SP/94/71, SP/104/187; BL, Add. 28053, Eg. 3354.

SP58.
STAFFORD, John (*fl*.1680s)

27 Mar. 1688*a* - Aug. 1689*g*   Envoy Extraordinary
Arrived: 18 Sept. 1688   £5/d

Instructions: PRO, SP/104/187, pp. 279-81.
Correspondence: BL, Add. 41842.

SPANISH NETHERLANDS
(FLANDERS)

As Spanish control over the whole of the Low Countries began to wane at the end of the sixteenth century, and a true, if only *de facto* separation emerged between the autonomous United Provinces to the north and the areas in the south controlled by Spain, the English government began sending envoys specifically to the Spanish court, located in Brussels.

SN1.

EDMONDES, Thomas (later Sir Thomas; *c.*1563-1639)*

20 Dec. 1599[b] - 29 Jan. 1600[f]	[Special Ambassador]
Audience: 9 Jan. 1600	40s/d

Instructions: BL, Stowe 179, f. 24; Sawyer, E. (ed.), *Memorials of Affairs of State...*(1725), i, p. 139.
Correspondence: BL, Stowe 179; PRO, SP/77/6.

SN2.

1 Mar. 1600[a] - 13 Apr. 1600[b]	[Special Ambassador]
Audience: 22 Mar. 1600	

He returned to England, and then went directly to Boulogne, France (q.v.), to become one of the peace commissioners at the meetings he had previously arranged on this mission.

Instructions: BL, Stowe 167, ff. 163-7, 179, f. 48; Birch, T. (ed.), *An Historical View of the Negotiations...*(1749), p. 198.
Correspondence: BL, Stowe 167 (summary), 179.

SN3.

1 Nov. 1604[a] - 30 Sept. 1609[b]	Resident Ambassador
Audience: 30 Apr. 1605	66s 8d/d
Secretary: William Trumbull	

Edmondes undertook this assignment in conjunction with Hertford, (below), and then remained in residence.

Instructions: (Which are separate from Hertford's) PRO, SP/77/7, ff. 133-46, SP/77/8, f. 204-05; BL, Cotton Galba B.i, ff. 296-9.
Correspondence: PRO, SP/77/7-9; BL, Harl. 1875, Stowe 169; HMC *Salisb.*, xvii-xxi; Birch, T. (ed.) *An Historical View of the Negotiations...*(1749); Birch, T. (comp.), *The Court and Times of James I...*(1849).

SN4.
SEYMOUR, Edward, Earl of Hertford (1539?-1621)*

1 Jan. 1605[a] - 20 May 1605[a] Envoy Extraordinary
Audience: 29 Apr. 1605 £6/d

Hertford travelled to this assignment with Edmondes (see immediately above).

Instructions: PRO, SP/77/7, ff. 97-115, SP/77/8, ff. 204b-221 (joint instructions for Hertford and Edmondes); BL, Harl. 1579, ff. 65-7.

Correspondence: PRO, SP/77/7; BL, Add. 32092, Stowe 168; HMC *Salisb.*, xvii.

SN5.
TRUMBULL, William (*d.*1635)*

*c.*29 Aug. 1609[h] - 2 Nov. 1625[a] Agent, then Resident Ambassador
20s/d, then 40s/d

Trumbull returned to England, at least in early 1613, and possibly several other times as well. In early 1621, he was apparently sent to various German States (q.v.).

Correspondence: PRO, SP/77/9-18; BL, Stowe 174-6; Berkshire Record Office, Downshire Mss., Trumbull Alphabetical Series; HMC *Eglinton, Maxwell*...; Birch, T. (comp.), *The Court and Times of James I*...(1849), i; Sainsbury, W., *Original Unpublished Papers...of Sir Peter Paul Rubens*...(1859); Boyd, D., 'Sir Francis Nethersole...' Unpublished PhD Dissertation, Temple University, 1972; Richards, S. (ed.), *Secret Writing*...(1974).

SN6.
BENNET, Sir John (*c.*1553-1627)*

1 Mar. 1617[a] - 25 June 1617[b] Ambassador Extraordinary
Audience: 1 May 1617 66s 8d/d

Instructions: BL, Harl. 1579, ff. 59-60; implied in *CSPV, 1615-17*, p. 485.
Credentials: PRO, SP/77/12, ff. 297, 306-07.
Correspondence: PRO, SP/77/12; BL, Lansd. 151, 157, Harl. 1579.

SN7.
HAY, James, 1st Viscount Doncaster (later Earl of Carlisle; *c.*1580-1636)*

On his journey to the Imperial Court and various German States (qq.v.), he had audience with the Archdukes 22 May 1619.

SN8.
WESTON, Sir Richard (later 1st Earl of Portland; 1577-1635)*
CONWAY, Sir Edward (later Viscount Conway; *d.*1631)*

They visited the Archdukes in Brussels *c.*10 July 1620 on an embassy to various German States (q.v.). They also stopped at the Hague in the Low Countries (q.v.).

Instructions: BL, Add. 35832, ff. 10-77, 38597, f. 15.

SN9.
DIGBY, John, Baron Digby (later 1st Earl of Bristol; 1580-1653)*

6 Feb. 1621*b* - *c*.10 Apr. 1621*c*　　　Ambassador Extraordinary
Audience: *c*.16 Mar. 1621　　　　　　£6/d

Instructions: BL, Add. 36445, f. 53.
Correspondence: PRO, SP/77/14.

SN10.
CHAWORTH, Sir George (later Viscount Chaworth of Armagh; *d*.1639)*

20 Aug. 1621*a* - *c*.1 Nov. 1621*c*　　　Ambassador Extraordinary
Audience: 13 Oct. 1621　　　　　　　66*s* 8*d*/d
Steward: Mr. F. Parker

Instructions: Kempe, A. (ed.), *The Loseley Mss...*(1835), pp. 437-9; also
　inferred in *CSPD, 1611-18*, p. 514.
Correspondence: PRO, SP/77/14.

SN11.
DIGBY, John, Baron Digby (later 1st Earl of Bristol; 1580-1653)*

He visited the Archduke Albert in Brussels, in late Oct. 1621, on his return from
　a mission to the Emperor (q.v.).

SN12.
WESTON, Sir Richard (later 1st Earl of Portland; 1577-1635)*

20 Mar. 1622*a* - *c*.27 Sept. 1622*e*　　　Ambassador Extraordinary
Audience: 6 May 1622　　　　　　　£6/d

Credentials: PRO, SP/77/15, f. 103.
Correspondence: PRO, SP/77/15.

SN13.
HAY, James, Earl of Carlisle (*c*.1580-1636)*

1 Jan. 1628*a* - 28 Jan. 1629*c*　　　Ambassador Extraordinary
Audience: late Dec. 1628　　　　　　£8/d

He visited Brussels while on a mission that included Savoy, Switzerland, and the
　Low Countries (qq.v.).

Instructions: PRO, SP/92/13, ff. 70, 202, SP/92/14, f. 246.
Correspondence: PRO, SP/77/19, SP/104/169; *CSPD, 1628-9*; Sainsbury, W.,
　Original Unpublished Letters...of Sir Peter Paul Rubens...(1859).

SN14.
PORTER, Endymion (1587-1649)*

On this embassy to Spain (q.v.), Porter stopped in both the Low Countries (q.v.)
　and at Brussels, *c*.Sept - Oct. 1628.

SN15.
GERBIER, Sir Balthazar (1591?-1667)*

1 Jan. 1631[a] - 17 Apr. 1641[c]   Resident Agent
Audience: 20 June 1631   40s/d
Secretary: Sidney Bere, George Gerbier

Instructions: PRO, SP/77/20, ff. 40-8.
Correspondence: PRO, SP/77/19-31, SP/104/170, SP/105/7-18; BL, Add. 33587, Eg. 2597; *CSPD, 1639-40, 1640*; Sainsbury, W., *Rubens*; De Fonblanque, *Lords Strangford*; Richards, S. (ed.), *Secret Writing...*(1974).

SN16.
BALFOUR, Sir William (*d.*1660)*

28 Sept. 1631[g] - late Oct. 1631[h]   Ambassador Extraordinary

He was sent to pay compliments to Marie de Medici in the Spanish Netherlands.

Correspondence about: *CSPD, 1631-3.*

SN17.
MURRAY, William (later 1st Earl of Dysart; 1600?-1651)*

*c.*20 Nov. 1632[h] - *c.*26 Dec. 1632[c]   [Special Ambassador]

He seemingly undertook this mission as a private embassy on behalf of the King, going primarily to meet with the French Queen Mother in Flanders.

Instructions: PRO, SP/78/92, f. 210-14.
Correspondence: PRO, SP/77/22.

SN18.
PORTER, Endymion (1587-1649)*

23 Nov. 1634[f] - 2 Jan. 1635[a]   Ambassador Extraordinary
Audience: *c.*5 Dec. 1634   £1,000 (approx. total)

Instructions: PRO, SP/77/24, ff. 506-07.
Correspondence: PRO, SP/77/24; Townshend, D., *Life and Letters of Mr. Endymion Porter*; De Fonblanque, *Lives of the Lords Strangford.*

SN19.
TAYLOR, John (1600?-1665)*

On his journey to England from the Emperor (q.v.), he apparently stopped in Brussels *c.*Apr. 1639.

SN20.
DE VIC, Sir Henry (later Bart.; *d.*1671)

23 Aug. 1641[f] - 14 Mar. 1661[a]   Agent
Arrived: 3 Sept. 1641   40s/d

His initial audience was delayed until long after his first arrival, owing to the illness of the Cardinal Infanta. During the greater part of this time he represented the exiled Charles II at Brussels, although what his role or even location was between 1643 and 1649 is in doubt.

Instructions: From 1649, when he seemingly assumed the residence for the exiled Charles II—BL, Add. 37047, f. 15.

Correspondence: PRO, SP/77/31, 33, SP/81/56, SP/105/144; BL, Add. 15857, 18982, 28558, 37047, Eg. 2533-7; Nicholas, E. (ed.), *The Nicholas Papers...*, Camden 3rd ser., xxxi (1920); Carte, T. (ed.), *A Collection...found among the Duke of Ormonde's papers...*(1759).

SN21.
THELWALL, Peter (*fl.*1640s-1650s)

Spring 1646[h] - early 1651[h]	Agent
	£300/an.

He resided there in behalf of Parliament.

Correspondence: Bodl., Tanner Mss. 56, 57, Rawlinson Mss. A.2; *ThSP*, i.
Correspondence about: *CSPD, 1649-50, 1650*.

SN22.
DIGBY, George, 2nd Earl of Bristol (1612-1677)*

On his journey to Parma (Italy, q.v.) he had audience in the Spanish Netherlands, 22 Feb. 1661.

SN23.
COTTERELL, Sir Charles (1615-1701)*

14 Feb. 1665[b] - 24 Mar. 1665[a]	Envoy
Audience: 24 Feb. 1665	

Instructions: Implied from *CSPD, 1664-5*, p. 230.
Correspondence: PRO, SP/77/33.

SN24.
TEMPLE, Sir William, 1st Bart. (1628-1699)*

8 Oct. 1665[c] - 12 June 1668[a]	Resident Ambassador
Audience: 10 Nov. 1665	£100/mo.
Secretary: Thomas Downton	

He formally assumed his duties in Brussels on this date, although he had been in the area previously. He had been negotiating from Brussels with the Bishop of Münster (Germany, q.v.).

Credentials: PRO, SP/81/57, ff. 68-9.
Correspondence: PRO, SP/77/33-7, SP/104/174B; BL, Add. 9796-9800, 35852, 40795, Stowe 198; [Taafe, Karl Graf], *Memoirs of the Family Taafe* (Vienna, 1856); Bennet, H., *...The Earl of Arlington's Letters to Sir W. Temple, Bart., from July 1665...*(1701); Haley, K. H. D., *An English Diplomat in the Low Countries...*(1986); Temple, W., *The Works of Sir William Temple...*, ed. Swift (1754).

SN25.
TAAFE, Theobald, 1st Earl of Carlingford (*d*.1677)*

On a mission to the Emperor and the German States (qq.v.), he had audience at
   Brussels *c*.18 Sept. 1665.

SN26.
VANE, Sir Walter (*fl*.1660s-1670s)*

On a journey to Brandenburg, he had audience at Brussels, 5 Dec. 1665.

SN27.
SPRAGGE, Sir Edward (*d*.1673)*

27 Nov. 1668[a] - 29 Jan. 1669[b]   [Special Ambassador]
Arrived: 5 Dec. 1668

Instructions: Implied from Thibaudeau, A. (ed.), *The Bulstrode Papers* (1897),
   p. 87.
Correspondence: PRO, SP/77/38.

SN28.
CHICHELEY, Sir John (*c*.1640-1691)*

19 Sept. 1670[b] - 23 Nov. 1670[b]   [Special Ambassador]
Audience: *c*.8 Oct. 1670   £300 (total)

Correspondence: PRO, SP/77/39.

SN29.
SOUTHWELL, Sir Robert (1635-1702)*

20 Oct. 1671[b] - 13 Jan. 1672[c]   Envoy Extraordinary
Audience: 10 Nov. 1671   £4/d
Secretary: James Vernon?

Instructions: PRO, SP/77/39, ff. 170-3.
Correspondence: PRO, SP/77/39; *CSPD, 1671*.

SN30.
BULSTRODE, Sir Richard (1610-1711)*

14 July 1674[b] - *c*.Jun. 1689[h]   [Agent, then Resident Ambassador]
                                            20*s*/d, 50*s*/d (by 1684), 60*s*/d
                                            (beginning 13 Oct. 1687)

He returned to England in late 1675 and remained there through early 1676.

Correspondence: PRO, SP/77/44-54, SP/104/11, 56, 185-7, 190, 193; BL,
   Add. 15857, 23242, 28225-6, 28896, 32680, 34339, 34341, 34344, 35101,
   35104, 38847, 38849, 38855, 40861, 41832, 43688, 47899, Eg. 3326, Stowe
   199; *CSPD, 1685*; Bulstrode, R., *Original Letters...*(1712).

SN31.
PORTER, Thomas (*fl.*1670s)

9 Mar. 1675*b* - May? 1675*h*   Envoy Extraordinary
Audience: mid-Apr. 1675

Correspondence about: *CSPV, 1673-5.*

SN32.
GODOLPHIN, Sidney (later Baron Godolphin of Rialton, 1st Earl of
    Godolphin; 1645-1712)

*c.*10 Jan. 1678*g* - 23 Jan. 1678*c*   [Envoy Extraordinary]
Audience: 15 Jan. 1678

Instructions: BL, Add. 25119, ff. 21-33; Browning, A., *Thomas Osborne, Earl
    of Danby...*(Glasgow, 1944-51), i, pp. 598-61.
Correspondence: BL, Eg. 3324; Coventry Papers at Longleat, xli, lxiii; HMC,
    4th Report; Browning, *Danby.*

SN33.
BRISBANE, John (*fl.*1670s)

While agent in France (q.v.), he undertook a brief mission to Brussels, Feb.
    1678.

Instructions: PRO, SP/104/239, ff. 15-17; BL, Add. 25119, ff. 32-4.

SN34.
LEGGE, Capt. William (*c.*1650-*c.*1697)*

19 Nov. 1680*d* - 16 Dec. 1681*f*   Ambassador Extraordinary
He also travelled to Hesse-Cassel (Germany, q.v.).

Instructions: Inferred from PRO, SP/104/57, p. 122; Oxford, Mss. at All Souls
    Lib., 248, p. 90.
Correspondence about: PRO, SP/77/52.

SN35.
HOWARD, Thomas, Baron Howard of Norfolk (*fl.*1680s)

5 May 1682*d* - 9 June 1682*a*   [Special Ambassador]
Instructions: Suggested in *CSPD, 1682.*
Correspondence about: PRO, SP/77/53; *CSPD, 1682.*

SN36.
PORTER, James (1638-n.d.)*

*c.*1 May 1686*h* - Jun. 1686*h*   Ambassador Extraordinary
Audience: *c.*10 May 1686

Instructions: Suggested in *CSPD, 1686-7*, no. 452.
Correspondence: PRO, SP/77/55.

SWEDEN

S1.

BONNER, Edmund (later Bishop of Hereford, London; 1500?-1569)*
CAVENDISH, Richard (*fl.*1530s)

20 July 1535[b] - 27 Apr. 1536[a]   [Special Ambassadors]
                                           13*s* 4*d*/d (Cavendish)

Besides the court of Sweden, they visited Denmark, the Duke of Holstein and
    some of the Hanse towns (qq.v.).

Instructions: Inferred from *L&P*, x, nos. 24, 303.
Correspondence: *L&P*, vii-x; BL, Add. 48036, Cotton, Vitel. B.xxi, Nero B.iii;
    Merriman, R., *The Life and Letters of Thomas Cromwell* (1902).

S2.

ROGERS, Dr. John (*c.*1540-1603)*

Although this mission, 1580 - 1581, consisted primarily of contacts with Poland
    and the Hanse towns (qq.v.), he reputedly also visited the Swedish court.

S3.

GORGES, Thomas (later Sir Thomas; 1536-1610)*

Apr.? 1582[h] - late August 1582[h]   [Special Ambassador?]
Audience: *c.*20 July 1582
Correspondence about: *CSPF, 1582, 1583-4.*

S4.

CAREW, George (*d.*1612)*

He visited the Polish King, who claimed sovereignty over Sweden, in Sweden,
    12 Sept. 1598 (Poland, q.v.).

S5.

LEE, Sir Richard (*c.*1548-1608)*

On his return from Russia (q.v.), he visited Sweden, May 1601.
Correspondence about: HMC *Salisb.*, xi.

S6.

MERRICK, John (later Sir John; *d.*1638)*

He apparently visited Duke Charles of Sweden in Livonia on his return from
    Russia (q.v.), late summer 1602.

S7.

SPENCE, Sir James (*fl.*1600s-1620s)

May? 1609[h] - July 1613[a]   [Special Ambassador]
                                £3/d (from 20 Apr. 1611)

This included several returns to England.

Instructions: PRO, SP/95/1, f. 199.
Correspondence: PRO, SP/95/1-2.

S8.

*c.*1 Aug. 1620[h] - early summer 1622?[h] [Special Ambassador]
Correspondence: PRO, SP/95/2.

S9.

1 Mar. 1625[a] - mid-Aug. 1625[c]   [Special Ambassador]
                                      £4/d

Spence returned to London in 1625 to represent the Swedish King at the English
    court.

Instructions: PRO, SP/95/2, ff. 116-19.
Correspondence: PRO, SP/95/2.

S10.

28 Apr. 1627[a] - late 1628[h]   Ambassador Extraordinary
Audience: after 1 Aug. 1627
Secretary: Peter Young

Instructions: PRO, SP/95/2, ff. 165-71.
Correspondence: PRO, SP/95/2-3.

S11.

ROE, Sir Thomas (1581?-1644)*

2 Apr. 1629[a] - 4 July 1630[a]   Ambassador Extraordinary
Arrived (at peace negotiations):   £4/d
    29 Aug. 1629

This mission included visits to the courts in the United Provinces, the Palatinate,
    Denmark, Prussia, the Hanse towns and Poland (qq.v.).

Instructions: PRO, SP/88/5, ff. 42-9, SP/104/170, pp. 31-40; HMC *3rd Report*,
    p. 190; Gardiner, S. R., *Letters Relating to the Mission of Sir Thomas Roe to
    Gustavus Adolphus, 1629-30*, Camden n.s., xiv (1875), pp. 10-21.
Correspondence: PRO, SP/88/5-6, SP/104/170; *CSPD, 1629-31*; Gardiner,
    Letters Relating to the Mission of Roe.

S12.
VANE, Sir Henry (1589-1655)*

1 May 1631[a] - late Nov. 1632[c]   Ambassador Extraordinary
Audience (with Swedish King at   £6/d
  Würzburg): *c*.1 Dec. 1631
Secretary: William Curtius

He met with Gustavus Adolphus, not in Sweden, but rather in Germany, where
the King was campaigning. His mission also carried him to various German
states and to Denmark (qq.v.).

Instructions: Summarized in *CSPV, 1629-32*, pp. 550 & 552.
Correspondence: PRO, SP/81/37-8, SP/75/12; *CSPD, 1631-3, Add. 1625-40*;
  Baker, L. (ed.), *The Letters of Queen Elizabeth of Bohemia* (1953).

S13.
CURTIUS, William (later Sir William, Bart.; *fl.*1630s-1670s)

2 Oct. 1632[a] - 12 Dec. 1633[a]   Agent
                                          20*s*/d

He went to the Swedish King campaigning in Germany and then remained in
  Germany (q.v.) as an agent.

Instructions: BL, Eg. 2541, ff. 193-4.
Correspondence: PRO, SP/104/170.
Correspondence about: *CSPD, 1633-4*.

S14.
AVERY, Joseph (*fl.*1630s-1660s)

While an agent at Hamburg, 1631-49 (Hanse, q.v.) and to Denmark (q.v.),
  1632-9, he travelled to Sweden repeatedly in these years.

Correspondence: PRO, SP/95/4.

S15.
BERKELEY, John (later 1st Baron Berkeley of Stratton; 1606?-1678)*

1 Jan. 1637[a] - *c*.20 July 1637[c]   Agent
Audience: 13? May 1637   40*s*/d

Instructions: PRO, SP/95/4, ff. 162-70.
Correspondence: PRO, SP/95/4.

S16.
FLEETWOOD, Sir George (1605-1667)

c.1 Mar. 1637[h] - *c*.20 Apr. 1637[g]   [Special Ambassador]
                                          £200 (total?)

Instructions: *CSPD, 1636-7*, pp. 559; inferred from *CSPV, 1636-9*, pp. 189-90.
Correspondence about: *CSPD, 1636-7, 1637; CSPV, 1636-9*.

S17.
JENKS, Richard (*fl.*1640s)
BARKER, William (*fl.*1640s)

24 Nov. 1643^c - Apr. 1644^d [Special Ambassadors]

They also went to Denmark and the Hanse (qq.v.), at the direction of Parliament.

Instructions: Bodl., Tanner Mss. 62, f. 379.

S18.
LISLE, Daniel (*fl.*1650s)

2 June 1652^d - *c.*20 July 1652^c [Special Ambassador]
Accompanied by: John Durie

Credentials: *ThSP*, i, pp. 206-07.
Correspondence: Bodl., Tanner Mss. 53.
Correspondence about: *CSPD, 1651-2*; HMC *Portland*, i.

S19.
WHITELOCKE, Bulstrode (1605-1675)*

14 Sept. 1653^a - 7 July 1654^a Ambassador Extraordinary
Audience: 23 Dec. 1653   £100/mo.

He received £6,500 diets for the first six months, and £100/mo. thereafter.

Instructions: HMC *3rd Report*, p. 192; Whitelocke, B., *Journal of the Swedish Embassy in the Years 1653 and 1654* (1772), p. 85 et seq.
Correspondence: BL, Add. 4902, 4991A & B, 4992, 4995, 37346-7; Bodl., Rawlinson A.12, 24; *ThSP*, i-ii; Abbot, W., *The Writings...Oliver Cromwell*, (Cambridge, Mass., 1937-47), iii; Whitelocke, B., *Journal of the Swedish Embassy.*

S20.
ROLT, Edward (*fl.*1650s)

20 July 1655^a - 3 Apr. 1656^b [Special Ambassador]
Audience: 6 Nov. 1655

Instructions: *ThSP*, iii, p. 418-19; Abbott, *Writings...of Oliver Cromwell*, iii, pp. 774-5.
Correspondence: *ThSP*, iii-iv.
Correspondence about: *CSPD, 1655, 1655-6.*

S21.
JEPHSON, Col. William (1615?-1659?)*

25 Aug. 1657^a - *c.*15 Aug. 1658^c Ambassador Extraordinary
Audience: 9 Oct. 1657

He also went to Brandenburg (German States) and the Hanse towns (qq.v.).

Instructions: BL, Add. 4157, ff. 201-04; *ThSP*, vi, 471, 478-80.
Correspondence: BL, Add. 4158; *ThSP*, vi-vii; Jenks, E., 'Some Correspondence of Thurloe and Meadowe,' *EHR*, vii (1892), pp. 720-42.

S22.
MEADOW, Sir Philip (1626-1718)*

3 Sept. 1657[c] - c.1 Oct. 1659[e]	Ambassador Extraordinary
Audience: 10 July 1658	£1000/an.

Secretaries: William Godolphin and
John Werden

He was, in these years, an ambassador who had various diplomatic responsibilities in Denmark, Poland and the Hanse (qq.v.), besides in Sweden. He seems to have been in Sweden specifically from July through Aug. of 1658, and Aug. through Sept. of 1659.

Various Instructions for Sweden: PRO, SP/95/5A, ff. 66-74; *ThSP*, vii, pp. 63-4.

Correspondence: *ThSP*, vii; Jenks, 'Correspondence of Thurloe and Meadowe.'

S23.
MONTAGU, Edward (later 1st Earl of Sandwich; 1625-1672)*
SIDNEY, Algernon (1622-1683)*
HONYWOOD, Sir Robert (1601-1686)*
BOONE, Thomas (*fl.*1650s)

11 Mar. 1659[c] - c.1 Aug. 1660[e]	Plenipotentiaries

Audience (with Swedish King): 31 July
1659

While operating only at Elsinore in Denmark, these commissioners had as their reponsibility negotiating peace between Denmark and Sweden, and did meet with the Swedish King. See 'Conferences and Congresses' for the full citation.

S24.
HOWARD, Charles, 1st Earl of Carlisle (1629-1685)*

20 June 1663[b] - 31 Jan. 1665[c]	Ambassador Extraordinary
Audience: 14 Sept. 1664	*ad hoc*

Secretaries: Andrew Marvel and Guy
de Miege

They also went to Denmark and Russia (qq.v.).

Correspondence: PRO, SP/91/3, SP/95/5A-B, 7; Bodl., Clarendon Mss. 80-1; Konovalov, S., 'England and Russia: Three Embassies,' *Oxford Slavonic Papers*, x (1962), pp. 59-101; and a contemporary narrative, along with correspondence in: [Miege, G.,] *A Relation of Three Embassies...*(1669).

S25.
COVENTRY, Henry (*c.*1618-1686)*

1 Aug. 1664[a] - 21 Jun. 1666[a]	Ambassador Extraordinary
Audience: 3 Oct. 1664	£5/d

Secretaries (at various times): Thomas
Ross, Henry Thynne, William
Griffith and Charles Fanshawe

Major Edward Wood, whose status is unclear, accompanied him at the outset. He was later briefly joined by Thomas Clifford (see following).

Instructions: HMC *4th Report*, p. 251.
Correspondence: PRO, SP/95/5A-B, 6-7; BL, Add. 28937; Bodl., Clarendon Mss. 81-3; HMC *Bath*.

S26.
CLIFFORD, Sir Thomas (later 1st Baron Clifford of Chudleigh; 1630- 1673)*

29 Aug. 1665[b] - *c*.1 Feb. 1666[c]   Ambassador Extraordinary
Audience: 20 Nov. 1665
Secretary: Peter du Moulin

He also went to Denmark *c*.20 Oct. 1665 (q.v.).

Instructions: HMC *Leeds*...
Correspondence: PRO, SP/75/17.

S27.
SHUTTLEWORTH, George (*fl*.1660s)

c.May 1666[h] - Oct. 1670[h]   [Chargé d'Affaires]

He was chargé when a fully accredited ambassador was absent.

Correspondence: PRO, SP/95/6-7.

S28.
THYNNE, Sir Thomas (later 1st Viscount Weymouth; 1640-1714)*

12 Sept. 1666[b] - 13 Jan. 1669[a]   Ambassador Extraordinary
Audience: 15 Jan. 1667   £5/d
Secretary: George Shuttleworth

He visited the Dukes of Lüneburg (German States, q.v.) and Hamburg among the Hanse towns (q.v.) on his return journey.

Instructions: PRO, SP/95/6, ff. 103-10, SP/104/174B, pp. 106-10.
Correspondence: PRO, SP/78/18, SP/95/6-7; HMC *Bath*...; Bodl., Clarendon Mss. 85; *CSPD, 1667-8*.

S29.
HOWARD, Charles, 1st Earl of Carlisle (1629-1685)*

26 Nov. 1668[b] - 28 Oct. 1669[a]   Ambassador Extraordinary
Audience: 17 Apr. 1669   £10/d

Investment: 9 July 1669
Secretaries: Francis Vernon and Sir
  Edward Wood

He stopped in Denmark (q.v.) on his return journey.

Instructions: Inferred in *CSPV, 1666-8*, p. 300.
Correspondence: PRO, SP/95/7, SP/75/18; *CSPD, 1668-9*.

S30.
WYCHE, Sir Peter (1628-1699?)*

On his journey to Russia (q.v.) he stopped in Sweden, with an audience on 4 Oct. 1669.

S31.
WERDEN, John (later Sir John, 1st Bart.; 1640-1716)*

15 Feb. 1670[b] - 19 Sept. 1672[a]   Envoy Extraordinary
Audience: 17 Oct. 1670   £4/d, £5/d (after 7 July 1670)
Secretary: William Blathwayt
Correspondence: PRO, SP/95/7.

S32.
COVENTRY, Henry (c.1618-1686)*

12 July 1671[a] - 27 June 1672[b]   [Ambassador Extraordinary]
Audience: c.6 Oct. 1671   £10/d
Secretary: Thomas Ross

Instructions: PRO, SP/95/12, ff. 77-83?; HMC *4th Report*, p. 235, 251.
Correspondence: PRO, SP/95/7-8.

S33.
WOOD, Sir Edward (fl.1670s)

8 July 1672[a] - 15 Dec. 1679[a]   Envoy Extraordinary
Audience: 3 Sept. 1672   £5/d
Secretaries: Thomas Chudleigh to 1675,
    William Allestree to 1678, John
    Robinson to 1679

Instructions and Commission: BL, Add. 28949, f. 229; *CSPD, 1672*, pp. 320-1.
Correspondence: PRO, SP/81/65-9, 71, 73, 74, SP/95/9-11, SP/104/56, 152-3;
    BL, Add. 25118, 31043, Eg. 3354, Sloane 3299.

S34.
ROBINSON, John (later Dr. John, Bishop of Bristol, London; 1650- 1723)*

1 Aug. 1679[a] - 1 Sept. 1680[b]   [Chargé d'Affaires]
                                             20s/d

Correspondence: PRO, SP/95/11; BL, Add. 37985; *CSPD, 1680-1*.

S35.
WARWICK, Sir Philip (d.1683)*

17 June 1680[e] - d.20 Mar. 1683   Envoy Extraordinary
Audience: 20 Sept. 1680   £5/d
Secretary: John Robinson

Instructions: PRO, SP/104/153, pp. 14-16.
Correspondence: PRO, SP/95/11-12, SP/104/153; BL, Add. 35104, 37985;
    Oxford, Mss. at All Souls Lib., ccxviii, ccxl; *CSPD, 1680-1, 1683*.

S36.

ROBINSON, Dr. John (later Bishop of Bristol, London; 1650-1723)*

1 Feb. 1683[a] - 12 Oct. 1687[a]   Agent
                                     20s/d

Credentials: PRO, SP/104/153, pp. 74-5.
Correspondence: PRO, SP/104/153; BL, Add. 41831; *CSPD, 1683*; HMC *7th Report*; Singer, S. (ed.), *The Correspondence of Henry Hyde...and Laurence Hyde...*(1828), i.

S37.

POLEY, Edmund (*fl.*1670s-1680s)

27 Oct. 1686[e] - 3 July 1689[a]   Envoy Extraordinary
Audience: summer 1687   £5/d

Instructions: PRO, SP/104/153, pp. 146-9.
Correspondence: PRO, SP/95/12, SP/104/187; BL, Add. 4573, 41831.

SWITZERLAND

SWZ1.
PACE, Richard (later Sir Richard; 1482?-1536)*

10 May 1514[b] - 6 Aug. 1514[f]   [Special Ambassador]
Audience (Zürich): 19 June 1514

He was accompanied by the merchant Ryng. They joined with Knight and
   Woodhouse, (below). Upon conclusion of his responsibilities in Switzerland,
   he continued to Rome on private business.

Correspondence: *L&P*, i, 2.

SWZ2.
KNIGHT, Dr. William (later Bishop of Bath and Wells; 1476-1547)*
WOODHOUSE, Richard (*fl.*1510s)

May? 1514[h] - *c.*21 Aug. 1514[e]   [Special Ambassadors]
They joined with Pace (above).

Instructions: Inferred from *L&P*, i, 2, no. 2997.
Correspondence and correspondence about: BL, Cotton, Vesp. F.i; *L&P*, i, 2.

SWZ3.
PACE, Richard (later Sir Richard; 1482?-1536)*

24 Oct. 1515[g] - *c.*15 Dec. 1517[c]   [Special Ambassador]
Audience (Constance): 22 Nov. 1515
Audience (Zürich): 24 Nov. 1515

This was a mission to the Emperor (q.v.) with extended responsibilities in
   Switzerland. He was back with the Emperor by February of 1516, and
   remained with him until Pace's return to Switzerland in October of 1516.
   Pace remained in Switzerland thereafter for an unknown time. He also visited
   the Low Countries (q.v.) both going to and returning from his assignment.

Instructions: BL, Cotton, Vitel. B.xviii, ff. 193-4; Harl., 283, ff. 39b-43.
Correspondence: BL, Cotton, Vitel. B.xviii-xix.

SWZ4.
KNIGHT, Dr. William (later Bishop of Bath and Wells; 1476-1547)*

*c.*29 Jan. 1522[g] - *c.*13 Apr. 1522[c]   [Special Ambassador]
From a mission to the Emperor (q.v.) in the Low Countries accompanied by Sir
   Robert Wingfield, Knight continued alone to Switzerland.

Instructions: Inferred in *L&P*, iii, 2, nos. 2026, 2035, 2104.
Correspondence about: *L&P*, iii, 2.

SWZ5.
WAKE, Sir Isaac (1580-1632)*

While an agent at Savoy (q.v.), he visited the Swiss cantons, Feb. - May 1617, negotiating, it would seem, mostly on behalf of the Duke of Savoy.

Correspondence: PRO, SP/96/2, SP/99/26.

SWZ6.

While ambassador at Venice (q.v.), he visited the Swiss cantons, Aug. - Oct. 1625 (during a trip to Savoy, q.v.). He had audience at Zürich 24 Aug. 1625, and at Berne *c.*10 Sept. 1625.

Correspondence: PRO, SP/96/2.

SWZ7.
HAY, James, Earl of Carlisle (*c.*1580-1636)*

1 Jan. 1628*a* - 28 Jan. 1629*c*	Ambassador Extraordinary
Audience (Basle): 26 June 1628	£3/d
Audience (Zürich): 30 Sept. 1628	
Secretary: William Boswell	

This diplomatic mission included stops in Venice, the Spanish Netherlands, the Low Countries, Lorraine (France) and Savoy (qq.v.).

Correspondence: PRO, SP/96/2; *CSPD, 1628-9.*

SWZ8.
FLEMING, Sir Oliver (*fl.*1620s-1640s)*

2 Mar. 1629*a* - *c.*1 Dec. 1641*h*	Agent
Audience (Geneva): *c.*10 Nov. 1629	40*s*/d

There is every indication that Fleming was acting as an agent, under Wake's direction, in Geneva, perhaps as early as 1626. The given dates represent an assumption of official duties, as directed from London. During 1638, he was sent to the Duke of Saxe-Weimar (German States, q.v.). He returned to England Mar. - Apr. 1639, at which point he was knighted.

Instructions: PRO, SP/96/3, f. 45.
Correspondence: PRO, SP/81/56, SP/96/2-6; BL, Eg. 2597; *CSPD, 1629-31, 1635*; Richards, S. (ed.), *Secret Writing...*(1974).

SWZ9.
FEILDING, Basil, Viscount Feilding (later 2nd Earl of Denbigh; *c.*1608-1674)*

On his journey to assume the residency at Venice (q.v.), he had audience at Geneva c.mid-Dec. 1634.

SWZ10.
PELL, John (1611-1685)*

c.2 Mar. 1654[h] - 17 Aug. 1658[c]   [Agent]
Audience (Zürich): 19 May 1654   £800/an.
Conference (Arran): c.13 June 1654
Audience (Geneva): 25 Aug. 1655

He was accompanied at the outset by John Durie, who was sent to Switzerland
and parts of Germany to coordinate a common religious policy among the
chief Protestant states. The audience at Arran involved a group of Protestant
delegates to explore such an objective. Pell's responsibilities were more
secularly diplomatic. His base of operations was Zürich.

Instructions: Implied in Abbott, W., *The Writings and Speeches of Oliver
Cromwell* (Cambridge, Mass., 1937-47), iv, p. 234.
Correspondence: BL, Add. 4364; *ThSP*, iii-v; Abbott, *Writings*, iv; Vaughan,
R. (ed.), *The Protectorate of Oliver Cromwell...* (1838), i-ii.

SWZ11.
MORLAND, Sir Samuel (later Bart.; 1625-1695)*

23 May 1655[c] - 8 Jan. 1657[a]   [Resident Ambassador]
Audience (Geneva): 15 July 1655

This mission also included contact with the courts of France and Savoy (qq.v.).

Instructions: Inferred from Morland, S., *History of the Evangelical Churches...*
(1658), pp. 563-5; *ThSP*, v, p. 616.
Correspondence: Bodl., Rawlinson Mss. A.48; *ThSP*, iii-v; Morland, *History*
(based on the ambassador's experiences in Geneva); Abbott, *Writings*, iv;
Vaughan, *The Protectorate*, i-ii.

SWZ12.
DOWNING, George (later Sir George, 1st Bart.; 1623-1684)*

28 July 1655[d] - 25 Oct. 1655[a]   Ambassador Extraordinary
Audience (Geneva): 2 Sept. 1655
Secretary: Edmund Warcup

He also visited France on this mission (q.v.), but not Savoy, as originally
intended.

Instructions: BL, Add. 4364, ff. 1-6; *CSPD, 1655*, p. 247.
Correspondence: *ThSP*, iii-iv; Vaughan, *The Protectorate*, i.
Correspondence about: *CSPD, 1655, 1655-6*.

TURKEY

The first substantial English contact with the Levant came through trade in the early sixteenth century. Commercial relations increased through the century, usually under the auspices of the French. The Sultan granted the English their first independent trading rights in 1553 when he gave such a concession to Anthony Jenkinson. Subsequently, trade burgeoned, and in 1578, William Harborne, already familiar with Mediterranean commerce, was granted quasi-official status to establish a formal trading/diplomatic relation with the Porte.

T1.
HARBORNE, William (1552-1617)*

1 July 1578[f] - early 1582[h]   [part Special Ambassador,
Audience: *c*.28 Oct. 1578   part commercial agent]
                               £200/an.

Instructions: Inferred from Hakluyt, R., *The Principal Navigations* (1903), v, p. 178, (where concessions secured by Harborne are detailed).
Correspondence and relevant documents: Skilliter, S., *William Harborne and the Trade with Turkey*...(Oxford, 1977); BL, Cotton, Nero, B.xi; Harl 6993; *CSPF, 1578-9, 1579-80, 1581-2*.

T2.

20 Nov. 1582[b] - late Dec. 1588[c]   Resident Ambassador
Audience: 23 Apr. 1583   £200/an.
Secretary: Edward Barton

He visited Poland and the Hanse towns (qq.v.) on his way home.

Instructions: Hakluyt, R., *The Principal Navigations*...(1903), iii, pp. 85-7.
Correspondence: PRO, SP/97/1; BL, Cotton, Nero, B.viii, B.xi, Titus, B.vi, Harl., 295, Lansd. 42, 51 (summation), 61, 775; *CSPF, 1583, 1583-4, 1584-5, 1585-6, 1586-8, 1588* (vol. 22); Bodl., Tanner Mss. 77-9; HMC *Salisb.* xiiii, pp. 444-5 (summation of service); Read, C., *Mr. Secretary Walsingham*... (1925), iii, pp. 326-32.

T3.
BARTON, Edward (1562?-1597)*

5 Aug. 1588[c] - *d*.15 Dec. 1597   Agent (to 1593),
Audience (first public as accredited   Resident Ambassador
  resident ambassador): 14 Oct. 1593 £1500/an.
Secretaries: (variously) Henry Lello,
  John Sanderson, Thomas Wilcocks

Instructions: Bodl., Tanner Mss. 79, f. 77.
Correspondence: PRO, SP/97/1-3; BL, Cotton, Nero B.viii, ix, xi- xii, Lansd. 846; Bodl., Tanner Mss. 77; *CSPF, 1588* (xxii), *1589*; *L&A, 1589-90, 1590-*

1, 1591-2, 1592-3; HMC *Salisb.*, iv, vi; Rosedale, H., *Queen Elizabeth and the Levant Co.*...(1904).

T4.
LELLO, Henry *(fl.*1590s)

15 Dec. 1597[h] - c.June 1607[h]	Agent (to 1599), Resident
Audience (first public as accredited	Ambassador
resident ambassador): 14 Sept.1599	£1350/an.

He became agent/chargé d'affaires upon the death of Barton.

Correspondence: PRO, SP/97/3-5, SP/105/143; BL, Cotton, Nero, B.xi; HMC *Salisb.*, ix; Heeringa, K., *Bronnen tot de geschiedenis van den Levantschen Handel* (S'Gravenhage, 1910), i.

T5.
GLOVER, Sir Thomas *(fl.*1610s)

8 Nov. 1606[g] - 27 Jan. 1613[a]	Agent
Audience: c.3 Jan. 1607	£100/an.
Secretary: Hieronimo Meoli	

Correspondence: PRO, SP/97/5-6, SP/99/8, SP/105/143; BL, Stowe 178; HMC *Salisb.*, xix; Heeringa, K., *Bronnen tot de geschiedenis van den Levantschen Handel* (S'-Gravenhage, 1910), i; Richards, S. (ed.), *Secret Writing*...(1974).

T6.
PINDAR, Paul (1565?-1650)*

c.5 Nov. 1611[g] - 1620[h]	[Resident Ambassador]
Audience: c.1 Mar. 1612	

Instructions: Inferred from *CSPV, 1610-13*, pp. 295-8.
Correspondence: PRO, SP/97/6-7, SP/99/9-13, SP/105/143; BL, Stowe 175.

T7.
EYRE, Sir John *(fl.*1620s)

c.14 July 1619[h] - c.10 Apr. 1622[c]	[Resident Ambassador]
Audience: c.21 Apr. 1620	

He was abruptly relieved of his duties by John Chapman (see below) on 12 Dec. 1621.

Instructions: BL, Add. 38597, f. 7 (a version modifying his original instructions).

Correspondence: PRO, SP/97/7-8; BL, Add. 35897, 36444-5, Harl. 1580.

T8.
CHAPMAN, John *(fl.*1620s)

Sept. 1621[g] - Feb. 1622[h]	Chargé d'Affaires
Arrived: 12 Dec. 1621	

He was designated to serve Eyre with his immediate recall, and to take charge of the embassy until Eyre's successor might arrive.

T9.
ROE, Sir Thomas (1581?-1644)*

6 Sept. 1621[c] - mid-Jan. 1629[c]   [Resident Ambassador]
Audience: 12 Feb. 1622   £1800/an.

While ambassador, he conducted negotiations with Transylvania and with various princes in North Africa (q.v.).

Instructions: Roe, Sir T., *The Negotiations of Sir Thomas Roe in His Embassy to the Ottoman Porte...,*ed. Carte (1740), pp. 2-4. Also see: PRO, SP/97/8, f. 117.

Correspondence: PRO, SP/97/8-14, SP/104/167, SP/105/102; BL, Add. 18979, Lansd. 1054, Harl. 416, 1579-80; Bodl., Tanner Mss. 73; *CSPD, 1619-23, 1623-5, 1625-6, 1627-8, 1628-9*; Roe, *Negotiations*; Baker, L., *The Letters of Queen Elizabeth of Bohemia* (1953); Richards, S. (ed.), *Secret Writing...* (1974).

T10.
WYCHE, Sir Peter (*d.*1643)*

20 Mar. 1627[d] - by autumn 1639[h]   [Resident Ambassador]
Audience: *c.*19 Apr. 1628

Letter of Appointment and Commission: PRO, SP/105/143, ff. 32-3; BL, Add. 21993.
Correspondence: PRO, SP/97/14-16, SP/105/143; *CSPD, 1639.*

T11.
CROWE, Sir Sackville (later Bart.; *d.*1706)

9 Apr. 1634[b] - 1 Jan. 1648[e]   Resident Ambassador
Arrived: 13 Oct. 1638
Audience: mid-1639

Due to disputes about remuneration and status, it was some four years from the date of his appointment to his arrival in Constantinople. Subsequently, he had to be removed forcibly from his ambassadorship, which he refused to surrender to a Parliamentarian successor.

Instructions: PRO, SP/97/16, f. 154, SP/105/143, ff. 63-6; BL, Eg. 2541, f. 204; Add. 15856, ff. 15-16.
Correspondence: PRO, SP/97/16, SP/104/170, SP/105/143; BL, Eg. 2541, 2533; *CSPD, 1639*; Bendish, T., *Newes from Turkie...*(1648).

T12.
BENDISH, Sir Thomas, Bart. (*c.*1607-*c.*1674)*

29 Jan. 1647[b] - *c.*7 June 1661[e]   [Resident Ambassador]
Audience: 1 Oct. 1647

Instructions: PRO, SP/105/143, ff. 126-31.
Correspondence: PRO, SP/97/17, SP/105/103, 143-4; BL, Add. 15750, Eg. 2537; Bodl., Tanner Mss. 52; *CSPD, 1649-50, 1650, 1651, 1651-2, 1653-4,*

1654, 1655, 1655-6, 1656-7, 1657-8, 1658-9, 1659-60; *ThSP*, ii, iv-vii; Bendish, T., *Newes from Turkie*...(1648); Bendish, T., *A Brief Narrative and Vindication of Sir T. Bendish*...(1660?).

T13.
LAURENCE, Richard (*fl*.1650s)

16 Aug. 1653[d] - Sept.? 1656[h]   [Resident Ambassador]

Although accredited by the English Council of State in 1653, Laurence was refused permission, once he had arrived in Constantinople, to assume his diplomatic responsibilities. This was attributable to the influence of Bendish with the Grand Signor.

Instructions: PRO, SP/97/17, f. 115-6, SP/105/144, ff. 59-61; *CSPD, 1653-4*, p. 123.
Correspondence: PRO, SP/97/17; Bodl., Rawlinson Mss. A.48, A.56; *ThSP*, ii; *CSPD, 1654, 1655*.

T14.
FINCH, Heneage, 2nd Earl of Winchilsea (1627/8-1689)*

23 Aug. 1660[b] - 7 July 1669[a]   Ambassador Extraordinary
Audience: 26 Jan. 1661
Secretary: Paul Rycaut, Dartes

He paid his compliments at the courts of Portugal (q.v.) and Algiers (North Africa, q.v.) on his voyage to Constantinople.

Instructions: PRO, SP/97/17, f. 150-5; BL, Eg. 2542, ff. 439-42.
Correspondence: PRO, SP/97/17-19, SP/71/1, SP/44/1, SP/99/45; BL, Add. 23120, 32093-4, 34174, 40698, 40710, Eg. 2537, 2539, Stowe 744-5; *CSPD, 1661-2, 1663-4, 1664-5, 1665-6, 1666-7, 1667, 1667-8*; Richards, S. (ed.), *Secret Writing*...(1974).

T15.
HARVEY, Sir Daniel (1631-1672)*

22 Feb. 1668[b] - d.26 Aug. 1672   [Resident Ambassador]
Arrived: 23 Dec. 1668   £3000/an.
Audience: 27 Nov. 1669.
Secretaries: George Etherege to 1671;
   John Newman after 1671

Instructions: PRO, SP/97/19, ff. 25-8, SP/104/174B, ff. 163-4; Bodl., Rawlinson Mss. A.255, f. 68.
Correspondence: PRO, SP/97/19; BL, Add. 22910, 28937, 38015; *CSPD, 1668-9, 1670*.

T16.
NEWMAN, John (*fl*.1670s)

25 Aug. 1672[h] - n.d.   Chargé d'Affaires
Correspondence: PRO, SP/97/19.

T17.

FINCH, Sir John (1626-1682)

9 Nov. 1672[a] - *c*.10 July 1682[c]   [Resident Ambassador]
Audience: 20 Mar. 1674   £2800/an.
Secretary: Possibly Mr. Dereham, and/
   or William Carpenter, and/or
   Thomas Coke

He apparently resided briefly in Genoa, July - Oct. 1673, on his way to his
   assignment in Constantinople. He also visited Florence on this same journey
   (Italian States, q.v.).

Instructions: BL, Add. 28937, pp. 167-9; Bodl., Rawlinson Mss. A.256, f. 51;
   additional instructions: PRO, SP/104/88, ff. 24-6.
Correspondence: PRO, SP/79/2, SP/97/19, SP/104/188; Oxford, Mss. at All
   Souls Lib., ccxxxix; BL, Add. 17017, 22910, 23215, 23898, 25121, 38855,
   Lansd. 841, Sloane 2439, Stowe 219; *CSPD, 1673*; Abbott, G., *Under the
   Turk in Constantinople...*(1920).

T18.

BRYDGES, James, 8th Baron Chandos of Sudeley (1642-1714)*

6 Jan. 1681[b] - *c*.10 Feb. 1687[c]   [Resident Ambassador]
Audience: Aug. 1681   £1800/an.
Secretary: Thomas Coke

Instructions: PRO, SP/105/145, pp. 93-5.
Correspondence: PRO, SP/97/19-20, SP/104/188 & 190, SP/105/154; BL,
   Stowe 219-21.

T19.

SOAME, Sir William (*fl*.1670s)

15 Sept. 1685[b] - *d*.June 1686   [Resident Ambassador]

He also visited Algiers and Tunis (North Africa, q.v.) on his way to
   Constantinople. He died in Malta on this journey.

T20.

TRUMBULL, Sir William (1639-1716)*

Nov. 1686[h] - *c*.1 Oct. 1691[e]   [Resident Ambassador]
Audience (private): 3 Sept. 1687
Audience (public): 16 Jan. 1688
Secretary: Thomas Coke;
Personal secretary: Jacques Dayrolle

Instructions: PRO, SP/105/145, pp. 135-43.
Correspondence: PRO, SP/97/20, SP/105/145; BL, Eg. 3678, Add. 34799
   (memoirs of embassy), 40771, Stowe 220; HMC *Downshire*, i.

V1.

SHEFFIELD, Sir Thomas (*fl*.1510s)
NEWPORT, Sir Thomas (*d*.1522)*

Summer 1513[h] - *c*.5 Nov. 1513[g]   [Special Ambassadors]
Audience: 3 Sept. 1513

They went to Rhodes after visiting Venice.

Instructions: Suggested in *L&P*, i, 2, nos. 2254, 2263.
Correspondence: *L&P*, i, 2.

V2.

PACE, Richard (later Sir Richard; 1482?-1536)*

While on a mission principally to Rome, 1521-5 (q.v.), he also visited Venice
    several times. He had audience 21 Aug. 1522, and returned to Venice July
    1523 and Feb. 1525.

Instructions: BL, Harl. 283, ff. 35-8; suggested in *L&P*, iii, 2, no. 2498.
Correspondence: BL, Stowe 147, 149; *L&P*, iii, 2.

V3.

CASALE, John Baptiste da (*d*.1536)

16 Jan. 1526[h] - *died c*.Aug. 1536   [Resident Ambassador]
Audience: Jan. 1526   13*s* 4*d*/d

Correspondence: BL, Arundel 151, Add. 28584, Cotton, Julius E.iii, Nero
    B.vi-vii, Vitel. B.viii, x-xi; *L&P*, iv, 1 - xi.

V4.

GARDINER, Dr. Stephen (later Bishop of Winchester; 1483?-1555)*

On a 1528 mission to Rome (q.v.) with Fox, Gardiner visited Venice in July to
    solicit favorable opinions regarding the divorce.

V5.

STOKESLEY, Dr. John, Bishop of London (1475?-1539)*
CROKE, Richard alias 'Johannes Flanorensis' (1489?-1558)*

On a mission to gather opinions about the divorce throughout Italy and France, a
    mission that may have included negotiations with the Pope (q.v.), Stokesley
    joined with Richard Croke to have an audience at Venice, June 1530.

Correspondence: BL, Cotton, Vitel. B.xiii; *L&P*, iv, 3.
Correspondence about: BL, Arundel 151.

V6.
HARVEL, Edmund (*died c.*1550)

Feb. 1535[h] - *d.* before 7 Jan. 1550   [Agent, then Resident Ambassador]

Correspondence: BL, Cotton, Nero B.vi-vii, Harl. 283-4; *L&P*, viii - xxi; *CSPF, 1547-53*; Merriman, R., *The Life and Letters of Cromwell* (1902).

V7.
VANNES, Peter (*d.*1563)*

19 May 1550[d] - Jan. 1557[g]   [Resident Ambassador]
Audience: *c.*10 Aug. 1550   40*s*/d

While resident, he visited Lucca c.Nov. 1551 (Italian States, q.v.).

Correspondence: BL, Cotton, Nero B.vii, Harl. 284; Bodl., Tanner, no. 90; *CSPF, 1547-53, 1553-8*; *CSPV, 1556-7*; *APC, 1552-4*.

V8.
BROWNE, Anthony, Viscount Montague (1528-1592)*
THIRLBY, Dr. Thomas, Bishop of Ely (1506?-1570)*

While on their embassy to re-establish English relations with the Papacy (q.v.), they visited Venice, and received an audience in late June 1555.

V9.
STANDEN, Sir Anthony (*fl.*1580s-1610s)

1 June 1603[a] - 22 Jan. 1604[b]   Special Ambassador
Audience: 30 Aug. 1603   40*s*/d

This mission also took him to Florence (Italy, q.v.).

Instructions: Inferred from PRO, PRO/31/9, bundle 87 (30 July 1603); BL, Royal, King's 124, ff. 11 et seq.
Correspondence: PRO, SP/99/2.

V10.
WOTTON, Sir Henry (1568-1639)*

26 Dec. 1603[a] - 31 Mar. 1611[a]   Resident Ambassador
Audience: 1 Oct. 1604   66*s* 8*d*/d
Secretaries: Albert Morton, William
   Parkhurst

He stopped in France (q.v.) on his return from this mission.

Instructions: HMC *7th Report*, p. 516.
Correspondence: PRO, SP/99/2-6, SP/105/105; BL, Add. 12504, 19402, Harl. 1875, Stowe 168-9; HMC *8th Report*, App. 2, p. 102; HMC *Salisb.*, xix, xxi; Sawyer, E., (ed.), *Memorials of Affairs of State...Winwood State Papers* (1725), i; Birch, T., (comp.), *The Court and Times of James I...*, ed. R. Williams (1849), i; Watson, C., 'Letters from Sir Henry Wotton to King

James I and others...,' *Archaeologia*, xl, pp. 257-84; Smith, L. P., *The Life and Letters of Sir Henry Wotton* (Oxford, 1907); Crino, A., *Fatti e Figure del Seicento Anglo-Toscano*...(Florence, 1957); Richards, S. (ed.), *Secret Writing*...(1974).

V11.
CARLETON, Sir Dudley (later Baron Carleton of Imbercourt, Viscount Dorchester; 1573-1632)*

1 Apr. 1610[a] - 30 Nov. 1615[b] Resident Ambassador
Audience: *c*.26 Nov. 1610 66*s* 8*d*/d
Secretary: Isaac Wake, Gregorio Monti
 (Italian secretary)

He spent approximately the last year of his mission (Dec. 1614 to Nov. 1615) in Turin, Duchy of Savoy (q.v.), although he technically remained the English ambassador to Venice. He returned to England through the Palatinate (q.v.).

Instructions: Inferred in PRO, SP/92/2, ff. 186-200.
Correspondence: PRO, SP/99/6-17, SP/105/106; BL, Add. 34079, Cotton, Nero B.vii, Eg. 2813 (letterbook), Stowe 171-5; Bodl., Tanner Mss. 74; *CSPD, 1611-18*; HMC *Eglinton, Maxwell*...; Birch, *Court and Times of James I*..., i; Sainsbury, W., *Original Unpublished Papers...of Sir Peter Paul Rubens*...(1859); Richards, S. (ed.), *Secret Writing*...(1974); Carleton, D., *Dudley Carleton to John Chamberlain, 1603-1624*..., ed. M. Lee (New Brunswick, N.J., 1972).

V12.
PINDAR, Paul (later Sir Paul; 1565?-1650)*

He visited Venice in Nov. 1611, on his way to Turkey (q.v.).

V13.
WAKE, Isaac (1580-1632)*

c.4 Oct. 1614[h] - *c*.Dec. 1614[f] [Chargé d'Affaires]

He ran the embassy until Carleton returned, and then they both went to Savoy.

V14.
WOTTON, Sir Henry (1568-1639)*

17 Oct. 1615[b] - 31 Aug. 1619[a] Ambassador Ordinary
Audience: 27 June 1616 66*s* 8*d*/d
Secretary: Rowland Woodward?,
 Gregorio Monti (Italian secy.)

He visited Turin, Savoy, (q.v.) on his way to Venice, and the Palatinate (q.v.) on both the outbound and return journey.

Correspondence: PRO, SP/99/20-22; BL, Add. 34727, 35837, Harl. 1579; Bodl., Tanner Mss. 74; *CSPD, 1611-18*; Smith, *Life and Letters*, i; Wotton, Sir H., *Letters and Dispatches...to James I*...(Roxburghe Club, 1850).

V15.
MONTI, Gregorio (*d.*1622)

25 Apr. 1619*ᵃ* - Mar. 1621*ʰ*	Chargé d'Affaires
	£7 10*s*/mo.

Correspondence: PRO, SP/99/23; Wotton, *Letters*.

V16.
WOTTON, Sir Henry (1568-1639)*

3 Jun. 1620*ᵇ* - 11 Dec. 1623*ᶜ*	[Resident Ambassador]
Audience: 20 Mar. 1621	£4/d

Secretary: John Dynely, Michael
    Branthwaite?

He went to Venice by way of the Imperial Court at Vienna (q.v.). He withdrew
    to Padua from Apr. 1621 through Jan. 1622.

Correspondence: PRO, SP/99/23-5; Oxford, Mss. at All Souls Lib., ccxviii;
    Smith, *Life and Letters*, vol. ii.

V17.
BRANTHWAITE, Michael (*fl.*1620s)

27 Sept. 1623*ᵃ* - 11 Apr. 1625*ᵃ*	Agent
	30*s*/d

Correspondence: PRO, SP/99/25

V18.
WAKE, Sir Isaac (1580-1632)*

1 Nov. 1624*ᵃ* - *c.*1 Mar. 1631*ᶠ*	Ambassador Ordinary
Audience: *c.*30 Dec. 1624	£4/d

Secretary: John Jacob (early), Thomas
    Rowlandson (Italian secy.), John
    Wilkinson, Anthony Hales, Francis
    Grevile, Richard Browne (at various
    times)

His accreditation shifted between Venice and Savoy (q.v.), but the English
    government continued to pay him through 1631, under the privy seal warrant
    for Venice. He visited Switzerland (q.v.) in late 1625. From 1628 through
    1631, he was principally in Savoy. He went directly to an assignment in
    France (q.v.).

Instructions: PRO, SP/99/25, ff. 176-83.
Correspondence: PRO, SP/99/25-30, SP/104/167, 169; BL, Add. 33935,
    34310-11 (letter-books), 36447; Bodl., Tanner Mss. 72, 73; Oxford, Mss. at
    All Souls Lib., ccxviii; HMC *2nd Report*, p. 44; Richards, S. (ed.), *Secret
    Writing*…(1974).

V19.
WILKINSON, John (*fl.*1620s)

1 Aug. 1625[a] - autumn 1626[h]	Chargé d'Affaires £10/mo.

He functioned as chargé during Wake's extended absences.

Correspondence: PRO, SP/99/26-7.

V20.
HAY, James, Earl of Carlisle (*c.*1580-1636)*

1 Jan. 1628[b] - 28 Jan. 1629[c]	Ambassador Extraordinary
Audience: 26 Aug. 1628	£8/d

Secretary: William Boswell, Thomas
  Rowlandson (Italian secy.)

This mission included visits to courts in the Spanish Netherlands, Savoy, Lorraine and Switzerland (qq.v.).

Instructions: PRO, SP/92/13, ff. 70, 202, SP/92/14, f. 246.

Correspondence: PRO, SP/99/30, SP/104/169; BL, Add. 34311; *CSPD, 1628-9.*

V21.
ROWLANDSON, Thomas (*fl.*1620s-1630s)

1 Nov. 1629[a] - 15 May 1636[a]	[Chargé d'Affaires] 20*s*/d

He was responsible for the mission during Wake's extensive absences. Rowlandson was in England from Jun. to Oct. 1631.

Correspondence: PRO, SP/99/30-35; BL, Eg. 2597; Richards, S. (ed.), *Secret Writing...*(1974).

V22.
WESTON, Jerome (later 2nd earl of Portland; 1605-1633)*

6 Dec. 1631[a] - 12 Mar. 1633[a]	Ambassador Extraordinary
Audience: *c.*1 Nov. 1632	£6/d

This mission included visits to the courts of France, Savoy and Florence, Italy (qq.v.).

Correspondence: PRO, SP/99/33; BL, Eg. 2597.

V23.
FEILDING, Basil, Viscount Feilding (later 2nd Earl of Denbigh; *c.*1608-1674)*

16 Sept. 1634[a] - 17 May 1639[b]	Ambassador Extraordinary
Audience: 27 Jan. 1635	£6/d

Secretary: Gilbert Talbot, Thomas
  Raymond, Peter Morton

Although remaining as resident to Venice, he spent the greater part of the period between Nov. 1637 and early Jan. 1639 as the English representative at Savoy (q.v.) and visited during the same period other Italian states (q.v.). He returned briefly to Venice, 19 Jan. 1639. He had his public audience this second time 19 Mar. and left Venice permanently 15 Apr. 1639. He tried, but was not permitted to visit the French court on his journey home.

Instructions: PRO, SP/99/34, ff. 288-91; HMC *8th Report*, App. 2, p. 54.

Correspondence: PRO, SP/92/20-3, SP/99/34-43; *CSPD, 1635-6*; HMC *4th Report*, pp. 257-9; HMC *6th Report*, pp. 277-85; HMC *7th Report*, pp. 221-3.

Correspondence about: *CSPV, 1636-9*.

V24.

TALBOT, Sir Gilbert (*c.*1606-1695)*

25 Feb. 1638[h] - 19 Jan. 1639[c] Chargé d'Affaires

He assumed the residency while Feilding was in Savoy.

Correspondence: PRO, SP/99/41-2.

V25.

5 Apr. 1639[d] - *c.*15 June 1644[e] Chargé d'Affaires
Secretary: Rafael Chias

After substituting for Feilding during his absences, he became a permanent chargé d'affaires after Feilding's departure, 5 Apr. 1639. He returned as a fully accredited ambassador in 1645.

Correspondence: PRO, SP/81/56, SP/99/41-5, SP/104/170; BL, Harl. 7001; *CSPD, 1644*; HMC *3rd Report*, p. 184; HMC *6th Report*, pp. 284-7.

V26.

5 Jan. 1645[d] - *c.*15 June 1645[c] Resident Ambassador
Audience: 2 Apr. 1645

Correspondence: PRO, SP/99/45.

V27.

BELASYSE, Thomas, Viscount Fauconberg (1627-1700)*

18 Nov. 1669[a] - 14 Nov. 1670[a] Ambassador Extraordinary
Audience: 28 June 1670 £10/d
Secretary: John Dodington, Dr.
  Yerburgh (during Dodington's
  disgrace), Mr. Hyde

He also visited the courts at Savoy and Florence (qq.v.). On his return journey, he attended the court at Treves and perhaps saw other German princes (q.v.).

Instructions: PRO, SP/99/46, ff. 318-25, SP/104/88, ff. 3-6; BL, Stowe 191, ff. 18-19.

Correspondence: PRO, SP/81/58-9, SP/92/24, SP/99/47-8, SP/104/88; BL., Sloane 2752, Stowe 191; Bodl., Rawlinson Mss. A.477; *CSPD, 1670*; HMC *8th Report*, App. 2, pp. 102-03; Ramsey, R., *Studies in Cromwell's Family Circle...*(1930); also see his memoirs of the embassy, found in Ellis, 'Relation of the Lord Fauconberg's Embassy...' *Archaeologia*, xxxvii, pp. 158-88, as drawn from BL, Sloane 2752.

V28.
DODINGTON, John (*d.*1674)

9 Oct. 1670[a] - 22 Feb. 1673[a]   Resident Ambassador
Audience: 12 Nov. 1670   50*s*/d
Secretary: Mr. Russel

He remained after Viscount Fauconberg's departure. He returned to England by way of the Palatinate (q.v.).

Correspondence: PRO, SP/99/47-52; BL, Add. 4716-18, 38849; Bodl., Rawlinson Mss. A.478; Ramsey, R., *Studies in Cromwell's Family Circle...* (1930).

V29.
HIGGONS, Thomas (1624-1691)*

10 Sept. 1673[a] - 16 June 1679[a]   Envoy Extraordinary
Audience: 1 Sept. 1674   £5/d

Instructions: PRO, SP/104/88, ff. 32-3; BL, Stowe 191, ff. 36-7; HMC *8th Report*, App. 2, p. 103.
Correspondence: PRO, SP/99/52-4; BL, Add. 25121, 32094-5; *CSPD, 1673*; HMC *3rd Report*, p. 198; HMC *4th Report*, p. 248; HMC *5th Report*, pp. 316-17.

AFTER Higgons' embassy, virtually all contact and permanent relations of any nature were handled by officers of consular status.

INDEX OF PERSONS

The names of all *English* diplomatic personnel are included. Those names that are combined with dates represent the men who headed or who had significant responsibilities in specific embassies.

Abbot, Maurice (1565-1642), LC119, LC122

Aldrich, Dr., F52

Allen, Edmund (1519?-1559), E68

Allen, Richard (*d.*1602), DK11, G39

Allestree, William, S33

Anstruther, Robert (Sir; *fl.*1600s-1640s), DK 31-6, E88-92, G81-2, G86, H17, LC124, LC127, LC139

Arundell, Henry (3rd Baron Arundell of Wardour; 1608-1694), F250, F253

Ascham, Anthony (*d.*1650), SP44

Ascham, Roger, E53

Ashby, William (d.1593), SC74

Aston, Walter (1st Baron Aston of Forfar; 1584-1639), SP31, SP41

Augier, Réné (fl.1620s-1670s), F211, F221, F226, F229, F232

Avery, Joseph (fl.1620s-1660s), DK36, DK42, DK43, E95, G90, H17, H20, H25, S14

Bainbridge, Christopher (Archbishop of York, Cardinal; 1464?-1514), IT1

Baker, John (Sir; *c.*1489-1558), DK1

Balfour, Michael (1st Baron Balfour of Burleigh; 1567-1619), IT28

Balfour, William (Sir; *d.*1660), SN16

Bancroft, Richard (Dr., Bishop of London, Archbishop of Canterbury; 1544-1610), DK27

Barker, William (*fl.*1640s), DK45, S17

Barlow, William (Dr.; Bishop of St. Asaph, St. David's, Bath and Wells, Chichester, *d.*1569), SC16, SC17

Barnaby, Thomas, F114

Barnes, Robert (1495-1540), G13, DK5

Barrett, Edward (Sir; 1581-1645), F199

Barton, Edward (1562-1597), T2-4

Batemanson, John (1500s-1510s), SC1

Battier, James, F221

Beale, Robert (1541-1601), C9, G40, LC68, LC97

Beaulieu, Jean, F170, F183

Beckwith, Leonard, SC24

Beecher, William (*fl.*1600s-1620s), F179, F182, F187, G79-80, R16

Belasyse, John (1st Baron Belasyse of Worlaby; 1614-1689), F258

Belasyse, Thomas (Viscount Fauconberg, Earl of Fauconberg; 1627-1700), F234, F254, F261, G104, IT38, SAV25, V27-8

Belinge, Richard (Sir; *d.*1716), F250, F253

Belknap, Sir Edward, F9

Bell, Henry (Capt.; 1620s-1630s), G85

Bellingham, Edward (Sir; by 1507-1550), E49, LC42

Bendish, Thomas (Sir, Bart.; *c.*1607-*c.*1674), T12-13

Benet, William (Dr.; *d.*1533), E23-24, F37, IT17, IT20-1

Bennet, Henry (Earl of Arlington; 1618-1685), C15, F266, LC156, LC161, SP46

Bennet, John (Sir; *c.*1553-1627), SN6

Berde, Richard (*fl.*1530s), G16-17

Berde, Sidney, SN15

Berkeley, Charles (Viscount Fitzhardinge of Berehaven, Earl of Falmouth; (1630-1665), F238, F245

Berkeley, John (1st Baron Berkeley of Stratton; 1606?-1678), C17, F274, S15

295

Crofts, William (Baron Crofts of
Saxham; c.1611-1677), F235, F238
Croke, Richard (alias 'Johannes
Flanorensis,' 1489?-1558), V5
Crowe, Sackville (Sir, Bart.; d.1706),
T11
Curtius, William (Sir, Bart.; fl.1630s-
1670s), E96-8, G92, G96, S12-3

Dacre, Edward (fl.1620s), SAV18
Dacre, Thomas (Baron Dacre of
Greystoke; 1467-1525), SC4
Dacre, Thomas (Baron Dacre; c.1527-
1566), SC25
Dale, Valentine (Dr.; by 1527-1589),
C8, F124, F130, LC56, LC101
Dannet, Thomas (c.1525-1569), E70,
F80, F106
Darcy, Edward (1543-1612), LC85
Darius, Sylvester (fl.1520s), E22
Dartes, T14
Davison, William (c.1541-1608), LC67,
LC74, LC76, LC89-90, SC38, SC53,
SC66, SC68, p. 15
Dayrolle, Jacques, F285, T20
De Vic, Henry (Sir, Bart.; d.1671),
DK43, F210-12, F220, H20, SN20
Dereham, Thomas (fl.1670s-1680s),
IT47, IT50, T17
Dickenson, John (fl.1610s), G62,
LC115-7, PL13
Digby, George (2nd Earl of Bristol;
1612-1677), IT36, SP47, SN22
Digby, John (Baron Digby, 1st Earl of
Bristol; 1580-1653), E86-7, G77,
SP27, SP30, SP32, SN11
Digby, Kenelm (Sir; 1603-1665), IT33
Digby, Simon (fl.1620s-1640s), E86-7,
R23, SP27, SP32, SN9
Digges, Dudley (Sir; 1583-1639),
LC122, R17
Docwra, Thomas (Sir; d.1527), E11-2,
F1, F3, F9
Dodington, John (d.1674), E101, G108,
IT38, IT42, V27-8
Dorislaus, Isaac (1595-1649), LC144-5
Douglas, George (Sir; d.1636), PL16
Douglas, George (1st Earl of
Dumbarton; 1636?-1692), F282
Douglas, James (Earl of Arran, 4th Duke
of Hamilton; 1658-1712), F283

Downing, George (Sir, 1st Bart.; 1623-
1684), F231, LC148, LC155, SWZ12
Downton, Thomas, LC151, SN24
Drury, Robert (Sir; by 1456-1535), SC1-
2, SC5-6
Drury, William (Sir; 1527-1579), SC45,
SC47-50
Dudley, Andrew (Sir; c.1507-1559),
E55, LC47
Dudley, John (Viscount Lisle, Duke of
Northumberland; 1504/06-1553), F71,
F74, F81
Dunn, Daniel (Sir; c.1550-1617), C10
Duras, Louis (2nd Earl of Feversham;
1640?-1709), F277, F281
Durie, John, E92, SWZ10,
Dyer, Edward (1543-1607), DK20,
LC87
Dynely, John, V16

Edmondes, Clement (1564?-1622),
LC119
Edmondes, Thomas (Sir; c.1563-1639),
C9, F142, F158, F160, F164, F167-
8, F170, F174-5, F177, F183, F210,
F212, SN1-4
Eger, David, H26
Elyot, Thomas (Sir; c.1490-1546), E27
Errington, Nicholas (fl.1570s-1580s),
SC48, SC50-1, SC57-9, SC63
Etherege, George (Sir; 1635-1691),
E105, T15
Eure, Ralph (3rd Baron Eure; 1558-
1617), C10
Eure, Baron, F81
Ewers, Isaak (fl.1650s), DK49-50
Eyre, John (Sir; fl.1620s), T7-8

Fanshawe, Charles (4th Viscount
Fanshawe of Dromore; 1643-1710),
POR18, S25
Fanshawe, Lionel, SP48
Fanshawe, Richard (Sir, 1st Bart.; 1608-
1666), POR8-9, POR11, SP41-2,
SP47-8
Feilding, Basil (Viscount Feilding, 2nd
Earl of Denbigh; c.1608-1674), F219,
IT34, SAV20-2, SWZ9, V23, V25
Ferrers, Thomas (fl.1590s), DK25
Finch, Heneage (2nd Earl of Winchilsea;
1627/8-1689), NA8, POR5, T14

Waldegrave, Henry (1st Baron Waldegrave of Chewton; 1661-1689), F287

Wallop, John (Sir; d.1551), F33, F49, F52, F54, F67, G3, LC26, PL1

Walls, Christopher, SC3

Walsingham, Francis (Sir; c.1532-1590), F117-8, F121-2, F141, LC81, SC67

Warcup, Edmund, SWZ12

Warren, Thomas (fl.1660s), NA11, NA13

Warwick, Philip (Sir; d.1683), S35, p. 14

Watson, William, SEE Brende, John

Wayte, George (fl.1650s), G93

Welsborne, John (c.1498-1548), F43

Werden, John (1st Bart.; 1640-1716), SP49-50, S22, S31

West, Nicholas (Dr., Bishop of Ely; 1461-1533), E11, F1, F3, F6, F9, F16, SC3-5

Weston, Jerome (2nd Earl of Portland; 1605-1663), F217, IT32, SAV19, V21

Weston, Richard (1st Earl of Portland; 1577-1635), G74, SN8, SN12

Westphalus, Mr., C11

White, Ignatius (Marquis d'Albeville; d.1694), LC174, SP54

Whitehead, Hugh (fl.1530s), SC14

Whitelocke, Bulstrode (1605-1675), S19

Wilcocks, Thomas, T3

Wilkes, Thomas (Sir; c.1541-1598), F124, F130, F159, F161, F171, G36, LC80, LC83, LC94-5, LC104, SP20, p. 15

Wilkinson, John (fl.1620s), V18-9

Williams, Roger (Sir; 1540?-1595), F163

Williamson, Joseph (Sir; 1633-1701), C15-6, F266, LC156, LC160

Willis, Timothy (c.1560-1615?), R11

Willoughby, Hugh, p. 273

Wilson, Thomas (Dr.; 1523-1581), LC61, LC71, POR1, p. 15

Wilson, Thomas (1560?-1629), SP23

Wiltshire, John (Sir; fl.1520s), H1

Windebank, Thomas (c.1612-n.d.), E69, F222

Wingfield, Richard (Sir; 1469?-1525), E2-3, E10, E14, E18, F6, F8, F11, LC4-5, LC13, LC19, SP3

Wingfield, Robert (Sir; c.1470-1539), E1, E6, E13-4, IT3, LC2, LC20, LC24, SWZ4

Winwood, Ralph (Sir; 1563?-1617), F172-3, G61, G63, LC113, LC115, LC117

Wolsey, Thomas (Archbishop of York, Cardinal; 1475?-1530), E11, F29

Wood, Edward (Sir; fl.1670s), S25, S29, S33

Woodford, John, F183, F191, F195

Woodhouse, Richard (fl.1510s), SWZ1-2

Woodward, Rowland, V14

Wotton, Edward (Baron Wotton; 1548-1628), F148, F184, POR2, SC69, SP21

Wotton, Henry (Sir; 1568-1639), E85, F185, G65, G67, G71, G73, LC118-9, SAV5, SAV11, V10, V14, V16

Wotton, Nicholas (Dr., Sir; 1497?-1567), C2-4, C6, E42, E44, E47, E54, F71, F74-5, F85-7, F89, G16, G20, G22, LC36, LC45, LC53, SC30

Wriothesley, Thomas (later Earl of Southampton; 1505-1550), F30, G2, LC22, LC31-2

Wroth, John (d. after 1616), E78, G54-6, H14

Wyatt, Thomas (Sir; 1503-1542), E31, E33-5, F66, SP10

Wyche, Peter (Sir; d.1643), SP36, T10

Wyche, Peter (Sir; 1628-1699?), DK63, E101, H31, H33, PL17, POR13, R28, S30

Wyche, Thomas (fl.1630s), R21

Wynter, William (Sir; c.1528-1589), F115-6, LC68-9

Yard, Robert, PL17, R28, SP52

Yerburgh, Dr., IT38, V27

Yetswert, Nicasius, F77

Yorke, Edmund (fl.1590s), F157

Young, John (Dr.; 1467-1516), E2, F2, LC4, SP3

Zouche, Edward la (11th Baron Zouche; 1556?-1625), DK23, SC79